# ENVIRONMENTAL LAW AND REGULATIONS TO PROTECT PEOPLE

Second Edition

By Terence J. Centner
*University of Georgia*

cognella® | ACADEMIC PUBLISHING

Bassim Hamadeh, CEO and Publisher
Miguel Macias, Senior Graphic Designer
Carrie Montoya, Manager, Revisions and Author Care
Kaela Martin, Project Editor
Alia Bales, Associate Production Editor
Natalie Lakosil, Licensing Manager
Natalie Piccotti, Senior Marketing Manager
Kassie Graves, Director of Acquisitions and Sales
Jamie Giganti, Senior Managing Editor

Cover image copyright © 2016 iStockphoto LP/stellalevi.

Printed in the United States of America.

ISBN: 978-1-5165-2079-4 (pbk) / 978-1-5165-2080-0 (br)

# CONTENTS

# Section Three. Precluding Environmental Degradation

# Section Four. Safeguarding Environmental Quality

# Section Five. Regulations for Public Health

# Section One

---

# Introduction and Constitutional

# Proscriptions

# CHAPTER ONE

## Introduction to Law

## Learning Objectives

- *Identify the foundations of law.*
- *Sketch the parts of a lawsuit.*
- *Appraise the structure and function of legal disputes.*
- *Examine how to work with legal counsel.*
- *Evaluate how to avoid legal problems.*

L aw is a system of enforceable rules governing relationships among persons, along with obligations to society. Societies develop their law to coincide with the majority's concepts of right and wrong. These concepts are expressed in common law, which developed from decisions of courts and tribunals over time, as well as legislative directives by persons elected by the people. Law establishes rights, duties, and privileges that are representative of the values and beliefs of a society. Because newly elected officials are able to change the law, it is continually changing. And as our society changes, it may be expected that our laws will also change.

## Federal System with State Rights

In the United States, we are guided by a federal system, under which the US Constitution and the constitutional amendments serve as written foundations of our law. Our conduct is also governed by common law as adopted by each individual state. Moreover, each state also has a constitution that serves as a foundation for state law.

Federal and state legislative bodies enact laws that are referred to as *statutes*. Under the authority of a statute, governmental agencies enact rules and regulations. Local governments—including cities, counties, towns, villages, boroughs, parishes, districts, and others—enact and adopt local ordinances and laws governing local issues. The term *law* may refer to a single statute or may refer collectively to all of the legal provisions delineated by statutes, regulations, ordinances, laws, and common law.

At the federal level, Congress adopts statutes that become part of the law governing the entire country. Congress is limited in its actions by the federal Constitution, as it only has authority to regulate matters enumerated in the Constitution. As set forth in the Tenth Amendment, all powers not delegated to the federal government are reserved to the states or the people. Under parameters provided by statutes, federal agencies proceed to adopt rules and regulations that also become part of our federal law. Actions by state and local governments cannot be contrary to the dictates set forth by federal laws and regulations.

At the state level, state legislatures, sometimes called general assemblies, enact statutes for the people of the state. Pursuant to statutory directives, state agencies adopt rules and regulations to further govern conduct and activities. A state's constitution provides directives on powers given to local governments.

The substantial reserved powers of individual states mean that considerable variation may exist among various state laws. Yet good legislative ideas are copied by other states. Moreover, a National Conference of Commissioners of Uniform State Laws has drafted numerous "model" statutes for adoption by the states. Because state legislatures have been receptive to many of these model statutes, many laws are similar among different states. This is especially true for laws governing business arrangements, where every state has adopted provisions modeled after a Uniform Commercial Code.

Given the details desired to govern environmental quality and encourage public health and safety, federal and state agencies have considerable power in drafting regulations that apply to our conduct. To guide the actions of agencies, governments have adopted rules governing their conduct. Federal and state administrative law oversees the activities of administrative agencies. At the federal level, the provisions of the Administrative Procedure Act govern the way in which all federal agencies propose and establish regulations. Administrative actions include both rulemaking and adjudication. Rulemaking involves the agency process of formulating the rules and regulations needed to carry out legislative mandates.

---

**Our Division of Governmental Powers**

Federal—Enumerated Powers
States—Reserved Powers

Adjudication involves an agency's authority to issue decisions on controversies between an agency and regulated individuals. States have adopted provisions from a model state administrative procedure act to oversee their administrative activities.

# Criminal and Civil Law

A discussion of the law of the United States may also include divisions between civil and criminal laws. Criminal law provisions are under the authority of the government in charge of enforcing the statutory commands. A government brings a charge by accusing a suspect directly in a "bill of information" or by presenting evidence to a grand jury. The latter allows the grand jury to decide whether to proceed in a prosecution. A federal or state attorney general files criminal cases involving federal and state violations. At the local level, police and prosecutors are able to issue criminal complaints and prosecute local criminal actions. Local prosecutors are often referred to as district attorneys.

Civil lawsuits may be filed by any person, which includes corporations, organizations, and other entities. The person filing a case is generally referred to as the *plaintiff*, and the person against whom the charges are levied is known as the *defendant*. Most of the litigation involving environmental and health issues involves civil lawsuits, so nearly all of the textual materials will be related to civil issues. These materials will be introduced with a brief text, and for some a legal case will be used to show how a controversy about an issue evolved and was addressed by the judiciary. The cases are abridged to delete unnecessary information and extemporaneous issues that are not pertinent to the topic being discussed.

Most of the cases used in this book are appeals from a lower tribunal in which the appealing party, known as the *appellant*, claims an error. Because judges write their opinions for lawyers and other judges, they often use legal terms that are not always familiar to nonlawyers.

# The Development of a Case

Lawsuits develop from factual situations in which a person is unsatisfied with the current state of affairs. In many cases, the plaintiff is aggrieved and feels that some type of restitution should be made for the damages caused by a defendant's actions. Each plaintiff must tie the facts to a legal *cause of action*. This will involve facts that give a person the right to seek judicial redress against another. While common-law causes of action are important—especially negligence and nuisance causes of action—many

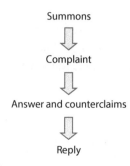

Fig. 1.1 Summons flow chart

environmental and health lawsuits involve a violation of a statute or regulation. All noncriminal causes of action should be brought in a single lawsuit, and the following documents are used.

A lawsuit commences when a plaintiff or a court issues a *summons*. This is a document that tells the defendant about the power of a court to hear and determine the charges being filed. A summons must be properly served on or delivered to the defendant. A plaintiff may hire a process server to serve the summons on the defendant.

Plaintiffs relate their facts to causes of action in their *complaint*. This is the written document that sets forth the information necessary to support each cause of action. The defendant will file an *answer* to the complaint. The answer must be filed within the appropriate time period and must address each of the plaintiff's allegations. This may involve denying some or all of the allegations, admitting some, or pleading the lack of sufficient information to admit or deny allegations. The defendant should also assert any affirmative defenses and counterclaims that may apply. A defendant also may file a *third-party complaint* that names another person as a party to the action, due to the belief that this third party should be liable for some or all of the alleged damages. If the defendant's answer includes a defense or counterclaim that needs a response, the plaintiff files a reply.

Lawyers normally draft the summons, complaint, and answer. These documents are collectively known as *pleadings*, and may be supplemented by other legal documents that also become part of the pleadings. With the initial pleadings, the parties' lawyers can go about collecting information to support their arguments. Pretrial discovery is a time when lawyers seek information to clarify the lawsuit and engage in pretrial motions regarding the issues. This often includes securing affidavits, interrogatories, and depositions. If the pleadings show that either a plaintiff does not have a valid case or a defendant does not have a defense, the opposite party may make a motion for *summary judgment*. The parties may also seek to end the case through negotiation or settlement. At some point, a lawyer can request a trial. With this introduction, we can set forth a time line describing important components of a lawsuit.

Things happen, and there
is an unresolved dispute.

Decision to file a lawsuit;
commences with a summons.

Complaint drafted and filed with at
least one viable cause of action.

Answer and counterclaims.

Reply if needed.

Discovery and pretrial motions;
efforts to settle.

Trial with various motions.

Court decision.

Appeal and higher appeals.

Fig. 1.2 Court procedure flow chart

# The Case Method

When reading case summaries, it is necessary to figure out how the appeal relates to the original lawsuit. Thus, before the text of each case, there are four questions with spaces for answers.

- *Who is bringing the lawsuit? The appellation used to denote the plaintiff, which may be the plaintiff's name, appellant, appellee, or other nomenclature used by the judge.*
- *Who is being sued? The appellation used to denote the defendant.*
- *For what? What is the plaintiff requesting?*
- *What is the issue on appeal? This is related to an error in the trial court's decision.*

The last question is the most difficult. It involves enumerating the appellant's argument about how the lower court erred in rendering its decision. This will provide assistance with understanding the case. Reread the case so that you can see how motions and efforts to settle fit together. Discern how the judge's decision relates to the issues.

The following case, *Underwood v. Wind*, introduces us to reading judicial decisions. It involves a violation of a state statute. The Pennsylvania legislature adopted a statute that overturned common-law rules for dog bites. The statute allows courts to find liability for a dog's first bite. In some states, a dog has one free bite before an owner incurs liability for damages. The case discloses that an error by a trial court may lead to a reversal of the trial court's judgment. The pertinent part of Pennsylvania's dangerous dog statute is set forth below.

*§ 459–502-A. (a) Summary Offense of Harboring a Dangerous Dog.*

*Any person who has been attacked by one or more dogs, … the State dog warden or the local police officer may file a complaint before a magisterial district judge, charging the owner or keeper of [the] dog with harboring a dangerous dog. The owner or keeper of the dog shall be guilty of the summary offense of harboring a dangerous dog if the magisterial district judge finds beyond a reasonable doubt that the following elements of the offense have been proven:*

*(1) The dog has done any of the following: (i) Inflicted severe injury on a human being without provocation on public or private property, (ii) Killed or inflicted severe injury on a domestic animal, dog or cat without provocation while off the owner's property, (iii) Attacked a human being without provocation, (iv) Been used in the commission of a crime.*

*(2) The dog has either or both of the following: … (ii) A propensity to attack human beings and/or domestic animals, dogs or cats without provocation. A propensity to attack may be proven by a single incident of the conduct described in paragraph (1)(i), (ii), (iii) or (iv).*

*(3) The defendant is the owner or keeper of the dog.*

### Underwood v. Wind
Superior Court of Pennsylvania

*Who is suing?* _____

*Who is being sued?* _____

*For what?* _____

*What is the issue on appeal?* _____

Two pit bull dogs owned by appellant Dana Wind escaped from the home she rented from her aunt, appellant Sherry Kasprzyk, and attacked the minor child, appellee Racquel Underwood, as well as the good Samaritans, appellees Shauna McInnes and Andrew Dash, who attempted to rescue the child. A jury entered awards of $65,000,

Fig. 1.3 Different opinions exist on liability for bites from dangerous dogs.

$85,000, and $80,000, respectively, in favor of the appellees. Appellants Kasprzyk and Wind filed notices of appeal.

According to the evidence of record, Kasprzyk entered into a lease agreement with her niece, Wind, for the rental of an apartment located on Sigel Street in Pittsburgh's North Side. The terms of the Sigel Street month-to-month lease included clauses stating that no animals were allowed absent the express, written consent of the lessor. At trial, landlord Kasprzyk testified that she also had a verbal agreement with tenant Wind that Wind's two pit bulls would not reside at the Sigel Street home. Wind admitted that she failed to advise her aunt that the dogs were indeed living at the Sigel Street address from April until the time of the attack in November. Wind testified that she took the two pit bulls with her when she moved into the Sigel Street residence despite knowing that her aunt, lessor Kasprzyk, disapproved. Wind admitted that two months prior to the attack in question, the unlicensed dogs had escaped the house through the front door, due to a faulty latch. On November 20, the dogs escaped through this same door once again. It was Kasprzyk's testimony that she was unaware the dogs were living at the Sigel Street rental and Wind had told her the dogs were gone.

On the day of the attack, according to the testimony of the child, Underwood, she was walking down the street, when first one dog and then the other attacked her and knocked her to the ground, both biting her and breaking the skin. While she lay on the ground, a car approached and stopped. Appellees McInnes and Dash exited the car and tried to help Underwood, and both were attacked by the dogs. With the dogs' focus on McInnes and Dash, Underwood was able to break free and run home where her mother called the paramedics. McInnes testified that as she and Dash tried to escape the vicious attack and get back into their vehicle, owner Wind arrived, followed by the paramedics.

There are two appeals before this Court. Wind, the tenant who owned the dogs that escaped from the house and attacked the appellees, argues the trial court erred by instructing the jury that the dogs' actions in this incident could be considered by the jury in determining the dogs' dangerous propensities. As we have stated in previous cases: we are convinced that proof of negligence, in contrast to holding one absolutely liable, is the vehicle by which accountability for injury sustained because of a dog bite is to be established.

We find the charge with regard to this specific argument was legally sound and adequately informed the jury of the law of liability as it applies to dog owners whose dogs escape and harm someone. The crux of the instruction advised the jurors to consider whether Wind's explanation for the dogs' escape was reasonable, or whether their escape and the subsequent harm they caused were due to Wind's negligence. Where proof of negligence rests upon a violation of the Dog Law, liability does not attach unless the violation is a substantial factor in bringing about the injuries sustained. This is exactly the law with which the jury was charged.

Wind also contends the court erred by instructing the jury that the dogs' actions on the day in question could be considered in determining whether the dogs had "violent propensities." In *Commonwealth v. Hake*, the court interpreted the 1996 amendments to the Dog Law and concluded that the propensity to attack may be proven by a single incident of the infliction of severe injury or attack on a human being, clearly finding a "propensity" to attack human beings by virtue of the attack in question, even if it is only the first attack. The 1996 amendments effectively removed the previous "one free bite" interpretation of the Dog Law and the Statute now permits liability for the dog's first bite. On that basis, we agree the trial court did not err by instructing the jury it may consider the attack upon the appellees as evidence of the dogs' dangerous propensities. Having found appellant Wind's arguments devoid of merit, we affirm the judgment of damages as entered against her.

We turn now to the three arguments presented by the landlord, appellant Kasprzyk. Kasprzyk's second and third allegations of error both relate to the jury charge and challenge the adequacy and accuracy of the court's instructions regarding the liability for negligence of an out-of-possession landlord. Kasprzyk argues the court's refusal to give the requested instructions is cause for a new trial. Appellant's two issues are:

> I. Charging the jury on the dog law without making a clear distinction between its application to a dog owner or a landlord out of possession was misleading and confusing to the jury and, thus defendant Kasprzyk is entitled to a new trial.
>
> II. Refusal to charge the jury on the duty of care of a landlord out of possession is a prejudicial error. Therefore, defendant Kasprzyk is entitled to a new trial.

Kasprzyk argues the court's charge misstated the law as to an out-of-possession landlord's duty of care by wrongly referencing and applying to the landlord the Dog Law, which is applicable only to an owner or keeper of dogs. We have reviewed the jury charge and we find the jury charge was confusing and, at worst, a misstatement of the law requiring a new trial. Our review of the instruction which discusses liability for negligence and negligence per se with regard to "dangerous" dogs reveals, however, that the court failed to make a distinction between the two defendants, the tenant Wind and "keeper of the dog" versus the landlord Kasprzyk, resulting in reversible error. The referenced portion of the charge follows.

> –*Pennsylvania's dog law … provided in part that it is unlawful for the owner or keeper of any dog to fail to keep at all times such dog confined within the premises of the owner. This state law dictates the duty of care required of someone in the same situation as Defendants. If you find that there was a violation of this state law, you must find Defendant negligent as a matter of law. …*
> –*The Pennsylvania dog law … provided in part that when a dog owner's dog has inflicted severe injury on a human being without provocation, the dangerous propensities of the animal are established by a single incident of attacking the human being. This state law dictates the duty of care required of someone in the same situation as the Defendants.*
> –*Pennsylvania's dog law … provides in part that the owner or keeper of any dog that aggressively attacks and causes severe injury or death of any human through the intentional, reckless or negligent conduct of the dog's owner has violated the Pennsylvania dog law. This state law dictates the duty of care required of someone in the same situation as the Defendants.*

This critical excerpt of the court's charge is confusing at it relates to the tenant/owner's responsibility versus that of the landlord, Kasprzyk. The court discusses the responsibility of the "owner keeper," but then instructs the jury with the plural "defendants," which necessarily includes landlord Kasprzyk. Moreover, landlord Kasprzyk is not the "owner keeper" of the dogs at issue, as defined by the Pennsylvania Dog Law, and therefore she is not subject to the provisions of that Law. Further, establishing proof of an excused violation of the Dog Law was the sole burden of tenant/dog owner Wind, not Kasprzyk, who was neither charged with nor convicted of any violation of the Dog Law. Not only is the charge confusing as to the law, it is erroneous, and mandates the award of a new trial. Accordingly, we reverse the finding of liability as to appellant Kasprzyk. We affirm the judgment of damages against appellant Wind and her case is remanded for proceedings not inconsistent with this Opinion.

## Questions

1.  Under the Pennsylvania dog law, does the plaintiff need to prove negligence?

2. When doesn't a defendant owner of a dog get "one free bite?"
3. Does the Pennsylvania dog law require "violent propensities" of a dog to establish liability?
4. What is an out-of-possession landlord?
5. What was the problem with the jury charge concerning Kasprzyk?
6. Can an out-of-possession landlord ever incur liability under the Pennsylvania dog law?
7. What does "remanded for proceedings not inconsistent with this Opinion" mean?

# Hiring a Lawyer

For our personal lives, as well as for persons with businesses involved with environmental and health services, it is important to know when to secure professional legal advice. This includes seeking advice before you get into a problem and using professional assistance when it is needed. Knowing when to consult an attorney is just as important as having a competent lawyer to consult. Finding the right attorney for you and your business should involve more than just choosing from the yellow pages or the Internet. Since many transactions are complex, you may benefit from an experienced attorney's services.

Whenever you are involved in activities that involve legal processes, a sizable investment, or potentially involve serious consequences, you have reason to secure professional assistance. Timely assistance can avoid problems, point out potential difficulties, and help both sides of a transaction understand the provisions of the arrangement. This will help you avoid risks and may provide you with a basis for recourse if something does go wrong. Individuals should plan to consult counsel for the following.

1. **Commencement of a Business:** The formation of a business organization, including partnerships, corporations, or joint ventures, requires a good foundation. This is even true when a person is forming a business with a parent, brother, sister, or other relative. Legal counsel may help explain business options, tax considerations, and offer ideas concerning protection of assets against liability from injuries and accidents. Although business arrangements may be consummated without an attorney, legal advice generally offers additional insurance and protection that more than pays for an attorney's fee.
2. **Significant Contracts:** When you enter a significant contract or lease, you may want to hire legal counsel. Although verbal contracts are binding, they are much more likely to involve misunderstandings. Individuals entering contracts offered by large companies and governmental agencies may need assistance in understanding the meaning of special terms and provisions. Legal representation may be particularly important, given liability for environmental contamination.
3. **Real Estate:** Buyers and sellers of real estate or who enter into significant lease obligations may benefit from consulting with an expert who can identify risks and recognize potential problems.

# Finding an Attorney

Once you decide you need legal advice, you should seek a competent attorney. First, who is conveniently available? Next, do you need help with a relatively simple business assignment, or do you require specialized business law expertise? To find an attorney to represent yourself:

- *Talk with your business associates, neighbors, and friends for their recommendations.*
- *Call the lawyer referral service sponsored by local and state bar associations.*
- *Ask professionals you deal with for their advice: bankers and lenders, for example.*
- *Check legal directories that disclose specialties and backgrounds.*

For routine matters, a general practitioner may provide satisfactory counsel. For more exacting problems, you may need a specialist. It is important that your attorney be someone you can feel comfortable communicating with and trust with your confidences. To find such a person, you may want to interview several lawyers. A lawyer may grant a free initial interview or may charge a nominal fee for an initial meeting. During the interview, ask appropriate questions of what subjects or client business the attorney has previously handled. If the lawyer has not handled a similar legal problem, you may ask for a recommendation of someone who is more familiar with the topic. You should also inquire about fees to learn something about the cost of the services or how the fee will be derived, before you employ the attorney.

One suggestion for learning more about an individual attorney is to hire one to handle a simple transaction such as preparing a will or the deed for the purchase of real estate. You can then evaluate the performance of your counsel and decide whether you would feel comfortable with this attorney for further transactions.

When you work with an attorney, an attorney-client privilege protects the confidentiality of communications. This privilege encourages clients to disclose all pertinent information by protecting disclosures from discovery at trial. Attorneys rely upon their clients for pertinent and timely information in order to develop the best strategy for the issue or problem. You should be honest and open with your lawyer, but obviously your communications are not entitled to protection if they contribute to the commission of a crime or fraud. Since fees are often based upon the time the attorney spends on the transaction, being prepared and helpful may save money. Be aware that most attorneys use support staff, secretaries and paralegals, in order to reduce their overhead costs. Be supportive and cooperative with the staff. Often, they can answer nonlegal questions and assist you with procedures and paperwork.

Realize that your lawyer may not be an expert in all legal matters and that you may need to use other experts. Feel free to inform your lawyer when you believe additional expertise is required for a difficult task, and seek advice in locating an expert. Of course, you must be prepared to pay for additional expertise: specialists will charge more than general practitioners.

# Attorneys' Code of Ethics

Lawyers are governed by a professional code of ethics. This code contains a number of provisions that are very important for clients, and a few are highlighted below.

1. **Crime or fraud.** Rule 1.2(d). A lawyer shall not counsel a client to engage, or assist a client, in conduct that the lawyer knows is criminal or fraudulent, but a lawyer may discuss the legal consequences of any proposed course of conduct with a client and may counsel or assist a client to make a good faith effort to determine the validity, scope, meaning or application of the law.
2. **Conflicts of interest.** Rule 1.7(a). Except as provided in paragraph (b), a lawyer shall not represent a client if the representation involves a concurrent conflict of interest.
3. **No business with clients.** Rule 1.8(a). A lawyer shall not enter into a business transaction with a client or knowingly acquire an ownership, possessory, security or other pecuniary interest adverse to a client [except for special situations].
4. **No frivolous lawsuits.** Rule 3.1. A lawyer shall not bring or defend a proceeding, or assert or controvert an issue therein, unless there is a basis in law and fact for doing so that is not frivolous, which includes a good faith argument for an extension, modification or reversal of existing law.
5. **Reporting dishonesty.** Rule 8.3(a). A lawyer who knows that another lawyer has committed a violation of the Rules of Professional Conduct that raises a substantial question as to that lawyer's honesty, trustworthiness or fitness as a lawyer in other respects, shall inform the appropriate professional authority.

# Litigation and Fee Structures

Lawyers are bound by rules of professional conduct that require all fees to be reasonable. The fee must be based on the complexity of the case, time spent on it, expertise required to handle it, and the economic costs associated with resolving the issues. Generally, fees will be set under one of the following four options.

- *Hourly*
- *Fixed or task*
- *Statutory*
- *Contingency*

Your attorney should discuss the fee with you early in your case, including how it will be calculated and collected. In addition to paying the fee, you may be expected to pay incidental costs. These include charges for depositions, doctors' reports, photographs, and expert witnesses. In contingency-fee lawsuits, you are obligated to pay incidental costs whether you win or lose. Although written fee agreements are not required in every case, ask your lawyer for a written statement of all of the fees and costs you might incur as a result of this legal matter.

Lawyers bill clients for legal services in a variety of ways. The most common is a time-based fee (an hourly fee). It is based on an hourly rate times the number of hours or portions of an hour spent on your legal matter, including telephone calls. The hourly rate generally takes into consideration the attorney's overhead, costs for staff, rent, and other expenses. This means the hourly rate needs to be high enough to cover these costs.

A second fee structure is a fixed fee or task-based fee. A fixed fee is a specific amount of money for a specific service, such as drafting a power of attorney, handling a DUI (DWI) case, or preparing a will. The fee is for that service only. A task-based fee might include writing a letter regarding a legal matter or a commission fee for a task such as a percentage of a probate estate. For a few legal issues, legislative bodies have established statutory-based fees. Legislative bodies decide how much certain tasks assigned to lawyers should cost.

Contingency fees are generally used for tort and litigation matters. A contingency fee is a percentage of monies that are obtained in the case, whether through settlement, trial, or negotiation. The attorney's fee comes off the top before the client receives any monies, as do any incidental costs not paid in advance. Thus, contingency fees are not based on time spent; they are based on the risks involved in taking the case. Generally, the fee is about 30 percent of the amount recovered. Ask your lawyer for a written fee agreement that sets forth the amount of the contingency fee and what will happen if the case is appealed.

Contingency fees may be preferred to charging by the hour because they provide incentives for attorneys to be efficient in handling tort cases. Under an hourly rate fee arrangement, the lawyer has no incentive to work quickly and efficiently. A survey of Wisconsin lawyers showed a wide variability in the hourly rates reflected by contingency-fee cases, but supported a finding that most contingency-fee cases result in reasonable attorney fees. Moreover, lawyers charging contingency fees placed considerable emphasis on satisfied clients. Many accepted fee reductions as part of a strategy for garnering future referrals.

## Litigation Is Costly

While a person's ability to use the judicial system to address wrongs is admirable, it can go too far. It may become too expensive. One report claims our country spends $328 billion per year on our tort system but that it costs $865 billion. The costs begin with the static costs of litigation, including annual damage awards, plaintiff attorneys' fees, defense costs, and administrative costs. But other costs are related to our legal system, including dynamic costs consisting of changes in behavior, research and development spending, costs of defensive actions, and the loss of output due to excess liability. Defensive medicine is an example of a dynamic litigation cost. Excessive liability hampers innovation by redirecting research and development funds to cover litigation expenses. In addition, public access to a court system with nominal filing fees places considerable judicial costs on governments. Significant attorney fees necessarily accompany individualized lawsuits. This explains why no-fault systems have been adopted in other countries.

Beyond fiscal concerns, if dissatisfied individuals can reap potential windfalls by filing lawsuits, we may not achieve meaningful justice. Evidence suggests our judicial system has difficulties discouraging false and frivolous suits. Millions of Americans are scared that someone will claim they did something wrong. Numerous cases abound of lawsuits that should never have been brought. Plaintiffs with unfortunate problems are blaming others for their mishaps. These cases force defendants to expend considerable time and money in defending themselves. Moreover, they also require a governmentally financed court system to expend resources in responding to the allegations. Our legal rules governing tort lawsuits are costly for defendants and taxpayers.

Yet a problem exists in that injured plaintiffs with small amounts of damages are not able to find an attorney to take their cases. Lawyers cannot afford to invest hours of preparation for small payouts. Lawyers reject more than half of the contingency-fee cases presented by persons seeking representation. Injured persons with valid claims that tend to be difficult to prove lose under our tort system. They cannot find an attorney willing to take the case. An estimated 90 percent of accident claims are not litigated. Nearly 98 percent of people negligently injured by a health care provider may never advance their claims. Our tort system is not perfect.

# Group Presentation Problem Set: Key Environmental Issues of the World

To enable each member of the class to get to know one or two fellow classmates, the class will have group presentations. The following exercise also allows everyone to learn more about some of the current environmental issues. Sign up with one or two classmates for one of the following topics.

## Team Topics:

1. Global warming
2. Loss of biodiversity
3. Energy
4. Invasive species

5. Chemicals and toxins
6. Ocean pollution
7. Air pollution
8. Waste management
9. Potable water
10. Deforestation
11. Acid rain
12. Plant and animal extinction
13. Earth's ozone
14. Pollution of rivers, lakes, and reservoirs
15. Soil degradation
16. Population growth
17. Industry: Globalization
18. Genetically modified organisms
19. Encouraging green construction
20. Brownfields
21. Heavy metals

Your environmental team has been invited to join a panel of experts to set the agenda for an upcoming United Nations' conference intending to draft an international environmental protocol. The presentations will be given in a formal setting, but without handouts, overheads, or PowerPoint slides. In an oral presentation no longer than three minutes, convince your fellow panel members that your topic is the most pressing global environmental issue.

For each presentation, appropriate dress, organization, and delivery are important. As a persuasive speech, you need to secure the audience's attention and convince listeners about the importance of your topic. This should include an introduction that draws in the audience to be interested in your topic and to think about it while you are presenting your facts. You also need a conclusion.

# Grading Rubrics for Presentations

Six categories (first column). Exemplary = 40 points

| Criteria | Exemplary | Satisfactory | Unsatisfactory |
|---|---|---|---|
| **Greeting and Introduction** | Complete welcome; grabs attention and completely delineates the issue – 10 | Perfunctory greeting; notifies audience and introduces the issue – 9 | Incomplete greeting; weak introduction without defining the actual issue – 6 |
| **Analysis** | Excellent and orderly; covers all pertinent details – 10 | Hard to follow; relevant components omitted – 9 | Not clearly organized; missing components – 7 |
| **Accuracy** | Excellent facts and figures; good sources – 6 | Good but questionable information and sources – 5 | Some inaccuracies and few good sources – 4 |
| **Conclusion** | Clear and complete – 5 | Noted but weak – 4 | Ambiguous – 3 |
| **Persuasiveness** | Very convincing – 6 | Convincing – 5 | Not persuasive – 4 |
| **Time** | Within 15 seconds –3 | Within 30 seconds – 2 | > 30 seconds off – 0 |
| **Total Points** | 40 | 34 | 24 |

# Discussion Questions

1. How might a state legislature attempt to reduce the costs of litigation?
2. Should a state consider moving away from contingency fees? Why or why not?
3. You visit a lawyer and explain your legal problem. What should you do if the lawyer fails to tell you how the fee for handling your legal matter will be determined?

# Image Credit

# CHAPTER TWO

## The American Legal System and Jurisdiction

### Learning Objectives

- *Identify the origins of American law.*
- *Recite major constitutional provisions that impact environmental and public health law.*
- *Describe options that can reduce the need for litigation.*
- *Contrast requirements for federal and state jurisdiction.*
- *Report several different concepts under which a state would have personal jurisdiction over a defendant.*

## The Legal System

The American legal system is a federal system, under which the US government has the powers enumerated by the federal Constitution and the constitutional amendments. Powers that are not enumerated are reserved for the states. Congress does what it deems necessary to exercise its enumerated powers. Under the reserved powers, each state regulates behavior and enforces order within its territory under its "police power" by making laws and regulations for the improvement of the health, safety, morals, and general welfare of its inhabitants. The federal Constitution restricts the police powers so that governments do not go too far in enacting laws that deny citizens basic rights.

States also have *parens patriae* powers, under which the state acts as the legal guardian for persons within its borders. As legal guardian, the state acts as the parent of each child or individual who is in need of protection, as well as incapacitated individuals. In most states, parens patriae powers require the protection of the best interests of a minor or incapacitated person. States also have responsibilities in safeguarding public health and reducing public nuisances.

Various constitutional provisions of our federal Constitution, as well as state constitutions, are important in providing protections to people, public health, and environment quality. As a federal system, our federal Constitution, statutes, and regulations are supreme and govern everyone in every state. Any rights, obligations, and requirements delineated by the federal government preempt inconsistent state and local actions. While the Commerce Clause of the Constitution is often noted as the authority for environmental and public health regulations, other provisions are also important.

The federal government contains three parts: the executive branch, Congress, and the court system. The executive branch executes and enforces the law. It does this by using administrative agencies. The legislative branch makes the law. Congress passes statutes that generally authorize administrative agencies to proceed with more details to oversee the congressionally passed provisions. The judicial branch interprets the law, although many administrative tribunals also interpret facts and issue orders.

The first ten amendments to our federal Constitution—known as the Bill of Rights—delineate limitations on actions by governments. An understanding of how the provisions are interpreted requires a balancing of personal freedoms with the common good of the majority. A quick review of some of these amendments provides a background for delving into more applicable Due Process and Taking issues that greatly affect environmental quality and public health.

1.  **First Amendment.** Congress shall make no law respecting an establishment of religion, or prohibiting the free exercise thereof; or abridging the freedom of speech, or of the press; or the right of the people peaceably to assemble, and to petition the Government for a redress of grievances.
2.  **Fourth Amendment.** The right of the people to be secure in their persons, houses, papers, and effects, against unreasonable searches and seizures, shall not be violated, and no Warrants shall issue, but upon probable cause, supported by Oath or affirmation, and particularly describing the place to be searched, and the persons or things to be seized.
3.  **Fifth Amendment.** No person shall … be subject for the same offence to be twice put in jeopardy of life or limb; nor shall be compelled in any criminal case to be a witness against himself, nor be deprived of life, liberty, or property, without due process of law; nor shall private property be taken for public use, without just compensation.

4. **Tenth Amendment**. The powers not delegated to the United States by the Constitution, nor prohibited by it to the States, are reserved to the States respectively, or to the people.

To discern how governments protect public health and safeguard the environment from being denigrated by firms that fail to internalize negative externalities, several constitutional issues may be highlighted. Negative externalities are costs imposed on society when persons do not pay for pollutants or wastes disposed of in common water, air, and land resources. First, the "Necessary and Proper" Clause of the federal Constitution grants Congress authority to enact statutes providing federal oversight over environmental protection, infectious diseases, and public health and safety. In making a determination whether a statute is sanctioned by the Necessary and Proper Clause, courts look to see whether the provisions constitute a means rationally related to the implementation of a constitutionally enumerated power.

Three other federal constitutional provisions are important for granting the federal government authority to regulate environmental and public health problems. The Commerce Clause serves as the authority for numerous federal statutes and regulations. The preemption clause is significant, as it allows Congress to preclude states from regulating certain issues to achieve uniformity throughout the country. The treaty clause empowers the president to propose and negotiate agreements between the United States and other countries. However, the United States only enters into treaties with other countries after the advice and consent of a super-majority of the Senate.

# Lawsuits and Liability Rules

Although the American legal system developed out of legal principles from Great Britain and English common law, many of our legal concepts governing accidents are in response to injuries that accompanied the Industrial Revolution. Most of the concepts were developed after we were an independent country. Our tort system evolved to respond to the sudden proliferation of injuries caused by dangerous machines and motorized transport. Injured persons could receive damages from wrongdoers through lawsuits.

Our reliance on negligence lawsuits may be contrasted with events in England and Germany. England adopted a workers' compensation program that extended social insurance coverage to other injured persons. Germany moved to a strict-liability workers' compensation program, followed by additional welfare programs. Today, most of the developed world has adopted welfare programs that eliminate the need to use tort law to address injuries from accidents. However, the United States relies on negligence litigation to provide damages for many injuries. Rather than adopt social insurance programs for non–work-related injuries, we remain obsessed with litigation. We only use workers' compensation laws and no-fault insurance to address some accidents.

## 1. Too Much Litigation

Most of us have all heard accounts that Americans bring too many lawsuits, and that a well-organized plaintiff's bar and generous juries have caused our legal system to get out of control. However, contrary to popular belief, we are not suing more than ever before. Research suggests that the filings of tort cases peaked in the 1980s. One survey from Georgia shows that tort filings have been decreasing since the late 1990s. Moreover, studies have shown that tort cases comprise a relatively small percentage of civil lawsuits. The study from Georgia estimated that tort claims only comprised 5.1 percent of the civil cases. Another study concluded that there are ten contract disputes for every tort lawsuit. Disputes over mortgages, business agreements, domestic relations, and other civil matters are five times as prevalent as a tort lawsuit.

Yet our concern should not simply be the number of lawsuits filed, but rather the number of aggrieved persons who should be able to recover damages. We should strive to implement a liability system that fairly assigns responsibilities for injuries so that wrongdoers are deterred from engaging in injurious activities. One difficulty with assignments of liability is that over time, our expectations have changed. In more and more cases, we expect injured persons to receive compensation. In other cases, our belief of what is fair has changed as well. Legislatures have enacted laws to establish rights that were not recognized a generation ago.

Due to more dangerous conditions, improved medical knowledge, and new laws to protect people, we might expect more lawsuits. If greater numbers of people are being wronged, we need to address these problems. Lacking other remedies—such as social programs or insurance—lawsuits constitute the vehicle for compensating deserving victims. We also rely on the threat of liability as a way to deter potential injurers from creating unsafe situations. Thus, it is not clear that too many lawsuits are the problem. Rather, it is our dependence on lawsuits for getting funds to injured victims. Persons with tort claims under $100,000 may not be able to find counsel willing to bring a lawsuit, and thus remain uncompensated for their injuries. Some people believe we should do more to assist persons with unfortunate injuries without resorting to litigation.

Some researchers have attempted to quantify selected items about lawsuits. Most of the evidence suggests that the public has been grossly misinformed about our litigious society. While the press has painted a picture of unrestrained litigation with excessive damage awards, the facts suggest otherwise. Tort claims are not that prevalent and, in most cases, damages are reasonable. The real problems are the expenses involved with individual litigation and the animosity that accompany lawsuits in an adversarial system. An analysis of negligence law shows that too much money is spent in lawsuits resolving disputes. Moreover, our tort system fosters divisiveness, rather than encouraging the fair resolution of differences in opinions.

When considering what we know about tort law, we need to realize that our newspapers and other media report news rather than objective stories. News consists of anecdotal reports and sensational accounts to garner attention. To remain competitive, the line between news and entertainment fades. Often, we do not receive an objective review. Exposés of legal issues often present only one side of the story, yet the media often imply that their reports have considered both sides. Many politicians also fall into this mode. They relate stories to support their views without an analysis of all the facts. In reporting the news, there is a blurring of fact and fiction.

This means we may not be receiving objective analyses of our litigation system. Even assuming the press reports true stories (which does not always happen), they generally are about unusual cases. We lack a meaningful assessment of how our litigation system is performing, as it is impossible to gather meaningful information on why litigants commence and settle civil disputes or the factors that are determinative of jury verdicts. Consequently, we may not have sufficient information to understand possible shortcomings of our litigation system.

## 2. Confusing Laws

Under the rule of law, people should be able to understand laws. They should also have a good idea of what courts will do in responding to a case. Today, this is no longer true. We have so many laws with legislatively created exceptions that no one knows what they mean. We have adopted specific laws to assure common treatment and to preclude governmental discretion. Yet detailed regulations create problems. They do not allow people to be free. Governments cannot regulate human activity without judgment by humans. In the absence of judgment, we preclude people from being themselves and from being able to live their lives.

As we look at our legal landscape, we see a preoccupation with rights and the imposition of practices that waste resources. In protecting individuals and their property rights, we denigrate the rights of neighbors and society as a whole. Communities remove playground equipment so they will not be sued for negligence. Recreation providers decline to allow persons to use their property because of liability concerns. In fear of charges concerning molestation, church and scout groups have to avoid situations where one adult is left alone with a child. Volunteers shy away from civic activities due to concerns about being sued. Doctors have to take defensive practices and order numerous medical tests, even though their expertise suggests that the tests will not disclose anything meaningful.

Yet our rules for tort lawsuits have not remained static. In attempts to be fairer and to achieve other objectives, federal and state governments have been active in revising negligence rules to alter liability outcomes. Economic analyses of tort law have been used to devise rules to promote more efficient resource allocation. Under various principles of fairness, rules are adopted that shift victims' losses to persons causing accidents. Negligence law continues to change as legislatures and courts respond to the altered needs of our society. In later chapters, tort law and litigation issues will be examined.

# Jurisdiction

Our governmental system, with separate federal and state governments, means there are separate federal and state court systems. As might be expected, these systems have different rules. Persons wishing to use the judicial system to secure relief need to know which court system is appropriate for their lawsuit. Established rules delineate which courts are able to hear cases. An understanding of these rules is important in assisting with using our legal system to protect property interests and environmental quality.

For any controversy, before a court will hear a lawsuit, there must be jurisdiction over the defendant and over the subject matter. Jurisdiction over a person in a state court requires some type of relationship of the person to the state so that it is reasonable for the court to adjudicate the dispute. Subject matter jurisdiction means the government has granted the court authority to hear the subject matter of the controversy. Some courts have general jurisdiction, so the subject matter they can hear is very broad. Other courts are more specialized or are limited in the subject matter or types of cases they can hear. Legal counselors are responsible for filing a lawsuit in a court that has jurisdiction. No court should hear a case that falls outside of its subject-matter jurisdiction.

For some appellate courts, there is discretionary jurisdiction. These courts can choose which cases to hear from among cases presented on appeal. Courts with discretionary jurisdiction often limit cases to those expected to resolve important and controversial issues.

# Federal Court Jurisdiction

Federal courts are courts of limited jurisdiction. This means that they only have jurisdiction bestowed by Article III of the Constitution or as created by Congress as "necessary and proper" to the exercise of legislative powers under Article I. The requirements include that there be a case or controversy and standing.

> *Case or Controversy. There must be an actual dispute before the court in the traditional, common-law sense of the term. If the dispute is merely academic, if the court is unable to act upon the legal rights and obligations of the parties, or if the dispute has become moot, there is no case or controversy.*

> *Standing. The party raising an issue must be suffering or threatened with suffering of a legal wrong, or have a legally protected right arguably being affected by some action or inaction undertaken or threatened by the opposing party. In addition, there cannot be any constitutional or statutory prohibition to the judicial resolution of the dispute.*

# 1.  Federal Subject Matter Jurisdiction

Federal courts have jurisdiction whenever the subject matter of the lawsuit's claim arises under the federal Constitution, laws, or treaties of the United States. Furthermore, some topics have been deemed to only be appropriate for federal courts to decide so that only federal courts have jurisdiction. The following are a few topics for which there is exclusive federal jurisdiction.

- *Admiralty or maritime civil cases.*
- *Proceedings in bankruptcy.*
- *Federal patent, copyright, and trademark law.*
- *Action against the United States.*
- *Action against consuls and vice consuls of foreign countries.*
- *Crime against the United States (treason).*

Concerns about the bias of state courts to persons from other states led Congress to authorize diversity jurisdiction in federal courts. When the defendants are from a different state than the plaintiffs, the lawsuit may proceed in a federal district court if there is a sufficient amount of money in controversy. Jurisdiction of suits where the amount in controversy, exclusive of interest and costs, must exceed $75,000 and be between:

- *Citizens of different states;*
- *Citizens of a state, and foreign states or citizens or subjects thereof; or*
- *Citizens of different states and in which foreign states or citizens thereof are additional parties.*

There are ninety-four federal judicial districts with at least one district in every state. Each federal district court has the authority to hear cases for which there is jurisdiction. Decisions rendered by a judge of a district court only apply in that district. If a party is unhappy with the district court's ruling, appeals go to the appropriate Circuit Court of Appeals. There are twelve regional circuits and an additional Circuit Court of Appeals for the federal circuit, with nationwide jurisdiction to hear specialized cases. A ruling by a three-judge panel of a circuit court only applies in the circuit. This means that different circuits may have different case law.

Appeals from circuit courts go to the US Supreme Court. In most instances, this court has discretion on whether to hear a case. The Supreme Court grants a writ of certiorari for each case it wants to hear from federal circuit courts, as well as the highest court of each state. The Court generally limits itself to cases that involve significant legal principles and in cases where two or more federal courts have different interpretations of federal law.

## 2. Standing

For nonprofit organizations and others to bring a lawsuit in a federal court, the plaintiff must have *standing*. This requires an injury that can be addressed by the court. The following case highlights a challenge concerning standing to describe its requirements.

***Natural Resources Defense Council v. EPA***
US Court of Appeals for the Ninth Circuit, San Francisco

*Who is suing?* _____

*Who is being sued?* _____

*For what?* _____

*What is the issue on appeal?* _____

The Federal Insecticide, Fungicide, and Rodenticide Act (FIFRA) prohibits the sale of any pesticide that has not been "registered" with the Environmental Protection Agency (EPA). Through the registration requirement, EPA ensures that no pesticides that will cause "unreasonable adverse effects" on human health or the environment are sold in the United States. This case involves EPA's conditional registration of two pesticides, AGS-20 and AGS-20 U (collectively AGS-20), that applicant-intervenor HeiQ Materials AG seeks to apply to manufactured textiles such as clothing, blankets, and carpet. After receiving comments from the public, EPA conducted a risk assessment of AGS-20 that it published in its decision document, where it granted HeiQ's application for conditional registration. Natural Resources Defense Council, Inc. (NRDC) petitions us to vacate EPA's decision to conditionally register AGS-20.

Fig. 2.1 Children's clothes may be treated with unhealthy pesticides.

FIFRA permits EPA to conditionally register a pesticide like AGS-20 that contains a new active ingredient until the agency receives sufficient data from an applicant such as HeiQ to decide whether to issue an unconditional registration. Under FIFRA's conditional registration provision, the administrator may conditionally register a pesticide containing an active ingredient not contained in any currently registered pesticide for a period reasonably sufficient for the generation and submission of required data on the condition that by the end of such period the Administrator receives such data and the data do not meet or exceed risk criteria enumerated in regulations issued under this subchapter, and on such other conditions as the Administrator may prescribe. A conditional registration under this subparagraph shall be granted only if the Administrator determines that use of the pesticide during such period will not cause any unreasonable adverse effect on the environment, and that use of the pesticide is in the public interest. Pursuant to this statutory framework, EPA conditionally registered AGS-20.

Before conditionally registering AGS-20, EPA assessed the risks that the product might pose to workers who apply it to textiles, consumers who use goods treated with AGS-20, and the environment. NRDC's challenges focus on the effects on consumers. EPA's assessment assumes that the consumer is a three-year old because it deemed toddlers to be the subpopulation that is most vulnerable to the possible harmful effects of the product. Among other things, EPA examined a hypothetical toddler's potential dermal, oral, and aggregate dermal and oral exposure to AGS-20. EPA's conditional registration of AGS-20 shall be sustained if it is supported by substantial evidence when considered on the record as a whole.

As a threshold matter, we hold that NRDC has standing to challenge EPA's conditional registration of AGS-20. In order to satisfy Article III's standing requirements, a petitioner must demonstrate that (1) it has suffered an "injury in fact" that is concrete and particularized and actual or imminent, not conjectural or hypothetical; (2) the injury is fairly traceable to the challenged action of the defendant; and (3) it is likely, as opposed to merely speculative, that the injury will be redressed by a favorable decision.

EPA argues that NRDC's members do not face an injury that is "actual or imminent" as opposed to "conjectural or hypothetical." Yet, EPA's decision to conditionally register AGS-20 increases the threat of future harm to NRDC's members. Absent EPA's authorization, there is roughly no chance that the children of NRDC members will be exposed to AGS-20. Conditional registration of the product increases the odds of exposure. As with many Article III standing cases, the threatened harm is by nature probabilistic. Our goal in these cases is to ensure that the concept of "actual or imminent" harm is not stretched beyond its purpose, which is to ensure that the alleged injury is not too speculative for Article III purposes. We have consistently held that an injury is "actual or imminent" where there is a "credible threat" that a probabilistic harm will materialize.

NRDC has carried its burden to demonstrate that there is a "credible threat" that its members' children will be exposed to AGS-20 as a consequence of EPA's decision to conditionally register the product. The ubiquity of textiles and the lack of public information concerning the chemical treatments applied to them during the manufacturing process would combine to make it nearly impossible for NRDC members to eliminate AGS-20-treated textiles from their children's lives, particularly in light of the expansive scope of permissible applications of AGS-20 acknowledged by EPA. NRDC's members cannot reasonably assure that the carpets at the daycare center, the jackets worn by a caretaker, or the seats on the school bus have not been treated with AGS-20.

We conclude that NRDC has shown a "credible threat" that its members' children will be exposed to AGS-20, meaning that the purported injury is "actual or imminent." Neither Supreme Court precedent nor the out-of-circuit cases relied on by EPA dictate that we hold otherwise. NRDC has standing to sue under Article III and so we must proceed to consider the merits of its petition.

## Questions

1. Who would have challenged NRDC's standing?
2. To what does the court refer when it notes Article III's standing requirements?
3. Who has to prove they have standing?
4. How might the children of NRDC members be affected by AGS-20?

# Subject Matter Jurisdiction in State Courts

Each state has its own rules for jurisdiction that delineate when a court has authority to hear a case and issue a judgment. States have a variety of courts, from local courts to the state's supreme court. State trial courts have subject matter jurisdiction over all cases, except those that must be heard exclusively in other courts. The court must also have personal jurisdiction over the defendant. Georgia's courts serve an as example of state court systems and basis requirements for jurisdiction.

## 1. Georgia Supreme Court

The Georgia Supreme Court has limited jurisdiction. It has appellate jurisdiction from lower courts, with appeals taken on selected important matters from superior courts, juvenile courts, constitutional city courts, and state courts. The Georgia Supreme Court also has appellate jurisdiction from the Court of Appeals by way of certiorari (discretionary appeal) in cases involving grave and important questions of law of general public concern. Finally, the court has jurisdiction to hear certified matters from the Court of Appeals if the appellate court is equally divided on an issue of importance, or when the Court of Appeals certifies a legal question.

## 2. Georgia Court of Appeals

The Georgia Court of Appeals is an intermediate court that has appellate and certiorari jurisdiction in all cases from superior courts, juvenile courts, constitutional city courts, and state courts where jurisdiction has not been conferred on the Georgia Supreme Court.

## 3. Trial Courts

The Georgia court system has five classes of trial-level courts, including magistrate, probate, juvenile, state, and superior courts. Each of Georgia's 159 counties has a superior court, which is the trial court of general jurisdiction. A number of these courts have concurrent jurisdiction in certain civil cases. Moreover, superior courts have appellate and certiorari jurisdiction from lower tribunals.

# Jurisdiction over the Person or Things

## 1. Personal Jurisdiction

Each court needs to have jurisdiction over the person or property before it can decide a case. Personal jurisdiction is based on territorial concepts, with the defendant needing to be within or connected to the territory for the court to have jurisdiction. In most states, the defendant must fit within one of the following categories for there to be personal jurisdiction.

I.   Presence in state when served the summons, if not privileged or fraudulently induced. Thus, any person traveling through a state on business or for personal reasons who is served a summons in the state is subject to personal jurisdiction.

II.  A person can always consent to being sued in a state. Furthermore, defendants who come to the state to respond to a lawsuit must object to jurisdiction in a timely fashion or else they are subject to personal jurisdiction.

III. A natural person who is domiciled within the state is subject to jurisdiction. Domicile refers to where persons say they live. Obviously, if a person is registered to vote or has a driving license, they are a domiciliary of that state.

IV.  Each state has adopted a Non-Resident Motorist Statute, under which drivers agree they are subject to jurisdiction for vehicle mishaps in the state.

    V.   Every corporation is incorporated in some state, which may be a foreign country. States have adopted special rules called long-arm statutes that prescribe rules for jurisdiction over corporations and other business entities.

    VI.  Torts (civil wrongs) occurring within the state by someone outside the state.

The major consequences of a court's personal jurisdiction over a defendant are that the judgment may be satisfied out of any property owned by the defendant. The judgment also is entitled to full-faith-and-credit enforcement in other states. To enforce a judgment, the successful plaintiff sends an exemplified copy of the judgment to the clerk's office in the state and locality where the judgment debtor lives. The clerk will docket the judgment.

State courts have concurrent jurisdiction on some issues with federal district courts. Moreover, under federal law, a defendant has the right to remove a case from a state court to federal court if there is federal jurisdiction. The following case shows how a court will determine whether there is jurisdiction over an out-of-state defendant.

***Fischbarg v. Doucet***
Court of Appeals of New York

*Who is suing?* _____

*Who is being sued?* _____

*For what?* _____

*What is the issue on appeal?* _____

In this appeal, we are asked to determine whether a trial court properly exercised personal jurisdiction over defendants, an individual and corporation, both residents of California, who retained a New York attorney to represent the corporation in an action brought in an Oregon federal court. Because we conclude that defendants' retention and subsequent communications with plaintiff in New York established a continuing attorney-client relationship in this state and thereby constitute the transaction of business under Civil Practice Law and Rules (CPLR) § 302(a)(1), we hold that the exercise of jurisdiction was proper.

In February, defendant Suzanne Bell-Doucet, a California resident and president of defendant Only New Age Music, Inc. (ONAM), a California corporation, placed a telephone call to plaintiff, attorney Gabriel Fischbarg, a member of the New York bar, at his New York office. During the ensuing conversation, the parties discussed plaintiff's potential representation of ONAM in a lawsuit alleging breach of contract, fraud and copyright infringement claims against Allegro Corp., a nonparty Oregon corporation. On February 23, Ms. Bell-Doucet sent a letter to plaintiff's New York office to confirm that he "offered to take this case on a one-third contingency" and that she would pay him a $2,000 deposit "against expenses." Enclosed with the February 23 letter were "contracts, copyrighted material, an outline of events, and copies of correspondence" for plaintiff's review. According to plaintiff, after receiving these materials, he entered into a retainer agreement with defendants by telephone from his New York office.

On May 30, Allegro filed suit against ONAM in the United States District Court for the District of Oregon. Plaintiff conducted his work pertaining to the Oregon action—allegedly 238.4 hours worth—from New York. He appeared at depositions and court conferences, and argued a motion for summary judgment via telephone from New York. In addition, defendants repeatedly communicated with plaintiff in New York. According to plaintiff, he spoke with defendants by telephone at least twice per week over nine months regarding their case. Plaintiff's time records also show that on at least 31 occasions defendants sent e-mails regarding the Oregon case to plaintiff, that on three occasions they faxed materials to him, and that defendants sent plaintiff documents, by either mail or e-mail, seven times.

The following January, a dispute regarding the terms of plaintiff's retainer agreement arose. That same day, defendants accepted plaintiff's e-mailed resignation as their attorney. While the Oregon action was still pending, plaintiff moved the Oregon court for an order awarding him $57,906.05 for services rendered prior to his resignation. The court denied plaintiff's motion. Plaintiff initiated the present lawsuit seeking damages for breach of contract and unjust enrichment. His complaint alleged that defendant Bell-Doucet "is an individual residing in Los Angeles, California" and that defendant ONAM "is a California corporation doing business in this State." Defendants responded with a motion to dismiss for lack of personal jurisdiction under CPLR § 3211(a)(8).

The New York trial court denied defendants' motion. It held that it could properly exercise personal jurisdiction over defendants pursuant to CPLR § 302(a)(1) because their activities in retaining plaintiff, a New York attorney, situated in New York, to represent them in the Oregon Action were purposeful and a sufficient nexus exists between that retention and the instant claim regarding allegedly unpaid legal fees. The Appellate Division agreed. The majority reasoned that by seeking out plaintiff's representation in New York and by working with plaintiff on a consistent basis, defendants "transacted business" in New York sufficient to subject themselves to this State's jurisdiction. Thereafter, the Appellate Division granted defendants leave to appeal to this Court and certified to us the question whether its order which affirmed the order of the Supreme Court was properly made? We answer that question in the affirmative.

Defendants argue that they have transacted no business in New York because they have not purposefully availed themselves of the privileges and protections of our state's laws. According to them, their retention of plaintiff and their communications—by telephone, facsimile and e-mail—with him are, as a matter of law, insufficient predicates for long-arm jurisdiction. Plaintiff argues to the contrary. We agree with plaintiff. CPLR § 302(a)(1) jurisdiction is proper, even though the defendant never enters New York, so long as the defendant's activities here were purposeful and there is a substantial relationship between the transaction and the claim asserted. Purposeful activities are those with which a defendant, through volitional acts, avails itself of the privilege of conducting activities within the forum State, thus invoking the benefits and protections of its laws.

Not all purposeful activity, however, constitutes a "transaction of business" within the meaning of CPLR § 302(a)(1). The case before us concerns defendants' purposeful attempt to establish an attorney-client relationship here and their direct participation in that relationship via calls, faxes and e-mails that they projected into this state over many months. A continuing relationship was contemplated and created here even though defendants never entered New York. There is a substantial relationship between plaintiff's action for fees accrued during his representation of defendant ONAM in the Oregon action, defendants' solicitation of plaintiff in New York to represent ONAM in that action and defendants' communications with plaintiff in this state with respect to the Oregon matter. When defendants projected themselves into New York via telephone to solicit plaintiff's legal services, they purposefully availed themselves of the benefits and protections of New York's laws governing lawyers. Requiring them to defend the present suit properly comports with traditional notions of fair play and substantial justice. Accordingly, the order of the Appellate Division should be affirmed, with costs, and the certified question answered in the affirmative.

## Questions

1. What is the CPLR? What is it similar to in your state?
2. Does a person have to be physically present in a state for a court in the state to exercise personal jurisdiction?
3. Where was the work concerning the Oregon lawsuit conducted? Is this important?
4. Does the court suggest that every attorney-client relationship between a New York attorney and a foreign defendant suffices to establish jurisdiction?
5. Could a New York accountant handling an audit of a Pennsylvania corporation lead to a relationship that could justify jurisdiction by a New York court if they disputed the fee?

## 2. In Rem Jurisdiction

When litigation concerns an object, in rem jurisdiction (*res* = thing) affects the interests of all persons in the property, rather than effecting personal liability. The judgment is upon the property and not the person. In rem jurisdiction is significant when there is a dispute over property in a state but the property's owner is not subject to personal jurisdiction.

**Burns v. State of Florida**
Court of Appeal of Florida

*Who is suing?* _____

*Who is being sued?* _____

*For what?* _____

*What is the issue on appeal?* _____

Chase Burns and others (Appellants) challenge a non-final order: (1) finding probable cause that their out-of-state bank accounts and out-of-county cars are contraband in violation of the Florida Contraband Forfeiture Act (FCFA) and (2) denying their motion for return of the seized property. Appellants argue the trial court lacked in rem jurisdiction over the bank accounts and the automobiles. We agree and, therefore, vacate the probable-cause order and remand for the trial court to grant Appellants' motion for return of property.

The Seminole County Sheriff seized 23 bank, investment, and insurance accounts of the Appellants in other states. The Seminole County Sheriff also seized four automobiles: two in Volusia County, one in Pinellas County, and one in Duval County. Appellants requested an adversarial preliminary hearing pursuant to section 932.703(2)(a), Florida Statutes. They sought return of their property, arguing that the Seminole County Sheriff did not have probable cause to seize the property and the trial court did not have in rem jurisdiction over the seized property. The trial court denied Appellants' motion to return seized property.

In Florida, forfeiture is an in rem proceeding. To have subject matter jurisdiction in an in rem proceeding, a court must have both the jurisdictional authority to adjudicate the class of cases to which the case belongs and jurisdictional authority over the property which is the subject matter of the controversy. Florida courts do not have in rem or quasi in rem jurisdiction over foreign property. In this case, because the bank accounts are located in foreign jurisdictions, the trial court does not have jurisdiction over the property in the forfeiture proceeding.

We similarly conclude that the Seminole County Circuit Court did not have jurisdiction to authorize continued seizure of the automobiles seized in other counties. Section 30.15(1), Florida Statutes (2013), provides for a sheriff's territorial authority, in pertinent part:

> *Sheriffs, in their respective counties, in person or by deputy, shall: ... (b) Execute such other writs, processes, warrants, and other papers directed to them, as may come to their hands to be executed in their counties. (e) Be conservators of the peace in their counties.*

The Seminole County Sheriff cannot wrongfully seize personal property outside Seminole County and bring it within the county so the trial court can exercise in rem jurisdiction. The order finding probable cause and denying the return of the bank accounts and automobiles is vacated, and we remand for the trial court to grant the motion to return the property.

## Questions

1. What properties were the subjects of the in rem jurisdiction?
2. Were the properties located in Florida or elsewhere? Why is this important?
3. Why didn't the circuit court have jurisdiction over the four automobiles?

## Discussion Questions

1. Does the Bill of Rights or any other provision of the federal Constitution provide a right to environmental protection?
2. Does the Bill of Rights or any other provision of the federal Constitution provide a right to public health services?
3. What provisions for jurisdiction would you write into a long-arm statute?
4. Should firms be subject to personal jurisdiction for their Internet sales?
5. How might a state legislature attempt to reduce the costs of litigation?
6. How might a legislature attempt to reduce problems dealing with confusing laws?

## Image Credit

# CHAPTER THREE
## Due Process and Takings

## Learning Objectives

- *Assess constitutional constraints to environmental and health problems.*
- *Illustrate personal rights against governmental interferences with private property.*
- *Explain the limits of governmental regulation of private property.*
- *Predict the legality of a governmental regulation that adversely affects property rights.*

Challenges to governmental action based upon the Due Process and Takings clauses of applicable constitutional authorities are important for several environmental law topics, especially zoning and land use planning. Challenges involve agency actions and governmental performance of duties.

This text includes both the federal Due Process and Takings clauses. The "without

---

**Fifth Amendment:**
No person shall ... be deprived of life, liberty, or property, without due process of law; nor shall private property be taken for public use, without just compensation.

---

due process of law" provision involves reasonable notice and fairness in governmental actions that impact a person's life, liberty, or property. "Without just compensation" delineates the takings provision to prevent governments from confiscating property without making fair payment. Applying both of these clauses to governmental activities is challenging, given that governments enjoy police powers to provide for the health, safety, welfare, and morals of their citizenry.

# Due Process

Constitutional due process protections are provided by the Fifth Amendment and the Fourteenth Amendment to the federal Constitution and by state constitutions. The Fifth Amendment applies to the federal government; the Fourteenth Amendment applies to state and local governments. State Due Process Clauses apply to state and local governments. Only governments are restrained by the due process provisions: private businesses and persons are not. The judiciary has recognized that the Due Process Clause involves both procedural and substantive issues.

> **Procedural due process.** *This involves timely notice and a meaningful opportunity to be heard before the government acts to limit or take away a protected interest. Procedural due process generally deals with decisions by agencies, unelected governmental employees, and courts.*
>
> **Substantive due process.** *This means that orders, rules, and regulations of an agency cannot be arbitrary, discriminatory, or irrelevant to delegated matters.*

When considering challenges based on due process, five questions may be asked to determine whether there is a legitimate issue:

I.    Is there governmental involvement in limiting an interest?
II.   What is the protected life, liberty, or property interest being infringed by government action?
III.  What constitutes the unconstitutional deprivation?
IV.   Does a sufficient post-deprivation remedy exist?
V.    Is there egregious official conduct?

Although governments have broad latitude to proceed under duly adopted laws and regulations to regulate activities that may be accompanied by adverse effects on property rights, these rights are limited by the Due Process Clause. The following three cases present situations where courts were asked to find that a government had denied plaintiffs their due process rights. Often, a due process procedural issue also is accompanied by conduct that may be arbitrary or capricious, thereby constituting a substantive issue.

### *Sheep Mountain Cattle Company v. State of Washington*
Court of Appeals of Washington

*Who is suing?* _____

*Who is being sued?* _____

*For what?* _____

*What is the issue on appeal?* _____

The Washington Department of Ecology (DOE) issued an order declaring Sheep Mountain Cattle Company's right to use public waters pursuant to a certificate had reverted to the State. The Pollution Control Hearings Board (PCHB) and the Superior Court affirmed DOE's order. Sheep Mountain appeals claiming its due process rights were violated because it was deprived of its water rights without notice and opportunity to be heard. We agree and reverse.

Sheep Mountain owns a ranch along with appurtenant ground and surface water rights. Certificate 3 of the Sinlahekin Creek Adjudication was issued for this land in 1932, and confirmed a right to divert 2.26 cubic feet of water per second from Toats Coulee Creek for the purpose of irrigating 108.5 acres. Sheep Mountain acquired the land from an owner who had ceased the diversion and irrigated the acreage from a well. The waters authorized under certificate 3 were not used for 12 years.

When Sheep Mountain was contemplating the purchase, the director investigated the water rights by making inquiries of the realtor, owner, and Federal Land Bank officials. The director also made inquiry to DOE. DOE advised him by telephone that "class 1 rights showed on the record, but the area's water rights were very intertwined and a personal visit to the Department to examine the entire record would be advisable." No other information was given him by DOE. The director was satisfied with the telephone inquiry and his conversations about the subject and did not visit the DOE to examine the records.

After its purchase of the land, Sheep Mountain began making plans to utilize the water rights, and apprised the Whitestone Reclamation District Board of a proposal to irrigate some land with the water authorized by certificate 3. Sheep Mountain proposed building a dam and changing the point of diversion and place of use, but never filed an application with DOE to do so. Sheep Mountain also discussed various proposals with other public agencies. Without a hearing or prior notice, DOE entered findings of fact and concluded that the right to use public waters as embodied in Certificate No. 3 had reverted to the state as provided by Revised Code of Washington (RCW) § 90.14.160 and ordered that Certificate No. 3 be declared relinquished.

RCW § 90.14.130 provides that when the supervisor of water resources believes a person has not beneficially used his water rights, he must notify the person to show cause at a hearing before the supervisor why his rights should not be declared relinquished. Proceedings held pursuant to RCW § 90.14.130 are "contested cases." Subsequently, the Legislature established the PCHB to provide for a more expeditious and efficient disposition of appeals with respect to the decisions and orders of the department and director. The legislative action included RCW § 43.21B that specifically prohibits DOE from conducting hearings on the issuance, modification, or termination of any permit or license. With the enactment of RCW § 43.21B, the Legislature prohibited DOE from conducting any hearings, thus repealing public input previously provided for in RCW § 90.14.130. Since PCHB was only given the power to hear appeals from DOE's orders, the Legislature failed to provide any due process prior to a termination order by DOE. Here, Sheep Mountain's water rights were terminated by DOE without notice or hearing. We conclude that portion of RCW § 43.21B which prohibits DOE from conducting hearings as to the issuance, modification, or termination of any permit or license is unconstitutional.

Property owners have a vested interest in their water rights, and these rights are entitled to due process protection. It is well established that prior to an action affecting an interest in life, liberty or property protected by the due process clause, notice must be given which is reasonably calculated to apprise interested parties of the pendency of the action and afford them an opportunity to present their objections. The order terminating Sheep Mountain's vested property right prior to notice and hearing does not comport with these principles. DOE's order of relinquishment was entered in violation of Sheep Mountain's constitutional right to due process and must be set aside.

DOE's actions, here, were particularly grievous because DOE in its finding stated: No facts exist to support an exemption from the application of the relinquishment and revision provisions of RCW § 90.14.160 as set forth in RCW § 90.14.140. The unfairness of this finding is demonstrated by the following evidence submitted at the PCHB appeal hearing that Sheep Mountain (1) made inquiries to DOE regarding the status of the certificate 3 water rights prior to purchasing the land; (2) apprised the Whitestone Reclamation District Board of a proposal for irrigating the property; (3) proposed building a dam and changing the point of diversion and place of use of the certificate 3 water; and (4) discussed various proposals for the use of the certificate 3 water with other public agencies. This evidence supports the exemption of determined future development under RCW § 90.14.140 so DOE's findings were wrong. The DOE's order is reversed and remanded for a hearing before the Department of Ecology.

## Questions

1. In providing for more expeditious disposition of appeals, the Legislature created the PCHB and prohibited DOE from having hearings on proceedings involving the relinquishment of public waters. What was the fatal omission of this regulatory scheme?

2. Did Sheep Mountain conduct a meaningful investigation of water rights under Certificate 3 prior to the purchase of the ranch, and should this matter?

3. Under Washington State law, rights to use public waters revert to the state if not used. Why didn't Sheep Mountain's rights under Certificate 3 revert to the state?

4. Because due process requirements are costly, can governments find ways to circumvent some of the more detailed requirements that involve the costs?

### *Kar-McVeigh, LLC v. Zoning Board of Appeals of the Town of Riverhead*
Supreme Court of Suffolk County, New York

*Who is suing?* _____

*Who is being sued?* _____

*For what?* _____

*What is the issue on appeal?* _____

In the amended petition the petitioner asserts it owns the property located in the Town of Riverhead, New York, operates a restaurant business known as the Jamesport Manor Inn, and seeks to develop the premises consistent with two submitted site plan applications including the installation of a temporary tent for restaurant use and construction of a barn/catering facility to be installed or constructed in accordance with the applicable area setbacks.

The respondent Zoning Board of Appeals (ZBA) of the Town of Riverhead denied a use variance requested by Kar-McVeigh to establish catering as a principal use on the subject premises. The ZBA also found that catering is a type of restaurant use that can be a principal or accessory use and is a permitted use where a restaurant use is permitted. Based upon the Town Board's denial of petitioner's application for the catering facility at the premises, the petitioner seeks a judgment annulling, reversing, and vacating the resolutions of the ZBA. The ZBA denied the petition for failure to state a claim on which relief can be granted. On a motion of the ZBA to dismiss a petition, all of the petition's allegations are deemed to be true.

Procedural due process is designed to insure that there will be no deprivation of rights otherwise created without notice and opportunity to be heard. The requirements of procedural due process apply only to the deprivation of interests encompassed by the Fourteenth Amendment's protection of liberty and property. Whether a party's interest in a land-use regulation is protected by the Fourteenth Amendment depends upon whether it has a legitimate claim of entitlement to the relief being sought.

In order to establish a deprivation of a property right in violation of substantive due process, the claimant must establish a cognizable or vested property interest and that the municipality acted without legal justification and motivated entirely by political concerns. As for the second element of the test, only the most egregious official conduct can be said to be arbitrary in the constitutional sense. The denial of a permit is not tantamount to a constitutional violation. Moreover, the denial of an application for permission to develop property does not implicate a protectable property interest if the governmental authority has the discretion to grant or deny the application.

When a motion to dismiss a petition has been denied, the respondent must be given an opportunity to answer. It is error to grant a petitioner affirmative relief before a respondent has had an opportunity to respond to the allegations contained therein. If there are questions of law and fact to be determined, a party which unsuccessfully moves to dismiss the petition must be permitted to answer.

In petitioner's first cause of action asserting that the ZBA resolution is invalid and void, contrary to State and Town law, is arbitrary and capricious and constitutes an abuse of discretion, and is therefore null and void, the Court finds that the petitioner has stated a cognizable cause of action.

In the second cause of action wherein the petitioner seeks reversal of the ZBA's determination refusing to review the petition on the basis that the respondent violated Town Law § 267-a because the Town Planning Director failed to file his letter within five business days with the Town Clerk's Office, as required, the Court finds that the petitioner has stated a cognizable cause of action.

In the third cause of action asserting that the respondents violated Town Law § 267-a as the ZBA resolution was not filed within five business days of the ZBA public hearing in the Town Clerk's office, the Court finds that the petitioner has stated a cognizable cause of action.

In the fourth cause of action asserting that petitioner has been deprived of due process by the actions and determinations of the ZBA and Town officials acting under the color of state law and depriving the petitioner of its property and its development according to the Town Zoning Code, and due process, the Court finds that the petitioner has stated a cognizable cause of action. Accordingly, ZBA's motion for an order granting dismissal of the petition is denied.

## Questions

1. Does this case involve procedural or substantive due process, or both?
2. How did the ZBA go wrong in responding to this request for a use variance?
3. Does the court delineate a definitive shortcoming justifying the first cause of action?
4. For the second and third causes of action, what is the problem?
5. What is the meaning of "acting under the color of state law?"
6. If your responsibilities as a governmental employee involve responding to petitions, what happens if you miss a regulatory or statutory deadline?

### *Saffo v. Foxworthy, Inc.*
Supreme Court of Georgia

*Who is suing?* _____

*Who is being sued?* _____

*For what?* _____

*What is the issue on appeal?* _____

The appellants contend the trial court erred in relying on Official Code of Georgia Annotated (OCGA) § 48-4-47 to dismiss their complaint against the appellees to recover property sold at a tax sale to satisfy unpaid property taxes. Section 48-4-47 provides that once the right of redemption has been foreclosed by the providing of notice to the delinquent taxpayer and the passing of the barment date, the delinquent taxpayer cannot file or maintain suit to invalidate the tax deed without first paying or tendering to the new owner the full redemption amount. The appellants, who are delinquent taxpayers, did not pay or tender the redemption amount before or after filing suit against the new owner to challenge the validity of the tax sale of their residence and the resulting tax deed. The appellants argue that the trial court nevertheless erred in dismissing their complaint, because an exception to the statutory payment or tender requirement applies and because the payment or tender requirement of § 48-4-47 violates their constitutional due process rights. We reject those arguments and affirm.

The delinquent taxpayers, appellants Sallie and Forrest Saffo, purchased the property at issue in 1983. For the next seven years, the property taxes were paid out of an escrow account connected with the mortgage. The Saffos knew that they had to pay property taxes and knew that the taxes were no longer being paid from the escrow account after 1990. Nevertheless, from 1991 on, the Saffos did not pay property taxes. A tax lien attached to the property, which was later foreclosed, and on February 1, 2000, the Fulton County Sheriff sold the property at a tax sale to the highest bidder, appellee Foxworthy, Inc., for $51,406.88. Under § 48-4-40(1), the Saffos had an initial period of 12 months to redeem the property by paying the redemption amount to Foxworthy. They failed to do so. Foxworthy served the Saffos with a Notice of Foreclosure of Equity of Redemption on November 4, 2004. The barment date specified in the notice was December 28, 2004. The Saffos failed to redeem the property.

In 2008, the trial court conducted a hearing on the parties' cross-motions to dismiss and for summary judgment. The court entered an order finding that the Saffos' right to redeem the property was permanently barred because the Saffos had not paid or

Fig. 3.1 Foreclosure proceedings must be fair.

tendered the redemption amount. The trial court granted Foxworthy's motions to dismiss the complaint and for summary judgment. The Saffos raise two claims on appeal. First, they argue that the trial court erred in holding that § 48-4-47 bars their suit challenging the validity of the tax sale and resulting tax deed to Foxworthy. Second, they contend that § 48-4-47 violates their constitutional right to due process of law.

The article of the Georgia Code governing redemption of property following a tax sale to satisfy unpaid taxes grants the delinquent taxpayer the right to redeem the property by paying the amount required for redemption, the redemption price. The redemption price is the amount paid for the property at the tax sale, as reflected in the tax deed, plus certain other taxes, costs, and penalties that increase as time passes. The effect of redeeming the property is to place title back in the hands of the delinquent taxpayer, with the tax delinquency resolved. The delinquent taxpayer has an initial period of 12 months from the date of the tax sale in which to redeem the property. At the expiration of the 12-month period, the new owner has the ability to terminate and forever bar the delinquent taxpayer's right of redemption by setting a barment date and causing a notice of foreclosure to be served 30 days prior to the barment date. Service of the notice of foreclosure of the right of redemption bars the filing or continuance of any action to set aside, cancel, or in any way invalidate the tax deed referred to in the notice or the title conveyed by the tax deed, unless the plaintiff first pays or tenders the full redemption amount.

The Saffos concede that they received a Notice of Foreclosure of Equity of Redemption which specified a barment date of December 28, 2004. The Saffos clearly received much more than the requisite 30 days' notice, and § 48-4-47 bars not only the filing of a suit to set aside a tax deed without payment or tender of the redemption amount, but also maintaining such a suit. It is undisputed that the Saffos never paid or tendered the redemption amount. Accordingly, the trial court did not err in dismissing the Saffos' complaint for failing to pay or tender the redemption amount.

The Saffos note that in this case, the redemption amount of $112,516 dwarfs the original $2,000 in unpaid taxes the property was sold to satisfy, and it was more than double what Foxworthy paid for the property at the tax sale in 2000 due to the addition of taxes, costs, and penalties. They claim that requiring them to pay or tender this large sum in order to challenge the tax sale effectively deprived them of notice and an opportunity to be heard by a judicial officer before the taking of their property, in violation of their constitutional right to due process of law. Due process requires that the government provide notice reasonably calculated to apprise interested parties of the pendency of the action and afford them an opportunity to present their objections. Georgia's statutory scheme requires that notice of foreclosure of the right of redemption be personally served, if possible, on the delinquent taxpayer, any occupant of the property, and anyone else with an interest of record in the property, as well as by publication.

The enforcement and collection of taxes through the sale of the taxpayer's property can be a harsh procedure. But procedures may be harsh without being unconstitutional. In this case, the Saffos have failed to make out a valid claim that their due process rights have been violated. Accordingly, we reject their due process challenge to the constitutionality of § 48-4-47.

## Questions

1. What is an escrow account?
2. What is the right of redemption?
3. What is a barment date?
4. What is the "redemption price?" Why is this important?
5. Why are harsh penalties allowed?

# Governmental Takings

When a governmental enactment results in the destruction of a substantial part of a lawful property, it effects a "taking" of private property without just and adequate compensation and is void under the federal Constitution or a state constitution. There are three recognized categories of takings:

    I.   **Per se taking:** A physical invasion.
    II.  **Categorical taking:** A denial of all economically beneficial or productive use of land.
    III. **Regulatory taking:** An uncompensated governmental taking by regulation.

Physical invasions by governments constitute *per se* takings, so governments must compensate adversely affected property owners. In rare instances where a governmental law or regulation denies a property owner all economic value of the property, the government should compensate the owner for the categorical taking. Regulations that severely limit the value or activities available on a property pose a more difficult situation. Courts need to decide whether the government has gone too far in limiting the property and so should compensate the owner for the regulatory taking. This is the situation considered in *Norman v. United States* and *Mann v. Georgia Department of Corrections*.

### Norman v. United States
US Court of Appeals for the District of Columbia Circuit, Washington

*Who is suing?* _____

*Who is being sued?* _____

*For what?* _____

*What is the issue on appeal?* _____

The Normans are real estate developers who planned to develop commercial and industrial office space in Reno, Nevada, on a 2,425-acre property previously used for ranching and agricultural activities (Ranch). In 1986, a company called Southmark Corporation purchased the Ranch, intending to develop it for commercial and residential uses. Southmark prepared a "master plan" for the development of the property and submitted it to the Reno City Council for approval. In 1987, the city council conditionally approved the master plan, identifying 41 conditions that the developer was required to satisfy before final approval would issue. One of those conditions required the developer to submit to the council plans approved by the U.S. Army Corps of Engineers (Corps) delineating wetlands or any other lands the development of which were subject to the issuance of federal permits.

In 1988, the Corps sent a team of wetlands experts to conduct field work necessary to prepare a final wetlands delineation. On September 12, 1988, the Corps issued a delineation (the 1988 Delineation) prepared pursuant to the 1987 version of the Corps' Wetlands Delineation Manual. The 1988 Delineation identified 28 acres of jurisdictional wetlands on the Ranch property, of which 17 acres were located on the 470-acre parcel desired by the Normans. Following completion of the delineation, the Normans acquired the property. At the same time, Robert Helms purchased the 1,800-acre "residential" portion of the Ranch. The Normans and Helms then entered into an agreement whereby they agreed to develop their properties consistently with Southmark's Master Plan.

After the 1988 Delineation became public, a "storm of controversy" erupted as a variety of concerned entities criticized the delineation. The Corps then revoked the 1988 Delineation and conducted a new delineation under a more current version of the Corps' Wetlands Delineation Manual (1991 Delineation). The 1991 Delineation substantially increased the acreage of jurisdictional wetlands on the subject property, identifying 87 acres on the commercial portion of the parcel owned by the Normans. This increased their wetlands acreage by 70 acres. The 1991 Delineation allegedly forced the owners of the Ranch property to revise their master development plan. In 1994, following creation of a new development plan that provided for development in three phases, the Normans began purchasing properties adjacent to their 470-acre parcel, including Helms' 1,800-acre parcel. Plaintiffs owned approximately 2,280 acres of property intended for development in the three-phase master plan.

In 1998, appellants submitted another 404 Permit application seeking permission to impact wetlands throughout the 2,280-acre development site. The Corps responded that because appellants' proposed actions would result in significant environmental impacts, the Corps would have to prepare an Environmental Impact Statement in compliance with the National Environmental Policy Act of 1969, unless appellants provided a mitigation plan which clearly reduced the project impacts to a less than significant level. In July of 1999, appellants submitted a revised mitigation proposal that was a result of a negotiations process between the Corps and plaintiffs. Under the modified development plan, a substantial portion of the mitigation wetlands would be on lands that would not otherwise have been developed in any case. The Corps approved the proposal and, on August 31, 1999, issued the Normans a 404 Permit enabling them to proceed with their development plan (1999 Permit). Prior to and following issuance of the 1999 Permit, appellants continued to sell the developable parts of the 2,280-acre Development to various independent third parties.

In their appeal, the Normans challenge the trial court's rulings on their categorical and regulatory takings claims. A "categorical" taking is a regulatory taking in which government action deprives the landowner of all beneficial use of his property, such that the government action is the functional equivalent of a physical invasion. The trial court identified the parcel as a whole as the 2,280-acre Development that was designated for development. Without an effective challenge to the trial court's identification of the parcel as a whole, appellants cannot dispute that court's conclusion that the facts here do not sustain a categorical takings claim.

The trial court moved on to weigh the three factors of the *Penn Central Transportation Co. v. New York* (1978) ad hoc analysis to determine whether a regulatory taking of the plaintiff's 220.85 acres occurred. That analysis requires the court to balance (1) the extent to which the regulation has interfered with reasonable investment-backed expectations; (2) the economic impact of the regulation on the claimant; and (3) the character of the governmental action at issue.

After undertaking a meticulous analysis of the *Penn Central* factors as applied to the facts, the trial court concluded that appellants had reasonable investment-backed expectations with respect to only a 4.07-acre parcel which appellants purchased in 1989 but which was first delineated as wetlands in the 1991 Delineation. The trial court then concluded that the economic impact factor weighed against a finding of a taking, because the 1999 Permit actually increased the economic value of the parcel as a whole by allowing plaintiffs to fill valuable commercial property and develop that property in exchange for setting aside other, less valuable property for mitigation. Weighing all factors, the trial court concluded that no regulatory taking of property occurred, because the Corps' actions simply did not unduly burden plaintiffs. The Normans purchased most of the land with full knowledge that portions of it were not subject to development. We conclude that the trial court correctly found that the appellants had reasonable investment-backed expectations only with respect to the 4.07-acre parcel. We affirm the trial court's judgment in favor of the United States as to the Normans' takings claims.

## Questions

1. What is a categorical taking?
2. How often do governmental actions outside of eminent domain result in a categorical taking?
3. What is a regulatory taking?
4. Is it fair for the government to change its mind as occurred with the adoption of the 1991 Delineation?
5. Why did the Normans lose the regulatory taking argument?

6. What might the Normans have done differently to mount a more successful takings challenge?

### Mann v. Georgia Department of Corrections
Georgia Supreme Court

*Who is suing?* _____

*Who is being sued?* _____

*For what?* _____

*What is the issue on appeal?* _____

This case involves a constitutional takings challenge to Official Code of Georgia Annotated (OCGA) § 42-1-15, which prohibits registered sex offenders from residing or loitering at a location that is within 1,000 feet of any child care facility, church, school or area where minors congregate (the residency restriction), or being employed by any business or entity located within 1,000 feet of any child care facility, church or school (the work restriction). Appellant Anthony Mann is a registered sexual offender, who previously challenged the predecessor to § 42-1-15 when its application required him to vacate his residence at his parents' home. In *Mann v. State*, we rejected his takings challenge to the residency restriction on the basis that he had only a minimal property interest in the living arrangement he enjoyed at his parents' home. The record here establishes that appellant moved from his parents' home, got married and purchased, together with his wife, a home on Hibiscus Court in Clayton County in October 2003. It is uncontroverted that the home at the time it was purchased was not within 1,000 feet of any child care facility, church, school or area where minors congregate. Around October 2004, appellant became the half owner and day-to-day operator of a Clayton County business, a barbecue restaurant, where he cooks and runs the dining room among other duties. It is likewise uncontroverted that the business, at the time it leased its current premises, was not located within 1,000 feet of any child care facility, church or school.

However, child care facilities thereafter located themselves within 1,000 feet of both appellant's home and his business. Appellant's probation officer then demanded that appellant quit the premises of his business and remove himself from his home upon penalty of arrest and revocation of probation. Appellant brought this action seeking a declaration that § 42-1-15 is unconstitutional because it authorizes the regulatory taking of his property without any compensation as required by the Constitution of the United States, as well as the Constitution of the State of Georgia. The trial court rejected appellant's arguments and he appeals. We affirm in part and reverse in part the trial court's order.

We address first appellant's constitutional challenge to the residency restriction. Under the terms of that statute, it is apparent that there is no place in Georgia where a registered sex offender can live without being continually at risk of being ejected. Section 42-1-15 contains no "move-to-the-offender" exception to its provisions. Thus, even when a registered sex offender like appellant has strictly complied with the provisions of § 42-1-15 at the time he established his place of residency, the offender cannot legally remain there whenever others over whom the offender has no control decide to locate a child care facility, church, school or area where minors congregate within 1,000 feet of his residence. As a result, sex offenders face the possibility of being repeatedly uprooted and forced to abandon homes in order to comply with the restrictions in § 42-1-15.

Further, § 42-1-15 is part of a statutory scheme that mandates public dissemination of information regarding where registered sex offenders reside. Thus, third parties may readily learn the location of a registered sex offender's residence. The possibility exists that such third parties may deliberately establish a child care facility or any of the numerous other facilities designated in § 42-1-12 within 1,000 feet of a registered sex offender's residence for the specific purpose of using § 42-1-15 to force the offender out of the community.

Government regulation of private property may be so onerous that its effect is tantamount to a direct appropriation or ouster, and that such "regulatory takings" may be compensable under the Fifth Amendment. Regulations that fall short of eliminating property's beneficial economic use may still effect a taking, depending upon the regulation's economic impact on the landowner, the extent to which it interferes with reasonable investment-backed expectations, and the interests promoted by the government action. This language reflects the essentially ad hoc, factual inquiries set forth in *Penn Central Transportation Co. v. New York City* (1978), which rejected any set formula and instead listed certain factors to be used to identify regulatory actions that are functionally equivalent to the classic taking in which government directly appropriates private property or ousts the owner from his domain. Accordingly, the *Penn Central* test focuses directly upon the severity of the burden that government imposes upon private property rights.

Although we earlier determined appellant's property interest in his rent-free residence at his parents' home to be minimal, we find appellant's property interest in the Hibiscus Court residence he purchased with his wife to be significant. As a registered sex offender, the locations where appellant may reside are severely restricted by § 42-1-15(a). Nevertheless, appellant and his wife were able to find and purchase a house that complied with the residency restriction. The effect of § 42-1-15 is to mandate appellant's immediate physical removal from his Hibiscus Court residence. It is functionally equivalent to the classic taking in which government directly ousts the owner from his domain. We thus reject the State's position that appellant has failed to demonstrate a significant economic impact from application of § 42-1-15 to his situation.

Moreover, § 42-1-15 looms over every location appellant chooses to call home, with its on-going potential to force appellant from each new residence whenever, within that statutory 1,000-foot buffer zone, some third party chooses to establish any of the long list of places and facilities encompassed within the residency restriction. Section 42-1-15 positively precludes appellant from having any reasonable investment-backed expectation in any property purchased as his private residence. It effectively places the State's police power into the hands of private third parties, enabling them to force a registered sex offender like appellant, under penalty of a minimum ten-year sentence for commission of a felony, to forfeit valuable property rights in his legally-purchased home.

The Takings Clause is intended to prevent the government from forcing some people alone to bear public burdens which, in all fairness and justice, should be borne by the public as a whole. Looking to the magnitude and character of the burden § 42-1-15 imposes on the property rights of registered sex offenders, we conclude that justice requires that the burden of safeguarding minors from encounters with registered sexual offenders must be spread among taxpayers through the payment of compensation. We therefore find that § 42-1-15(a) is unconstitutional because it permits the regulatory taking of appellant's property without just and adequate compensation. Accordingly, we reverse the trial court's ruling denying appellant's request for declaratory relief in regard to the residency restriction.

Appellant also contends that the work restriction in § 42-1-15(b)(1) violates the takings clauses of the United States and Georgia Constitutions. Applying the analysis set forth above, we conclude the trial court did not err by rejecting appellant's challenge. The evidence presented by appellant established that he owns a half interest in a business that operates a barbeque restaurant. Appellant testified that he runs the dining room, does some cooking and performs accounting work. He testified that the restaurant has an accountant, one server, a full-time cook, and a part-time dish washer. Although appellant testified that the business suffered as a result of his absence from the restaurant, he also testified that he could take a computer and his papers and so forth and perform tasks without being physically present at the restaurant.

We hold that nothing in the statute prohibits a registered sex offender from owning a business or entity within the 1,000-foot buffer zone as long as that ownership does not involve the sex offender's physical presence at the business or entity. Although the statute's work restriction does directly deprive appellant of his right to work at the physical location of the business, there was no showing that appellant's property interest in the business depends on his physical presence; that the tasks he performs on site at the restaurant cannot be performed economically by others; and that other tasks he performs cannot be handled with comparable economic efficiency at a site outside any buffer zone. Appellant provided no evidence to quantify his claim that the restaurant had suffered as a result of his physical absence.

Thus, although § 42-1-15(b)(1) has the functional effect of ousting appellant physically from his business, appellant has not shown that the regulation has unduly burdened him financially or adversely affected his reasonable investment-backed expectations in his business. We therefore conclude that appellant failed to establish that the economic impact of the work restriction, as applied to him, effected an unconstitutional taking of appellant's property interest in his business. The trial court did not err by denying appellant's request for declaratory relief.

## Questions

1. What takings challenge was denied in the earlier lawsuit, *Mann v. State?*
2. What is the difference between a *per se* and a regulatory taking?
3. What is the distinction between the house and the business?
4. Did the appellant and his attorney fail to articulate his need to physically work at his restaurant?
5. If a similar case arises for another sex offender owning a business, what additional facts should the appellant argue about his business to support a different result?
6. How does this statute affect the ability of sex offenders to make meaningful contributions to the state's economy through their work?
7. Is this statute, as modified by the court, good for Georgia?

## Discussion Questions

1. Can a person receive "due process" in court without a lawyer?
2. Given the constitutional protection accorded by due process, should a state be able to enact a voting law under which all persons must present at least one valid form of state identification (such as a driver's license or a state ID), an original Social Security card, and at least one piece of mail received by that person at the address listed on their voter registration card? Why?
3. Given the constitutional protection accorded by due process, should legal representation be a guaranteed right for all people, rich or poor? Why?
4. Should legal services for the poor be a federal responsibility, should it be entirely in state or local hands, or is some other combination preferable? What supports your preference?

# CHAPTER FOUR

## Federal Regulation of Commerce and Preemption

## Learning Objectives

- *Assess the use of the Commerce Clause for federal regulation of public health and environmental quality.*
- *Defend federal powers and limitations in regulating commerce.*
- *Describe the three types of preemption that may preclude a lower authority from regulating an issue.*
- *Qualify the constitutional constraints of preemption to lower governmental actions.*

## Regulation of Interstate Commerce

The ability of Congress to regulate interstate commerce and preempt state action has been controversial. As a federal system of government, our country intended for states to have the reserved powers under which they would make decisions on how to regulate society. For environmental, health, and social issues, Congress may adopt regulatory programs that are intended to benefit the country. The Commerce Clause has been identified as the authority for a plethora of federal laws and regulations.

---

**Commerce Clause:**
*The Congress shall have power ... To regulate commerce with foreign nations, and among the several states, and with the Indian tribes. ...*

---

Dissatisfied individuals and others continue to ask courts to determine whether the federal actions can be justified under the Commerce Clause, and courts use a large body of jurisprudence in making their determinations. However, the scope of this power continues to be disputed. A brief accounting through an evaluation of two challenges to federal laws helps elucidate the scope of actions possible under the Commerce Clause.

### *United States v. Lopez*
United States Supreme Court

*Who is suing?* _____

*Who is being sued?* _____

*For what?* _____

*What is the issue on appeal?* _____

In the Gun Free School Zones Act, Congress made it a federal offense "for any individual knowingly to possess a firearm at a place that the individual knows, or has reasonable cause to believe, is a school zone." The Act neither regulates a commercial activity nor contains a requirement that the possession be connected in any way to interstate commerce. We hold that the Act exceeds the authority of Congress to regulate Commerce among the several States.

Respondent, who was a 12th grade student, arrived at Edison High School in San Antonio, Texas, carrying a concealed .38 caliber handgun and five bullets. Acting upon an anonymous tip, school authorities confronted respondent, who admitted that he was carrying the weapon. He was arrested and charged under Texas law with firearm possession on school premises. The next day, federal agents charged respondent by complaint with violating the Gun Free School Zones Act. A federal grand jury indicted respondent on one count of knowing possession of a firearm at a school zone, in violation of 18 U.S. Code § 922(q).

Respondent moved to dismiss his federal indictment on the ground that § 922(q) is unconstitutional as it is beyond the power of Congress to legislate control over our public schools. The District Court denied the motion, conducted a bench trial, found him guilty, and sentenced him to six months' imprisonment and two years' supervised release. On appeal, respondent challenged his conviction based on his claim that § 922(q) exceeded Congress' power to legislate under the Commerce Clause. The Court of Appeals for the Fifth Circuit agreed and reversed respondent's conviction. Because of the importance of the issue, we granted certiorari, and we now affirm.

The Constitution creates a Federal Government of enumerated powers. Those powers which remain in the State governments are numerous and indefinite. This constitutionally mandated division of authority was adopted by the Framers to ensure protection of our fundamental liberties. A healthy balance of power between the States and the Federal Government will reduce the risk of tyranny and abuse from either front.

The commerce power is the power to regulate; that is, to prescribe the rule by which commerce is to be governed. This power, like all others vested in Congress, is complete in itself, may be exercised to its utmost extent, and acknowledges no limitations, other than are prescribed in the constitution. In the watershed case of *NLRB v. Jones & Laughlin Steel Corp.* (1937), the Court held that intrastate activities that have such a close and substantial relation to interstate commerce that their control is essential or appropriate to protect that commerce from burdens and obstructions are within Congress' power to regulate. The scope of the interstate commerce power must be considered in the light of our dual system of government and may not be extended so as to embrace effects upon interstate commerce so indirect and remote that to embrace them would effectually obliterate the distinction between what is national and what is local and create a completely centralized government.

We have identified three broad categories of activity that Congress may regulate under its commerce power. First, Congress may regulate the use of the channels of interstate commerce. Second, Congress is empowered to regulate and protect the instrumentalities of interstate commerce, or persons or things in interstate commerce, even though the threat may come only from intrastate activities. Finally, Congress' commerce authority includes the power to regulate those activities having a substantial relation to interstate commerce, i.e., those activities that substantially affect interstate commerce. We conclude, consistent with the great weight of our case law, that the proper test requires an analysis of whether the regulated activity "substantially affects" interstate commerce.

We now turn to consider the power of Congress to enact § 922(q). The first two categories of authority may be quickly disposed of: § 922(q) is not a regulation of the use of the channels of interstate commerce, nor is it an attempt to prohibit the interstate transportation of a commodity through the channels of commerce; nor can § 922(q) be justified as a regulation by which Congress has sought to protect an instrumentality of interstate commerce or a thing in interstate commerce. Thus, if § 922(q) is to be sustained, it must be under the third category as a regulation of an activity that "substantially affects" interstate commerce. Section 922(q) is a criminal statute that by its terms has nothing to do with "commerce" or any sort of economic enterprise.

The Government argues that possession of a firearm in a school zone may result in violent crime and that violent crime can be expected to affect the functioning of the national economy. The Government also argues that the presence of guns in schools poses a substantial threat to the educational process by threatening the learning environment. A handicapped educational process, in turn, will result in a less productive citizenry. That, in turn, would have an adverse effect on the Nation's economic well-being. Under the theories that the Government presents in support of § 922(q), it is difficult to perceive any limitation on federal power, even in areas such as criminal law enforcement or education where States historically have been sovereign. We do not doubt that Congress has authority under the Commerce Clause to regulate numerous commercial activities that substantially affect interstate commerce and also affect the educational process. The possession of a gun in a local school zone is in no sense an economic activity that might, through repetition elsewhere, substantially affect any sort of interstate commerce. Respondent was a local student at a local school; there is no indication that he had recently moved in interstate commerce, and there is no requirement that his possession of the firearm have any concrete tie to interstate commerce.

To uphold the Government's contentions here, we would have to pile inference upon inference in a manner that would bid fair to convert congressional authority under the Commerce Clause to a general police power of the sort retained by the States. We decline here to proceed any further. To do so would require us to conclude that the Constitution's enumeration of powers does not presuppose something not enumerated, and that there never will be a distinction between what is truly national and what is truly local. For the foregoing reasons the judgment of the Court of Appeals is affirmed.

## Questions

1. In its warning about the expanding scope of the Commerce Clause, what was the danger the Supreme Court sought to avoid?
2. What three broad categories of activity can Congress regulate under the Commerce Clause?
3. What category applies to this case? Why?
4. Does the case have something to do with "commerce?"
5. What pushed the Court to its decision?

### *Rancho Viejo, LLC v. Norton*
US Court of Appeals for the District of Columbia Circuit, Washington

*Who is suing?* _____

*Who is being sued?* _____

*For what?* _____

*What is the issue on appeal?* _____

Rancho Viejo is a real estate development company that wishes to construct a 202-acre housing development in San Diego County, California. The U.S. Fish and Wildlife Service determined that Rancho Viejo's construction plan was likely to jeopardize the continued existence of the arroyo southwestern toad, which the Secretary of the Interior has listed as an endangered species. Rather than accept an alternative plan proposed by the Service, Rancho Viejo filed suit challenging the application of the Endangered Species Act (ESA) to its project as an unconstitutional exercise of federal authority under the Commerce Clause. The district court dismissed the suit. We conclude that this case is governed by our prior decision in *National Association of Home Builders v. Babbitt* (*NAHB*) and therefore affirm.

Finding that various species of fish, wildlife, and plants in the United States have been rendered extinct as a consequence of economic growth and development untempered by adequate concern and conservation, Congress passed the ESA to provide a means whereby the ecosystems upon which endangered species and threatened species depend may be conserved. The ESA directs the Secretary of the Interior to list fish, wildlife, or plant species that she determines are endangered or threatened. Section 9 of the Act makes it unlawful to "take" any such listed species without a permit. The term "take" means to harass, harm, pursue, hunt, shoot, wound, kill, trap, capture, or collect, or to attempt to engage in any such conduct.

Section 7 of the ESA requires all federal agencies to ensure that none of their activities, including the granting of licenses and permits, will jeopardize the continued existence of any endangered species or result in the destruction or adverse modification of habitat of such species which is determined by the Secretary to be critical. When an agency concludes that its activities may adversely affect a listed species, it must engage in a formal consultation with the Interior Department's Fish and Wildlife Service (FWS). If the FWS decides that the proposed action is likely to jeopardize the continued existence of a listed species or result in the destruction or adverse modification of critical habitat, the opinion must set forth "reasonable and prudent alternatives," if any, that will avoid such consequences.

The Secretary listed the arroyo toad as an endangered species. The toads live in scattered populations from California's Monterey County in the north to Mexico's Baja California in the south. Plaintiff Rancho Viejo plans to build a 280-home residential development around Keys Creek on a 202-acre site inhabited by arroyo toads. Because Rancho Viejo's plan would involve the discharge of fill into waters of the United States, the company was required by section 404 of the Clean Water Act to obtain a permit from the U.S. Army Corps of Engineers (Corps). The Corps determined that the project "may affect" the arroyo toad population in the area, and sought a formal consultation with the FWS pursuant to ESA § 7.

Rancho Viejo excavated a trench and erected a fence, each running parallel to the bank of Keys Creek. Arroyo toads were observed on the upland side of the fence. The FWS informed Rancho Viejo that construction of the fence has resulted in the illegal take and will result in the future illegal take of federally endangered arroyo toads in violation of the ESA. The FWS proposed an alternative that would, without jeopardizing the continued existence of the toad, allow Rancho Viejo to complete its development by obtaining fill dirt from off-site sources instead of from the proposed borrow area.

Rancho Viejo neither removed the fence nor adopted the FWS's proposed alternative. Instead, it filed a complaint in the U.S. District Court alleging that the listing of the arroyo toad as an endangered species under the ESA and the application of the ESA to Rancho Viejo's construction plans exceeded the federal government's power under the Commerce Clause. The parties filed cross motions for summary judgment. In ruling on those motions, the district court noted that in *NAHB* this circuit had recently sustained, against a Commerce Clause challenge, a determination by the FWS that hospital construction in San Bernardino County, California would likely lead to the take of the Delhi Sands Flower-Loving Fly in violation of the ESA. Holding that Rancho Viejo's case was indistinguishable from *NAHB*, the court granted the government's motion.

Fig. 4.1 Development in unique desert areas may threaten endangered species.

In *United States v. Lopez*, the Supreme Court held that the clause authorizes Congress to regulate three broad categories of activity. First, Congress may regulate the use of the channels of interstate commerce. Second, Congress is empowered to regulate and protect the instrumentalities of interstate commerce, or persons or things in interstate commerce, even though the threat may come only from intrastate activities. Finally, Congress' commerce authority includes the power to regulate those activities having a substantial relation to interstate commerce, i.e., those activities that substantially affect interstate commerce.

The regulation of commercial land development, quite apart from the characteristics or range of the specific endangered species involved, has a plain and substantial effect on interstate commerce. Rancho Viejo's 202-acre project, located near a major interstate highway, is one that is presumably being constructed using materials and people from outside the state and which will attract construction workers and purchasers from both inside and outside the state.

To survive Commerce Clause review, all the government must establish is that a rational basis exists for concluding that a regulated activity sufficiently affects interstate commerce. And there can be no doubt that such a relationship exists for costly commercial developments like Rancho Viejo's. The ESA acts to regulate commercial development of the land inhabited by the endangered species because it asserts a substantial economic effect on interstate commerce.

Rancho Viejo's attack on the constitutionality of the application of the ESA to its commercial housing development is indistinguishable from the attack we turned back in *NAHB*. Accordingly, *NAHB* controls our decision in this case, and the district court's grant of summary judgment in favor of Secretary Norton is therefore affirmed.

## Questions

1. Why was the ESA able to preclude Rancho Viejo from proceeding with its housing development?
2. Why didn't Rancho Viejo adopt the FWS's alternative for proceeding with its development?
3. Why does the court rely on the *NAHB* decision?
4. Does the court show how the housing development affects interstate commerce?
5. Is the court's cited "rational basis" requirement the same as we saw in the judicial analyses of due process and equal protection?

# Preemption

Major controversies are occurring over governments adopting laws to preempt sub-governmental regulations. Federal law may preempt state law or state law may preempt regulation by a lower authority. Three types of preemption may be discerned: express, field, and conflict preemption. Express preemption occurs when a statute includes a preemption clause explicitly withdrawing specified powers from sub-governments. Field preemption involves legislation that wholly occupies a particular field and withdraws from a sub-government lawmaking power over that field. Conflict preemption is ubiquitous in that it is agreed that even though a statute contains no express preemption clause or impliedly occupies a particular field, it preempts sub-governmental law with which it "actually conflicts." Such a conflict exists if either (1) compliance with both laws are "a physical impossibility"; or (2) the sub-governmental law stands as an obstacle to the accomplishment and execution of the full purposes and objectives of the superior legislative body.

## 1. Congressional Preemption of State Actions

In some instances, Congress adopts laws to guarantee national uniformity that preempt states from taking actions states feel are best for their citizens. State legislatures may have a similar belief that state uniformity is needed and that local governments closest to the people should be precluded from acting independently to address risks and dangers. In *Gonzales v. Oregon*, Oregon challenges a federal regulatory action that attempted to prohibit the use of regulated drugs for physician-assisted suicide.

*Gonzales v. Oregon*

United States Supreme Court

*Who is suing?* _____

*Who is being sued?* _____

*For what?* _____

*What is the issue on appeal?* _____

The question before us is whether the Controlled Substances Act allows the United States Attorney General to prohibit doctors from prescribing regulated drugs for use in physician-assisted suicide, notwithstanding a state law permitting the procedure. As the Court has observed, Americans are engaged in an earnest and profound debate about the morality, legality, and practicality of physician-assisted suicide. The dispute before us is in part a product of this political and moral debate, but its resolution requires an inquiry familiar to the courts: interpreting a federal statute to determine whether executive action is authorized by, or otherwise consistent with, the enactment.

In 1994, Oregon became the first State to legalize assisted suicide when voters approved a ballot measure enacting the Oregon Death with Dignity Act (ODWDA). ODWDA exempts from civil or criminal liability state-licensed physicians who, in compliance with the specific safeguards in ODWDA, dispense or prescribe a lethal dose of drugs upon the request of a terminally ill patient. The drugs Oregon physicians prescribe under ODWDA are regulated under a federal statute, the Controlled Substances Act (CSA or Act). The CSA allows these particular drugs to be available only by a written prescription from a registered physician. In the ordinary course, the same drugs are prescribed in smaller doses for pain alleviation.

A November 9, 2001, Interpretive Rule issued by the U.S. Attorney General addresses the implementation and enforcement of the CSA with respect to ODWDA. It determines that using controlled substances to assist suicide is not a legitimate medical practice and that dispensing or prescribing them for this purpose is unlawful under the CSA. The Interpretive Rule's validity under the CSA is the issue before us.

We turn first to the text and structure of the CSA. Enacted in 1970 with the main objectives of combating drug abuse and controlling the legitimate and illegitimate traffic in controlled substances, the CSA creates a comprehensive, closed regulatory regime criminalizing the unauthorized manufacture, distribution, dispensing, and possession of substances classified in any of the Act's five schedules. The Act places substances in one of five schedules based on their potential for abuse or dependence, their accepted medical use, and their accepted safety for use under medical supervision. Congress classified a host of substances when it enacted the CSA, but the statute permits the Attorney General to add, remove, or reschedule substances. He may do so, however, only after making particular findings, and on scientific and medical matters he is required to accept the findings of the Secretary of Health and Human Services (Secretary).

The present dispute involves controlled substances listed in Schedule II, substances generally available only pursuant to a written, nonrefillable prescription by a physician.

A 1971 regulation promulgated by the Attorney General requires that every prescription for a controlled substance be issued for a legitimate medical purpose by an individual practitioner acting in the usual course of his professional practice.

To prevent diversion of controlled substances with medical uses, the CSA regulates the activity of physicians. To issue lawful prescriptions of Schedule II drugs, physicians must obtain from the Attorney General a registration issued in accordance with the rules and regulations promulgated by him. The Attorney General may deny, suspend, or revoke this registration if, as relevant here, the physician's registration would be inconsistent with the public interest. The CSA explicitly contemplates a role for the States in regulating controlled substances.

For Oregon residents to be eligible to request a prescription under ODWDA, they must receive a diagnosis from their attending physician that they have an incurable and irreversible disease that, within reasonable medical judgment, will cause death within six months. Attending physicians must also determine whether a patient has made a voluntary request, ensure a patient's choice is informed, and refer patients to counseling if they might be suffering from a psychological disorder or depression causing impaired judgment. A second "consulting" physician must examine the patient and the medical record and confirm the attending physician's conclusions. Oregon physicians may dispense or issue a prescription for the requested drug, but may not administer it. Physicians who dispense medication pursuant to ODWDA must also be registered with both the State's Board of Medical Examiners and the federal Drug Enforcement Administration (DEA). In 2004, 37 patients ended their lives by ingesting a lethal dose of medication prescribed under ODWDA.

In 2001, John Ashcroft was appointed Attorney General. On November 9, 2001, without consulting Oregon or apparently anyone outside his Department, the Attorney General issued an Interpretive Rule announcing his intent to restrict the use of controlled substances for physician-assisted suicide. The Attorney General ruled: "Assisting suicide is not a 'legitimate medical purpose' within the meaning of 21 CFR 1306.04 (2001)." There is little dispute that the Interpretive Rule would substantially disrupt the ODWDA regime. Every prescription filled under ODWDA has specified drugs classified under Schedule II. A physician cannot prescribe the substances without registration, and revocation or suspension of the registration would be a severe restriction on medical practice. Dispensing controlled substances without a valid prescription, furthermore, is a federal crime.

In response, the State of Oregon joined by a physician, a pharmacist, and some terminally ill patients, challenged the Interpretive Rule in federal court. A divided panel of the Court of Appeals for the Ninth Circuit held the Interpretive Rule invalid. It reasoned that, by making a medical procedure authorized under Oregon law a federal offense, the Interpretive Rule altered the usual constitutional balance between the States and the Federal Government without the requisite clear statement that the CSA authorized such action. We granted the Government's petition for certiorari.

Post-enactment congressional commentary on the CSA's regulation of medical practice is at odds with the Attorney General's claimed authority to determine appropriate medical standards. In 1978, in preparation for ratification of the Convention on Psychotropic Substances, Congress decided it would implement the United States' compliance through the framework of the procedures and criteria for classification of substances provided in the CSA. It did so to ensure that nothing in the Convention will interfere with ethical medical practice in this country as determined by the Secretary on the basis of a consensus of the views of the American medical and scientific community. The structure of the CSA, then, conveys unwillingness to cede medical judgments to an executive official who lacks medical expertise. In interpreting statutes that divide authority, we presume here that Congress intended to invest interpretive power in the administrative actor in the best position to develop these attributes. This presumption works against a conclusion that the Attorney General has authority to make quintessentially medical judgments.

As we have noted before, the CSA repealed most of the earlier antidrug laws in favor of a comprehensive regime to combat the international and interstate traffic in illicit drugs. In doing so, Congress sought to conquer drug abuse and to control the legitimate and illegitimate traffic in controlled substances. In deciding whether the CSA can be read as prohibiting physician-assisted suicide, we look to the statute's text and design. The statute and our case law amply support the conclusion that Congress regulates medical practice insofar as it bars doctors from using their prescription-writing powers as a means to engage in illicit drug dealing and trafficking as conventionally understood. Beyond this, however, the statute manifests no intent to regulate the practice of medicine generally. The structure and operation of the CSA presume and rely upon a functioning medical profession regulated under the States' police powers.

Oregon's regime is an example of the state regulation of medical practice that the CSA presupposes. Rather than simply decriminalizing assisted suicide, ODWDA limits its exercise to the attending physicians of terminally ill patients, physicians who must be licensed by Oregon's Board of Medical Examiners. The statute gives attending physicians a central role, requiring them to provide prognoses and prescriptions, give information about palliative alternatives and counseling, and ensure patients are competent and acting voluntarily. Any eligible patient must also get a second opinion from another registered physician, and the statute's safeguards require physicians to keep and submit to inspection detailed records of their actions.

In the face of the CSA's silence on the practice of medicine generally and its recognition of state regulation of the medical profession it is difficult to defend the Attorney General's declaration that the statute impliedly criminalizes physician-assisted suicide. This difficulty is compounded by the CSA's consistent delegation of medical judgments to the Secretary and its otherwise careful allocation of powers for enforcing the limited objects of the CSA. When Congress wanted to extend the CSA's regulation to substances not obviously habit forming or psychotropic, moreover, it relied not on executive ingenuity, but rather on specific legislation.

The Government's interpretation of the prescription requirement also fails under the objection that the Attorney General is an unlikely recipient of such broad authority, given the Secretary's primacy in shaping medical policy under the CSA, and the statute's otherwise careful allocation of decision-making powers. For all these reasons, we conclude the CSA's prescription requirement does not authorize the Attorney General to bar dispensing controlled substances for assisted suicide in the face of a state medical regime permitting such conduct. The judgment of the Court of Appeals is affirmed.

## Questions

1. What is the professional background of an attorney general?
2. On what basis did the attorney general decide Oregon physicians could not prescribe lethal doses of drugs?
3. Who should decide what constitutes a medical procedure?
4. What federal official deals with medical policy?
5. Does the case favor states' rights?
6. How does the CSA regulate medical practice?

## 2. State Preemption of Local Governmental Action

For a number of environmental issues, state legislatures have debated the merits of precluding local governments from enacting provisions on an issue covered by state statute. Perhaps the most noteworthy environmental issue is local regulation of the application of biosolids, also known as sewage sludge. The EPA considers land application of biosolids to be a safe, effective means of recycling these materials as a fertilizer or soil conditioner. Thus, the EPA and some state legislatures feel the land application of biosolids should be encouraged. However, numerous local governments have felt that biosolids pose health issues so have sought to adopt local laws and ordinances that preclude application on lands within their jurisdiction. While American law generally supports local health legislation, the prohibition of the disposal of biosolids posed a problem to statewide policies of promoting recycling over other disposal methods for solid waste.

Another area of preemption has been state legislation preempting local controls over unconventional oil and gas development due to public concerns about contamination from hydraulic fracturing. The Pennsylvania legislature adopted Pennsylvania Act No. 13 in 2012 to preempt zoning requirements for oil and gas wells by local governments. This act was challenged and struck down by the Pennsylvania Supreme Court in 2013. The derogation of local laws regulating negative externalities that accompany oil and gas drilling activities may expose citizens to more risks and damages. Hydrocarbon extraction is not always beneficial for a community so that precluding local laws to address problems accompanying fracturing can lessen the quality of life of citizens and impose costs. Other environmental topics for the preemption of local regulations by state governments include agricultural nuisances, forestry practices, genetically engineered seed, and water contamination.

### *City of Los Angeles v. County of Kern*
Federal District Court, California

*Who is suing?* _____

*Who is being sued?* _____

*For what?* _____

*What is the issue on appeal?* _____

Plaintiffs City of Los Angeles, Orange County Sanitation District, and County Sanitation District No. 2 of Los Angeles County generate large amounts of sewage treatment residues known as "sludge" or "biosolids," some substantial portion of which they ship to farmland located in unincorporated areas of Kern County for use as fertilizer. This arrangement has aroused substantial local opposition in Kern County even though EPA considers land application to be a safe, effective means of recycling biosolids. That opposition reached a fever pitch in 2006 when a local state senator sponsored a ballot initiative known as Measure E, which sought to ban land application of biosolids in the unincorporated areas of the County. The ordinance passed overwhelmingly, and therefore threatened to permanently ban Plaintiffs from further land application at their Kern County facilities.

In an effort to preserve their biosolids recycling programs, the government Plaintiffs, along with private firms and individuals that handle the material, filed suit against Defendants Kern County and Kern County Board of Supervisors on a variety of constitutional and statutory grounds. After dismissing some of their claims, this Court preliminarily enjoined enforcement of Measure E, as it concluded that Plaintiffs demonstrated irreparable harm and a likelihood of success on their claim that Measure E was preempted by the California Integrated Waste Management Act. Kern has now moved for summary judgment, and Plaintiffs have filed a cross motion for summary judgment on the California Integrated Waste Management Act claim.

Plaintiffs present the same argument that the Court accepted in granting the preliminary injunction: that the California Integrated Waste Management Act expresses a statewide policy of promoting recycling over other disposal methods for "solid waste," which the statute defines to include biosolids. Therefore, Plaintiffs argue, a ban on land application frustrates this statutory purpose and thus is invalid because of conflict preemption. Though Kern advances a barrage of arguments to the contrary, each is fairly easily rejected.

EPA regulations define "sewage sludge," also referred to as "biosolids," as the solid, semi-solid, or liquid residue generated during the treatment of domestic sewage in a treatment works. Municipalities typically dispose of sewage sludge in one of several ways, one of which is known as "land application." Land application means the spraying, spreading or other placement of biosolids onto the land surface, the injection of biosolids below the surface, or the incorporation of biosolids into the soil. EPA's regulations of biosolids are codified at 40 C.F.R. § 503 and are known commonly as the "Part 503" regulations. Part 503 differentiates between Class A and Class B sewage sludge depending on the concentration of pathogens, disease causing micro-organisms, remaining after treatment. In addition to pathogens, the Part 503 rules also limit the amounts of trace metals that can be found in biosolids at the parts per million level.

The collection and treatment of wastewater, and the resulting generation of biosolids that must be recycled or disposed of, is a constant, non-discretionary governmental function. In other words, government agencies cannot decide to stop producing biosolids and instead must find ways to manage those that are produced. Government agencies generally regard land application to be the best way to manage the material. The parties agree that land application constitutes a "beneficial use" of biosolids, and indeed EPA explains that it adopted the term "biosolids" so as to emphasize the beneficial nature of this valuable, recyclable resource (i.e., the use of the nutrients and organic matter in biosolids as a fertilizer or soil conditioner). EPA has also stated that beneficial use of biosolids reclaims a wastewater residual, converting it into a resource that is recycled to land. EPA therefore promotes land application.

Plaintiff City of Los Angeles has been land applying biosolids in Kern County since 1994. The City collects wastewater and then treats this wastewater at its treatment and water reclamation plants. The wastewater treatment process generates solid residuals, which are then further treated and eventually reconstituted into biosolids. The City then sends its biosolids to a site known as "Green Acres" in the unincorporated area of Kern County. The site is a 4,700-acre, functioning farm that mainly grows crops used for animal feed. The Green Acres biosolids program is administered by Plaintiff Responsible Biosolids Management, Inc. Experts have opined that the biosolids operation at Green Acres presents no threat to the environment that is discernable—at least based on current science. Though remote, Green Acres impacts negatively on certain activities. It emanates strong odors and attracts an unusual amount of flies. Green Acres also lies adjacent to the Kern Water Bank, which sits atop an underground aquifer used to store water for extraction during dry years.

Because the incorporated areas of the County necessarily lie beyond Kern's jurisdiction, Kern has never regulated the land application of biosolids by the several cities in the County that land apply biosolids on farm land within city limits. Dubbed the "Keep Kern Clean Ordinance of 2006," Measure E's initiative campaign made clear that the target was sludge from out-of-county. It included such statements as: "Measure E will stop L.A. from dumping on Kern." Not surprisingly, the voters of Kern County adopted Measure E to prohibit the land application of all biosolids in the unincorporated areas of Kern County.

Plaintiffs contend Measure E is preempted because it thwarts the California Integrated Waste Management Act's express purpose of promoting recycling of wastes such as biosolids before other methods of disposal. The preemption analysis under state law is analogous to that under federal law. A county or city may only make and enforce ordinances and regulations that are not in conflict with general laws. Local legislation in conflict with general law is void. Conflicts exist if the ordinance duplicates, contradicts, or enters an area fully occupied by general law, either expressly or by legislative implication. Local legislation is contradictory to general law when it is inimical thereto. The party claiming that general state law preempts a local ordinance has the burden of demonstrating preemption.

When enacted in 1989, the California Integrated Waste Management Act required local governments to adopt waste management plans to divert 25% of the solid waste produced in their jurisdictions from landfills by 1995 and 50% by 2000. Additionally, the California Integrated Waste Management Act provides:

> In implementing this division, the board and local agencies shall do both of the following: (a) Promote the following waste management practices in order of priority: (1) Source reduction. (2) Recycling and composting. (3) Environmentally safe transformation and environmentally safe land disposal, at the discretion of the city or county. (b) Maximize the use of all feasible source reduction, recycling, and composting options in order to reduce the amount of solid waste that must be disposed of by transformation and land disposal.

It is undisputed that land application of biosolids, therefore, constitutes recycling of solid waste within the meaning of the statute. The California Integrated Waste Management Act thus uses mandatory language to require that local agencies such as Kern recycle solid wastes—including biosolids—that cannot be eliminated through source reduction. Moreover, it mandates that they "maximize" all "feasible" methods of recycling, and it does so specifically to further the goal of diverting solid waste from landfills. Given California Integrated Waste Management Act's mandate to recycle solid waste, Measure E's ban on land application of biosolids amounts to a ban on activity that the state statute attempts to promote, therefore, the Court concludes that Measure E is inimical to the goals of the California Integrated Waste Management Act, contradicts it, and is therefore preempted. Plaintiffs' motion for summary adjudication of this claim is granted and Kern's is denied.

## Questions

1. Was Measure E proposed by a federal, state, or local level of government? What is the best clue to this?
2. What does the federal EPA recommend for the disposal of biosolids?
3. Why was Measure E proposed?
4. Was Measure E valid?
5. Could the California general assembly have used discretionary language concerning local regulation of recycling solid waste?
6. Why is it important for a state or federal government to enact a law that preempts lower regulation?

# Discussion Questions

1. Amy grew and used marijuana at her home for medicinal purposes, which was legal in her state. Federal agents from the Drug Enforcement Agency seized Amy's marijuana plants and charged her with violating federal laws. Amy claimed the federal government violated her rights since she was not engaged in interstate commerce. Is this true? Why or why not?

2. Should the federal government preempt states from regulating the labeling of genetically engineered foods?

3. Should a state legislature preempt local governments from precluding timber harvesting operations in certain areas adjacent to streams, restricting helicopter timber harvesting operations to certain areas, or determining that timber harvesting should be excluded from certain areas?

# CHAPTER FIVE
## Equal Protection and Administrative Law

## Learning Objectives

- *Identify the three different tests to examine laws and regulations providing unequal treatment.*
- *Illustrate when governments can adopt environmental regulations that discriminate.*
- *Explain justifications for treating people and property differently.*
- *Discuss why governments employ agencies.*
- *Describe the rulemaking and adjudicative functions of agencies.*

## Equal Protection

Challenges to environmental and public health statutes, ordinances, and regulations often are grounded upon a perceived unfairness in differentiating among various categories of interests and persons. This may lead disgruntled individuals to allege that they are being discriminated against and as such are violations of their equal protection rights guaranteed by the federal Constitution. Actions of the federal government that classify individuals in a discriminatory manner will violate the Due Process Clause of the Fifth Amendment. The Fourteenth Amendment sets forth an equal protection provision that protects persons from state governmental actions that discriminate against various groups.

*14th Amendment: No state shall make or enforce any law which shall ... deny to any person within its jurisdiction the equal protection of the laws.*

State constitutions also contain equal protection clauses. Over the second half of the twentieth century, equal protection emerged as a powerful argument to challenge all kinds of governmental regulations, including environmental regulations, which did not apply to everyone equally. Federal courts developed three tests to determine whether a governmental statute or regulation offends equal protection. These tests depend upon the classification of the protected interest.

I. **Rational basis test.** This test is used unless the classification is found by the judiciary to be suspect. The statutory classification is presumed valid and will comport with constitutional standards as long as it bears reasonable relationship to a legitimate governmental purpose.

II. **Intermediate level of scrutiny.** For a quasi-suspect classification, the differentiation of groups by gender and legitimacy of birth must be substantially related to an important governmental objective.

III. **Strict judicial scrutiny.** For suspect classifications based on race, alienage, sex, or socially stigmatic inequities, the government classification will fall unless it demonstrates the classification is necessarily related to a compelling governmental interest.

For a majority of the governmental actions that distinguish among persons when addressing environmental and health issues, the rational basis test applies. The following cases show how questions of equal protection are evaluated. The first case concerns an ordinance that protects people's health from secondhand smoke. The second case involves an ordinance that grants certain property owners a windfall by forgiving indebtedness.

### *Goodpaster v. City of Indianapolis*
US Court of Appeals for the Seventh Circuit, Chicago

*Who is suing?* _____

*Who is being sued?* _____

*For what?* _____

*What is the issue on appeal?* _____

Appellants, who own bars in Indianapolis-Marion County, Indiana, filed suit seeking injunctive and declaratory relief against enforcement of the 2012 Indianapolis-Marion County smoking ordinance. The district court denied the bar owners' motion for a preliminary and permanent injunction and entered judgment in favor of the City. The bar owners now appeal.

In 2005, the City-County Council of Indianapolis and Marion County passed an ordinance prohibiting smoking in most buildings frequented by the general public. The City-County Council excepted several businesses from the ban. Seven years later, in 2012, the City-County Council expanded the 2005 ordinance by eliminating many of its exceptions. As amended, the ordinance included exceptions for private residences, retail tobacco stores, tobacco specialty bars, and private clubs that voted to permit smoking. The amended ordinance thus prohibited smoking in most Indianapolis bars and taverns.

A group of Indianapolis-Marion County bar owners affected by the ordinance brought suit seeking declaratory and injunctive relief from the ordinance. In their amended complaint, they asserted due process, equal protection, takings and freedom of association claims under both the federal and Indiana constitutions. The bar owners filed a motion for a preliminary injunction, and the City filed a motion to dismiss for failure to state a claim. The district court consolidated the hearing on the preliminary injunction with a hearing on the merits. At the hearing, several of the bar owners testified about the negative economic effects of the ordinance. All who were asked denied they were facing insolvency. After the hearing, both the bar owners and the City filed their proposed findings of fact and conclusions of law. The district court entered judgment in favor of the City, finding that the bar owners could not establish actual success on the merits of their claims.

The bar owners argue the ordinance denies them equal protection of the laws because while it bans smoking in traditional bars, smoking remains lawful in tobacco specialty bars. The ordinance defines "tobacco specialty bars" as businesses that do not sell cigarettes or permit cigarette smoking on their premises, that sell food only as an incident to cigars or hookah, and that earn at least 20% of their revenue from the sale of cigars or hookah. The bar owners acknowledge this distinction does not rest on a suspect or quasi-suspect classification and is thus subject to rational basis review.

Rational basis review requires us to presume an ordinance is valid and to uphold it so long as it bears a rational relation to some legitimate end. Once we identify a plausible basis for the legislation, our inquiry is at its end. When dealing with local economic regulation, it is only the invidious discrimination, the wholly arbitrary act, which cannot stand consistently with the Fourteenth Amendment. The bar owners suggest that because the council members could not articulate a reason for the cigar bar exception, the legislation lacked a rational basis. But they mischaracterize the nature of rational basis review. To uphold a legislative choice, we need only find a "reasonably conceivable state of facts that could provide a rational basis" for the classification. The actual motivation (or lack thereof) behind the legislation is immaterial.

The bar owners also argue that because cigars are at least as harmful as cigarettes, permitting cigar smoking while banning cigarette smoking is arbitrary and capricious. Illogical reasons for a distinction, however, will not doom a classification supported by other rational reasons. In this case, the City could have been trying to protect public health by decreasing secondhand smoke exposure but simultaneously trying not to close all businesses where tobacco was sold or used. This was rational: while the City wants to decrease involuntary exposure to secondhand smoke, it does not want to ban smoking and tobacco use in its entirety. An effort to decrease involuntary exposure to secondhand smoke will naturally not be as concerned with bars whose business model is predicated on tobacco. Presumably, the patrons of cigar bars and hookah bars are not being involuntarily subjected to secondhand smoke because they chose to patronize bars where smoking is a necessary and essential part of the experience.

The City thus drew a line between traditional bars, for whom tobacco sales and usage are incidental to their primary business of alcohol and food sales, and tobacco specialty bars, whose business models depend on tobacco sales. The bar owners essentially argue that this line was drawn incorrectly because it does not include their businesses, which also depend significantly upon on-site tobacco usage. But legislation does not violate the Equal Protection Clause merely because the classifications it makes are imperfect. A law can be underinclusive or overinclusive without running afoul of the Equal Protection Clause. Because the bar owners cannot establish that the ordinance lacked a rational basis, their equal protection claim must fail. We affirm the district court's judgment in favor of the City.

## Questions

1. Does the ordinance discriminate against a group, and whom?
2. Does the governing body have to articulate the rational basis for its discrimination?
3. What did the court identify as the rational basis for the discrimination?
4. Could the governing body have also exempted pool (billiard) halls?
5. If the court had considered a substantive due process argument about the discrimination against bar owners, how would it have responded?

### *Armour v. City of Indianapolis*
United States Supreme Court

*Who is suing?* _____

*Who is being sued?* _____

*For what?* _____

*What is the issue on appeal?* _____

For many years, an Indiana statute, the "Barrett Law," authorized Indiana's cities to impose upon benefitted lot owners the cost of sewer improvement projects. The Law also permitted those lot owners to pay either immediately in the form of a lump sum or over time in installments. In 2005, the city of Indianapolis (City) adopted a new assessment and payment method and it forgave any Barrett Law installments that lot owners had not yet paid. A group of lot owners who had already paid their entire Barrett Law assessment in a lump sum believes that the City should have provided them with equivalent refunds. And we must decide whether the City's refusal to do so unconstitutionally discriminates against them in violation of the Equal Protection Clause, Amendment 14. We hold that the City had a rational basis for distinguishing between those lot owners who had already paid their share of project costs and those who had not and there is no equal protection violation.

Indiana's Barrett Law permitted cities to pay for public improvements, such as sewage projects, by apportioning the costs of a project equally among all abutting lands or lots. When a city completed a project, the board would issue a final lot-by-lot assessment. The Law permitted lot owners to pay the assessment either in a single lump sum or over time in installment payments with interest. In 2005, the City adopted a new system, called the Septic Tank Elimination Program (STEP), which financed projects in part through bonds, thereby lowering individual lot owners' sewer-connection costs. This case concerns the Brisbane/Manning Sanitary Sewers Project for which the Indianapolis Board of Public Works sent 180 affected homeowners a formal notice of their payment obligations in July 2004. The notice made clear that each homeowner could pay the entire assessment—$9,278 per property—in a lump sum payment or under an installment plan paid over 10, 20, or 30 years.

The next year, however, the City decided to abandon the Barrett Law method of financing. It thought that the Barrett Law's lot-by-lot payments had become too burdensome for many homeowners to pay. The City's new STEP method of financing would charge each connecting lot owner a flat $2,500 fee and make up the difference by floating bonds eventually paid for by all lot owners citywide. The City's Board of Public Works enacted a further Resolution to forgive all assessment amounts established pursuant to the Barrett Law Funding due and owing from the date of November 1, 2005 forward. In its preamble, the Resolution said that the Barrett Law may present financial hardships on many middle to lower income participants who most need sanitary sewer service in lieu of failing septic systems; it pointed out that the City was transitioning to the new STEP method of financing; and it said that the STEP method was based upon a financial model that had considered the current assessments being made by participants in active Barrett Law projects as well as future projects.

The upshot was that those who still owed Barrett Law assessments would not have to make further payments but those who had already paid their assessments would not receive refunds. This meant that homeowners who had paid the full $9,278 Brisbane/Manning Project assessment in a lump sum the preceding year would receive no refund, while homeowners who had elected to pay the assessment in installments, and had paid a total of $309.27, $463.90, or $927.80, would be under no obligation to make further payments.

Thirty-one of the 38 Brisbane/Manning Project lump-sum homeowners brought this lawsuit seeking a refund of about $8,000 each. They claimed in relevant part that the City's refusal to provide them with refunds at the same time that the City forgave the outstanding Project debts of other Brisbane/Manning homeowners violated the Federal Constitution's Equal Protection Clause. The trial court granted summary judgment in their favor. The State Court of Appeals affirmed that judgment. But the Indiana Supreme Court reversed. In its view, the City's distinction between those who had already paid their Barrett Law assessments and those who had not was rationally related to its legitimate interests in reducing its administrative costs, providing relief for property owners experiencing financial hardship, establishing a clear transition from the Barrett Law to STEP, and preserving its limited resources. We granted certiorari to consider the equal protection question.

As long as the City's distinction has a rational basis, that distinction does not violate the Equal Protection Clause. This Court has long held that a classification neither involving fundamental rights nor proceeding along suspect lines cannot run afoul of the Equal Protection Clause if there is a rational relationship between the disparity of treatment and some legitimate governmental purpose. We have made clear in analogous contexts that, where ordinary commercial transactions are at issue, rational basis review requires deference to reasonable underlying legislative judgments. And we have repeatedly pointed out that legislatures have especially broad latitude in creating classifications and distinctions in tax statutes.

Indianapolis' classification involves neither a "fundamental right" nor a "suspect" classification. Its subject matter is local, economic, social, and commercial. It is a tax classification. Hence, this case falls directly within the scope of our precedents holding such a law constitutionally valid if there is a plausible policy reason for the classification, the legislative facts on which the classification is apparently based rationally may have been considered to be true by the governmental decisionmaker, and the relationship of the classification to its goal is not so attenuated as to render the distinction arbitrary or irrational.

In our view, Indianapolis' classification has a rational basis. The City had decided to switch to the STEP system. After that change, to continue Barrett Law unpaid-debt collection could have proved complex and expensive. It would have meant maintaining an administrative system that for years to come would have had to collect debts arising out of 20-plus different construction projects built over the course of a decade, involving monthly payments as low as $25 per household. To have added refunds to forgiveness would have meant adding yet further administrative costs, namely the cost of processing refunds. The Indiana Supreme Court wrote that the City's classification was "rationally related" in part "to its legitimate interests in reducing its administrative costs," and petitioners have not "negatived" this justification. We conclude that the City has not violated the Federal Equal Protection Clause, and the Indiana Supreme Court's similar determination is affirmed.

## Questions

1. Why did the city adopt the STEP method of financing?
2. Why were the petitioners unhappy with the city's STEP solution?
3. What does "granted certiorari" mean?
4. What is the significance of finding that the city's ordinary commercial transaction involved neither a "fundamental right" nor a "suspect" classification?

5. Did the city have to show that the administrative costs under the Barrett Law would be complex and expensive?

6. How did the trial court reach a contrary result?

# Administrative Law

Every government depends on persons to perform its activities. Governmental agencies and officials are given responsibilities to implement the law, administer its requirements, enforce the law, and reconcile disputes. American jurisprudence has a non-delegation doctrine under which legislative bodies cannot delegate legislative or judicial functions to the executive branch. However, it has been recognized that agencies can establish reasonably clear standards for agency rulemaking and for actions to enforce agency requirements. A brief overview of federal administrative law will highlight some of the issues that are important to public health and environmental quality.

The federal government has adopted the Administrative Procedure Act (APA) to oversee the activities of all federal agencies. The act governs the way in which federal agencies propose and establish regulations. Agencies have legislative power to create rules. Agencies, as part of the executive branch of the government, have executive power to investigate problems and violations. Investigations that show violations call for adjudication of the issue and a resolution. This is part of the agency's judicial power to settle disputes.

Administrative actions include (1) implementing and enforcing the law; (2) rulemaking, the agency process of formulating rules and regulations needed to carry out legislative mandates; and (3) adjudication, an agency's authority to issue decisions on controversies. State legislatures have adopted state administrative procedure acts to oversee the administrative activities of their state agencies.

Agencies of the federal government are part of the executive branch and therefore report to the president. A government implements its laws through agencies and the regulations developed by agencies. Through agencies, governments develop and maintain technical expertise and specialization to oversee activities and subjects that Congress has decided to regulate. Under rulemaking authority, agencies adopt regulations as part of their quasi-legislative function. With adjudication, agencies have decision-making power similar to judicial tribunals.

Several reasons have been advanced to explain the use of agencies in regulating our society. Agencies reduce the need for detailed legislation; agencies develop the rules that implement the broad mandates of legislation. Agencies allow for specialization. They hire persons who can provide the technical expertise to implement rules and oversee regulated firms. The personnel and rules of agencies provide uniformity of rules on a given subject and continuity of programs, regardless of who is president. Agencies provide some room for experimentation. If a new rule does not work out, the agency can change it without waiting for congressional action. Adjudication at agencies requires most actions against the government start at the agency level and so relieves court congestion.

## 1. Implementation and Enforcement of Laws

The president appoints the heads of each executive agency, and they are generally referred to as "secretaries." This means that when a new president is elected, the leadership of agencies changes; new secretaries are appointed. The president also issues executive orders, which may affect the implementation of federal laws. The Office of Management and Budget is important in recommending funding for each agency.

Governments have laws for many reasons. With respect to environmental and public health concerns, governments seek to preserve environmental quality; eliminate profits from noncompliance; safeguard public health and well-being; deter violations of adopted laws; and oversee regulatory provisions that are beneficial for society. Congress often passes laws on a given subject, so there are many laws that address environmental and public health issues. These will be discussed in later chapters.

Legislation passed by Congress will need to identify an agency for implementing the legal provisions and grant enforcement powers. Agencies are thereby limited by the enabling legislation enacted by a legislative body. Agencies proceed to develop regulatory provisions governing the subject matter. This will include civil remedies that delineate various types of relief.

All criminal penalties must be adopted by the legislative body. For federal actions against alleged crimes, the US Department of Justice has prosecutorial authority. A United States attorney has plenary authority exercised under the supervision and direction of the attorney general and his or her delegates.

Turning to the enforcement of laws, several terms are important for describing some of the actions that may be taken by administrative agencies. Whenever there is an alleged civil violation, the agency will refer to its regulations to select appropriate enforcement remedies.

    I.   Notice letters—alleged violations, remedial actions, deadlines, etc.
    II.  Consent agreements—informal adjudication.
   III.  Consent decrees—formal adjudication.
   IV.  Modifications or revocations of permits—may require a hearing.
    V.  Administrative fines.
   VI.  Injunctions to prohibit future actions or activities.
  VII.  Administrative orders with fines or require remedial measures or other relief.

## 2. Federal Rulemaking

An agency needs a legislative grant of power before it can enact regulations. For our purposes, regulations developed by agencies may also be referred to as *rules*. A rule is an agency statement to implement law, including rulemaking. The particular law that grants authority to an agency to manage a certain issue is called an *enabling act*. With a grant of power of an enabling statute, agencies engage in the legislative function of rulemaking. Rulemaking powers involve an agency process for formulating rules and regulations needed to carry out the legislative mandate. The APA sets minimum rulemaking standards that each agency must follow. If an agency fails to follow required procedures, it may be challenged in federal court. The cause of action may be a violation of the APA or an allegation of a due process violation.

There are three alternatives for making federal rules. (1) Informal rulemaking imposes minimum notice and comment requirements, which facilitate agency action in an expeditious fashion. Hearings may be over the phone, with a subsequent signed consent agreement. (2) Hybrid rulemaking requires greater opportunity for public input. (3) Formal rulemaking requires a full hearing and provides the public the greatest opportunity to present information on the merits of a proposed rule. An administrative law judge may preside over the hearings.

Whenever an agency proposes a new rule, it must be published in the *Federal Register* so that the public is aware of all regulatory changes. There are also requirements in allowing the public to participate in the development of new rules. Public participation and opportunity to be heard may be through the submission of written comments or through public hearings. Failure to follow these rules may result in a legal challenge, and an agency will be forced to conform to legal requirements. Agencies cannot make rules that define crimes. The definition of a crime is a legislative function that cannot be delegated to an agency.

After opportunities for public input, an agency considers all comments and information before adopting a final regulation. Each final regulation is published in the *Federal Register*. Final regulations are also published in the *Code of Federal Regulations* (CFR). Persons wanting to know what regulations apply to their business would look to the CFR. This compendium of regulations is organized by subject and contains all applicable federal regulations. A violation of a federal regulation is a violation of federal law. Every final regulation is subject to judicial review.

## 3. Adjudication

Adjudication is the ability of a federal agency to hear claims and respond to violations. The agency must comply with all constitutional principles and the requirements established by statutes and regulations. The agency will develop an administrative record that documents the transactions so that the agency can be held accountable for its actions. Aggrieved persons may seek judicial review if the agency has not followed its rules and proscriptions. In reviewing the actions of an agency, four major arguments form the basis for most actions.

I. A violation of a constitutional standard such as due process or equal protection.
II. The statute fails to delegate administrative authority to the agency, so it lacks the power to engage in its action.
III. The adoption of a regulation was procedurally flawed, so it should not be given effect.
IV. An allegation of a vague enabling statute or an insufficient limitation on an agency's actions that renders the agency's action invalid or void. Vague provisions do not provide adequate notice to persons about conduct that is prohibited.

## 4. Standards of Review under Administrative Law

A duly adopted regulation is presumed to be valid. We rely on agencies to implement our laws and the regulations they adopt have the force of law. Anyone who challenges a regulation needs to establish a basis for a judicial body to find that the regulation is not valid. This might involve a showing that a regulation was not adopted pursuant to the requisite procedure or that it is arbitrary and capricious. To avoid being considered arbitrary and capricious, the evidence must show a rational basis for the agency's action. The arbitrary or capricious test chiefly relates to whether a particular action is justified and whether the administrative action is without foundation. Actions need to be consistent with prior agency policies; otherwise, they open the door for being found to be arbitrary and capricious.

Agency actions are reviewed under the substantial evidence standard. Competent substantial evidence is tantamount to legally sufficient evidence. Moreover, the substantial evidence standard of review requires that the reviewer not reweigh the evidence or substitute judgment for that of the initial fact finder. Instead, an agency action is upheld if there is substantial evidence supporting its determination. The following case involved a challenge to a governmental action in which the State of California took drastic action to help save sharks. Chinese and Asian Americans argued that the prohibition was discriminatory but the court found a rational basis for the state's action.

### *Chinatown Neighborhood Association v. Harris*
US District Court, N.D. California

*Who is suing?* _____

*Who is being sued?* _____

*For what?* _____

*What is the issue on appeal?* _____

Fig. 5.1 Cities with immigrants often offer cultural specialities for sale

The State of California has made it unlawful for any person to possess, sell, offer for sale, trade, or distribute a shark fin (the Shark Fin Law). The official findings of the California legislature cited environmental, humanitarian, and health reasons in support of the Shark Fin Law. Plaintiffs Chinatown Neighborhood Association and Asian Americans for Political Advancement challenge the Shark Fin Law because it allegedly discriminates against Chinese Californians, since shark fins are a significant part of Chinese culture, and contend that it is unconstitutional.

Defendants Attorney General of the State of California and Director of the California Department of Fish and Wildlife (collectively, defendants), who are responsible for enforcing the California Fish and Game Code, move to dismiss the First Amended Complaint. Because none of the claims is plausibly alleged, I grant the motions to dismiss.

The Shark Fin Law makes it unlawful for any person to possess, sell, offer for sale, trade, or distribute a shark fin in California. Although the law contains limited exceptions, a violation of the Shark Fin Law is a misdemeanor and may be punished by up to six months' imprisonment and a fine up to $1,000. Before the Shark Fin Law was enacted, California law already banned the practice of shark finning by prohibiting the trading or possession on any commercial fishing vessel of any shark fin or shark tail or portion thereof that has been removed from the carcass. In enacting the law, the California legislature made official findings included as part of the Shark Fin Law that supported their action.

Shark fins, which are primarily used to make shark fin soup, are a significant part of Chinese culture. They are a traditional symbol of respect, honor, and appreciation, and are a ceremonial centerpiece of traditional Chinese banquets and holidays. Before the Shark Fin Law was enacted, the shark fins traded and consumed in California were harvested from sharks caught by fishers both within California and in other jurisdictions, including federal waters.

The plaintiffs allege that although the proponents of the Shark Fin Law ostensibly sought to address shark finning (the specific practice of cutting a shark's fin off and discarding the remainder of the shark at sea), shark population endangerment, and mercury consumption by people, those justifications were ruses. The plaintiffs claim the law violates the Equal Protection Clause under the Fourteenth Amendment and other causes. The Equal Protection Clause of the Fourteenth Amendment commands that no State shall deny to any person within its jurisdiction the equal protection of the laws, which is essentially a direction that all persons similarly situated should be treated alike.

The plaintiffs are mistaken. Nothing in the Shark Fin Law's text discriminates on the basis of race, ethnicity, cultural background, or national origin. Rather, it is a broadly applicable law that prohibits the possession or sale of shark fin. Every person in California is subject to the law. Because the Shark Fin Law is facially neutral, the plaintiffs must plead sufficient facts to show that the Shark Fin Law was enacted for the purpose of discriminating on account of race in order to subject the law to strict scrutiny. The plaintiffs have not done this.

The plaintiffs allege that the Shark Fin Law has a disparate impact on people of Chinese origin because it bears almost exclusively on people of Chinese national origin by suppressing the practice of Chinese ceremonial and cultural traditions. However, a law is not unconstitutional simply because it has a racially disparate impact. Even if a neutral law has a disproportionately adverse effect upon a racial minority, it is unconstitutional under the Equal Protection Clause only if that impact can be traced to a discriminatory purpose. Discriminatory purpose implies that the decisionmaker, in this case a state legislature, selected or reaffirmed a particular course of action at least in part "because of," not merely "in spite of," its adverse effects upon an identifiable group.

Because the Shark Fin Law need not be strictly scrutinized, it must only have a rational basis to be sustained. Under the rational basis review, a law must be rationally related to the furtherance of a legitimate governmental interest. In other words, the law must be upheld against equal protection challenge if there is any reasonably conceivable state of facts that could provide a rational basis for the classification. Courts are compelled under rational-basis review to accept a legislature's generalizations even when there is an imperfect fit between means and ends.

Humanitarian, conservationist, and health goals are legitimate government interests. The law bans all shark fins, regardless of origin or point of sale. While the plaintiffs suggest that the law is not well-tailored to its purported ends, that is insufficient to invalidate the law. Under rational basis review, a court should not expect the legislature to design a scheme that perfectly addresses the court's own concerns, nor should a court impose other methods that it would prefer. The plaintiffs have not carried their burden of plausibly alleging the lack of any rational basis by negating every conceivable basis supporting the law or showing that it is wholly irrational. Accordingly, I will dismiss the Equal Protection cause of action.

## Questions

1. Was it significant that the legislature made specific findings on shark population endangerment and conservation as part of the Shark Fin Law? Why?
2. Does the Shark Fin Law discriminate on the basis of cultural background or national origin? If so, why did the court find it to be constitutional?
3. Can a law have a racially disparate impact yet not offend the Equal Protection Clause, and if so, when?
4. The court noted that laws with a rational basis imperfectly addressing an issue may not violate the Equal Protection Clause and will be upheld despite their discrimination. Is this review standard similar to how our laws address due process challenges?

# Alternatives to Litigation

Although Americans have a special attachment to tort litigation, alternatives do exist. We might want to consider whether we can reduce or eliminate some litigation by adopting one or more alternative options. Many states have already moved to a reformed tort system with caps on damages, shortened time periods for initiating malpractice litigation, allowing collateral source offsets, and limiting attorneys' contingency fees. Other approaches for providing redress for medical malpractice include enterprise liability, no-fault, voluntary no-fault, mediation or binding arbitration, and early offers.

We have not been very receptive to dispute resolution methods other than litigation. We fear change. Rather than adopt no-fault insurance and other enterprise liability programs, we hang on to our tort system and attempt to address problems piecemeal through legislative amendments. We enact new exceptions to negligence rules and consider other changes, but established interest groups, including the plaintiffs' bar, make tort reform difficult.

## 1. No-Fault Insurance

No-fault insurance is an alternative to litigation. Although no-fault weakens the deterrent effect of tort law and has other problems, it can replace some litigation. One option is to move to a strict liability regime similar to workers' compensation programs. Under workers' compensation, injured persons receive benefits for injuries incurred on the job without proving fault. Workers' compensation replaces tort lawsuits with a state-sponsored insurance system providing payments to injured employees. While workers' compensation eliminates some incentives for workers to use sufficient care, it may be less costly than the alternative of individual lawsuits for each injury.

Alternatively, a no-fault system would not need to replace all tort cases with a strict liability scheme. Rather, it might differentiate among selected types of accidents and select those that are better handled outside of regular tort litigation. Another idea is to allow medical practitioners and patients to voluntarily agree to be bound by a no-fault compensation system. Patients would be compensated for injuries, but would not be able to file any additional claims against the practitioners.

## 2. Alternative Dispute Resolution Processes

American jurisprudence is attempting to encourage disagreeing parties to do more in resolving their disputes without going to court through alternative dispute resolution processes. Due to judicial costs, legislative bodies attempt to reduce litigation in the courts and alleviate court congestion. Parties find that alternative dispute resolution (ADR) offers a more economical solution to a controversy. Persons with small claims may have better access to justice if they do not need to proceed with an expensive trial. For some issues, alternatives to litigation may offer better solutions, as the procedures usually generate less animosity and may facilitate compromise solutions.

Alternative dispute resolution may employ one or more of several available techniques. Legislative directives or the selection by litigants determine which techniques are employed.

    I.   Voluntary or mandatory participation.
    II.   Involvement of counsel or no counsel.
    III.  Decisions by disputants or a third party.
    IV.  Formal or informal procedure.
    V.   Decisions based on law or additional criteria permitted.
    VI.  Settlements legally enforceable or not.

The four most common processes used in ADR are mediation, arbitration, case evaluation, and negotiation.

    I.   **Mediation.** Mediation is a process in which a neutral facilitates settlement discussions between parties. The neutral has no authority to make a decision or impose a settlement upon the parties. The neutral attempts to focus the attention of the parties upon their needs and interests, rather than upon rights and positions. Although in court-annexed or court-referred mediation programs the parties may be ordered to attend a mediation session, any settlement is entirely voluntary. In the absence of settlement, the parties lose none of their rights to a jury trial.

    II.  **Arbitration.** Arbitration differs from mediation in that an arbitrator or panel of arbitrators renders a decision after hearing an abbreviated version of the evidence. In nonbinding arbitration, either party may demand a trial within a specified period. The essential difference between mediation and arbitration is that arbitration is a form of adjudication, whereas mediation is not.

III. **Case evaluation.** Case evaluation or early neutral evaluation is a process in which a lawyer with expertise in the subject matter of the litigation acts as a neutral evaluator of the case. Each side presents a summary of its legal theories and evidence. The early neutral evaluation of the case may also provide a basis for settlement discussions.

IV. **Negotiation.** Negotiation is a dialogue between the parties intended to reach an understanding and produce an agreement. Negotiation is intended to result in a compromise that will end the dispute.

## 3. EPA's Alternative Dispute Resolution

The EPA's primary resource for services and expertise in the areas of consensus-building, collaborative problem solving, alternative dispute resolution, and environmental conflict resolution is the Conflict Prevention and Resolution Center. To achieve better governance, the agency adopted a memorandum calling for a commitment to employ collaboration to minimize and potentially avoid environmental and natural resource conflicts, as well as to enhance the use of environmental conflict resolution to manage and resolve conflicts that arise. This approach supports other transparency and good government initiatives such as the Executive Order on Improving Performance of Federal Permitting and Review of Infrastructure Projects, which encourage early collaboration among agencies, project sponsors, and affected stakeholders to incorporate and address their interests and minimize delays in making informed and timely federal permitting and review decisions.

## Discussion Questions

1. You are a manager for a company and an area under your management is cited for an Occupational Safety and Health Act (OSHA) violation. What does this mean for your job?

2. You are a governmental inspector. On an inspection, you note a problem beyond your responsibilities. What do you do?

3. What should we require of governing agencies in their development of rules governing safety and environmental quality?

4. Who should participate when an agency develops new rules?

5. As a representative of an environmental group, what rights do you have to participate in the development of new federal rules?

6. Why should we study administrative law?

# CHAPTER SIX
## Ownership and Use of Property

### Learning Objectives

- *Recognize different types of joint ownership in property.*
- *Explain the meaning of the different types of deeds.*
- *Describe various liens that may be placed on real property.*
- *Justify a state law recognizing adverse possession.*
- *Assess the policy implications of allowing the defense of property by the use of deadly force.*

Private property ownership is a fundamental aspect of democracy. Individuals are able to buy and sell property and can accumulate wealth through the ownership of real estate. Over the centuries, we have encouraged property ownership through tax incentives and have adopted laws that support the use of real property for productive purposes.

### Ownership Shares

In the United States, we allow more than one person to own real estate under several distinct title-document options. These options involve different ownership rights so buyers have choices in relationships with cotenants. Unless more is said, multiple owners will own property as "tenants in common." However, for situations where co-owners feel restrictions on transfers of the interests of a co-owner are desirable, they can acquire property under the auspices of a state law that limits cotenants from transferring ownership rights.

## 1. Tenancy in Common

A tenancy in common is created wherever two or more persons are entitled to the simultaneous possession of a given parcel of property. Tenants in common may have equal or unequal shares. Every tenant in common has the right to possess the joint property in accordance with the designated share.

A cotenant cannot withdraw from the joint property any of its essential value, such as mineral deposits, and is not liable for accounting for rent to cotenants. A tenant in common is liable to account to a cotenant for the receipt of rent or other profit from the joint property, waste committed, deprivation of a cotenant of the use of a fair proportion of the joint property, appropriation of the joint property to exclusive use, or use of the joint property in a manner which necessarily is exclusive. If one tenant in common receives more than an appropriate share of the rents and profits, the cotenant is liable therefore as the agent of the other cotenant.

## 2. Joint Ownership

If co-owners want the survivor to inherit the property, this is possible under a state statute through special language in the title document. Each state has its own statutory provisions for creating joint ownership with survivorship, and more than one option may exist in a state. Under statutory provisions, the instrument of title usually refers to the takers as *joint tenants, joint tenants and not as tenants in common, joint tenants with survivorship*, or as taking *jointly with survivorship*. The right of survivorship means that when joint tenants die, their interests in the joint property pass to the other joint tenants and not to the heirs of the deceased.

In most states, four conditions are required to create a joint tenancy: (1) All tenants acquire the property at the same time; (2) all tenants have an equal interest in the property; (3) all tenants acquire title by the same instrument (deed or will); and (4) all tenants have an equal right to possession of the entire property. If a joint tenant transfers his or her ownership share before death, the new share owner is not a joint tenant due to not acquiring an interest in the property at the same time. The new share owner would have a tenancy in common with the other joint tenants. The remaining joint tenants would have a joint tenancy with each other but a tenancy in common with the new owner.

In most states, married individuals may own property as a *tenancy by the entirety*. This is a special type of shared ownership of property under which both the husband and wife own an undivided interest in the property, have full rights to occupy and use the property, and have the right of survivorship. The important difference with other statutory joint tenancies is that tenants by the entirety cannot transfer their interest in the property during their lifetime without the consent of the other spouse. Thus, a spouse cannot unilaterally sever the tenancy, dispossess the other spouse, or make any transfer to someone else. At the death of a spouse, the property automatically goes to the surviving spouse and not to the heirs of the deceased.

# Deeds to Real Property

A deed is the name of the instrument used to transfer title in real estate from a grantor to a grantee during the grantor's lifetime. In most states, a deed must be made on valuable (generally money) or good (generally love and affection) consideration, signed by the maker, attested by two witnesses, and delivered so it is no longer in control of the maker. There are different types of deeds, with the following four types of deed being the most common.

1. **Warranty Deed.** A warranty deed includes covenants of a right to sell, freedom from encumbrances except as noted, and quiet and peaceful possession.
2. **Quit Claim Deed.** A quit claim deed conveys to the grantee the interest the grantor had to convey. The grantor does not make the promises that are present in a warranty deed.
3. **Security Deed.** When a grantor borrows funds to purchase real property, title passes to the grantee (lending institution). Upon payment of the debt, the grantee then reconveys title back to the grantor. A state may have a statute requiring lenders to cancel security deeds within a few weeks of receipt of full payment of the debt.
4. **Personal Representative's Deed.** A deed signed by an individual who is looking after the sale of real estate on behalf of another is called a personal representative's deed. This type of deed is used by executors of decedents' estates and administrators of the affairs of persons who are incapacitated.

A deed should be recorded in the clerk's office of the superior court in the county where the land is located. Deeds that are not recorded may be valid, but if the grantor makes a subsequent transfer of the same property interest, the subsequent grantee may acquire a superior interest. Grantors must have the requisite mental capacity to transfer property. The following case discusses some issues involving conflicting claims to a small portion of real estate involving a roadway.

### *Chackal v. Staples*
Court of Appeal of Florida

*Who is suing?* _____

*Who is being sued?* _____

*For what?* _____

*What is the issue on appeal?* _____

The Chackals timely appeal the trial court's ruling that a portion of a roadway that borders their property is owned by Palm Beach County pursuant to § 95.361, Florida Statutes. Having carefully considered all of the arguments raised on appeal, we hold that the County has satisfied its statutory burden in all respects as to the majority of the disputed strip, except for the grassy area west of the guardrail. Thus, we affirm in part and reverse in part.

Upland residents of the waterfront Carleton neighborhood originally filed this action against waterfront residents, the Chackals and the Hechts, and the County to enforce their deeded easement rights of access to the Intracoastal Waterway. The Chackals and the Hechts counterclaimed against the plaintiffs and cross-claimed against the County to quiet title based upon their warranty deeds to the disputed property. During these proceedings, the County and the plaintiffs adopted the shared position that the County owns the disputed portion of the road. At the trial, the County presented evidence of statutory presumed dedication. After a two-day bench trial, the trial court entered final judgment in favor of the County holding that it had acquired title to the land at issue by statutory presumed dedication pursuant to Florida Statutes § 95.361(1). The court found the evidence was undisputed that the County had constructed, maintained and repaired the roadway continuously and uninterruptedly for more than four years, which included the utilization of the entire disputed strip.

Ernest Carleton had developed the Carleton subdivision comprised of multiple lots around Suzanne Circle, a road that was originally constructed out of shell rock. At the west end of South Suzanne, the original shell rock road sloped downward to the Intracoastal Waterway and was historically used as a boat ramp by the Carleton residents. The portion of South Suzanne located between lot 10 (Hecht) and lot 11 (Chackal), described in this case as "the disputed strip," measures approximately 151' long by 34' wide and extends west from the southwest corner of Suzanne Circle to the Intracoastal Waterway. In each of the original Carleton deeds, Carleton granted an easement that provided a right-of-way over the disputed strip to access the Intracoastal Waterway. In its written order, the trial court acknowledged and defined the residents' deeded easement rights as private easement rights for pedestrian access for ingress and across the disputed strip to the Intracoastal Waterway right of way. On appeal, the Chackals do not dispute the trial court's findings concerning the residents' easement rights and those findings remain undisturbed by the holding reached by this court.

In 1972, all property owners in the Carleton subdivision voluntarily executed quitclaim deeds to the County for their portions of Suzanne Circle as part of the County's Courtesy Maintenance program. Due to an apparent oversight by Carleton, title to the disputed strip was never included in the original deeds to lots 10 and 11. Consequently, when the predecessor owners of lots 10 and 11 attempted to convey their interests in the disputed strip, title did not pass to the County because it was not theirs to convey. Unaware that the owners of lots 10 and 11 failed to effectively convey title to the disputed strip, the County removed the property from the tax rolls (as if it had been conveyed to the County), along with the rest of Suzanne Circle, in 1972.

In 1984, the County undertook "Suzanne Circle Street Improvements." The County paved all of Suzanne Circle and updated the drainage system. In the disputed strip portion of South Suzanne Circle, the County raised and leveled the roadbed; constructed a three-foot cement outflow pipe beneath the road; paved 137' by 34' of the road's surface; installed a 25' guardrail where the pavement ends, and planted sod on the approximately 15' by 34' of land lying to the west of the guardrail. Additionally, at the end wall of the road, which was created when the County elevated the roadbed, the County installed bags of "riprap" or sand cement around the outflow pipe for reinforcement. Following the 1984 improvement project, the upland Carleton residents continued to utilize the disputed strip to access the Intracoastal Waterway for recreation purposes. Thereafter, the Chackals purchased lot 11, and the Hechts purchased lot 10 and both lots border the disputed strip.

After conducting a title search, the Chackals discovered that the disputed strip was never conveyed to the County. In an attempt to obtain dominion over the property, the Chackals and the Hechts purchased special warranty deeds to the disputed strip from Carleton's widow. Following completion of the 1984 road improvement project, the County continued to conduct maintenance to the disputed strip. According to the undisputed testimony, over that same period, the Chackals and the Hechts jointly maintained the grassy portion of the disputed strip located west of the guardrail.

The appellants argue that the County failed to meet its burden under Florida Statutes § 95.361 because the County did not "construct" the portion of the road at issue, as it was already a pre-existing shell rock road. We disagree and hold that the trial court's finding that the County "constructed" the road was amply supported by competent substantial evidence in the record. We therefore hold that competent substantial evidence supports the trial court's finding that the County maintained the road east of, and up to, the guardrail continuously and uninterruptedly for a period of over four years.

Nevertheless, the trial court's findings, as they relate to the County's maintenance of the grassy area west of the guardrail, are not supported by competent substantial evidence. We find no evidence in the record indicating that the County ever maintained the grassy portion of the road west of the guardrail and that there was unrefuted testimony and evidence that the Chackals and the Hechts maintained that area to the extent appropriate under the circumstances. Since we find that the County has not met its burden of proving presumed dedication with respect to the grassy portion of the disputed strip located west of the guardrail, the Chackals and the Hechts retain fee simple ownership therein, subject to the easement rights of the Carleton residents and the County. Affirmed in part and reversed in part.

## Questions

1. On appeal, what property was in dispute?
2. What was the purpose of the quit claim deeds in 1972?
3. What is the difference between counterclaims and cross-claims?

4. Who owned the property under the disputed strip in 1983 and from whom had they acquired the property?
5. What may happen when a grantor fails to convey property to a government for a road but government proceeds and develops a road?

# Liens

A lien is any official claim or charge against property or funds for payment of a debt or an amount owed for services rendered. Liens generally are formal documents signed by the party to whom money is owed. A mortgage or a security is a form of a lien. Any lien against real property must be recorded in the county where the property is located.

There are numerous types of liens, including mechanics' liens against the real property upon which a workman, contractor, or supplier has provided work or materials, attorneys' liens for fees to be paid from funds recovered by the attorney's efforts, medical liens for medical bills to be paid from funds recovered for an injury, landlords' liens against a tenant's property for unpaid rent or damages, and tax liens to enforce a government's claim of unpaid taxes. Most liens are enforceable in the order in which they were recorded, except tax liens, which have priority over other liens.

# Adverse Possession

Adverse possession is a doctrine under which a person in possession of land owned by someone else may acquire valid title to it. This only occurs if the adverse possessor meets the requirements of state law and is in possession for a sufficient period of time as defined by a statute of limitations. Most states have multiple adverse possession statutes to encourage the beneficial use of property and to resolve disputes between persons with different claims to the same property.

Regular adverse possession by prescription occurs when a possessor acquires the property by reason of the continuance of possession for a period of twenty years or more. In order for possession to be the foundation of a prescriptive title, four conditions for occupation are enumerated: (1) continuous; (2) hostile; (3) open and notorious to the true owner; and (4) actual so that the true owner has an action for trespass. Permissive possession cannot be the foundation of a prescription until there are an adverse claim and actual notice to the other party.

In some cases, multiple parties may have separate written evidence of title to property under different warranty or quit claim deeds. Under "color of title," a possessor must occupy the property adversely for a period of seven years. This will confer good title by prescription to the property against everyone except the state and those persons laboring under the disabilities. Property held by governments cannot be taken by adverse possession. This includes lands owned by local governments. The following case shows how an adverse possessor of property can acquire superior title.

### *Steinichen v. Stancil*
Supreme Court of Georgia

*Who is suing?* _____

*Who is being sued?* _____

*For what?* _____ _____

*What is the issue on appeal?* _____

At issue is title to a rectangular-shaped piece of real property measuring 25 feet by 75 feet. Appellant Karen Steinichen filed a petition to quiet title against all the world with regard to four contiguous parcels of real property, and appellee Larry Stancil, the owner of property adjacent to that of appellant, filed an answer and counterclaim in which he contended he held fee simple title to the property at issue. Pursuant to the Official Code of Georgia Annotated (OCGA) § 23-3-63, the case was submitted to a special master who quieted title to three of the four tracts in Stancil after ruling that Steinichen had failed to present evidence establishing title to those parcels. As to the fourth parcel, the special master ruled that Steinichen had failed to carry her burden of proof to establish title, and that Stancil had presented sufficient evidence to establish adverse possession under color of title as well as prescriptive title without color of title. The trial court entered an order adopting the findings and the recommendation of the special master and declared Stancil as the holder of fee simple title to all the property in dispute. This appeal follows the denial of Steinichen's motion for new trial.

Steinichen does not take issue with the trial court's determination that she failed to establish title to the disputed tract. Instead, she asserts only that the evidence was insufficient to support the conclusion that Stancil had acquired the property by adverse possession.

> *To establish title by adverse possession, whether by twenty years or seven years under color of title, a party must show possession not originated in fraud that is public, continuous, exclusive, uninterrupted and peaceable, and accompanied by a claim of right. In an action to quiet title under OCGA § 23-3-60 et seq., the findings of the Special Master and adopted by the trial court will be upheld unless clearly erroneous. If there is any evidence to support the trial court's judgment, it will not be disturbed on appeal.*

There was evidence that the disputed property was part of a lot Stancil acquired by deed in 1999 from the DeLaPerriere estate. Prior to his purchase of the property, Stancil used the property in connection with the garage and wrecker service he operated on contiguous property he leased from the estate from 1985 to 1999. He placed two school buses on the tract and used them to store engines and other parts. From 1971 to 1984, the estate leased to Lendgrin Maddox another portion of the building in which Stancil's business was located, and authorized Maddox to use and maintain the real property at issue. Maddox testified he openly, continuously, and exclusively used the disputed tract for his business during the entire term of his tenancy, and he maintained the tract by "bush-hogging" it and keeping it clean. Maddox testified the tract was separated from the neighboring property by a deep drainage ditch. Stancil testified he has openly, continuously and exclusively used the property in dispute since Maddox's departure, and that there is a fence on the tract.

In order to constitute the element of continuity which is essential to adverse possession as the foundation of a good prescriptive title, it is not necessary that adverse possession be maintained for the statutory period by the same person, since continuity may just as effectively be shown by the successive bona fide possessions of several persons, provided the requisite privity exists between them, so as to thus permit a tacking of their unbroken successive possessions. In order to show privity between successive occupants, all that is necessary is that one shall have received his possession from the other by some act of such other or by operation of law.

The unrefuted testimony that Maddox and Stancil used the disputed property as tenants from 1971 until 1999 inures to the benefit of the landlord. Accordingly, the DeLaPerriere estate possessed the tract from 1971 to 1999, by and through its tenants, and that possession can be tacked onto Stancil's possession as owner from 1999 until the present. Thus, the special master's finding that Stancil acquired the property by adverse possession is supported by some evidence, and the trial court's judgment adopting that finding is not clearly erroneous.

In light of our affirmance of the trial court's judgment based on the finding that Stancil acquired prescriptive title by possession for more than 20 years, we need not address the additional finding that Stancil also established adverse possession for seven years under color of title. Judgment affirmed.

## Questions

1. What is the meaning of a petition to quiet title?
2. What are the differences between prescriptive adverse possession and adverse possession by color of title?
3. Who owned the disputed property from 1971 to 1999?
4. Did the evidence show that Stancil himself had established adverse possession?
5. What is the policy basis for adverse possession?

## Defense of Property

State legislatures have passed statutes concerning the amount of force a person may lawfully use to defend property. The lawful amount of force depends on the type of property and the belief that the force employed was necessary. In general, persons are justified in threatening or using force against others when they reasonably believe that such threat or force is necessary to defend themselves or a third person against the imminent use of unlawful force.

Persons are justified in using force against another when they reasonably believe that such threat or force is necessary to prevent or terminate such other's unlawful entry into a habitation. Persons are not justified in using force if they initially provoke the use of force by another or they are attempting to commit, committing, or fleeing after the commission or attempted commission of a felony. Persons are justified in using force which is intended or likely to cause death or great bodily harm only if they reasonably believe that such force is necessary to prevent death or great bodily injury or to prevent the commission of a forcible felony.

Three categories of state laws prescribing rules governing the use of force may be noted: duty to retreat, castle doctrine, and stand your ground. The duty to retreat applies to situations where persons are required to diffuse the situation without resorting to deadly force. This includes retreating if the person is safely inside a habitation. Approximately one-half of the states recognize the castle doctrine under which you can use deadly force to protect real property, including your home, yard, or private office. More than twenty states have passed legislation known as "stand your ground" laws. Under these laws, persons have no duty to retreat prior to use of force in self-defense, including the use of deadly force.

## Transfers and Brokerage Relationships

Transfers of real property generally involve considerable money so that buyers and sellers may choose to engage the skills provided by real estate brokers and lawyers. Each state legislature has adopted statutory provisions concerning licensing and obligations of real estate brokers. For most areas, the general rule is that a broker who performs services under a brokerage engagement for another is a limited agent. Unless a broker enters into a brokerage engagement with a person, it is presumed that the person is a customer of the broker rather than a client. This means that the broker is not employed by a client and is not a seller's or buyer's broker. However, a different legal relationship between the broker and the person may be documented by a writing.

A broker engaged by a seller will promote the interests of the seller, will timely disclose to prospective buyers with whom the broker is working all material adverse facts pertaining to the physical condition of the property, including but not limited to material defects in the property, environmental contamination, and facts required by statute or regulation to be disclosed which are actually known by the broker and which could not be discovered by a reasonable diligent inspection of the property by the buyer. A broker engaged by a seller does not breach any duty or obligation by showing alternative properties to prospective buyers.

A broker engaged by a buyer shall promote the interests of the buyer and will timely disclose to a prospective seller all material adverse facts actually known by the broker concerning the buyer's financial ability to perform the terms of the sale. A broker engaged by a buyer does not breach any duty or obligation by showing properties in which the buyer is interested to other prospective buyers.

# Instruments Accompanying the Purchase and Sale of Real Estate

The purchase and sale of property is often complicated by the existence of one or more instruments that affect the rights of the owner of the property. The buyer's lawyer will assist the buyer in discerning the meaning of these instruments and in executing the necessary paperwork to successfully complete the purchase of the property.

Fig. 6.1 "For Sale" signs are used to alert potential buyers of available properties.

1. **Sales Contract.** This is the agreement that commits you to transfer real estate. Although a contract for sale is often presented to buyers by a broker and signed without consultation with a legal expert, buyers might benefit from consulting a lawyer. This contract usually includes "earnest money" that is not returned if the buyer declines to complete the agreement. Contracts for sale include miscellaneous provisions (known as fine print) concerning fixtures, financing, title, closing procedures, and other terms. Since one or more of these terms may not provide what the buyer wants and may have a significant impact on the contract, the buyer should use care before signing the contract.

2. **Loan Agreement.** Buyers needing additional funds will need to secure a loan. The lending institution will probably have a standard loan agreement containing terms on paying back the borrowed moneys.

3. **Lien Releases.** If there are any liens against property being purchased, requisite arrangements should be made to secure releases prior to closing or to diminish the sales price by the amounts of unpaid liens.

4. **Mortgages.** If the buyer needs to borrow money, a clause can be included in the sales contract stating that the contract is dependent upon obtaining a mortgage. A mortgage will provide the lender a security interest in the property.

5. **Easements.** An easement is the right to use the property of another. Easements may already exist on the property or may be created by a deed, an express grant, or common-law action. Buyers will want to know what easements affect their rights on property being purchased.

6. **Covenants.** A covenant is an agreement concerning the use of property affecting quality, value, or mode of enjoyment. Protective covenants dealing with real estate are used to prescribe conditions and rules governing the use of property to be sold as part of a new subdivision to enhance the character and property values. In this manner, property owners of a subdivision are assured that their neighbors cannot engage in certain objectionable activities or deviate too far from certain community standards. Examples might include the construction of outbuildings and parking campers or mobile homes on the property. In most states, covenants governing real estate have a limited duration of twenty years. Covenants are enforced by owners of property burdened with the covenant.

7. **Leases and Usufructs.** A lease is an agreement whereby one person conveys real estate for a term of years or at will to another. The owner of the property is the lessor, while the person acquiring an interest is the lessee. Historically, leases have been divided into four major categories: tenancy for years; tenancy from year to year; tenancy at will; and tenancy by sufferance. In some states, existing law divides leases into two major categories: leases under five years and leases for more than five years. Leases under five years are called usufructs. Leases for more than five years are known as estates for years. A usufruct is a mere license to use or enjoy the use of property without conveyance of an interest in the land. It differs from a

leasehold estate or an estate for years due to no grant in an interest in land. Rather, a usufruct is a mere right to use property, not an interest in that property.

8. **Termite and Utility Inspections.** The buyer should have structures checked for termites and a guarantee should be made by an inspector. Buyers may hire someone to perform a utility inspection or may make such an inspection themselves.

9. **Title and Recording the Deed.** A qualified professional should check title to ascertain that there are no problems with the documentation needed for closing. After the closing, the deed should be recorded.

## Specific Performance and Closing

Due to the unique nature of property, each state has decided that either the buyer or the seller should be able to compel the other to complete a contract for sale. This can be controversial in situations where persons change their mind and do not want to proceed with the sales transaction. Generally, the seller and the buyer will get together at closing at the office of the buyer's attorney. At this time, the purchase price will be given to the seller, the buyer will receive a deed, and the mortgage will be signed so that it may be immediately filed along with the deed. Although buyers and sellers may contract otherwise, traditionally, most counties have established closing costs that are borne by each party. The following case shows a seller changing his mind about a contract for sale and a buyer seeking to enforce the contract.

### *Kennedy v. The Droughton Trust*
Court of Appeals of Georgia

*Who is suing?* _____

*Who is being sued?* _____

*For what?* _____

*What is the issue on appeal?* _____

Mark Kennedy sued The Droughton Trust and David Droughton, trustee for The Droughton Trust (collectively the Trust), to compel them to specifically perform a contract for the sale of land owned by the Trust. The trial court granted the Trust's motion for summary judgment and Kennedy appeals. We reverse.

Viewed in the light most favorable to Kennedy, the evidence shows that on November 10, 2013, Kennedy offered to purchase a vacant lot from the Trust for $64,500 cash. The form contract contained the following language with regard to the closing date:

> *This transaction shall be closed on December 10, 2013, or on such other date as may be agreed to by the parties in writing, provided, however, that: (1) the loan described herein is unable to be closed on or before said date; or (2) Seller fails to*

*satisfy valid title objections, Buyer or Seller may by notice to the other party (which notice must be received on or before the closing date) extend this Agreement's closing date up to seven days from the above-stated closing date.*

Kennedy left the portion of the contract allowing him to place a time limit for acceptance of his offer blank.

On December 11, 2013, one day after the closing date specified in the contract, the Trust signed the form contract and returned it to Kennedy through its real estate agent. The contract that was returned to Kennedy was marked by hand with an acceptance date of "December 11, 2013." The contract also has what appears to be a hand-drawn line though the closing date of December 10, 2013. Droughton testified in his deposition that he did not know whether he marked through the date before the contract was returned to Kennedy or if the line was created when the document was faxed. Kennedy testified that he did not make this mark.

Two or three days after he signed the contract with Kennedy, Droughton received a phone call from another bidder. The following day, an employee in the real estate agent's office called Droughton and told him there was a problem with the contract because it was signed the day after the closing date. Droughton then explained to the agent there was another problem, because the other bidder still wanted to buy the property.

Kennedy testified that he notified the Trust in writing that he accepted their offer of December 11, 2013. When Kennedy called the Trust's real estate agent to schedule the closing date, the agent informed him, "there is some monkey business going on," that he did not want to get into it. Kennedy called another person in the real estate agent's office and was told that Droughton was very upset with the agent's performance and wanted to get out of the contract. On December 16, 2013, Kennedy sent the following letter to the Trust:

*This letter is to serve notice to you that the Buyer(s) of the property in keeping with the terms of the certain sales contract dated December 11, 2013 are hereby notifying you the Seller that since the closing could not take place on December 10, 2013, the Buyer(s) are under the provisions set forth in Section 4, Paragraph C, of the contract notifying you in writing that we are attempting to contact you to schedule and set a new closing date as is our option per the contract. We are notifying you in writing that we request a new closing date of December 22, 2013 at the latest. Failure to close on this contract or respond to this notice will result in immediate legal action and a claim against the property.*

Later that day, Kennedy sent another letter to the Trust scheduling the closing for December 23, 2013. Because the trust received another higher offer after signing the contract on December 11, 2013, Droughton refused to schedule a closing date with Kennedy. There is no evidence the Trust withdrew its December 11, 2013 counteroffer in writing before December 16, 2013. Droughton acknowledged receiving a copy of the closing papers on December 19, 2013. Kennedy scheduled a closing for December 23, 2013 with the closing attorneys specified in the contract, and placed the purchase price funds in the closing attorney's escrow account. The Trust did not cooperate or participate in Kennedy's attempted closing. On December 30, 2013, Droughton signed a contract to sell the property to the other bidder for $75,000. Kennedy filed suit for specific performance of his contract on January 2, 2014. The trial court granted summary judgment to the Trust based on its conclusion that the contract expired by its own terms on December 10, 2013 and that, even if there had been a valid contract, Kennedy could not obtain specific performance because he had failed to prove he tendered the purchase price. Kennedy appeals and asserts that there is a jury question as to the existence of a contract and that the trial court erred when it concluded that he was required to tender the purchase price as a matter of law.

We agree with Kennedy's assertion that the parties entered into a valid contract for the sale of the property. The fact that Kennedy's offer was signed the day after the closing date specified in the offer does not support the trial court's conclusion that the contract expired by its own terms. Kennedy's December 16, 2013 letter manifested his acceptance of the counteroffer. The lack of a specific closing date in the contract does not render it too vague and indefinite to be enforced. If a contract does not contain a specific time for performance, it should be construed as requiring performance within a reasonable time. Kennedy made numerous attempts to schedule the closing. The Trust refused to cooperate, even though every contract imposes upon each party a duty of good faith and fair dealing in the performance of their respective duties and obligations. The trial court erred when it granted summary judgment based on its conclusion that a contract between the parties had expired by its own terms.

We also find the trial court erred by granting summary judgment based on its conclusion that Kennedy's claims are barred because he failed to make a proper tender of the purchase price to the Trust. It is true that to be entitled to specific performance on a real estate contract, the purchaser must make an unconditional tender of the purchase money due. This tender is excused or waived where the seller, by conduct or declaration, proclaims that if a tender should be made, acceptance would be refused. The law does not require a futile tender or other useless act. In this case, the Trust ignored Kennedy's requests to schedule a closing date and refused to participate in the closing. These facts create, at a minimum, a genuine issue of material fact as to whether Kennedy's tender obligation was excused. Judgment reversed.

## Questions

1. Why does the court view the facts in the light most favorable to Kennedy?
2. For real estate contracts, are dates for closing important?
3. Was Kennedy represented by good legal counsel?
4. What obligations do real estate agents own to buyers and sellers when there is a higher bid after a signed contract for sale?

5.  Did the court resort to equity in its decision?

# Discussion Questions

1.  What is the significance of the adoption of a "stand your ground" law by a state legislature?
2.  Which category of law concerning the defense of property has your state adopted? Is it optimal?
3.  You engage a broker to sell your house. While showing the broker your property, he asks about a remodeled part, and you disclose that there had been termite damage so it was repaired and all was fine. Is your broker obligated to share the existence of past termite damage with perspective buyers? Why or why not?

# Section Two

## Establishing Liability
## to Seek Redress

# CHAPTER SEVEN

## Strict Liability and Intentional Torts

## Learning Objectives

- *Summarize tort causes of actions for damages.*
- *Describe the intentional torts important to environmental quality.*
- *Identify examples of strict liability situations.*
- *Explain why injured persons prefer strict liability and intentional torts over negligence causes of action.*
- *Define the criteria evaluated to determine whether strict liability should apply.*

A tort is often defined as a civil wrong other than a breach of a contract for which relief is sought. Remedies are usually in the form of recompense for injuries from accidents caused by other persons. Tort actions force wrongdoers to provide restitution and act to deter persons from actions and activities that inflict harm on others. Tort actions are pursuant to state law, with the elements being prescribed by state legislation and common law.

Torts must be distinguished from crimes. Whereas a tort provides a private person with a remedy in civil law, a crime is an offense against the sovereign authority. Criminal prosecution is therefore by the government and is a separate lawsuit. However, wrongful action by a person may constitute both a tort and a crime. Moreover, a judgment against a defendant in a criminal case may be used as evidence against the defendant in a civil case. For example, assume that the defendant ran a stop sign and caused an accident.

Conviction of a traffic violation (not stopping for a stop sign) may be used as evidence in a civil action concerning damages for injuries arising from the accident.

# Strict Liability under Statutes and Common Law

Strict liability is a cause of action that makes persons liable for damages due to their engagement in an activity without fault. Plaintiffs do not have to prove negligence, and strict liability reduces the defenses that may be raised to defeat an action for damages. Each state has its own laws and rules on when a strict liability standard applies to an activity.

Many American states have adopted their doctrine of strict liability from the English case of *Rylands v. Fletcher* for abnormally dangerous conditions and activities. For other states, the definitive basis for strict liability is the doctrine for abnormally dangerous activities delineated by the *Restatement (Second) of Torts*. Restatements of the law are treatises on US legal topics published by the American Law Institute. This is an organization of legal academics and practitioners that prepares scholarly refinements of law to address uncertainty in the law through restatements of basic legal subjects that tell judges and lawyers what the common law provides for our legal system.

The *Restatement (Second) of Torts* § 519 provides that:

I.   One who carries on an abnormally dangerous activity is subject to liability for harm to the person, land or chattels of another resulting from the activity, although he has exercised the utmost care to prevent such harm.

II.  Such strict liability is limited to the kind of harm, the risk of which makes the activity abnormally dangerous.

*Restatement (Second) of Torts* § 520 lists the factors to be used when determining what constitutes an abnormally dangerous activity:

I.    Existence of a high degree of risk of some harm to the person, land or chattels of others;

II.   Likelihood that the harm that results from it will be great;

III.  Inability to eliminate the risk by the exercise of reasonable care;

IV.   Extent to which the activity is not a matter of common usage;

V.    Inappropriateness of the activity to the place where it is carried on; and

VI.   Extent to which its value to the community is outweighed by its dangerous attributes.

The application of these sections of the *Second Restatement* can be gleaned from a lawsuit in which the plaintiffs sued for injuries from fireworks.

### *Colangelo v. Bay View Improvement Association*
Superior Court of Connecticut

*Who is suing?* _____

*Who is being sued?* _____

*For what?* _____

*What is the issue on appeal?* _____

The defendant moves the court to strike all counts of the complaint because illegal fireworks displays are not, as a matter of law, an ultrahazardous activity imposing strict liability under Connecticut law. On July 4, the defendant owned, possessed and controlled Bayview Beach, a private beach in Milford, Connecticut. The defendant promoted and allowed its residents and their guests to ignite fireworks on Bayview Beach on July 4th of each year. On July 4, the plaintiffs were at Bayview Beach to watch the fireworks display as guests and/or business invitees of a resident. A resident, guest, member agent, servant and/or employee of the defendant ignited a firework that went straight into the crowd, striking the plaintiffs and detonating on their bodies resulting in serious injuries.

Each plaintiff alleges negligence, recklessness, and strict liability. In their strict liability claims, the plaintiffs allege that the promotion and allowance of illegal fireworks displays is an ultrahazardous activity, plaintiffs were injured as a proximate result of such activity and, therefore, the defendant is strictly liable for the harm the plaintiffs suffered. The defendant filed a motion to strike counts five and six for failure to state a legally sufficient cause of action for strict liability arising out of an ultrahazardous activity. The purpose of a motion to strike is to contest the legal sufficiency of the allegations of any complaint to state a claim upon which relief can be granted. A motion to strike challenges the legal sufficiency of a pleading, and, consequently, requires no factual findings by the trial court. In ruling on a motion to strike, the court is limited to the facts alleged in the complaint.

It is fundamental that in determining the sufficiency of a complaint challenged by a defendant's motion to strike, all well-pleaded facts and those facts necessarily implied from the allegations are taken as admitted. The role of the trial court in ruling on a motion to strike is to examine the complaint, construed in favor of the plaintiff, to determine whether the pleading party has stated a legally sufficient cause of action. The defendant moves to strike counts five and six on the ground that strict liability does not apply in this case, as the allegation of an "illegal fireworks display" is not an ultrahazardous activity as a matter of Connecticut law. Counts five and six are pleaded on the doctrine of strict liability imposed on persons who engage in what the *Restatement (First) of Torts* refers to as "ultrahazardous activity," and the *Restatement (Second) of Torts* terms "abnormally dangerous activity." Our Appellate Court has adopted the "abnormally dangerous activity" language, and standard, of the *Second Restatement*. In addition, the defendant contends that the plaintiffs fail to allege facts that would support a conclusion that the circumstances were such that they were necessarily or obviously exposed to the danger of a probable injury.

Strict liability imposes legal responsibility without regard to fault. To impose liability without fault, certain factors must be present: an instrumentality capable of producing harm; circumstances and conditions in its use which, irrespective of a lawful purpose or due care, involve a risk of probable injury to such a degree that the activity fairly can be said to be intrinsically dangerous to the person or property of others; and a causal relation between the activity and the injury for which damages are claimed. Thus, a plaintiff must allege not only that a dangerous instrumentality was used but also that it was used under such circumstances and conditions as necessarily and obviously to expose the person or property of another to probable injury even though due care was taken. The issue of whether an activity is ultrahazardous is a question of law for a court to decide. The courts in Connecticut and other jurisdictions which recognize the doctrine of strict liability for dangerous activities impose it only in narrow circumstances. In Connecticut, it has traditionally been applied in cases involving blasting and explosives.

The factors for a court to consider in determining whether an activity is abnormally dangerous are listed in § 520 of the *Second Restatement*: (a) existence of a high degree of risk of some harm to the person, land or chattels of others; (b) likelihood that the harm that results from it will be great; (c) inability to eliminate the risk by the exercise of reasonable care; (d) extent to which the activity is not a matter of common usage; (e) inappropriateness of the activity to the place where it is carried on; and (f) extent to which its value to the community is outweighed by its dangerous attributes. Comment (f) of § 520 clearly states that all of the factors need not be present for an activity to be considered abnormally dangerous. Comment (f) also states that any one of them is not necessarily sufficient of itself in a particular case, and ordinarily several of them will be required for strict liability.

*Lipka v. DiLungo* is the only Connecticut case addressing whether the allegation of illegal fireworks displays states a legally sufficient cause of action. In *Lipka*, the court analyzed each of the *Second Restatement* § 520 factors in the context of ruling on the defendant's motion to strike the plaintiff's cause of action for strict liability. The court adopts the reasoning of *Lipka* in this matter. In discussing the first factor, the "existence of a high degree of risk of some harm," the *Lipka* court stated that even jurists opposing the imposition of strict liability with respect to lawful fireworks displays have acknowledged that such displays satisfy this factor. The *Lipka* court found the second factor, the "likelihood that the resulting harm will be great," satisfied as well because fireworks are capable of causing extremely serious injuries. Factor three addresses the inability to eliminate the risk by the exercise of due care. The *Lipka* court, noting the legislative efforts prohibiting illegal fireworks displays and highly regulating all legal fireworks displays, concluded that, even with due care, an unavoidable risk of harm remains even in the case of legal displays of modern fireworks, but the risk of harm inevitably increases with the unlawful or illegal fireworks displays. Therefore, the *Lipka* court found that the first three factors of *Second Restatement* § 520, were satisfied.

The *Lipka* court only considered common usage, addressed in factor four, to the extent of stating that, although the illegal fireworks displays are common, it would be anomalous for the law to condone common illegal activity simply because it is common. The *Lipka* court did not consider factor five, the inappropriateness of the activity to the place where it is carried on, however this court notes that in Connecticut General Statutes § 29–357(b), the legislature delegates the issuance of permits to the State Fire Marshal's Office after the site is inspected and approved by the local fire marshal and approval by both the police and fire chiefs or other controlling local authorities. The *Lipka* court determined that factor six, the value to the community, was satisfied because the legislature determined, by enacting § 29–357, that the value of unlawful displays of fireworks is outweighed by their dangerousness.

After analyzing the factors and concluding that four of the six were satisfied, the court decided that the plaintiff had appropriately stated a case of strict liability in tort, and denied the defendant's motion to strike. This court finds the logic and reasoning of the *Lipka* court is persuasive. The allegations of an illegal fireworks display in this complaint are legally sufficient to state a cause of action arising out of an abnormally dangerous activity or an ultrahazardous activity which, if proved, imposes strict liability on the defendant for harm proximately caused to the plaintiffs. Following the analysis provided by the court in *Lipka*, the plaintiffs have sufficiently alleged a cause of action sounding in strict liability in tort. Accordingly, the court denies the defendant's motion to strike counts five and six of the complaint.

## Questions

1. What is the meaning of striking counts five and six?
2. Why is the *Restatement (Second) of Torts* important to this case?
3. Why did the court refer to a section of the Connecticut General Statutes?
4. What are three examples of activities subject to strict liability in Connecticut?
5. Which two factors for strict liability were not satisfied by the facts of the case?
6. Could a court in another state reach a different result given these facts and interpretations?

# Statutory Strict Liability Torts

For environmental problems involving the discharge of pollutants, statutes and regulations often enunciate a strict liability standard. The following case shows how polluters do not always realize the exacting requirements of water pollution statutes and regulations.

### *State ex. rel. Miller v. DeCoster*
Supreme Court of Iowa

*Who is suing?* _____

*Who is being sued?* _____

*For what?* _____

*What is the issue on appeal?* _____

Austin J. DeCoster appeals a district court ruling finding him in violation of several water pollution and animal waste control requirements at hog confinement facilities. He also contests the imposition of $59,000 in civil fines. He claims the district court did not have substantial evidence to support its rulings and abused its discretion in imposing the fines. We affirm.

DeCoster owned more than thirty hog confinement facilities in Iowa. Most of DeCoster's facilities are leased to other producers, but DeCoster is responsible for management and disposal of manure. The violation of improper spray irrigation was alleged. The attorney general brought this action to seek civil penalties and enjoin DeCoster from violating his permits, the administrative rules, and statutes. The district court imposed various civil fines which DeCoster challenges.

The most hotly contested issue is the challenge to the district court's imposition of a $5,000 fine on finding the spray irrigation incident violated statutes enacted to protect water quality. On April 27, DeCoster Farms began spraying irrigating water and manure from the storage basin at its finishing unit number three site. The irrigation equipment used consisted of a pump at the lagoon, aluminum piping to the irrigation equipment, and a sprinkler and hose. After the sprinkler finishes its 180 degrees arc application the equipment must be turned around in the opposite direction and the process completed. A DeCoster employee, Robert Polzin, was performing the application and completed the first 360 degrees turn, called a "pull," while it was still daylight. During the evening Polzin stayed in his truck while irrigating and used a spotlight to ascertain if there were any problems.

There were three large deep tiles underlying the DeCoster farm, all of which originated at unknown locations south of DeCoster's land and all of which were approximately three-to-four feet underground. Two of the three converged at some point on the DeCoster farm, so there were only two outlets. During the second "pull" that evening, Polzin noted that water and manure started to pool in the low spots. Irrigation continued until about 9 or 10 a.m. on April 28. A local person, Joe Haugen, found both tile outlets running a dirty darkish color, with a strong odor of hog manure. Both outfalls were identical in appearance, contained significant suspended solids, and created foam in the water in the ditch. The two outlets discharge into a stream that, in another 743 feet, joins the Iowa River.

Jeff Vansteenburg, a field agent for the Iowa Department of Natural Resources (DNR), arrived on April 28 and drove with Polzin around a portion of the field. No standing water or ponding on the irrigated land was noted when Vansteenburg arrived. Vansteenburg concluded the source of the discharge in the tiles was a result of DeCoster farms' spray irrigation. A DNR engineer, Ubbo Agena, concluded there must have been holes or other direct access to the tiles. We affirm the trial court's finding that the polluted discharge from the tile outlets flowed from the spray irrigation. The trial court's finding on the point is easily supported by substantial evidence. The record establishes, to a near certainty, that the spray irrigation conducted by DeCoster on April 27 and April 28 caused the pollution.

It is the State's claim that DeCoster's actions rendered him subject to the civil punishment imposed under Iowa Code § 455B.191(1) not to exceed five thousand dollars for each day of such violation. The State points particularly to Code § 455B.186(1) which provides:

> *A pollutant shall not be disposed of by dumping, depositing, or discharging such pollutant into any water of the state, except that this section shall not be construed to prohibit the discharge of adequately treated sewage, industrial waste, or other waste pursuant to a permit issued by the director.*

We hold these provisions call for strict liability, and this holding renders some of the factual disputes irrelevant. Prohibitions involved in § 455B.186(1) are not grounded on fault. Matters of negligence and foreseeability are thus not at issue. The statute is violated when the operator places the pollutant so that its introduction into the state's water results. Under any theory of this record, the pollutant at the tile outlets could only be traced to DeCoster's spray irrigation. No one else in the area was applying manure, and examination of the area revealed no other possible source of the pollutants at the outlets. The State established that DeCoster, through his agents, knowingly took the steps that introduced the waste pollutant onto the soil so that it was introduced into the waters of the state.

The trial court also found that the spray irrigation violated Iowa Administrative Code rule 567–65.2(7). That administrative rule provides that all manure removed from an animal feeding operation or its manure control facilities shall be land-applied in a manner which will not cause surface or groundwater pollution. DeCoster's argument is that the rule is not violated until some pollution occurs and again he contends the State has failed to show actual pollution resulted from his irrigation on April 27. The record shows that surface pollution, in the form of "pooling," occurred on April 27, during the irrigation. This also contributed to the pollution in the tile outfall the following day.

DeCoster also assails the civil penalties imposed. Review of the district court's assessment of civil penalties is for abuse of discretion. Deference is generally given to an agency's judgment unless the penalty is so harsh and unconscionably disproportionate to the offense that it amounts to an abuse of discretion. Matters committed to the discretion of a trial court are not reviewable upon appeal; only the alleged abuse of that power is reviewable. We find no abuse in the fines, totaling $59,000, for the various violations. Liberally construing the remedial nature of both Iowa Code § 455B.186(1) and Iowa Administrative Code rule 567–65.2(7), the district court was correct in its application of the law. Substantial evidence has been defined as evidence which would justify refusal to direct a verdict. DeCoster certainly could not have received a directed verdict, therefore the case should be and is affirmed.

## Questions

1. What evidence is needed to support the $59,000 fine?
2. What is the significance of Joe Haugen's testimony?
3. Is the fact that the two outlets drained into a stream and then the Iowa River significant? If so, in what manner?
4. What causes of action doomed Mr. DeCoster?
5. What was the burden of proof?
6. Assuming employee Robert Polzin watched the irrigation system and shut it off prior to any land pooling, should the defendant incur liability?
7. How did the appellate court handle the argument about excessive civil penalties?
8. What can we say about liability under Iowa common law, as opposed to Iowa regulatory law?

# Intentional Torts

Other than strict liability and nuisance, torts are generally classified as either intentional or unintentional torts. Intentional torts are those in which the person had an intent to do the act. Unintentional torts do not have intent as a prerequisite, but rather are based upon negligence or breach of duty. Seven intentional torts are discussed in this section: battery, assault, infliction of emotional distress, false imprisonment, trespass to land, trespass to chattels, and conversion.

An intentional tort requires: (1) an act; (2) intent; and (3) causation. There is no requirement of real damages; nominal damages may be awarded.

## 1. Battery

A battery is the intentional touching of another without consent or legal justification. Stated differently, a battery is the intentional, unpermitted, unprivileged contact with the person of another. The touching does not have to be by the physical self, but may involve an object controlled by the person committing the battery. For example, if a thief pokes a gun in the victim's ribs, the thief has committed a battery. In addition, if the thief shoots a person, the act may constitute a battery by reason that the thief caused the bullet to strike the victim. Damages may be recovered by the injured party, the spouse, or the parents of a minor.

Some activities by their nature involve consent, and therefore, consent serves as a defense to a cause of action for a battery. All contact sports involve some type of consent, although litigation concerning ice hockey raises a question concerning the permissible force. Self-defense is another defense that may defeat a cause of action for battery. A person who believes there exists a threatened injury may use reasonable force to prevent personal harm. A person may use deadly force if he or she feels threatened with death or serious physical harm.

## 2. Assault

Assault is intentionally causing another person to be in apprehension of a battery. For example, pointing a gun at a person and causing apprehension could constitute an assault. The defenses of consent and self-defense, as discussed for battery, apply to actions for assault.

## 3. Infliction of Emotional Distress

The intentional infliction of emotional distress through outrageous conduct may constitute a tort. For example, profane language by employees of an innkeeper or a common carrier (bus or plane) may subject the company to liability for the intentional infliction of mental distress.

## 4. False Imprisonment

The unlawful detention of a person depriving that person of their liberty gives rise to a cause of action for false imprisonment. This cause of action may be troublesome for treating persons suffering mental problems.

## 5. Trespass to Land

Trespass is the unauthorized entry to property of another. Generally, no intent to enter is required, only knowledge of entry to property. Whenever a tangible object physically invades property of another without permission, there is a trespass. Invasions by nonphysical intangible objects such as spray drift, gases, vibrations, and odors present more challenging issues. State courts are not consistent in allowing the use of the trespass cause of action for invasions of intangible objects.

### *Babb v. Lee County Landfill SC, LLC*
Supreme Court of South Carolina

*Who is suing?* _____

*Who is being sued?* _____

*For what?* _____

*What is the issue on appeal?* _____

The plaintiffs, six individuals residing near a landfill operated by defendant Lee County Landfill SC, LLC (the Landfill) in Bishopville, South Carolina, initiated this action seeking to recover for substantial interference with the use and enjoyment of their property caused by odors emanating from the landfill. The plaintiffs asserted nuisance, trespass, and negligence claims based on the odors. Following a trial, the jury awarded the plaintiffs actual or compensatory damages totaling $532,500 on their claims. The Landfill filed motions for judgment as a matter of law or alternatively for a new trial. After determining that South Carolina precedent was not clear on state law issues raised in the post-trial motions, the federal District Court certified five questions to this Court. Question 2 is:

> Does South Carolina law recognize a cause of action for trespass solely from invisible odors rather than a physical invasion such as dust or water?

The plaintiffs argue South Carolina has abandoned the traditional rule that a trespass requires an invasion of property by a physical, tangible thing, and thus, the Court should recognize odors as constituting a trespass.

We first note the relevant distinctions between the trespass and nuisance causes of action which presumably give rise to the plaintiffs' arguments that intangible intrusions should be sufficient to constitute a trespass. First, recovery under a nuisance claim

Fig. 7.1 Landfills may be smelly and are accompanied by birds and other pests.

requires proof of actual and substantial injury, whereas trespass entitles a plaintiff to nominal damages even in the absence of any actual injury. Also, in order to rise to the level of an actionable nuisance, the interference or inconvenience must be unreasonable. For trespass, there is no requirement of unreasonableness. Rather, any trespass, however small and insignificant, gives rise to an actionable claim.

The traditional common-law rule, the "dimensional test," provides that a trespass only exists where the invasion of land occurs through a physical, tangible object. Under that rule, intangible matter or energy, such as smoke, noise, light, and vibration, are insufficient to constitute a trespass. More specifically, under that rule, courts have held that odors do not give rise to a trespass cause of action because they are intangible. In reaction to modern science's understanding of microscopic and atomic particles, a divergent line of decisions has discarded the dimensional test and permitted recovery for trespass without regard to whether the intrusion was by a tangible object, but rather by considering the nature of the interest harmed.

The first seminal case in this line of decisions was *Martin v. Reynolds Metals Co.* (Oregon 1959). There, the plaintiffs brought a trespass action against an aluminum smelter for fluoride gases and microscopic particulates they alleged the smelter emitted, which traveled through the air and settled on the plaintiffs' property. Dispensing with the dimensional test, the Oregon Supreme Court held the intrusion of fluoride was a trespass despite its intangible nature. The court reasoned that each particle that entered the plaintiffs' property was a physical intrusion, and but for their size, would undoubtedly give rise to a trespass action. In light of those considerations, the *Martin* court held the determination of whether an invasion of the right to exclusive possession occurred, and thus whether a trespass occurred, is best determined by consideration of the energy and force of the thing intruding upon a plaintiff's land. The court imposed a "substantiality test" to distinguish trespassory intrusions from non-trespassory intrusions, holding that in order to constitute a trespass, an intrusion must be of sufficiently substantial force and energy as to interfere with the right to exclusive possession.

The next seminal decision in the divergent line was *Borland v. Sanders Lead Co., Inc.* (Alabama 1979), where the plaintiffs sued a lead smelter for lead and sulfoxide emissions they alleged settled on and damaged their property. Adopting the *Martin* rejection of the dimensional test, the court set forth a two-tiered concept of trespass. Where a trespass is "direct," as formerly required for a trespass to exist and including physical, tangible intrusions, there is no substantiality requirement and nominal damages may be awarded. However, where the intrusion is indirect, including where the intrusion is intangible, the intrusion constitutes a trespass only if the plaintiff can show: (1) an invasion affecting an interest in the exclusive possession of his property; (2) an intentional doing of the act which results in the invasion; (3) reasonable foreseeability that the act done could result in an invasion of plaintiff's possessory interest; and (4) substantial damages to the Res.

However, we find persuasive the Michigan Court of Appeals' rejection of this divergent line of decisions in *Adams v. Cleveland-Cliffs Iron Co.* There, the court adhered to the dimensional test, holding that intangible invasions are properly characterized as giving rise to nuisance or negligence actions and cannot give rise to a trespass action. The court first noted that courts rejecting the dimensional test have been troubled by the principle that nominal damages are available for trespass, and in order to avoid subjecting manufacturing plants to potential liability to every landowner on whose parcel some incidental residue of industrial activity might come to rest, these courts have grafted onto the law of trespass a requirement of actual and substantial damages. But in adopting the substantiality requirement, those courts transmute the trespass cause of action into the nuisance cause of action.

We acknowledge that the dimensional test is an imperfect rule. It does not comport with modern science's understanding of matter and the relationship between matter and energy. However, we question whether any rule can perfectly distinguish between those things that intrude upon the right to exclusive possession of land and those that do not. The right to exclusive possession is an artificial construct incapable of precise definition or measurement and thus, defies the creation of a perfect rule to measure intrusions upon it.

Imperfections also plague the divergent line of decisions rejecting the dimensional test and their new form of trespass. The initial imperfection and that from which the others arise is that trespass is a strict liability theory under which a plaintiff may collect nominal damages for any intrusion regardless of whether it caused harm. Without the dimensional test, even the most ephemeral intrusion would constitute a trespass and an entitlement to at least nominal damages. In order to avoid that absurd result and the arresting effect it would have on modern life, those courts rejecting the dimensional test are compelled to adopt a substantiality requirement to distinguish between those intrusions substantial enough to constitute a trespass and those too insubstantial to do so.

Lacking a perfect measure of when one's right to exclusive possession has been infringed and comparing the merits and demerits of the dimensional test and the divergent view with its substantiality requirement, we conclude the dimensional test is superior to the divergent view. The dimensional test, while not perfect, possesses the virtues of clarity, ease of implementation, and ability to serve as a guide for future conduct. The substantiality requirement is a fact-specific, case-by-case rule. Thus, the dimensionality test gives members of the public some idea of what constitutes a trespass and enables them to conform their conduct to the standard. The substantiality test would leave them uncertain as to whether they would be liable in trespass for certain actions. The rule would thus result in inefficient behavior because persons would forego some legally permissible and socially and economically beneficial activities due to uncertainty as to whether the activities would constitute a trespass under the substantiality test.

South Carolina does not recognize a trespass cause of action for invisible odors. Rather, South Carolina hews to the traditional dimensional test and only recognizes intrusions by physical, tangible things as capable of constituting a trespass. For the reasons stated, we hold a trespass exists only when an intrusion is made by a physical, tangible thing.

## Questions

1. In what court did the plaintiffs commence their lawsuit?
2. What is the traditional rule of trespass?
3. What is the advantage of the "dimensional test?"
4. What is the advantage of the "substantiality test?"
5. In situations of physical invasions, can the same conduct constitute a trespass and a nuisance?
6. The court noted with disfavor the substantiality requirement because it requires a fact-specific, case-by-case rule; but if an invisible particle is not a trespass, how will it be handled under nuisance law?

## 6. Trespass to Chattels

The intentional interference with the possession or physical condition of a chattel of another constitutes a trespass to chattels. Chattels are movable personal property. Thus, trespass to chattels involves interference with personal property.

## 7. Conversion

The intentional interference with the dominion or control over a chattel is a conversion. For example, taking the wrong umbrella from a restaurant would constitute a conversion. A more common knowledge of conversion may come from criminal law, as conversion may be both a tort and a crime. Criminal prosecution for a bad check is usually based upon conversion; the thief took money from the rightful owner of the check.

### *AgSouth Farm Credit v. Gowen Timber Company, Inc.*
Court of Appeals of Georgia

*Who is suing?* _____

*Who is being sued?* _____

*For what?* _____

*What is the issue on appeal?* _____

On appeal from a jury verdict for defendant Gowen Timber Company (Gowen Timber) in this action for timber conversion, plaintiff AgSouth Farm Credit (AgSouth) argues that the trial court erred when it denied AgSouth's motion for judgment notwithstanding the verdict because no evidence showed that Gowen Timber received written consent to cut the timber at issue. We agree that the trial court erred when it admitted parol evidence as to AgSouth's alleged consent.

The jury is the final arbiter of the facts, and the verdict must be construed by the trial and appellate courts in the light most favorable to upholding that verdict. The record shows that AgSouth sued Gowen Timber for timber conversion pursuant to the Official Code of Georgia Annotated (OCGA) § 51-12-51(a), which provides that a holder of "legal title" to an interest in land as security for debt may recover the unpaid portion of the secured indebtedness, interest thereon, and a reasonable attorney's fee from any person who converts trees growing or grown on such land to his own uses without the written consent of the secured party.

The unpaid portion of the secured indebtedness at issue in this case arose after George Gowen and Shirley Bluff, LLC defaulted on the residue of a $2 million loan first extended by AgSouth. In exchange for the loan, George Gowen and Shirley Bluff provided AgSouth with a promissory note, a deed to secure the debt in favor of AgSouth, and a security agreement. By means of the deed to secure debt, Shirley Bluff, LLC conveyed a 1,057-acre parcel of land in Charlton County, known as the Shirley Bluff tract, as collateral for the loan. The deed provided in relevant part that the borrowers will not, except with the written consent of AgSouth, cut, use or remove, or permit the cutting, use or removal of, any timber or trees on the parcel for sawmill, turpentine or other purposes, except for firewood and other ordinary farm purposes. The security agreement identified the collateral securing the loan as all merchantable or pre-merchantable standing, felled and harvested pine, hardwood, or other timber growing or to be planted on the property.

As the parties negotiated for a third renewal of the loan, AgSouth reviewed a tax return from Shirley Bluff, LLC indicating that Gowen Timber had harvested timber that year without AgSouth's written consent, for which it paid Shirley Bluff, LLC $276,523.40. The parties were unable to agree to a third renewal and the loan went into default. AgSouth gave George Gowen and Shirley Bluff, LLC, notice of the default as well as its intention to collect attorney fees under OCGA § 13-1-11.

AgSouth's principal argument on appeal is that the trial court erred when it denied its motion for judgment notwithstanding the verdict because undisputed evidence showed that Gowen Timber cut timber to which AgSouth held legal title by virtue of its security interest in the Shirley Bluff property and it did not give Gowen Timber written consent to cut timber, which was required under both the timber conversion statute and the original loan documents. We agree with these contentions.

Given the undisputed facts showing that Gowen Timber cut timber on the Shirley Bluff tract, to which AgSouth held legal title by virtue of the deed to secure debt, the only question before this jury was whether AgSouth ever granted its written consent to any such removal efforts, as required by both OCGA § 51-12-51(a) and the unambiguous terms of the deed to secure debt and the renewals of that deed. Gowen Timber asserts that the jury was authorized to determine that verbal consent to cut timber was given to vary the explicit terms of the deed and the parties mutually departed from the explicit terms of the closing documents. We disagree. Any verbal consent to George Gowen's expressions of intent to cut timber on the property was inadequate as a matter of law to grant Shirley Bluff, LLC or Gowen Timber the right to harvest any timber on the Shirley Bluff property. The record provides no evidence of a prior or contemporaneous oral agreement to vary the explicit terms of the original loan documents or of any subsequent agreement so as to vary those terms. The trial court erred when it denied

AgSouth's motions for directed verdict and for judgment notwithstanding the verdict as to Gowen Timber's liability for converting the Shirley Bluff timber.

## Questions

1. What was converted by Gowen Timber Company and why did it qualify as a conversion?
2. Why did AgSouth include a term in the security agreement that written permission was required to cut timber?
3. Why did Gowen Timber Company cut timber in violation of the security agreement?
4. Why was oral consent to cut timber not relevant to the jury's determination?
5. Should a breach of a security agreement be able to trigger default on the loan with the entire balance being due?

# Discussion Questions

1. Can a defendant be liable for assault if in fact she is not capable of inflicting harmful contact on the plaintiff?
2. Adrian, a sixteen-year-old, vandalizes Tom's home. Should Adrian's parents incur liability for the damages?
3. Mary owns a dangerous dog that has bitten one person. The dog attacks Johnny and causes severe injuries. Should Mary be liable under strict liability for the injuries to Johnny?
4. Why should a debt need to be paid in full after conversion by the borrower?

# Image Credit

Copyright in the Public Domain.

# CHAPTER EIGHT

## Negligence

## Learning Objectives

- *Describe the policy justifications for different duties of care.*
- *Apply the different duties of care to negligent situations.*
- *Illustrate injuries that are proximate to an activity.*
- *Explain the attractive nuisance doctrine.*
- *Summarize comparative and contributory negligence.*

Negligence is the failure to exercise due care when there exists a foreseeable risk of harm to others. This tort may involve an unreasonable act or the omission of an act. Negligence is generally recognized as having four requirements: (1) duty of care; (2) breach of the duty; (3) damages; and (4) proximate causation.

Negligence embodies the concept of fairness involving shifting an injured person's financial losses to the person causing the damages. However, by relying on lawsuits and the threat of litigation, this tort markedly influences human behavior. Fears of being sued permeate activities and business relationships. Governments have enacted legislation that revises negligence rules to alter liability outcomes in attempts to achieve fairness as well as preferred economic solutions.

In some situations, a statute may delineate the applicable standard of care to be applied in a particular action that establishes negligence per se. To establish liability as a result of a statutory violation, a plaintiff must satisfy two conditions. First, the plaintiff must be within the class of persons protected by the statute. Second, the injury must be of the type for which the statute was intended to prevent. Negligence per se operates to engraft a particular legislative standard onto the general standard of care imposed by traditional tort law principles. In a negligence per se case, the jury needs not decide whether the defendant acted as an ordinarily prudent person would have acted under the circumstances; rather, it decides whether the relevant statute or regulation has been violated. If it has, the defendant was negligent as a matter of law.

## Legislative Expansion of Exceptions to Liability

Persons and groups have sought exceptions from tort liability for hundreds of years. Under common law, a doctrine of sovereign immunity developed whereby governments did not incur liability for torts. Other immunity principles have become part of common law and have been expanded by state statutes. Good Samaritan laws allow persons to assist others without incurring liability for mistakes that may injure the victim being helped. During the past fifty years, groups have petitioned state legislatures to adopt additional laws to provide immunity from tort actions to qualifying individuals. Three major categories of laws may be identified that provide exceptions to common law tort: recreational use, equestrian immunity, and sport responsibility statutes. The immunity provisions form a confusing set of rules which are then complicated by state laws specifically making governments liable for injuries from selected activities.

Legislative bodies have employed several distinguishable strategies to assist qualifying persons in avoiding liability for injuries and property damages. One strategy is to provide that qualifying individuals are not liable for damages except in certain situations. Good Samaritan statutes are the classic example of an immunity statute incorporating this strategy. Physicians assisting others without pay are not liable for negligence but remain liable for gross negligence. A second strategy is to alter the duty owed to selected persons to reduce situations under which an aggrieved plaintiff qualifies for damages. For example, under a state recreational use statute, an owner of land owes a minimal duty of care to recreational users. A third strategy employed for dangerous sport activities, such as horseback riding, provides that participants assume risks related to the sport. They are responsible for injuries that are a part of the inherent danger of the sport.

## Duty of Care

People have a duty not to engage in conduct which involves an unreasonable risk of causing harm to others. This obligation exists due to common law or by statute to protect people from unreasonable risks. While the duty applies in all aspects of life, it is especially important for persons offering specialized services. Professionals owe their clients or patients a duty to employ the degree of skill and knowledge common for experts in the profession. When a person owes others a duty, an omission of an act constitutes a breach of the duty of care. For example, doctors have a duty to provide reasonable medical care. Any failure to provide proper care constitutes negligence and the doctor may be sued for medical malpractice.

Under American negligence law, liability depends on a breach of the duty of care. Many state legislatures have adopted different duties of care dependent on the relationship between persons. Property owners and occupiers of property owe care based upon the entrant status of the plaintiff. Nearly one-half of the states differentiate distinct duties for invitees, licensees, recreational users, and trespassers. When there is a relationship under which a property owner invites others to come onto property for business purposes, there exists a greater duty to keep these entrants safe as opposed to entrants who are trespassers. Landowners owe the highest duty of care to invitees, a lesser duty to licensees, and the lowest duty to trespassers. Every state has further altered negligence rules with exceptions for Good Samaritans and others engaged in good deeds.

Due to complexity and confusion, some states have abolished the historic distinction between invitees and licensees. Generally, these states impose a duty on landowners to exercise reasonable care in the maintenance of their premises for the protection of all lawful visitors. This means that the court looks at what is reasonable under the circumstances. In these states, the status of an entrant is no longer relevant in determining a landowner's duty of care. Distinct duties may remain, however, for trespassers and recreational users.

## 1. Invitees

An invitee is a person who is induced or invited to come upon the premises of the owner for any lawful purpose. Customers in a store are invitees. Invitees are owed the greatest amount of care. Property owners are liable to invitees for failure to exercise reasonable care in keeping their property safe. A similar duty is owned to entrants by persons renting property, managing property, or who are in charge of property. They must keep the property under their control safe for others.

## 2. Licensees

A licensee is a person who is neither a customer, servant, or trespasser. A licensee does not stand in any contractual relationship with the owner of the premises and is expressly or impliedly permitted to go on the premises. Social guests, including friends visiting your apartment, are licensees. A property owner owes a licensee the duty to avoid wanton or willful injury. This duty of care that is not as exacting as the duty owed to invitees. It involves refraining from creating a dangerous condition and may include disclosing hidden defects that could cause an accident.

## 3. Recreational Users

In the mid-1960s, state legislatures began to encourage property owners to make natural and rural areas available for appropriate recreational activities. Recreational use statutes were enacted to reduce situations in which qualifying recreational providers could incur liability for damages to injured participants. Subsequently, all states have adopted recreational use statutes with differing coverage of properties and recreational activities, often for hiking, hunting, and fishing. These statutes provide incentives for property owners to allow others to use their property by altering the duties providers owe recreational users. Many of the state recreational use statutes have restrictions on compensation so that landowners charging a fee do not qualify for protection.

Recreational use statutes delineate a lesser duty of care for qualifying recreational providers. The statutes often say that qualifying recreational users are not licensees or invitees. Instead, the duty owed to recreational users is more analogous to the duty a property owner owes to a trespasser. Under these provisions, persons making lands available to others do not owe recreational users a duty of care to keep premises safe. By redefining the duty of care, the recreational use statutes make it less likely that a property owner will be liable for damages to an injured recreational user.

## 4. Trespassers

Although trespassers are breaking the law, persons in charge of property have duties with respect to these persons. An owner of property has a duty not to injure trespassers wantonly and willfully. If an owner knows trespassers are entering his property, willful or malicious failure to guard or warn against dangerous conditions may lead to liability. It is considered willful or wanton not to exercise ordinary care to protect anticipated trespassers from dangerous activities or hidden perils on the premises. State legislatures have also adopted numerous statutes covering trespass actions.

## 5. Attractive Nuisances

A majority of states have adopted an attractive nuisance doctrine whereby a special duty is prescribed to protect trespassing children who are unable to perceive possible dangers. In many cases, states adopted a version of the attractive nuisance doctrine from the *Second Restatement of Torts*. The doctrine generally is restricted to trespassing children who are physically injured due to an artificial condition of the land. Thus, injuries to children from natural and common objects (such as rocks, ponds, and trees) are not governed by the attractive nuisance doctrine. Section 339 of the *Restatement* establishes five requirements for qualifying under the attractive nuisance doctrine. The five-part foreseeability test governing determinations of attractive nuisance liability is enumerated in the *Rubio v. Davis* case below.

# Breach of a Duty of Care

Negligence only applies if there was a breach of a duty of care. The standard of care is often referred to as the reasonable man standard: was the defendant's behavior reasonable for an ordinary person in the position? If the defendant has some type of disability (such as blindness), was the behavior reasonable for a person with such a disability? A defendant is liable for negligence only if it was foreseeable that consequences of an injurious nature would result from an act or omission. The following case highlights duties of care for property owners and persons supervising others. The child was a social guest and so under state law was considered a licensee.

### *Hemphill v. Johnson*
Georgia Court of Appeals

*Who is suing?* _____

*Who is being sued?* _____

*For what?* _____

*What is the issue on appeal?* _____

Lesa Hemphill, the mother and administrator of the estate of Niki Hemphill, appeals the superior court's grant of summary judgment to defendant Judy Johnson in this wrongful death drowning case. Although the superior court properly granted the motion on Hemphill's premises liability claim, issues of material fact remain on Hemphill's negligent supervision claim. Therefore, we reverse in part. In order to prevail at summary judgment, the moving party must demonstrate that there is no genuine issue of material fact and that the undisputed facts, viewed in the light most favorable to the nonmoving party, warrant judgment as a matter of law.

The record reveals during one afternoon in May, Lesa Hemphill's 11-year-old daughter, Niki Hemphill, drowned in Judy Johnson's pool. Niki and her seven-year-old sister Teda were invited over to swim by Chase Brumagin, a seven-year-old boy who was in Johnson's care during the day. Another friend of Chase's, seven-year old Gary Wyms, also came to play in the pool. Teda and Niki had never been in Johnson's pool before. Before Johnson allowed them to go swimming, she sent them home to get permission to swim, a swimsuit, and a towel. Both Hemphill and Teda state in their depositions that Niki called Hemphill at work and got permission to swim.

When the children returned to the pool with their towels and swimsuits, Johnson inquired of the children's swimming abilities. Niki told Johnson that she could swim, but that Teda could not. Johnson restricted Teda to the shallow end of the pool, with Gary and Chase. Johnson said Niki demonstrated her swimming ability by swimming across the shallow end of the pool. Therefore, Niki was not restricted to the shallow end. Johnson admitted that although she considered herself a good swimmer, she had no underwater swimming ability when she undertook to supervise the children. Johnson also did not have any lifesaving equipment, like a shepherd's hook, which would enable her to pull a child from beneath the eight feet of water at the deep end of her pool.

After she determined the children's swimming abilities, Johnson walked to the edge of the shallow end of the pool to help the younger children inflate a float. According to Johnson, Niki was the only child in the water at the time. Johnson said she watched the pool area continuously from the time the children arrived and did not go inside the house. Within moments of Niki's swimming across the pool, Johnson heard Gary and Chase say that Niki was drowning. Teda told Johnson that Niki was just kidding, that she could hold her breath underwater. Johnson walked around to the deep end of the pool and saw that Niki was not kidding, that she was sinking under the water. Johnson, realizing she could not pull the child from the water, ran next door to call 911 and to get a neighbor to pull the child from the pool. The neighbor, however, was unable to pull Niki from beneath the water.

Niki's sister, Teda, recalls the incident somewhat differently. Johnson asked Teda and Niki if they could swim and restricted Teda to the shallow end. Teda recalled that Johnson went inside the house to turn on a radio at some point during the afternoon. As Teda stood by the side of the pool, Niki was going under the water. When Teda saw Niki's eyes blinking as she drifted further underwater, she realized something was seriously wrong. As this was happening, Johnson walked up behind Teda, looked down into the pool, and then took her shoes off. Johnson then started screaming and ran to the front yard, calling for help.

Johnson admits she undertook to supervise Niki and the other children who came to her house to swim. When a person undertakes to control and watch over a young child, even without compensation, he becomes responsible for injury to the child through his negligence, and his duty to use reasonable care to protect the child is not measured by what his duty would have been to a social guest or licensee. However, the measure of duty of a person undertaking control and supervision of a child to exercise reasonable care for the safety of the child is to be gauged by the standard of the average responsible parent; such person is not an insurer of the safety of the child and has no duty to foresee and guard against every possible hazard. The measure of precaution which must be taken by one having a child in his care, who stands in no relation to the child except that he has undertaken to care for it, is that care which a prudent person would exercise under like circumstances. As a general rule, a person who undertakes the control and supervision of a child, even without compensation, has the duty to use reasonable care to protect the child from injury. Such person is required only to use reasonable care commensurate with the reasonably foreseeable risk of harm.

Evidence exists which would authorize a finding that Johnson failed to use reasonable care commensurate with the reasonably foreseeable risk of harm to Niki under these circumstances. Although Niki could swim, she was only 11-years old and unfamiliar with Johnson's pool. Further, Johnson had never supervised Niki before and knew very little about her physical abilities. Johnson admits she could not swim underwater and had no life-saving equipment with which to pull a child from beneath the water of the deep end of her pool. Johnson also admitted she did not jump into the pool when Niki began to drown because she knew she was not strong enough to pull Niki from the water. Though Johnson knew or should have known that she could not rescue Niki from beneath the water in the foreseeable event of the child's drowning, she let Niki swim in the deep end of the pool. Given these circumstances, a jury could find that Johnson's decision to let Niki swim in the deep end was both unreasonable and a proximate cause of Niki's death. We cannot say, therefore, that Johnson's supervision of Niki was not negligent as a matter of law.

We hold that the trial court properly granted the defendant summary judgment on Hemphill's premises liability claim. Unlike the negligent supervision claim, the premises liability claim is based upon Johnson's allegedly permitting a defect or hazardous condition to exist upon the premises, and not upon Johnson's conduct as a supervisor. Niki, as Johnson's social guest, was a licensee. Under Georgia law, Johnson, as a landowner, owed a duty to Niki not to injure her willfully or wantonly. The existence and condition of Johnson's pool was open and obvious. Further, a swimming pool is not per se a mantrap. There is no evidence in this case that Niki's drowning was proximately caused by any defect in the pool, including the absence of safety or rescue equipment. Judgment affirmed in part and reversed in part.

## Questions

1. What two claims were raised by the plaintiff?
2. What duties does a property owner have when children are invited to one's property?
3. What if a jury had found no liability for all causes of action and the plaintiff appealed?
4. What if the plaintiff only advanced a premises liability claim and the jury had found for plaintiff?
5. What if a jury had found that the defendant was liable under the premises liability claim?
6. Should a pool without any life-saving equipment be considered to constitute premises for which there is no premises liability claim?

## Proximate Cause

There must be some connection between the defendant's negligent conduct and the plaintiff's injury. Two cases about litigation by patrons of restaurants show that plaintiffs must relate their ailment to the allegedly poisonous food. In *Doss v. NPC International, Inc.*, the trial court found that the plaintiffs failed to show that their illnesses were related to the defendant's food. In the second case, *Capps v. The Bristol Bar and Grille,*

*Inc.*, the court found sufficient evidence of food poisoning to allow the plaintiffs to continue with their lawsuit.

### *Doss v. NPC International, Inc.*
US Court of Appeals for the Fifth Circuit, New Orleans

*Who is suing?* _____

*Who is being sued?* _____

*For what?* _____

*What is the issue on appeal?* _____

In this consolidated action, the plaintiffs-appellants appeal the district court's summary judgment in favor of defendant-appellee NPC International, Inc. We affirm the district court's grant of summary judgment.

The plaintiffs-appellants, who were all members of the St. Paul Missionary Church in Itta Bena, Mississippi, participated in a "Daniel's Fast," in which they refrained from eating any food between 12:00 a.m. and 3:00 p.m. After completing the Daniel's Fast, the appellants ate a mid-afternoon meal at defendant-appellee NPC International, Inc.'s (NPC's) Pizza Hut restaurant. This meal included servings of chicken wings and meat lover's pizza. Within thirty to sixty minutes after the commencement of the meal, some of the appellants allegedly began to experience one or more of the following symptoms: vomiting, nausea, cramps, diarrhea, asthma attack, and headache. The appellants, including some who were not actually experiencing symptoms but wanted

Fig. 8.1 Group meals offer opportunities for food pathogens.

to be "checked out," then sought treatment at the Greenwood Leflore Hospital. Within twenty-four hours, however, nearly all of the appellants who actually experienced symptoms had recovered and only one appellant later returned to the hospital for additional treatment.

After the incident, the Mississippi State Department of Health (State Health Department) began investigating whether Pizza Hut caused the various symptoms allegedly suffered by the appellants. The State Health Department tested stool samples and samples of leftover food. The State Health Department also noted a "non-critical" violation involving raw chicken. The temperature of raw chicken located adjacent to the deep fryer was measured at 93 degrees Fahrenheit which exceeded the maximum cold holding temperature of 41 degrees Fahrenheit. The raw chicken was held at that temperature for an unknown length of time. The State Health Department made the following noteworthy conclusions:

> *Clinical laboratory results were not particularly useful, as specimens were collected after resolution of illness. Eight stool specimens were collected from members who ate at the restaurant; five from individuals who were ill and three from non-ill persons. Neither the S. aureus specimen typing nor exterotoxin testing were consistent from one specimen to the other, indicating unrelated organisms that were not from a single source. Results also indicated the presence of B. cereus in 2 non-ill persons. These bacteria can be found in up to 43% of well persons. Inspection of the restaurant was notable in that chicken wings were held at inappropriate temperatures for an unknown length of time. Food specimens that were evaluated in the Public Health Laboratories and FDA were negative for S. aureus, Staph[y] lococcal enterotoxins and volatile or semi-volatile chemicals.*
>
> *The results of this investigation do not clearly explain the illnesses among the persons who ate at Pizza Hut. If there was a toxin in the food prepared that afternoon, one would expect a higher attack rate among those who ate at or from Pizza Hut but were not associated with the church group. The only illnesses outside the church group were among one household, and their illness was very mild. Environmental investigation revealed raw chicken kept at inappropriate temperatures. The bacteria that produce toxins that can sometimes cause gastrointestinal illness with a short incubation period (S. aureus and B. cereus) are not the typical bacteria found in raw chicken. The evidence regarding this incident does not provide an answer to the cause of the illness among the persons involved.*

The district court granted NPC's motion for summary judgment, finding that the appellants had failed to establish the breach of duty and causation elements of their negligence action. Appellants contend that the district court erred in granting NPC's motion for summary judgment. We review a summary judgment viewing the evidence in the light most favorable to the non-moving party. If there is no genuine dispute as to any material fact, the movant is entitled to judgment as a matter of law. This standard provides that the mere existence of some alleged factual dispute between the parties will not defeat an otherwise properly supported motion for summary judgment; the requirement is that there be no genuine issue of material fact. A dispute as to a material fact is genuine if the evidence is such that a reasonable jury could return a verdict for the nonmoving party. Summary judgment must be entered against a party who fails to make a showing sufficient to establish the existence of an element essential to that party's case, and on which that party will bear the burden of proof at trial.

NPC offered as summary judgment evidence the State Health Department report, which concluded that the evidence regarding the Pizza Hut incident does not provide an answer as to the cause of the illness among the persons involved. Second, NPC presented an affidavit of its expert, Dr. Ernest Williams, who, upon review of the appellants' medical records and the State Health Department report, concluded that there were several inconsistencies with what the plaintiffs have put forth in terms of there being a direct illness being brought about due to consuming contaminated food while at Pizza Hut. Third, the appellants' medical records showed that not one appellant was diagnosed with food poisoning on the day they ate at Pizza Hut and many received diagnoses that were unrelated to food poisoning.

In order to survive summary judgment, the appellants were required to respond to NPC's evidence with contrary evidence to establish a genuine issue of material fact. The appellants failed to meet this burden. The appellants provided evidence from their medical records indicating that at least some of them claimed to have fallen ill after eating chicken wings at Pizza Hut. They also showed that some chicken, which was discovered by State Health Department, was kept for an unknown length of time at 93 degrees Fahrenheit in the Pizza Hut kitchen. Finally, the appellants presented the affidavit of a Pizza Hut employee who testified that Pizza Hut was having sewage issues on the date of the incident. This evidence fails to create a genuine issue of material fact regarding causation.

Most importantly, the appellants failed to present any scientific or medical evidence linking their alleged symptoms to the chicken. To the contrary, the summary judgment evidence overwhelmingly indicated that such a link was lacking. The State Health Department report, for example, explained that their tests did not reveal the presence of consistent types of bacteria in the appellants' stool samples and that such consistency would have been expected in a food poisoning case. Similarly, the State Health Department also reported that the vast majority of non-church group patrons of Pizza Hut the same day did not get sick, which is inconsistent with typical food poisoning cases. Critically, the State Health Department's report also concluded that it was unlikely the chicken wings caused the appellants' alleged symptoms because the bacteria that produce toxins that can sometimes cause gastrointestinal illness with a short incubation period (*S. aureus* and *B. cereus*) are not the typical bacteria found in raw chicken. The appellants' failure to rebut this evidence, which was largely corroborated by Dr. Williams, supports the district court's grant of summary judgment on causation.

In this negligence case, the appellants were required to show that NPC owed them a duty, breached that duty, and proximately caused their injuries and damages. NPC moved for summary judgment, relying on evidence that the meal at Pizza Hut did not cause the appellants' alleged symptoms. The appellants have failed to offer sufficient evidence in rebuttal. Accordingly, we affirm the district court's grant of summary judgment in favor of NPC.

## Questions

1. What is the significance of the violation involving raw chicken?
2. What is the significance of the conclusions of the department of health?
3. Why did NPC hire Dr. Ernest Williams?
4. What element of negligence did the court feel was not established?
5. Is our law sufficient for situations like the facts of this case where a person feels they became ill due to food ingested at a restaurant?

### *Capps v. The Bristol Bar and Grille, Inc.*
US District Court for Kentucky

*Who is suing?* _____

*Who is being sued?* _____

*For what?* _____

*What is the issue on appeal?* _____

This matter is before the court on motion of the defendant, The Bristol Bar and Grille, Inc. (Bristol or Defendant), for summary judgment. For the reasons set forth below, the motion will be granted in part and denied in part. For purposes of its motion for summary judgment, Defendant has conceded that the factual allegations in Plaintiffs' Amended Complaint are true.

The plaintiffs, Donald Capps, Betty Capps, and Jeannette Frazier (collectively, Plaintiffs), attended the rehearsal dinner for the wedding of David and Laura Setters. The rehearsal dinner was held in the private room of a Bristol Bar & Grille Restaurant located in Prospect, Kentucky (Prospect Restaurant). It was a buffet style dinner which consisted of a Bristol house salad, including Bristol salad dressing, fresh fruit trays, Kentucky Hot Browns, Yukon gold potatoes, and mixed desserts, including brownies. Within twelve to forty-eight hours of consuming the dinner, the bride, groom, and nearly all of the rehearsal dinner guests, including Plaintiffs, became violently ill. Plaintiff Jeannette Frazier was hospitalized for two nights due to her illness and suffered pregnancy complications. Plaintiffs Donald and Betty Capps were temporarily stranded on the side of the interstate and became violently ill in public.

A party moving for summary judgment has the burden of showing that there are no genuine issues of fact and that the movant is entitled to summary judgment as a matter of law. The disputed facts must be material. They must be facts which, under the substantive law governing the issue, might affect the outcome of the suit. The dispute must also be genuine. The facts must be such that if they were proven at trial, a reasonable jury could return a verdict for the nonmoving party. The disputed issue does not have to be resolved conclusively in favor of the nonmoving party, but that party is required to present some significant probative evidence which makes it necessary to resolve the parties' differing versions of the dispute at trial. The evidence must be construed in a light most favorable to the party opposing the motion.

Defendant first seeks summary judgment on Plaintiffs' negligence claims. Defendant argues that Plaintiffs are unable establish all the elements of a negligence claim against Defendant. Three elements are necessary to support a negligence action, including "a duty, a violation thereof, and consequent injury." Defendants argue that *Rutherford v. Modern Bakery* requires Plaintiffs to establish which food caused their illness in order to succeed on their negligence claim against Defendant. In *Rutherford*, the plaintiff became ill after consuming two pies produced by the defendant and purchased through a retailer. Although the plaintiff was hospitalized for vomiting, cramps, and diarrhea, he had previously undergone surgery for an ulcerated stomach and produced no medical testimony to prove that his illness was in fact caused by food poisoning. The court held that the mere possibility that the pies could have caused the illness was not sufficient to warrant submission of the case to the jury.

However, we find this case distinguishable from *Rutherford*. Upon reviewing the evidence in the light most favorable to Plaintiffs, there is sufficient evidence to establish that Plaintiffs suffered from food poisoning which was caused by their eating the rehearsal dinner meal at the Prospect Restaurant. Nearly all of the guests at the rehearsal dinner suffered from food poisoning. Although the symptoms began to occur the next day, only those who attended the rehearsal dinner became ill and not any of the other wedding guests who only attended the wedding reception. It is undisputed that Defendant provided items on the buffet at the rehearsal dinner which were consumed by Plaintiffs. Reviewing the evidence, we find that Plaintiffs have established that the rehearsal dinner caused them to suffer food poisoning and that Defendant provided food for the rehearsal dinner.

This circumstantial evidence is sufficient to support their claim of negligence against Defendant. Under Kentucky law, negligence may be inferred from circumstances properly adduced in evidence, provided those circumstances raise a fair presumption of negligence; and circumstantial evidence alone may authorize the finding of negligence. We find that Plaintiffs have presented sufficient circumstantial evidence to support their negligence claim against Defendant and withstand its motion for summary judgment. Plaintiffs have shown that they suffered from food poisoning upon consuming the rehearsal dinner meal at the Prospect Restaurant and that Defendant supplied food items for that meal. Under Kentucky law, strong circumstantial evidence can support a negligence claim, and therefore, we find that reviewing the evidence in the light most favorable to Plaintiffs, summary judgment is not proper.

Defendant also seeks summary judgment on Plaintiffs' breach of warranty claims. In Kentucky, claims for breach of implied warranty relating to the service of food are governed by the Uniform Commercial Code provisions relating to the sale of goods. Although some jurisdictions have abolished the privity requirement for breach of warranty claims, Kentucky law requires a buyer-seller relationship for such claims. Kentucky courts have interpreted the statutory language in Kentucky's enactment of the Uniform Commercial Code as requiring privity for breach of implied and express warranty actions. Plaintiffs have not alleged that they engaged in a buyer-seller relationship with Defendant or purchased any food product from Defendant. Plaintiffs argue that they were the intended consumers of the food purchased for the rehearsal dinner that they attended at the Prospect Restaurant. However, Kentucky courts have rejected this argument and strictly interpret the statutory language as requiring a privity relationship for breach of warranty claims, or that the plaintiffs fall within those class of persons specifically noted in *Kentucky Revised Statutes* § 355.2–318. Therefore, Plaintiffs' breach of warranty claims fail, and summary judgment is proper.

## Questions

1. Why were the factual allegations in Plaintiffs' complaint conceded to be true?
2. Why wasn't the *Rutherford* case controlling for this case?
3. Did the court find any direct evidence of negligence?
4. Why was the breach of warranty claim unsuccessful?
5. Given the different results in the above two cases (*Doss* and *Capps*), how many people need to become ill before a court declines to grant a defendant's motion for summary judgment?

# Negligence Defenses

American jurisprudence recognizes three major defenses to negligence: assumption of risk, contributory negligence, and comparative negligence. Other defenses also exist under common and statutory law.

## 1. Assumption of Risk

Persons who voluntarily subject themselves to a known risk assume the risk of injury arising by virtue of their actions. For example, spectators at a baseball game assume the risk of being hit by a stray or wild ball. The defense of assumption of the risk forecloses recovery when the evidence shows that the plaintiff, unprompted by the circumstances, takes a course of action fully appreciating the danger it poses and nonetheless voluntarily chooses to go forward or not to go forward in the act. In some states, a defendant asserting an assumption of the risk defense must establish that the plaintiff (1) had actual knowledge of the danger; (2) understood and appreciated the risks associated with such danger; and (3) voluntarily exposed herself to those risks.

Knowledge of the risk means both actual and subjective knowledge on the plaintiff's part. The knowledge requirement does not refer to a plaintiff's comprehension of general, nonspecific risks that might be associated with such conditions or activities. The knowledge that a plaintiff who assumes a risk must subjectively possess is that of the specific, particular risk of harm associated with the activity or condition that proximately causes injury.

## 2. Contributory Negligence

The defense of contributory negligence is not currently applicable in many states, including Georgia. However, since some concepts from contributory negligence may apply in some states, an understanding of this defense is important. Contributory negligence is a defense in situations where the plaintiff contributes to the injury. For example, suppose a plaintiff was driving an automobile and fails to use a turn signal when making a turn. A drunken driver is tailgating and fails to slow down and strikes plaintiff's car when plaintiff makes a left turn, causing back injuries to plaintiff. Even though it might be said that the drunken driver was the main cause of the accident, the fact that the plaintiff failed to use a turn signal may preclude the plaintiff from successfully suing the drunken defendant. Contributory negligence is a harsh rule and thus is no longer followed.

## 3. Comparative Negligence

The defense of comparative negligence, applicable in most states, reduces an award of damages to a plaintiff when the plaintiff was partly responsible for the injuries. A plaintiff may recover that percentage of damages attributable to the defendant. For example, if a plaintiff was 20 percent liable for an accident, the award of damages would be decreased by 20 percent, and the plaintiff could collect 80 percent from the defendant. Thus, comparative negligence acts as a defense for the defendant to reduce damages by 20 percent.

## 4. A Good Samaritan Defense

State statutes may delineate numerous Good Samaritan provisions that serve as a defense for negligent conduct of persons covered by the statutes. For example, Georgia law provides:

> *Any person, including any person licensed to practice medicine and surgery ... who in good faith renders emergency care at the scene of an accident or emergency to the victim or victims thereof without making any charge therefore shall not be liable for any civil damages as a result of any act or omission by such person in rendering*

*emergency care or as a result of any act or failure to act to provide or arrange for further medical treatment or care for the injured person.*

This Good Samaritan statute means that medical personal who voluntarily offer assistance at the scene of an accident in a reasonable manner will not incur liability for an unfortunate outcome.

## Discussion Questions

1. How might incentives be incorporated into negligence law to encourage persons not to place themselves in risky situations?
2. Should dangersome sports activities such as snow skiing have special liability provisions that place duties on participants, thereby reducing situations in which sports providers are liable? Why or why not?
3. Who should qualify for a Good Samaritan defense? Why?
4. Should we have special negligence provisions in a statute applicable to horseback riding?

# CHAPTER NINE
## Nuisance and Anti-Nuisance Law

## Learning Objectives

- *Critique problems associated with nuisance law.*
- *Describe the justifications for anti-nuisance legislation.*
- *Interpret legislative provisions limiting nuisance rights.*
- *Contrast qualifications states set for anti-nuisance protection.*
- *Criticize overzealous anti-nuisance protection by elaborating some negative consequences.*

Each state's common law includes principles of public and private nuisance law. If an activity is too objectionable for the location and interferes with surrounding property owners' use and enjoyment of their properties, courts may use equitable principles to ameliorate the offensive practice. Furthermore, activities that adversely impact the order and economics of the public at large may be enjoined as a public nuisance. While certain activities that are a private nuisance may also be a trespass, the causes of action are distinct. Under trespass law, there is an interference with a property owner's possession of property that gives rise to a cause of action. Under private nuisance, there is an interference with the use and enjoyment of property that constitutes a cause of action.

# Public and Private Nuisances

Public and private nuisances are separate and distinct causes of action. A private nuisance gives a right of action to the person injured, whereas under a public nuisance, the rights belong to the public. The definition of a public nuisance often relies on the *Restatement (Second) of Torts* to require an infringement or invasion of the rights of the public. This may mean that a public nuisance involves a process instituted in the name of the state or a statutory directive allowing others to recover. Unlike private nuisance, public nuisance does not necessarily involve an interference with a particular individual's use and enjoyment of land. Rather, a public nuisance typically arises on a defendant's land and interferes with a public right. The following case shows a court examining and differentiating private and public nuisances.

### *Whaley v. Park City Municipal Corporation*
Utah Court of Appeals

*Who is suing?* _____

*Who is being sued?* _____

*For what?* _____

*What is the issue on appeal?* _____

Ronald R. Whaley and Melanie A. Reif (Plaintiffs) appeal the trial court's grant of summary judgment on their nuisance claims. We affirm in part and reverse and remand with respect to Plaintiffs' nuisance.

This case is a noise dispute concerning amplified, outdoor concerts that were held near Plaintiffs' home in Park City. Park City authorized the concerts by issuing permits in 1999 and then by adopting ordinances in 2000 and 2001. The 1999 permits authorized concerts at a reasonable level as not to unduly disturb the surrounding neighborhood. The 2000 ordinance authorized outdoor music at the Town Lift Plaza and the Summit Watch Plaza each for up to five hours a day, two days a week, at a maximum sound level of ninety decibels. The 2001 ordinance eliminated Town Lift Plaza as one of the venues and concerts at Summit Watch Plaza continued at ninety decibels and were authorized from 5:00 p.m. to 8:00 p.m. Both before and after the Outdoor Music Ordinances were enacted, Randy Barton functioned as the concert promoter and sound controller for at least one of the concert venues at issue.

Plaintiffs live in the historic district of Park City. Both Town Lift Plaza and Summit Watch Plaza were developed after Plaintiffs moved into their home. Town Lift Plaza is located approximately 150 feet from Plaintiffs' home; Summit Watch Plaza is approximately 380 feet away. Because of Plaintiffs' close proximity to the venues, the outdoor concerts impeded Plaintiffs' sleeping, resting, relaxing, working, studying, reading, or doing anything that required concentration.

Plaintiffs repeatedly complained about the concerts to Barton, the permit holders, the Park City Police, the Park City Planning Commission, and the City Council. In 1999,

Park City revoked at least two sound permits for violations of the permit conditions that required sound levels to remain at a reasonable level as not to unduly disturb the surrounding neighborhood. Plaintiffs' complaints also prompted Park City to adopt Outdoor Music Ordinances, which provided more direct guidelines concerning the concerts. These ordinances were passed after several reports and hearings to properly set forth reasonable regulations and time limits to substantially mitigate the effects of such music upon neighboring residents and businesses.

Plaintiffs brought suit when no further action was taken by Defendants. Plaintiffs alleged nuisance claims, one claim alleging violations of the general noise ordinance, and one claim alleging violations of the 1999 permits. Before filing an answer, Defendants filed a Motion for Summary Judgment and to Dismiss. The trial court granted Defendants' motion and Plaintiffs appealed. Plaintiffs argue the trial court erred in granting summary judgment on their nuisance claims. Summary judgment should be entered only if there is no genuine issue as to any material fact and the moving party is entitled to a judgment as a matter of law.

Common law recognizes two types of nuisance claims: public and private. Utah law also recognizes both causes of action, and the legislature has adopted distinct statutory provisions codifying each of these theories. Here, Plaintiffs alleged, and the trial court dismissed, both nuisance causes of action. Specifically, the trial court ruled that the licenses and ordinances authorized by Park City barred Plaintiffs' claims.

A public nuisance is a crime against the order and economy of the state. The original remedies for a public nuisance were a prosecution for a criminal offense or a suit to abate or enjoin the nuisance brought by or on behalf of the state or other public authority. Nevertheless, while the civil redress of the societal wrong caused by a public nuisance is usually through an action for abatement by a public official, private actions for damages may also be pursued. However, the plaintiff in a private suit must establish additional elements beyond those required to be proven by a public entity. In this case, Plaintiffs must establish the following elements to recover on their claim: (1) the alleged nuisance consisted of unlawfully doing any act or omitting to perform any duty; (2) the act or omission in any way rendered three or more persons insecure in life or the use of property, (3) Plaintiffs suffered damages different from those of society at large, (4) Defendants caused or are responsible for the nuisance complained of; and (5) Defendants' conduct was unreasonable.

In this case, the trial court granted summary judgment on Plaintiffs' public nuisance claim because most of Defendants' actions were specifically authorized by license and, later, by the Outdoor Music Ordinances. Even though the law allows private individuals to assert public nuisance claims, by definition, public nuisances are only those occurrences that impact the order and economy of the state or the public at large. In this case, the public at large, through its elected officials, issued licenses and passed specific ordinances authorizing amplified, outdoor concerts. Park City's City Council expressly determined that the concerts have a positive effect on both the existing businesses around them and the community at large. Accordingly, we hold that Defendants' actions did not constitute a public nuisance to the extent they were specifically authorized by Park City.

However, Plaintiffs alleged and Defendants conceded that at least some of the 1999 concerts exceeded the regulations set forth by the permits. These few concerts were not specifically authorized but, instead, were in direct violation of the license requirement that sound levels remain at a reasonable level. Because these few concerts exceeded the authorization from Park City and were in violation of Park City's noise ordinances, the concerts were "unlawful." Accordingly, the trial court's grant of summary judgment is reversed with respect to the few 1999 concerts that exceeded the terms of the permits.

Unlike public nuisances, which are concerned with the rights of the community at large, the essence of a private nuisance is an interference with an individual's use and enjoyment of land. Plaintiffs allege a private nuisance claim based on an interference with the comfortable enjoyment of their property. Private nuisance claims do not require that the defendant's actions be unlawful and private nuisance law is not centrally concerned with the nature of the conduct causing the damage, but with the nature and relative importance of the interests interfered with or invaded. The doctrine of nuisance has reference to the interests invaded, to the damage or harm inflicted, and not to any particular kind of action or omission which has led to the invasion. Distinguished from negligence liability, liability in nuisance is predicated upon unreasonable injury rather than upon unreasonable conduct. Because unlawful conduct is not an element of a private nuisance claim we hold that the permits and ordinances at issue in this case do not prevent Plaintiffs from maintaining a private nuisance claim. We reverse the trial court's grant of summary judgment on Plaintiffs' claim for private nuisance and reverse in part the grant of summary judgment on Plaintiffs' claim for public nuisance.

## Questions

1. Before the 2000 ordinance was adopted, do you think the Park City Council (the governing body) was aware that some residents would find the concert noise offensive?
2. Why did Park City adopt its 2000 outdoor music ordinance?
3. Can neighbors maintain a public nuisance claim against noise authorized by a local government's ordinance?
4. Can neighbors maintain a public nuisance claim if the noise is above the prescribed level authorized by a local government?
5. Does a private nuisance require the same burden of proof as a public nuisance?
6. Can lawful activities constitute a private nuisance?
7. Assuming that Park City continued with concerts and kept the noise levels within the bounds of the Park City ordinance, what should Mr. Whaley and Ms. Reif do?

# Relief under Nuisance Law

A nuisance cause of action is important whenever a plaintiff wants to secure relief other than damages. Under nuisance law, injunctive relief is possible. A court may abate conditions likely to become hazardous or may enjoin an offensive activity so that it will no longer be offensive to the community. While the termination of an offensive activity is often the relief requested and granted, alternatives exist to offer more appropriate responses for the issues under consideration. In some cases, a court will enjoin the polluter, but allow the continuance of the polluter's activities if the polluter agrees and adopts suitable technology to reduce the problem. In other situations, a court may enjoin a polluter, but allow the polluter to operate if the polluter pays damages to permanently compensate aggrieved neighbors.

Other equities are also important. In some cases, volunteer activities, charitable events, or other good deeds may lead courts to fashion remedies to allow beneficial activities. The following case shows a court examining injunctive relief for a church that was providing a service to homeless people.

### *Fifth Avenue Presbyterian Church v. The City of New York*
US Court of Appeals for the Second Circuit, New York

*Who is suing?* _____

*Who is being sued?* _____

*For what?* _____

*What is the issue on appeal?* _____

Plaintiffs—a religious corporation which owns and operates a church at the corner of Fifth Avenue and 55th Street in Manhattan, New York City (Church); a member of the Church engaged in the Church's program toward the homeless population; and ten homeless persons—brought this action to obtain a permanent injunction preventing the City of New York (City) from dispersing homeless persons sleeping, at the Church's invitation, in the landings at the tops of the staircases leading up into the Fifth Avenue and the 55th Street entrances to the Church as well as for a declaration that the dispersal of such persons from such areas has violated plaintiffs' rights.

Homeless persons had been sleeping in the areas described above for some time when they were officially designated by the Church as places where the homeless might sleep at night. In November, however, the City notified the Church that it would no longer permit the homeless to sleep on the Church's outdoor property described above, and on three occasions in early December, the police removed the homeless from the Church's property during the night. By Memorandum and Order dated the following January, the Court granted a preliminary injunction against defendants, against their entering onto the property of the plaintiff Church for the purpose of dispersing or arresting any person who shall be sleeping or otherwise lawfully on that property, with certain exceptions not applicable here.

The preliminary injunction against defendants was limited to the staircases. The Court of Appeals affirmed the January Order. Plaintiffs move for summary judgment for the requested permanent injunction. Summary judgment is appropriate when, after reviewing the evidence in the light most favorable to the non-moving party, there is no genuine issue as to any material fact and the moving party is entitled to judgment as a matter of law. The burden of showing that no genuine factual dispute exists rests upon the moving party, and in assessing the record to determine if such issues do exist, all ambiguities must be resolved and all inferences drawn in favor of the party against whom summary judgment is sought.

The Court is not persuaded by defendants' claim that the City's actions were necessary to address a public nuisance. A public nuisance is conduct or omissions which offend, interfere with, or cause damage to the public in the exercise of rights common to all in a manner such as to offend public morals, interfere with use by the public of a public place or endanger or injure the property, health, safety or comfort of a considerable number of people. Panhandling, prostitution solicitation, littering, altercations, public urination and defecation, and operation of a de facto shelter that fails to meet minimum standards of habitability may constitute a public nuisance. That such conduct violates particular ordinances is not dispositive. Individualized instances of misconduct, not of a violent or aggressive nature, such as panhandling and soliciting a prostitute, cannot, without more, constitute a substantial and unreasonable interference with the public right.

The final factual allegation is that homeless persons who sleep on Church property engage in public urination and inappropriate disposal of sewage. As stated previously, to constitute a nuisance, conduct must offend public morals, interfere with use by the public of a public place, or endanger or injure the property, health, safety or comfort of a considerable number of people. Defendants do not contend that public urination and defecation by homeless persons sleeping on a Church's private property offends public morals, as most New York City residents can attest, homeless persons sleeping and performing basic human functions in public is not uncommon. Thus, that such activity occurs on Church property, with the full consent of the Church, is hardly the type of conduct likely to offend the community, but rather, is simply the reality of our life in a crowded metropolis.

The remaining ground for a public nuisance finding is that the property, health, safety or comfort of a considerable number of people have been endangered or injured. Although the conduct at issue violates the City's Health Code, that fact alone is insufficient to show that the health of a considerable number of people has in fact been endangered or injured. Mere speculation about danger or injury is not generally sufficient, and successful nuisance claims typically include evidence of the actual danger or injury resulting from challenged conduct. Defendants have not proffered any evidence that the conduct at issue endangers or injures anyone's health, and also do not dispute that the Church cleans the affected area on a daily basis, thereby abating some substantial portion of the alleged nuisance.

Finally, the concept of reasonableness is one that permeates the case law on nuisance. With respect to the conduct here, it is relevant that homeless persons live their lives in public places, sleeping, eating, and even relieving themselves in public because many have, or feel they have, no alternative. As a result, if the homeless persons who wish to sleep on Church property were prevented from doing so, many would simply move to another location and continue to engage in identical conduct. The City's actions thus would not prevent public urination and defecation, but would succeed only in relocating the conduct elsewhere. Moreover, if reasonableness is to prevail, organizations that work with homeless individuals by meeting with them, learning about their individual histories and needs, providing encouragement and assistance, and giving them a place to sleep at night, should be encouraged, not discouraged.

The Court turns to plaintiffs' request that the preliminary injunction be made permanent as to the Church staircases. It is ordered that the defendants are permanently enjoined from entering onto the property of the plaintiff Fifth Avenue Presbyterian Church described below for the purposes of dispersing or arresting any person who shall be sleeping or otherwise lawfully on that property, provided that nothing in this order shall limit the authority of the New York City Police Department to arrest any person for other conduct that is unlawful, or from removing from Church property anyone who is present there without the consent of the Church, or from removing homeless persons from Church property during a winter alert officially declared by the New York City Department of Health.

## Questions

1. Why did the city police remove homeless persons on three occasions?
2. Does the case involve a public nuisance or a private nuisance, or both?
3. Why was the city enjoined?
4. What is the purpose of the exception during a winter alert?
5. Are a few citations enough to show a public nuisance?
6. Is speculation enough to show a nuisance?
7. Do you agree that different nuisance standards should apply to activities by the homeless people in large cities, as opposed to other areas? Why?

## Anti-Nuisance and the Right to Farm

In the late 1960s, concern about new neighbors using nuisance law to stop farming activities led agricultural interest groups to advance anti-nuisance legislation. Subsequently, every state has passed anti-nuisance laws to preclude some nuisance actions. The original intent of the laws was to protect viable agricultural operations from new neighbors who moved to the country. Most anti-nuisance laws incorporated a "coming-to-the-nuisance" doctrine, under which established agricultural operations can continue with bothersome activities whenever a complainant neighbor moved into the area. Anti-nuisance laws modestly shift the balance of competing property rights, so that some agricultural activities are now condoned. In other situations, neighbors can employ nuisance law to stop objectionable practices and anticipated nuisances. These anti-nuisance laws are known as "right-to-farm" laws.

The legislative interference with property usage by right-to-farm laws is similar to a zoning provision. Both zoning ordinances and right-to-farm laws operate to circumscribe uses of land within an area. Zoning laws delineate zoning districts, proscribe land uses, and prohibit activities. For example, a commercial land use is not allowed in a residential zoning district. Right-to-farm laws operate to preclude persons with new land uses for which an agricultural operation is objectionable from employing nuisance law to enjoin the existing agricultural operation. Under right-to-farm laws, the land around the operation is an area where property owners who adopt new land uses are not protected by nuisance law. Under zoning and the right-to-farm laws, the governmental edicts reduce the rights of property owners in the district.

With a right-to-farm law, each state legislature has made a policy decision to support the retention of farmland by reducing situations whereby nuisance law can be used to end an activity. The typical scenario involves a residential subdivision being built near existing farms. After a few years, the new neighbors object to a farming activity and use nuisance law to forbid it. Under right-to-farm laws, neighbors moving to the nuisance cannot use nuisance law to seek judicial abeyance of the activity. Right-to-farm laws are especially important for farms with livestock. Raising animals involves manure and manure is smelly. Americans are generally unfamiliar with animal production and do not appreciate that the use of animal manure as a fertilizer on nearby cropland is a good husbandry practice. Right-to-farm laws have given many agricultural activities sufficient protection from nuisance lawsuits so that farmers there first could carry on with their operations. They embrace the concept that persons moving next to a smelly or dusty agricultural operation accept the annoying activities as part of their choice to live in the country.

Alternatively, citizens also have difficulties in evaluating whether an anti-nuisance law affects other issues. In responding to the following, recall the original purpose of anti-nuisance laws and the limitations prescribed by state legislatures in each law. How does an anti-nuisance law affect:

1. local taxation?
2. property and sales taxes?
3. local laws and ordinances?
4. zoning?
5. municipal service charges?
6. business licenses?
7. non-nuisance lawsuits?

8.   health ordinances?

## Contrasting Right-to-Farm Protection

No two state right-to-farm laws are the same. In fact, some are very different and have little in common with the previously noted generalized example. Some right-to-farm laws only protect specific activities, require the creation of agricultural districts, or depend on the use of generally accepted agricultural management practices. A few right-to-farm laws, however, adopt a strategy that agriculture should be favored to the detriment of other landowners. As might be expected, such inequality makes these laws controversial. An examination of the Indiana right-to-farm law shows how its anti-nuisance defense operates to enable a farm to continue its business operations.

### *Dalzell v. Country View Family Farms, LLC*
US Court of Appeals for the Seventh Circuit, Chicago

*Who is suing?* _____

*Who is being sued?* _____

*For what?* _____

*What is the issue on appeal?* _____

Don Leis acquired agricultural property in Randolph County, Indiana. The farm grew corn and beans. Within two years, Leis and entities he controlled had converted the property to a pig farm with 2,800 hogs. Neighbors who objected to the stench filed this nuisance suit under the diversity jurisdiction. The district court granted summary judgment for the defendants, ruling that the Indiana Right to Farm Act, Indiana Code § 32-30-6-9, blocks their claim. The law says:

> *(a) This section does not apply if a nuisance results from the negligent operation of an agricultural or industrial operation or its appurtenances.*
>
> *(b) The general assembly declares that it is the policy of the state to conserve, protect, and encourage the development and improvement of its agricultural land for the production of food and other agricultural products. The general assembly finds that when nonagricultural land uses extend into agricultural areas, agricultural operations often become the subject of nuisance suits. As a result, agricultural operations are sometimes forced to cease operations, and many persons may be discouraged from making investments in farm improvements. It is the purpose of this section to reduce the loss to the state of its agricultural resources by limiting the circumstances under which agricultural operations may be deemed to be a nuisance. ...*

*(c) An agricultural or industrial operation or any of its appurtenances is not and does not become a nuisance, private or public, by any changed conditions in the vicinity of the locality after the agricultural or industrial operation, as the case may be, has been in operation continuously on the locality for more than one (1) year if the following conditions exist:*

*(1) There is no significant change in the type of operation. A significant change in the type of agricultural operation does not include the following:*

*(A) The conversion from one type of agricultural operation to another type of agricultural operation.*

*(B) A change in the ownership or size of the agricultural operation.*

*(C) The: (i) enrollment; or (ii) reduction or cessation of participation; of the agricultural operation in a government program.*

*(D) Adoption of new technology by the agricultural operation.*

*(2) The operation would not have been a nuisance at the time the agricultural or industrial operation began on that locality.*

Plaintiffs contend that the record does not show any changed conditions in the vicinity of the locality after the agricultural operation has been in operation continuously for a year, as subsection (d) requires. They maintain that the Act's function is to change the common-law rule that a person "coming to the nuisance" could sue to abate it. They did not come to the pig farm, they observe, the pig farm came to them. The problem with this argument

Fig. 9.1 A hog waste lagoon may be smelly and particularly offensive.

is that the land appears to have been in agricultural use since 1956, long before plaintiffs bought their parcels. But plaintiffs say that the agricultural operation for the purpose of subsection (d) means the pig farm, not the prior use of the land. That argument won't fly. Subsection (d) says "the agricultural operation," not "the current agricultural operation" or anything similar. Subparagraph (d)(1)(B) illustrates the difference by providing that a change in ownership or size is not "significant." If, as plaintiffs assert, a change in ownership restarts the clock for the purpose of subsection (d), then subparagraph (d)(1)(B) would be useless. So would subparagraph (d)(1)(A), which says that a change in the type of agricultural operation is not significant. We read these subparagraphs to show that subsection (d) as a whole starts the one-year clock from the time any agricultural use began on a parcel of land. Only a "significant" change starts a new clock.

Plaintiffs contend that defendants have operated their pig farm negligently and that subsection (a), which provides that the entire Act "does not apply if a nuisance results from the negligent operation of an agricultural ... operation" applies. The district judge wrote that "ample evidence" (when viewed favorably to plaintiffs) shows that the defendants operated several aspects of the pig farm negligently. His opinion gives ten examples. But the judge added that the record would not permit a reasonable trier of fact to conclude that these shortcomings cause the stench that aggrieves plaintiffs. The judge concluded that every farm with 2,800 hogs, no matter how well operated, emits odors that plaintiffs would find obnoxious.

According to plaintiffs, several of the defendants' shortcomings in operating the pig farm contribute to odors. That suffices to show causation, plaintiffs insist—enough, at least, to create a material dispute whose resolution belongs to a jury. But if the odor from a well-operated pig farm would make plaintiffs' land unlivable (as they insist it has become), a small increment is irrelevant. Plaintiffs' experts did not make any attempt to quantify the extent of the odor-enhancing effects of the defendants' shortcomings. Indeed, they did not offer even a rough qualitative estimate, such as the difference between "a lot" and "a little." Plaintiffs have not attempted to identify any large, well-run pig farm that avoids emitting the sort of noxious odors that plaintiffs say makes this farm a nuisance. Without any effort to show that a well-run pig farm is not a nuisance, or even any effort to show that the shortcomings plaintiffs see in defendants' operations contribute materially to how surrounding landowners perceive the farm's odors, there is nothing for a jury to determine. The judgment therefore is affirmed.

## Questions

1. Would the Indiana law protect a property owner with a nonagricultural commercial activity that is a nuisance?

2. Given the statute's definition of "significant change in the type of agricultural operation," what is left to constitute a "significant change?"

3. Why didn't the ten examples of negligent operations effect to defeat the anti-nuisance defense?

4. What does this law mean for a homeowner who moves into a rural crop-growing area?

### *Gilbert v. Synagro Central, LLC*
York County Court, Pennsylvania

*Who is suing?* _____

*Who is being sued?* _____

*For what?* _____

*What is the issue on appeal?* _____

This matter is before the Court on the Joint Motion for Summary Judgment of Defendants, which is granted. The thirty-seven named Plaintiffs own or have resided at properties located in New Freedom, York County, Pennsylvania. The Plaintiffs' various properties are located adjacent to or near Defendant Hilltop Farms (Farm), a 220-acre farm business owned and operated by Defendant George Phillips (Phillips). Defendants Synagro Central, LLC and Synagro Mid-Atlantic (Synagro) recycle biosolids for public agencies for land application. Plaintiffs allege that the Defendants engaged in a combination of activities at or near the Farm during 2007, including farm operations, and hauling, spreading and applying "sewer sludge."

Plaintiffs allege that sludge is "the solid by-product of sewage treatment," containing various bacteria, viruses, pathogens, prescription drug products and pharmaceutical compounds, pesticides, thousands of synthetic and industrial chemicals, waste, heavy metals, and toxic runoff, and the sludge treatment process often raises the pH to a level where it is irritating to skin, nose, throat and lungs. Plaintiffs also allege that the sludge has an extremely offensive odor that can burn and irritate the lungs, eyes[,] throat, nose and skin, which gives offense to the senses, endangers life and health, violates the laws of decency and obstructs the reasonable and comfortable use of property. Plaintiffs claim that Defendants' sludge activities have interfered with their right to the use and enjoyment of their properties and homes and that they have suffered various medical problems as a result of exposure from the Defendants' conduct of the sludge activities at the Farm site beginning in mid-July 2007.

Plaintiffs allege that Defendants' activities and omissions have resulted in offensive conditions and created a health hazard for those living on the adjoining properties, in the nature of a private nuisance. Plaintiffs seek an injunction that modifies Defendants' conduct so that the injurious conditions do not continue, compensatory and punitive damages, counsel fees, and other costs. The Pennsylvania Department of Environmental Protection (DEP) filed a Brief of Amicus Curiae In Support of Defendants' Motion for Summary Judgment. Summary judgment is proper when the pleadings, depositions, answers to interrogatories, and admissions on file, together with any affidavits, show that there is no genuine issue as to any material fact and that the moving party is entitled to judgment as a matter of law.

Defendants argue that Plaintiffs' case is barred by the Right to Farm Act's (RTFA) statute of repose. Plaintiffs contend the RTFA does not apply because: (1) the use of sewer sludge constitutes a substantial change to the fertilization practices at the Farm; (2) it is disputed whether the application of biosolids is a normal agricultural operation, and so Defendants cannot invoke the RTFA based solely on their assertion that it is; and (3) Defendants have violated state law. Plaintiffs principally argue that the RTFA's statute of repose means that the one year limitation runs from the establishment of the agricultural operation, or in other words, from the establishment of the farm itself, and not from the commencement of the various activities on the farm.

The RTFA was enacted to protect agricultural land and operations from the encroachment of nonagricultural uses and nuisance suits. Specifically, the RTFA provides:

> (a) *No nuisance action shall be brought against an agricultural operation which has lawfully been in operation for one year or more prior to the date of bringing such action, where the conditions or circumstances complained of as constituting the basis for the nuisance action have existed substantially unchanged since the established date of operation and are normal agricultural operations, or if the physical facilities of such agricultural operations are substantially expanded or substantially altered and the expanded or substantially altered facility has either: (1) been in operation for one year or more prior to the date of bringing such action, or (2) been addressed in a nutrient management plan ... and is otherwise in compliance therewith: ...*
>
> (b) *The provisions of this section shall not affect or defeat the right of any person, firm or corporation to recover damages for any injuries or damages sustained by them on account of any agricultural operation or any portion of an agricultural operation which is conducted in violation of any Federal, State or local statute or governmental regulation which applies to that agricultural operation or portion thereof.*

At issue is whether the application of biosolids as fertilizer constitutes a normal agricultural operation. Defined by the RTFA, "normal agricultural operations" includes the activities, practices, equipment and procedures that farmers adopt, use or engage in the production and preparation for market of poultry, livestock and their products and in the production, harvesting and preparation for market.

The Right to Farm Act does not elucidate what may comprise activities, practices, equipment and procedures. Defendants aver that in the past 20 years, DEP has permitted approximately 1,500 sites, including farms, for the application of biosolids, and more than 700 of those sites had active permits as of 2010. Defendants further aver that DEP's statistics show that more than 70 sites in York County have been approved in the past 15 years. Furthermore, DEP, who regulates biosolids pursuant to the Pennsylvania Solid Waste Management Act, (SWMA), provided additional information on the land application biosolids program in its Amicus Brief, including facts, statistics, and the permit process.

The definition of "normal agricultural operation" states that the term includes new activities, practices, equipment and procedures consistent with technological development within the agricultural industry. Defendants have provided data that show biosolids have been in use in Pennsylvania for over 20 years. Based on the evidence, we find that Defendants have established an evidentiary record to show the land application of biosolids is a program that has been acknowledged and addressed by both the United States government and the government of the Commonwealth. Therefore, we find that the land application of biosolids does constitute an activity or practice that has been adopted or used by farmers, and is consistent with technological development, and accordingly, meets the RTFA's definition of a "normal agricultural operation."

We next consider whether Plaintiffs are time barred, pursuant to Section 954(a) of the RTFA, to bring a nuisance action against Defendants. Defendants argue that Plaintiffs are time barred under Section 954(a). Defendants state that they began the land application of biosolids at the Farm in March 2006, but Plaintiffs did not file their action until 2008. Defendants interpret the statute to mean that because Plaintiffs brought the action more than one year after the conditions complained of have existed substantially unchanged since the established date of operation, then Plaintiffs are barred.

In reading Section 954, we first review General Assembly's explicit intent in enacting the RTFA, which states it is the purpose of this act to reduce the loss to the Commonwealth of its agricultural resources by limiting the circumstances under which agricultural operations may be the subject matter of nuisance suits and ordinances. Correspondingly, Section 954(a) provides a defense to agricultural operations, or "farms," against nuisance actions. However, in order for the farm to use this defense, the farm must meet certain conditions. The farm must have been lawfully working, for a year or more prior to the date of the action either in a substantially unchanged manner, or if it had expanded or substantially altered, the farm must have an approved nutrient management plan for that expansion. Biosolids are a type of organic fertilizer and Defendants averred to using biosolids as fertilizer for corn, wheat and soybeans. We cannot find that the use of biosolids as a fertilizer is a substantial change to an agricultural operation. Therefore, we find that Plaintiffs are barred under Section 954(a) from bringing this nuisance action against Defendants.

In summary, we find that Plaintiffs are barred to bring a nuisance claim under Section 954(a), and have failed to allege any legal violations under Section 954(b). Therefore, Defendants' Motion for Summary Judgment is granted, and the case is dismissed as to all Defendants.

## Questions

1. Under common law, is the application of biosolids such as alleged in this lawsuit a nuisance?
2. Why didn't the application of biosolids constitute a substantial change?
3. Can a "normal agricultural operation" change over time, and if so, what did the legislation intend for interpreting this provision?
4. Did the plaintiffs' lawyer fail in developing the complaint?
5. Is this a fair result for these neighboring property owners?

## Discussion Questions

1. With the elementary discussion of provisions from the Indiana and Pennsylvania right-to-farm laws, how does the Indiana statute differ from the Pennsylvania statute?
2. If you were an agricultural producer, would you prefer the Indiana or Pennsylvania statute? Explain your reasons.
3. Given that nuisance law balances competing interests, does the Indiana or Pennsylvania right-to-farm law constitute an overzealous protection of nuisances that may adversely affect neighbors and a community? Explain your response.

## Image Credit

# CHAPTER TEN
## Agency and Independent Contractors

## Learning Objectives

- *Describe how the law defines an agency relationship.*
- *Diagnose factors that distinguish independent contractors from agents.*
- *Discuss how to qualify as an independent contractor.*
- *Examine how the law determines liability for acts of subcontractors.*
- *Explain how statutes redefine liability for principals.*

A fiduciary relationship, whereby a person consents to have another act on his or her behalf and the other person accepts, is an agency. The fiduciary relationship is one of trust and confidence by two parties: principals and agents. A principal authorizes the agent to act on his account subject to his control, and so trusts the agent to perform pursuant to their agreement. An agent is the person authorized by the principal to act subject to the principal's control. In a majority of agency relationships, agents place trust in the principal that they will receive some type of compensation for their efforts. Agency relationships may arise by agreement, operation of law, or employment. Agencies also exist under an employer-employee relationship.

Historically, the doctrine of *respondeat superior*, "let the master respond," meant that a master was liable for the torts committed by a servant within the scope of the servant's employment. Under the principles of agency, principals are liable for actions of agents performed within the scope of the agency relationship. In the same manner, employers are liable for actions of employees. If a business relationship is a joint venture, both parties may be liable for damages caused by the other.

Liability for employers who are principals is affected by state workers' compensation legislation. In many states, any employer with a requisite number of employees (often three) must pay moneys into a state workers' compensation fund. This fund is then used to pay workers injured on the job, or their surviving families. At the same time, workers' compensation limits employees' rights to sue under common-law negligence or other action for damages arising from work-related injuries. Thus, workers injured on the job do not sue their employers.

## Finding an Agency Relationship

In the following two cases, issues are presented whether there is an agency relationship. In *Anderson v. Turton Development, Inc.*, the issue is whether an agency relationship existed between a franchisor (motel chain) and a franchisee that would support liability for an accident. In *Robinson Oil Co., Inc. v. County Forest Products, Inc.*, the court evaluates the issue of an undisclosed principal and the liability of such a principal for a contractual obligation.

### *Anderson v. Turton Development, Inc.*
Georgia Court of Appeals

*Who is suing?* _____

*Who is being sued?* _____

*For what?* _____

*What is the issue on appeal?* _____

The Andersons appeal the grant of summary judgment to Choice Hotels International, Inc., franchisor of a Comfort Inn under the franchise agreement. The Andersons' action alleged that defendants' negligence caused Mrs. Anderson's slip and fall.

On the night of July 16, plaintiffs and their family checked into the motel. They requested a ground-floor room to accommodate Mr. Anderson, who was in a wheelchair. Mrs. Anderson was driving him in his truck, which she parked in a handicap parking space as authorized by his handicap parking sticker. She also had handicap parking privileges as a result of an automobile accident. The following morning, she departed her room to load her belongings into the truck but slipped and fell on a handicap parking ramp while walking to the parking lot.

Plaintiffs' expert, a professional engineer, testified that the handicap ramp fails to comply with American National Standards Institute (ANSI) standards for buildings and facilities for handicapped persons, in that it fails to have sufficient detectable warning textures for blind persons. It was his opinion that the ANSI standards were also violated because the color of the ramp, and the width and depth of the curb and flares, failed to give sufficient warning of any change in the elevation of the surface. The inn, constructed five years earlier, was required to comply with ANSI standards under a state statute (the Georgia Handicap Act) enacted to facilitate access to and use of facilities by physically handicapped and elderly persons.

The weather was very clear when Mrs. Anderson fell, and nothing obstructed her view of the ramp. She testified that as she was walking down the ramp, she was looking straight ahead. Although nothing prevented her from looking down, she did not do so as she placed her left foot on the ramp because she always looks ahead.

Plaintiffs first seek to hold Choice vicariously liable under an actual agency theory. A franchise contract under which one operates a type of business on a royalty basis does not create an agency or a partnership relationship. In order to impose liability on the franchisor for the obligations of the franchisee, it must be shown that: (a) the franchisor has by some act or conduct obligated itself to pay the debts of the franchisee; or (b) the franchisee is not a franchisee in fact but a mere agent or "alter ego" of the franchisor. Plaintiffs argue that an actual agency between Choice and Turton was created because the franchise agreement, along with certain rules and regulations that Turton was obligated to follow, provided Choice with the ability to control the time, manner, and method of Turton's business.

Under Georgia law, the relation of principal and agent arises wherever one person, expressly or by implication, authorizes another to act for him or subsequently ratifies the acts of another in his behalf. The historical test applied by Georgia courts has been whether the contract gives, or the employer assumes, the right to control the time and manner of executing the work, as distinguished from the right merely to require results in conformity to the contract. However, the need for controls over the use of a trade name, in a franchise agreement authorizing such use, has generally been recognized. Thus, a franchisor is faced with the problem of exercising sufficient control over a franchisee to protect the franchisor's national identity and professional reputation, while at the same time foregoing such a degree of control that would make it vicariously liable for the acts of the franchisee and its employees.

Plaintiffs rely on provisions in the franchise agreement requiring that the inn contain a specified number of rooms, that the form and content of local advertising conform to standards prescribed by Choice, that Turton retain on the premises records and data relating to room rentals and revenue for examination and audit by Choice, and that Turton permit Choice to inspect the inn at all reasonable times.

These terms of the franchise agreement, rules and regulations, would not support a finding that Choice had the right to exercise such control as to make it vicariously liable for the acts of its franchisee Turton in maintaining the premises in a safe condition. The agreement sets forth the terms and conditions under which Turton may be licensed to operate a hotel or motel using the name "Comfort Inn," and the rules and regulations impose various building, construction, and operational requirements, not to permit Choice to direct or control the time, manner and method of performance of the daily operations of the franchise but as a means of achieving a certain level of quality and uniformity within its system. The franchise agreement provides that no agency relationship exists between Choice and the franchisee and that nothing contained in the agreement would take away from the franchisee the right to exercise "ordinary business control" to the extent consistent with the specific terms of the agreement. Therefore, it is immaterial that the agreement was subject to termination if the inn were operated in a manner which violated the rules and regulations.

Plaintiffs also argue that Choice is directly liable because of its own negligence in the construction, design, and maintenance of the handicap ramps. The rules and regulations required the construction of handicap parking ramps and provided a suggested design, but they were in fact designed, built, and maintained by Turton. Although there is evidence that they met Choice's requirements, the evidence is that the drop-off from the sidewalk to the parking lot, and the lack of warning, were Turton's design and not Choice's. Franchisor Choice was entitled to summary judgment.

## Questions

1. Why is it significant that the ramp did not comply with the ANSI standards?
2. Why wasn't Choice liable under an actual agency theory?
3. Why wasn't Choice liable for the negligent construction of the ramp?
4. What lesson does this hold for parent corporations?
5. What might be said about the competency of the lawyer drafting the franchise agreement?
6. Should a state legislature change state law to make franchisors liable for accidents such as occurred in this case?

### *Robinson Oil Co., Inc. v. County Forest Products, Inc.*
Supreme Court of Maine

*Who is suing?* _____

*Who is being sued?* _____

*For what?* _____

*What is the issue on appeal?* _____

County Forest Products, Inc. and Galen R. Porter Jr. appeal from the District Court's judgment in favor of Robinson Oil Co., Inc. on Robinson's complaint seeking payment on a fuel products account. Porter and County Forest challenge the trial court's decision to hold them jointly and severally liable for the debt as well as its award of financing charges and attorney fees. We modify the judgment to remove the award of attorney fees and affirm as modified.

We present the evidence and the trial court's findings in the light most favorable to Robinson as the prevailing party. Porter is the sole shareholder in County Forest, a corporation. Porter spoke with a vice president of Robinson at a charity golf event. Subsequently, the two orally agreed that Robinson would begin delivering fuel products to G. R. Porter & Sons, another corporation with which Porter was involved. Porter next began operating a fuel delivery business as Porter Cash Fuel, but never registered that name with the Secretary of State. Porter testified that he intended to operate Porter Cash Fuel as a trade name of County Forest and not as a separate sole proprietorship. The record reveals that Porter ordered fuel and gas over the phone from Robinson in a series of transactions that continued for three years and eventually gave rise to this suit.

Several types of writings confirmed these oral agreements. Within two days after Robinson delivered its products, it mailed invoices directed to Porter Cash Fuel. Robinson also regularly sent Porter Cash Fuel statements of account. Further, an authorization for direct payment listed "Porter Cash Fuel" and bore two signatures, one of which belonged to Porter. None of the writings made any reference to County Forest and none indicated the corporate status of Porter Cash Fuel. All of Robinson's dealings were with Porter or with Porter Cash Fuel; it had no reason to believe it was dealing with County Forest.

Over the years of this business relationship, Robinson added terms to the bottom of its invoices asserting its entitlement to financing charges, collection costs, attorney fees, and court costs. Although Porter never expressly agreed to these terms, when Porter paid sporadically, some of the payments were applied to financing charges, and Porter never complained. Ultimately, the business relationship deteriorated, and Robinson refused to deliver any more products. Robinson sued County Forest and Porter seeking payment on the account. Following a non-jury trial, the court entered judgment for Robinson jointly and severally against County Forest and Porter in the amount of the invoices plus financing charges and attorney fees. County Forest and Porter appeal from the entry of that judgment. First, County Forest and Porter contend that the trial court erred in holding them jointly and severally liable for the debt. Porter testified at trial that he intended to operate Porter Cash Fuel as a trade name of County Forest, and he did not establish a separate sole proprietorship unrelated to County Forest. By operating under an unregistered assumed or trade name, Porter violated Maine corporation law.

Porter became personally liable, as did County Forest, based on principles of agency. In his transactions with Robinson, Porter, through Porter Cash Fuel, was acting as an agent for an undisclosed principal—County Forest. The Restatement (Third) of Agency, states that when an agent acting with actual authority makes a contract on behalf of an undisclosed principal unless excluded by the contract, the principal is a party to the contract, as is the agent. This rule is justified because "a third party's reasonable expectations will receive adequate protection only if an undisclosed principal is liable on a contract made on its behalf by an agent." Notably, however, an undisclosed principal only becomes a party to a contract when an agent acts on the principal's behalf in making the contract.

Here, Porter testified that he intended to operate Porter Cash Fuel as a trade name of County Forest. His brief to this Court reiterates that this was his intent. This testimony establishes that he was not operating Porter Cash Fuel as a separate sole proprietorship, which might have permitted County Forest to escape liability. Because Porter operated Porter Cash Fuel as an agent for County Forest without disclosing that County Forest was the principal, he and County Forest are parties to the contract. This result is consistent with the outcome of our prior cases. Thus, the trial court properly held Porter and County Forest jointly and severally liable.

Second, County Forest and Porter assert that the trial court erred in interpreting section 2-207 when it enforced the financing charges and attorney fees clauses added to Robinson's invoices over the course of the business relationship. We review the trial court's interpretation of a statute de novo. In a transaction between merchants for the sale of goods, additional terms contained within a written confirmation of an oral agreement become part of the contract unless those additional terms materially alter the oral agreement. The test for materiality is objective. An additional term materially alters the oral agreement if it would result in unreasonable surprise or hardship to the buyer. Even additional terms that materially alter the oral agreement become part of the contract, however, if they are consistent with trade usage or the parties' course of performance.

Here, the court correctly awarded financing charges to Robinson because within the meaning of section 2-207(2)(b), the addition of a financing charge does not materially alter an oral agreement between merchants. In addition, the course of performance followed by these parties included the payment of financing charges. A provision requiring payment of attorney fees in the event of a breach, however, does materially alter an oral agreement unless such charges are consistent with trade usage or the parties' course of performance. The record does not support a finding that the addition of the attorney fees provision was consistent with either trade usage or the parties' course of performance. Absent such evidence, the trial court erred in awarding attorney fees to Robinson. The judgment is modified to remove the award of attorney fees. As modified, judgment affirmed.

## Questions

1. What is an undisclosed principal?
2. Who is liable for the breach of a contract with an undisclosed principal?
3. Was Porter's testimony consistent with his claim that he was not liable?
4. Why did the court approve the payment of financing charges?
5. Why did the court refuse to sanction the attorney fees?

# Independent Contractors

It is necessary to distinguish agency relationships from independent contractors. An independent contractor refers to a person who contracts with others to deliver or perform, rather than enter into an agency relationship. Consequently, independent contractors are not controlled by a principal and are not subject to agency principles. If an arrangement is an independent contractor who is performing a contract for another, there is no employer-employee relationship, and the arrangement is not governed by an agency relationship.

The major significance of this distinction involves liability. Whereas principals are liable for the actions of their agents, persons are not generally liable for the actions of an independent contractor performing a task on their behalf. The classification of an individual as an independent contractor may be significant for liability in the areas of labor law, torts, and workers' compensation. There is no single rule or test for determining whether an individual is an independent contractor or employee; jobs cannot be easily categorized as constituting an independent contractor or employee status. Each decision must be decided on a case-by-case determination. This can lead to conflicting decisions by various federal and state courts and federal and state agencies, which must apply different laws and statutes.

An independent contractor is one who engages to perform services for another according to his own method and manner, free from the direction and control of the employer in all matters relating to the performance of the work, except as to the result or the product of his work. Under the common-law test, an independent contractor is distinguished from an employee by the degree to which the employer maintains control over the individual. The determination focuses primarily on whether the employer has a right to direct and control the means employed to achieve the desired result. When the employer dictates the time, place, manner, and method of obtaining the desired results, an independent contractor relationship cannot exist. If the employer has the right to direct the employee in what is to be done, when and how the service is to be done, and has control over the actual conduct of the individual doing the job, then employee status is inevitable. It must be remembered that the key is the right to control—but not necessarily the exercise of that right.

While courts have focused ultimately on the power to control, there are additional factors that are relevant to this determination. These include: the extent of the worker's personal investment in the business and his own risk of loss; the kind of occupation; the length of time for which the person is employed; the employment of others to assist the individual in his performance; the percentage of time the individual works for the employer; the method of payment; the parties' belief they are creating the relationship of master and servant; and the degree of skill required for the performance. However, the deciding factor is the right to control.

Various agencies and courts have reached different conclusions on whether an individual is an employee or independent contractor. The inconsistencies stem from the fact that decisions are made on a case-by-case basis. One reviewing body may find one particular factor important, while another reviewing body may not. A business agency may apply the right to control common-law test, while a labor agency may apply an economic reality test and reach a different conclusion. In both cases, however, the right to control remains the single most important factor. When there is control, the individual will probably be considered an employee.

The following case delineates a factual situation in which questions arise whether a defendant should incur liability for the actions of others. One question is whether a subcontractor is an independent contractor so that the contractor does not incur liability for the actions of the subcontractor's employees.

### *Adcox v. Atlanta Building Maintenance Company*
Georgia Court of Appeals

*Who is suing?* _____

*Who is being sued?* _____

*For what?* _____

*What is the issue on appeal?* _____

Timothy Adcox alleges that he slipped and fell on ice in his employer's parking lot. He brought suit against his employer's janitorial services contractor, Building Maintenance Company (BMC) and subcontractor, JMS Maintenance Services (JMS) because the ice allegedly formed when used mop water was discarded in the parking lot. Both contractor and subcontractor moved for summary judgment. The contractor (BMC) argued that it did not owe a duty to Adcox because it did not own or occupy the premises and it was not responsible for its subcontractor's actions. The trial court granted the contractor's motion and denied the subcontractor's motion. Adcox appeals the ruling in favor of the contractor. We affirm.

Construed in favor of Adcox, the evidence shows that he was employed by ADT Security as a service manager. On Sunday night in January between 8:00 and 10:00 p.m., the 44-year-old Adcox received a call that an alarm had gone off in the ADT building indicating that the back door sensor had been tripped. Adcox asked that the police be sent, and he went there himself after the police had a chance to inspect. It was a very cold and windy night, but it had not been raining. Adcox drove around back and parked near the back stairs. At the back of the ADT facility, there are two doors about one door width apart about loading dock height; they both open onto a small landing surrounded by a metal railing with about six or seven metal stairs running down from the middle of the landing to the parking area for the loading dock.

Adcox parked one car spot to the right of the stairs and walked directly left of his car toward the stairs. After about three or four steps, Adcox slipped and fell on ice and slid up against the bottom steps. He landed flat on his back. After he got up, he saw ice on the ground and ice on the steps. There was less ice on higher stairs and no ice on the landing. The ice on the pavement extended straight out from the stairs, with some under the bottom stairs as well. Adcox alleges that he suffered injuries as a result of the fall.

Some time prior to his injury, ADT had hired BMC to perform the janitorial services at the building. BMC, in turn, subcontracted the work to JMS. In that regard, BMC and JMS entered into an agreement entitled "Independent Contractor Agreement" signed by Carlos Mesa. Mesa testified that only one employee was on the ADT premises on the night in question. Mesa had trained that person on how to do his job, including telling him how and where to dispose of mop water. Mesa instructed that the dirty mop water should be dumped out the back door over the railing to the side of the building. Mesa did not give special instructions for disposing of the water in cold temperatures. Finally, Mesa admitted that the interior security camera system at ADT captured a picture of a JMS employee near a mop bucket; the picture is time stamped as 7:31 that evening. And Mesa admitted that his employee threw water somewhere out of the back of the building that night. Adcox alleges the water turned to ice and that he slipped on that ice.

Adcox contends the trial court erred by granting summary judgment in favor of BMC because BMC owed a duty of care to keep the premises safe and breached that duty. Adcox does not claim that BMC owed a duty as an "owner" or "occupier" under § 51-3-1 of the Official Code of Georgia (OCGA). Rather, he claims that BMC is liable because janitorial contractors, such as BMC and JMS, have a duty to use ordinary care in providing janitorial services and that there is an issue of fact as to whether it breached that duty. But even assuming the duty, Adcox has no evidence that BMC actually provided any janitorial services to ADT other than through its independent contractor.

Janitorial service contractors whose actions cause injury to a third party certainly can be held liable to those parties. But there is no allegation in this case that BMC threw out the mop water or otherwise acted negligently so as to cause Adcox's injuries. The only suggestion of BMC playing a role related to the alleged fall is Mesa's testimony that BMC said the mop water could be discarded in the back of the building. This is insufficient to support liability. Adcox has not shown that there was anything wrong with that instruction. Mesa did not aver that BMC told him where in the back of the building the water could be thrown nor give him any instruction on what to do in cold weather. Thus Adcox has not shown that BMC breached any duty by recommending that the mop water could be discarded somewhere out back, and, accordingly, Adcox has no claim against BMC for negligence arising out of its own actions.

Adcox contends there is a question of fact as to whether BMC is vicariously liable for JMS's actions. With regard to vicarious liability, in Georgia "an employer generally is not responsible for torts committed by his employee when the employee exercises an independent business and in it is not subject to the immediate direction and control of the employer" (OCGA § 51-2-4). This rule applies to janitorial contractors who retain independent subcontractors to actually perform the work.

In janitorial service cases, the standard test applies for determining whether the subcontractor is an independent contractor. That test asks whether the contract gives, or the employer assumes, the right to control the time, manner, and method of executing the work as distinguished from the right merely to require certain definite results in conformity to the contract. And, if the contract clearly denominates the other party as an independent contractor, that relationship is presumed to be true unless the evidence shows that the employer assumed such control. Adcox contends there is a conflict in the evidence regarding whether BMC retained or exercised sufficient control of the time, manner and method of cleaning the premises. We disagree. The agreement between BMC and JMS is entitled "Independent Contractor Agreement" and it states that the parties intended that JMS be an independent contractor. Although BMC retained a general power of supervision, to ensure that the work conforms to the contract, including the right of inspection and the right to request corrections of work as needed, retention of the right to require certain definite results in conformity to the contract does not defeat independent contractor status. It is well recognized that merely taking steps to see that the contractor carries out his agreement, by supervision of the intermediate results obtained, or reserving the right of dismissal on grounds of incompetence, is not such interference and assumption of control as will render the employer liable.

The contract provides that JMS was free to contract with others; that JMS was not an agent or employee of BMC and not entitled to BMC employee benefits; and that BMC had no right to control the manner in which the work is to be done and shall not be charged with the responsibility of preventing risk to the contractor or his/her employees. Rather, JMS had full authority and responsibility over its employees, including hiring and firing. The agreement provides that JMS would indemnify, defend and hold harmless BMC from any claims from any other source arising out of the contractor's actions and that JMS would obtain insurance to fully protect both JMS and BMC from such claims. In connection with services performed under the agreement, the contract states that the premises shall be under the exclusive management and control of JMS, except in connection with BMC's general power of supervision quoted above. These provisions clearly and thoroughly provide for an independent contractor relationship.

Under the contract, JMS was required to use its own materials, tools, and equipment except that JMS could borrow or rent equipment from BMC. Despite the contract language, BMC in fact provided all of the equipment that JMS used at the job site, such as vacuum cleaner, mop, and buckets. JMS provided only the labor. But, BMC's willingness to supply these materials to its agents does not intrude into the agents' ability to control the daily operations of his business.

Finally, Mesa had a conversation with BMC about where the used mop water would be discarded. He does not remember the content of the conversation, except he recalls that BMC indicated the water could be discarded in the back of the building. Jeremy Fort, the BMC manager of the ADT account, added that he never instructed Mesa to discard the water "over the rail at the stairs at the rear of the building." Given the explicit terms of the contract and the other facts and circumstances, we find BMC's indication that the mop water could be discarded in back of the building was insufficient as a matter of law to constitute an assumption of control by BMC so as to create the relation of master and servant or so that an injury results which is traceable to its interference (OCGA § 51-2-5). Rather, it is no more than a general indication that the mop water could be discarded in back of the building. Under the contract, BMC had delivered full and complete possession of the premises to its independent contractor JMS, and it was Mesa, on behalf of JMS, who gave the worker the specific instructions about where to discard the water. Judgment affirmed.

## Questions

1. Why didn't Adcox sue ADT?
2. Why was the evidence construed most favorably for Adcox?
3. What is the significance of the agreement between BMC and JMS?
4. What if BMC had told Mr. Mesa to throw the mop water at the bottom of the steps?
5. What if BMC's contract told JMS how to mop the floor and dump the mop water?
6. What does this case suggest for contracts for services?

# Statutory Liability for Dangerous Activities

The next case presents an exception to the independent contractor rules. In *Perry v. Soil Remediation, Inc.*, the court finds that a state statute precludes a firm from avoiding liability for the breach of a nondelegable duty. This may impose liability on employers for work conducted by independent contractors.

### *Perry v. Soil Remediation, Inc.*
Georgia Court of Appeals

*Who is suing?* _____

*Who is being sued?* _____

*For what?* _____

*What is the issue on appeal?* _____

Shawn Perry suffered injury when, according to his suit, a vehicle in another lane struck an accumulation of sand and oil on the road, lost control, and hit his motorcycle. Claiming that oily waste spilled from a transport truck en route to a landfill and caused the accident, Perry sued the owner-driver of the truck he claims caused the spill and Soil Remediation, the company he claims shipped the waste. Soil Remediation moved for summary judgment, claiming it had no vicarious liability for the acts of its truck

Fig. 10.1 Motorcycle accident.

driver, an independent contractor. The trial court agreed. We reverse because questions of fact remain as to whether Soil Remediation had a nondelegable duty to ensure proper transport of its waste products, bringing this case within an exception to the independent contractor rule.

Summary judgment is proper only if the pleadings, together with the affidavits, show that there is no genuine issue of material fact and the moving party is entitled to judgment as a matter of law. The trial court properly found the truck driver, Mitchell, to be an independent contractor. The true test whether a person employed is a servant or an independent contractor is whether the employer, under the contract, whether oral or written, has the right to direct the time, the manner, the methods, and the means of execution of the work, as contradistinguished from the right to insist upon the contractor producing results according to the contract, or whether the contractor in the performance of the work contracted for is free from any control by the employer in the time, manner, and method in the performance of the work. The key is to determine whether the contractor is truly independent or whether he is simply the employer's alter ego.

The affidavit of Soil Remediation's president alleged Mitchell to be an independent contractor and not an employee. A denial of the existence of an agency relationship may constitute an uncontradicted fact which will sustain a motion for summary judgment.

Whenever it needed to make a shipment, Soil Remediation contacted Mitchell or other independent truckers. It paid Mitchell by the job, on the basis of mileage and time spent at the various delivery sites. Mitchell owned or leased his own equipment to haul the waste and carried his own workers' compensation and liability insurance. The truck he drove bore his name on its door. Soil Remediation did not control the routes

Mitchell took to or from shipment sites, and Mitchell was free to work for others. Under these circumstances, the trial court did not err in finding Mitchell to be an independent contractor as a matter of law. Mitchell clearly functioned independently of Soil Remediation under the circumstances of this case.

Although Mitchell is an independent contractor, the evidence is insufficient to conclude Soil Remediation may not be held liable for any spill he caused. Pursuant to section 51-2-5(4) of the Official Code of Georgia (OCGA), an employer is liable for the negligence of an independent contractor who is performing the employer's nondelegable statutory duty. Soil Remediation may have had such a duty to ensure the transportation of its waste products in accordance with applicable laws and regulations. Soil Remediation is a "materials recovery facility" which must dispose of its wastes in compliance with the Georgia Comprehensive Solid Waste Management Act (OCGA § 12-8-20 et seq.) and regulations issued pursuant to it. The legislature enacted this law in furtherance of its responsibility to protect the public health, safety, and well-being of Georgia's citizens. Assuming Soil Remediation shipped waste by Mitchell, Mitchell was himself required to obtain a permit from the State and comply with the Act and its rules and regulations.

To properly dispose of its waste, Soil Remediation was required to comply with rule 391-3-4-.04(5) of the Georgia Comprehensive Rules and Regulations, which states:

> *The owner or occupant of any premises, ... industry, or similar facility shall be responsible for the collection and transportation of all solid waste accumulated at the premises ... to a solid waste handling facility operating in compliance with these Rules unless arrangements have been made for such service with a collector operating in compliance with these Rules.*

Accordingly, Soil Remediation had a statutory duty to transport the waste and could be relieved of this responsibility only if Mitchell complied with the rules. The record does not demonstrate Mitchell had the necessary permit. Furthermore, questions of fact exist as to whether he complied with Georgia Comprehensive Rules & Regulations r. 391-3-4-.06(3)(a)(3), which requires that vehicles or containers used for the collection and transportation of solid waste shall be loaded and moved in such manner that the contents will not fall, leak or spill therefrom.

These state regulations carry the force of law. They concern themselves with possible spills and leaks from vehicles transporting solid waste and are, therefore, applicable to this situation. It is apparent the regulations are designed to ensure that persons who dispose of solid waste do so only through properly regulated channels. If Soil Remediation did not ensure Mitchell was properly registered with the State, it remained responsible for any injury resulting from his transportation of its solid waste in violation of the regulations.

A person can be an independent contractor in one part of his activity and an employee in another. The regulations at hand dictate that, in the limited area of ensuring its waste is properly transported, Soil Remediation must either use a properly registered or permitted waste collector or remain "responsible" for the waste until it reaches a registered landfill. Although these regulations would not make Soil Remediation responsible for every possible catastrophe in transit, it would remain responsible for ensuring transportation of the waste in compliance with applicable rules and regulations and could be responsible for an injury proximately caused by Mitchell's violation of those regulations. Thus, the trial court erred in granting summary judgment to Soil Remediation. Judgment reversed.

## Questions

1. How was Soil Remediation related to the driver and accident?
2. Was the truck driver an independent contractor?
3. What should Soil Remediation have done to avoid liability?
4. Can a person be an independent contractor for some items and an agent for others?
5. Who should pay for damages due to the disposal of other people's waste?

# Discussion Questions

1. How should the law distinguish independent contractors from agents?
2. Why do states have different laws defining agency relationships?
3. How should a legislature protect employees of subcontractors who are injured?

# Image Credit

# CHAPTER ELEVEN
## Litigation and Damages

## Learning Objectives

- *Describe the compensatory damages that are recoverable in tort lawsuits.*
- *Critique damage awards for intangible environmental damages founded upon descriptions lacking dollar amounts.*
- *Explain how citizens can bring a lawsuit against someone for violating a federal statute.*
- *Define what is needed for a class action lawsuit.*
- *Assess Georgia's legislative provisions enacted to encourage settlements.*

Numerous policy decisions contribute to a pervasiveness of litigation and its costs. An initial concern is that damage awards are too large. Next, Congress has adopted provisions that provide significant strategies for bringing lawsuits against violators and tortfeasors. Citizen suit provisions allow citizens to help agencies enforce federal environmental law, and class action lawsuits allow consolidations of claims to lessen court congestion. Another group of responses to litigation costs are state legislative provisions that encourage settlements.

# Concerns about Damages

Some Americans feel that juries are out of control and are awarding too many damages in civil lawsuits. It is argued that excessive damages are leading insurance companies to raise their rates and in making medical care too expensive. For injuries to humans, some believe that overzealous attorneys are coercing juries into awarding huge awards for pain and suffering and punitive damages. If you select anecdotal evidence and fail to look at the total picture, you might arrive at this conclusion. But in-depth studies of damage awards show a different picture. Studies of damage awards generally show that persons who suffer major injuries due to the negligence of another need large amounts of money to cover their losses. Persons wrongfully injured in automobile accidents or the recipients of negligent medical treatment should receive sufficient compensation to continue with their lives.

## 1. Compensatory Damages

The normal damages in a tort lawsuit are compensatory. These damages cover the expenses incurred in seeking medical treatment, lost earnings, and a figure for pain and suffering. Looking at compensatory damages, studies show that in most cases they are modest. The most notable problem is that many injured persons do not secure compensation for their injuries. Some victims won't realize that someone else was responsible for their injuries. Others will decline to file suit. Plaintiffs with small claims will not be able to afford to litigate their claims, while a few lawsuits will wrongly deprive plaintiffs of recovery. Less than 3 percent of accident victims file lawsuits. A vast majority of negligent actions are not litigated. Furthermore, few of the legal problems of low-income households are ever addressed by our legal system.

The low rates for recovery of damages for tortious actions mean that the sum of compensatory damages awarded in civil lawsuits does not reflect the true harm being inflicted by injurers. Injurers do not pay damages to persons who never file lawsuits or successfully recover damages. Absent the need to pay for these damages, a rational response by injurers is to reduce the care they use in producing products and providing services. Injurers will cut corners because they do not have to pay the full amount on damages caused by their improprieties.

While our legal system is grounded on the award of compensatory damages to injured victims, there is debate about payments for pain and suffering. Considerable public support exists for legislation that establishes a cap for pain and suffering damages, although such a cap is irrelevant in most cases. Moreover, caps on pain and suffering adversely affect injured persons suffering severe damages such as brain damage and para/quadriplegia. Since most groups already admit that tort claimants with severe injuries are undercompensated, it is not clear that caps on pain and suffering contribute to a fair resolution for these injuries.

Another compensatory damage issue involves what is compensable. For litigation involving the destruction of natural resources, should owners of destroyed property recover intangible environmental damages? What should these damages include, how should they be calculated, and what proof should be required to establish the losses? The following case shows a response from California in which state law facilitated the recovery of environmental damages.

### *United States v. CB&I Constructors, Inc.*
#### US Court of Appeals for the Ninth Circuit, San Francisco

*Who is suing?* _____

*Who is being sued?* _____

*For what?* _____

*What is the issue on appeal?* _____

Defendant CB&I Constructors, Inc. (CB&I) negligently caused a wildfire that burned roughly 18,000 acres of the Angeles National Forest in Southern California. The United States brought a civil action against CB&I to recover damages for harm caused by the fire. CB&I does not contest its liability or the jury's award of roughly $7.6 million in fire suppression, emergency mitigation, and resource protection costs. It challenges only the jury's additional award of $28.8 million in intangible environmental damages. The district court denied CB&I's motions for judgment as a matter of law and a new trial. The court held that the government provided sufficient evidence for the jury to determine the amount of environmental damages. We affirm.

The Angeles National Forest covers roughly 650,000 acres just north of metropolitan Los Angeles. It is an important environmental and recreational resource for Southern

Fig. 11.1 Fires pose dangers in many forested areas.

Californians, representing about 70 percent of all open space in Los Angeles County. It is also a refuge for native plants and animals, including several threatened and endangered species.

A county water district hired Merco Construction Engineers, Inc. (Merco) to build four water storage tanks for a housing project. Merco subcontracted with CB&I to construct two of the steel tanks. The site was on private land, next to a brush-covered hillside about a half mile from the Angeles National Forest. A CB&I employee was on the roof of the tank operating an electric grinder to cut and smooth metal with a high-speed rotating abrasive disc that sends out a trail of sparks. The employee saw the sparks ignite a fire but by the time the crew descended from the roof the fire was out of control.

As the fire spread, it reached the National Forest where it burned another 18,000 acres. Federal, state, and county firefighters fought the fire for nearly a week before they contained it. The United States filed a civil action against CB&I and Merco to recover tort damages. During a five-day jury trial, the government presented evidence of monetary costs for its fire suppression, rehabilitation, and resource protection efforts. The government also called expert witnesses who testified about environmental harm. However, the government did not elicit testimony that put a dollar amount on the environmental harm. It maintained that the environmental damages are "not susceptible to empirical calculation" because they are measured by their value to the public and for posterity.

In its closing argument, the government described the intangible environmental harm as a category of damage that the jury needs to decide based on their assessment of the evidence. The district court instructed the jury that the United States does not have to prove the exact amount of damages that will provide reasonable compensation for the harm. "However, you must not speculate or guess in awarding damages." The court also instructed the jury not to include any punitive damages for the purpose of punishing or making an example of the defendant.

The jury returned a special verdict finding CB&I and Merco liable for negligence and trespass by fire, allocating 65% of the fault to CB&I and 35% to Merco. It awarded roughly $7.6 million for fire suppression, rehabilitation, and resource protection costs. The jury also awarded the government an additional $28.8 million for intangible environmental damages, or $1,600 per acre of burned National Forest land. CB&I's 65% share of the environmental damage's award was $18.72 million.

On appeal challenging its share of the $28.8 million jury award for intangible environmental damages, CB&I argues that intangible noneconomic damages are not compensable in tort suits alleging harm to property. Second, it contends that the government did not produce sufficient evidence for the jury to determine the amount of environmental damages in a rational way.

State law governs the federal government's recovery of damages for harm caused by fires in National Forests. California's general tort statute provides that the proper measure of damages "is the amount which will compensate the plaintiff for all the detriment proximately caused thereby, whether it could have been anticipated or not." There is no fixed rule for the measure of tort damages. The measure that most appropriately compensates the injured party for the loss sustained should be adopted. What is apparent from the cases is the flexibility employed in the approach to measuring damages and the broad scope of alternative theories applied to fit the particular circumstances of a case.

California also has a specific statutory provision governing liability for negligently set fires. It provides "Any person who personally or through another wilfully, negligently, or in violation of law, sets fire to, allows fire to be set to, or allows a fire kindled or attended by him to escape to, the property of another ... is liable to the owner of such property for any damages to the property caused by the fire." Based on the provision's broad language and "history of liberal construction," state law places no restrictions on the type of property damage that is compensable. Landowners in California may recover damages for all the harm, including environmental injuries, caused by negligently set fires. Under California law, the government may recover intangible environmental damages because anything less would not compensate the public for all of the harm caused by the fire. Accordingly, we agree with the district court that the government should be able to recover all of the damages caused by the fire, including the intangible environmental damages.

CB&I next argues that the government did not produce sufficient evidence for the jury to determine the amount of environmental damages. Where property has no commercial or market equivalent, its value must be ascertained in some other rational way, and from such elements as are attainable. As the district court observed, a "rational way" of ascertaining damages does not require mathematical precision. The district court acknowledged that the government in this case did not elicit any testimony that put a dollar amount on the intangible environmental damages. However, the court noted that the government produced evidence regarding the extent of damage to the Angeles National Forest, including testimony regarding the 18,000 acres of burned federal land that was not usable by the public as a result of the fire. The jury also heard testimony concerning the extensive destruction and harm to animal habitats, soils, and plant life. This testimony included the harm caused by the fire to the endangered California red-legged frog and the destruction of the historic Hazel Dell mining camp.

We agree with the district court that the trial provided sufficient evidence for the jurors to quantify the intangible environmental harm. Evidence about the "nature and character" of the damaged National Forest environment provided a rational way for the jury to calculate the award. Such evidence having been shown, the jury could determine the intangible environmental damages award in the exercise of sound discretion. That the government's environmental damages are "largely intangible" and not readily subject to precise calculation does not make them any less real. Under California law, the government was entitled to full compensation for all the harm caused by the fire, including intangible environment harm. Affirmed.

## Questions

1. What common law causes of action enable plaintiffs to collect awards of damages related to forest fires?
2. Were California's statutory provisions important to the recovery of damages by the federal government?
3. Why didn't CB&I need to pay all of the $28.8 million in environmental damages?
4. Why should societies allow the recovery of intangible noneconomic damages for harm to the environment?
5. Why should a plaintiff be required to proffer testimony with a dollar amount of intangible environmental damages?
6. Would the findings of this case be relevant to a similar lawsuit for a fire occurring in Oregon? Why or why not?
7. Should the Eleventh Circuit Court of Appeals in Atlanta adopt the policy that testimony without a dollar amount of environmental damages is sufficient to justify a damage award?

## 2. Punitive Damage Awards

A second category of damages is punitive damages. Punitive measures against wrongdoers have existed for millennia and are justified by the need to encourage deterrence to prevent future negligence. They are awarded in a few cases to make injurers pay more than compensatory damages. Punitive damages are available when there is aggravated misconduct on the part of the defendant. Generally, punitive damages are only awarded if there is clear and convincing evidence that the defendant's conduct was reckless or outrageous. Although an imperfect way to allocate costs, punitive damages attempt to make up for those compensatory damages that injurers never have to pay. Only about 5 percent of tort cases involve such awards so that most lawsuits never involve punitive damages.

## 3. Deterring Future Negligence

A major objective of our tort system is deterrence. We enact rules to encourage persons to take reasonable actions to avoid injuries and discourage persons from engaging in actions that might result in an accident. We want to deter manufacturers from making shoddy goods that would lead to injuries. We want to deter physicians from making mistakes while diagnosing or operating. We seek to deter providers of services from skimping on care so that we will have fewer injuries. Persons who fail to take appropriate action are punished by holding them liable for damages.

The incorporation of deterrence into our tort system means that providers of goods and services have incentives to use care to avoid accidents. By employing sufficient care to keep things safe, manufacturers, service providers, property owners, and others can avoid awards for injuries. Due to this system of deterrence, we have an outstanding safety record. Despite more dangerous equipment, chemicals, machines, and situations, personal injuries are low.

Simultaneously, our preoccupation with deterrence has created an obsession for litigation. We threaten people with lawsuits if they do fail to adopt sufficient deterrence. Plaintiffs argue that if the defendant had just employed a bit more care the accident could have been prevented. The result is that deterrence obliges people to overinvest in safety or buy more insurance to cover any claims they are forced to pay. Companies and individuals choose to use more than a reasonable amount of care to prevent accidents because they want to avoid situations where injured persons bring lawsuits. In providing this care, they spend billions to avoid injuries costing millions.

Alternatively, compensation schemes that involve payouts regardless of fault detract from deterrence. Workers' compensation, strict liability, and no-fault insurance systems are troublesome as each involves the lack of deterrence. Injured persons are compensated even when they are at fault. This opens up the possibility that individuals will underinvest in using care to reduce injury. If persons know they will be compensated for an injury, they are less likely to be careful. Thus, policy makers are hesitant to adopt rules that fail to incorporate deterrence.

## Citizen Suits

Citizen suit provisions in various federal environmental statutes open avenues for litigation to enforce environmental law provisions. Such suits permit citizens to stand in an agency's shoes and bring a suit when the agency responsible for enforcing environmental statutes is unwilling or unable to do so. In citizen suits, individuals act as "private attorneys general." They also induce agencies to do more in enforcing antipollution standards. When provided by in a statute, individuals have a right to file a citizen suit if they can establish (1) that they have suffered an actual or threatened injury as a result of the defendant's actions violating a federal law; (2) the injury is "fairly traceable" to the defendant's actions; and (3) the injury will likely be redressed if the individual prevails in the lawsuit. An organization can file suit on behalf of its members if some of its members are injured. Citizen suits have been permitted where an organization's members claimed harm as to aesthetic, environmental, or recreational interests.

At least sixty days prior to filing suit, the citizens must notify the alleged violator and responsible enforcement agency of the planned filing. The sixty-day notice serves two purposes. First, the notice allows the alleged violator to come into compliance. Second, it allows the agency to take action to remedy problems and alleviate the need of a citizen suit. Citizen suits are not appropriate if an agency is already diligently prosecuting the alleged violator. What constitutes diligent prosecution, however, is not entirely clear. In *Friends of the Earth, Inc. v. Laidlaw Environmental Services, Inc.*, the United States Supreme Court considered the issue under what circumstances citizen-plaintiffs may have "standing" to sue for civil penalties that are paid into the United States Treasury. The Court held that civil penalties may redress threatened injuries by deterring future violations, and hence that, in appropriate cases, litigants may have standing to sue for civil penalties.

### Friends of the Earth, Inc. v. Laidlaw Environmental Services, Inc.
United States Supreme Court

*Who is suing?* _____

*Who is being sued?* _____

*For what?* _____

*What is the issue on appeal?* _____

This case presents an important question concerning the operation of the citizen-suit provisions of the Clean Water Act. Congress authorized the federal district courts to entertain Clean Water Act suits initiated by a person or persons having an interest which is or may be adversely affected. To impel future compliance with the Act, a district court may prescribe injunctive relief in such a suit; additionally or alternatively, the court may impose civil penalties payable to the United States Treasury. In the Clean Water Act citizen suit now before us, the District Court determined that injunctive relief was inappropriate because the defendant achieved substantial compliance with the terms of its discharge permit. The court did, however, assess a civil penalty of $405,800.

The Court of Appeals vacated the District Court's order. We reverse the judgment of the Court of Appeals. The appellate court erred in concluding that a citizen suitor's claim for civil penalties must be dismissed as moot when the defendant, albeit after commencement of the litigation, has come into compliance. The Court of Appeals also misperceived the remedial potential of civil penalties. Such penalties may serve, as an alternative to an injunction, to deter future violations and thereby redress the injuries that prompted a citizen suitor to commence litigation.

In 1972, Congress enacted the Clean Water Act (Act), also known as the Federal Water Pollution Control Act. Section 402 provides for the issuance of National Pollutant Discharge Elimination System (NPDES) permits. NPDES permits impose limitations on the discharge of pollutants, and establish related monitoring and reporting requirements in order to improve the cleanliness and safety of the Nation's waters. Noncompliance with a permit constitutes a violation of the Act. Under § 505(a), a suit to enforce any limitation in an NPDES permit may be brought by any "citizen," defined as a person or persons having an interest which is or may be adversely affected.

Defendant-respondent Laidlaw Environmental Services bought a hazardous waste incinerator facility in Roebuck, South Carolina that included a wastewater treatment plant. Shortly after Laidlaw acquired the facility, the South Carolina Department of Health and Environmental Control (DHEC) granted Laidlaw an NPDES permit authorizing the company to discharge treated water into the North Tyger River. The permit placed limits on Laidlaw's discharge of several pollutants into the river, including mercury, an extremely toxic pollutant. Once it received its permit, Laidlaw began to discharge various pollutants. Repeatedly, Laidlaw's discharges exceeded the limits set by the permit. Laidlaw consistently failed to meet the permit's stringent daily average limit on mercury discharges. The District Court later found that Laidlaw had violated the mercury limits on 489 occasions during an eight-year period.

On April 10, plaintiff-petitioner Friends of the Earth (FOE) sent a letter to Laidlaw notifying the company of its intention to file a citizen suit against it after the expiration of the requisite 60-day notice period. Laidlaw's lawyer then contacted DHEC to ask whether DHEC would consider filing a lawsuit against Laidlaw. The District Court later found that Laidlaw's reason for requesting that DHEC file a lawsuit against it was to bar FOE's proposed citizen suit. DHEC agreed to file a lawsuit against Laidlaw; the company's lawyer then drafted the complaint for DHEC and paid the filing fee. On June 9, the last day before FOE's 60-day notice period expired, DHEC and Laidlaw reached a settlement requiring Laidlaw to pay $100,000 in civil penalties and to make "every effort" to comply with its permit obligations.

On June 12, FOE filed this citizen suit against Laidlaw alleging noncompliance with the NPDES permit and seeking declaratory and injunctive relief and an award of civil penalties. Laidlaw moved to dismiss the action on the ground that the citizen suit was barred by DHEC's prior action against the company. The District Court held that DHEC's action against Laidlaw had not been "diligently prosecuted." Subsequently, the court allowed FOE's citizen suit to proceed. The record indicates that after FOE initiated the suit, but before the District Court rendered judgment, Laidlaw violated the mercury discharge limitation in its permit 13 times. The District Court also found that Laidlaw had committed 13 monitoring and 10 reporting violations during this period.

Approximately five years later, the District Court issued its judgment. It found that Laidlaw had gained a total economic benefit of $1,092,581 as a result of its extended period of noncompliance with the mercury discharge limit in its permit. The court concluded, however, that a civil penalty of $405,800 was adequate in light of the guiding factors. FOE appealed the District Court's civil penalty judgment and Laidlaw cross-appealed. The Fourth Circuit held that the case had become moot. The court therefore vacated the District Court's order and remanded with instructions to dismiss the action. After the Court of Appeals issued its decision but before this Court granted certiorari, the entire incinerator facility in Roebuck was permanently closed, and all discharges from the facility permanently ceased. We granted certiorari to resolve the inconsistency between the Fourth Circuit's decision in this case and the decisions of several other Courts of Appeals, which have held that a defendant's compliance with its permit after the commencement of litigation does not moot claims for civil penalties under the Act.

Because the Court of Appeals was persuaded that the case had become moot, it simply assumed without deciding that FOE had initial standing. But because we hold that the Court of Appeals erred in declaring the case moot, we have an obligation to assure ourselves that FOE had Article III standing at the outset of the litigation. To satisfy Article III's standing requirements, a plaintiff must show (1) it has suffered an "injury in fact" that is (a) concrete and particularized and (b) actual or imminent, not conjectural or hypothetical; (2) the injury is fairly traceable to the challenged action of the defendant; and (3) it is likely, as opposed to merely speculative, that the injury will be redressed by a favorable decision. An association has standing to bring suit on behalf of its members when its members would otherwise have standing to sue in their own right, the interests at stake are germane to the organization's purpose, and neither the claim asserted nor the relief requested requires the participation of individual members in the lawsuit.

Focusing properly on injury to the plaintiff, the District Court found that FOE had demonstrated sufficient injury to establish standing. For example, FOE member Kenneth Lee Curtis averred in affidavits that he lived a half-mile from Laidlaw's facility and that he would like to fish, camp, swim, and picnic in and near the river between 3 and 15 miles downstream from the facility, as he did when he was a teenager, but would not do so because he was concerned that the water was polluted by Laidlaw's discharges. Other members presented evidence to similar effect. These sworn statements, as the District Court determined, adequately documented injury in fact.

The only conceivable basis for a finding of mootness in this case is Laidlaw's voluntary conduct: either its achievement by substantial compliance with its NPDES permit or its more recent shutdown of the Roebuck facility. It is well settled that a defendant's voluntary cessation of a challenged practice does not deprive a federal court of its power to determine the legality of the practice. The facility closure, like Laidlaw's earlier achievement of substantial compliance with its permit requirements, might moot the case, but only if one or the other of these events made it absolutely clear that Laidlaw's permit violations could not reasonably be expected to recur. The effect of both Laidlaw's compliance and the facility closure on the prospect of future violations is a disputed factual matter. FOE points out, for example, that Laidlaw retains its NPDES permit. These issues have not been aired in the lower courts; they remain open for consideration on remand.

FOE argues that it is entitled to attorney's fees on the theory that a plaintiff can be a prevailing party if it was the "catalyst" that triggered a favorable outcome. It is for the District Court, not this Court, to address in the first instance any request for reimbursement of costs, including fees. For the reasons stated, the judgment of the Court of Appeals is reversed, and the case is remanded for further proceedings consistent with this opinion.

## Questions

1. Why did the court decide that the plaintiff had standing?
2. How did Laidlaw attempt to bar FOE's citizen suit?
3. Why did the court decide that the state had not diligently prosecuted Laidlaw?
4. Why doesn't a defendant's compliance moot the case?
5. When should closure of an offensive facility moot a case?
6. When should a plaintiff in a citizen suit be awarded attorney's fees?

# Class Action Lawsuits

Another controversial subject has been the dramatic increase in the number of class action tort lawsuits. These are civil actions filed by numerous plaintiffs against defendants concerning products or actions that have caused injuries. They include class actions for disasters, contamination, and product liability damages. For environmental law, they often involve contamination events. Recent examples include Syngenta's GMO corn litigation and environmental damages from oil and gas development.

Governments have become involved in attempting to manage class action tort litigation lawsuits. In 2017, Congress proposed the Fairness in Class Action Litigation Act with provisions that should result in greater amounts of damages being paid to injured plaintiffs. Yet the provisions of this proposed legislation are debatable as they would replace provisions related to other policy issues that have been developed by state legislatures and courts.

The Federal Rules of Civil Procedure govern procedures used for civil lawsuits in federal courts. The federal rules are promulgated by the US Supreme Court and transmitted to Congress for approval. Although federal courts are required to apply the substantive law of the states as rules of decision in cases where state law is in question, the federal courts almost always use the federal rules as their rules of procedure. The following case shows how the federal rules affect class action tort litigation.

### *Butler v. Sears Roebuck and Co.*
US Court of Appeals for the Seventh Circuit, Chicago

*Who is suing?* _____

*Who is being sued?* _____

*For what?* _____

*What is the issue on appeal?* _____

The parties to this class action suit petitioned us to review separate orders by the district court ruling on motions for class certification filed by the plaintiffs. The suit is really two class actions because the classes have different members and different claims, and therefore they should have been severed, though both arise from alleged defects in Kenmore-brand Sears washing machines sold in overlapping periods. One class action complains of a defect that causes mold (the mold claim), the other of a defect that stops the machine inopportunely (the control unit claim). The district court denied certification of the class complaining about the defect that causes mold and granted certification of the class complaining about the defect that causes the sudden stoppage. The denial of certification of the mold class precipitated the petition for review by the plaintiffs who are complaining about the mold. The grant of certification to the plaintiffs (a different set of named plaintiffs) complaining about the stoppage precipitated Sears's petition for review.

We have accepted the appeals in order to clarify the concept of "predominance" in class action litigation. Federal Rules of Civil Procedure Rule 23(b)(3) conditions the maintenance of a class action on a finding by the district court that the questions of fact or law common to class members predominate over any questions affecting only individual members. If there are no common questions or only common questions, the issue of predominance is automatically resolved. Any other case requires "weighing" unweighted factors, which is the kind of subjective determination that usually— including the determination whether to certify a class—is left to the district court.

The mold claim pertains to all Kenmore-brand frontloading "high efficiency" washing machines sold by Sears during a cited time period. The claim is that because of the low volume of water used in these machines and the low temperature of the water, they don't clean themselves adequately and a mass of microbes forms where the washing occurs and creates mold, which emits bad odors. Roughly 200,000 of these Kenmore-brand machines were sold each year and there have been many thousands of complaints of bad odors by the owners.

Sears contends that there are a number of different models with different defects and therefore common questions of fact concerning the mold problem and its consequences do not predominate over individual questions of fact. Only five design changes relate to mold. The basic question in the litigation—were the machines defective in permitting mold to accumulate and generate noxious odors?—is common to the entire mold class, although the answer may vary with the differences in design. Should it turn out as the litigation progresses that there are large differences in the mold defect among the five differently designed washing machines, the judge may wish to create subclasses; but that possibility is not an obstacle to certification of a single mold class at this juncture.

Predominance is a question of efficiency. Is it more efficient, in terms both of economy of judicial resources and of the expense of litigation to the parties, to decide some issues on a class basis or all issues in separate trials? A class action is the more efficient procedure for determining liability and damages in a case such as this involving a defect that may have imposed costs on tens of thousands of consumers, yet not a cost to any one of them large enough to justify the expense of an individual suit. The class action procedure would be efficient not only in cost, but also in efficacy, if we are right that the stakes in an individual case would be too small to justify the expense of suing, in which event denial of class certification would preclude any relief.

We turn to Sears's appeal from the certification of a class of buyers of Kenmore-brand washing machines who incurred a harm because of the defective control unit. Each washing machine has a computer device that gives instructions to the machine's moving parts. This "central control unit" consists of circuit boards that are soldered together. The company that supplied the central control units altered its manufacturing process in a way that inadvertently damaged the layer of solder, causing some of the control units mistakenly to "believe" that a serious error had occurred and therefore to order the machine to shut down even though nothing was the matter with it. Sears is alleged to have known about the problem but to have charged each owner of a defective machine hundreds of dollars to repair the central control unit. The defect was corrected one year later but Sears continued to ship machines containing the earlier-manufactured, defective control units.

The principal issue is whether the control unit was indeed defective. The only individual issues concern the amount of harm to particular class members. It is more efficient for the question whether the washing machines were defective—the question common to all class members—to be resolved in a single proceeding than for it to be litigated separately in hundreds of different trials. Again the district court will want to consider whether to create different subclasses of the control unit class for the different states. That should depend on whether there are big enough differences among the relevant laws of those states to make it impossible to draft a single, coherent set of jury instructions should the case ever go to trial before a jury.

The denial of class certification regarding the mold claim is reversed and the grant of class certification regarding the control unit claim is affirmed.

## Questions

1. Why did the US Supreme Court develop a set of Rules of Civil Procedure?
2. Why do manufacturing firms object to the consolidation of lawsuits into class action lawsuits?
3. What does "predominance" have to do with class action lawsuits?
4. When all members of a class action lawsuit do not have to have identical allegations, how does a class action court enter its judgment?
5. What consumer advantage is citied for class action lawsuits?

# Settlements

Another litigation issue involves the use of settlements to reduce the number of cases that need to be tried. Settlements allow attorneys and their clients to opt out of the all-or-nothing lawsuit. They normally involve partial recoveries of damages agreed by the parties that resolve the dispute. Attorneys preparing a case make decisions on its merits and the likelihood of a favorable jury decision. If there are major problems with the proof, a settlement involving a reduced award of damages may be a good option for the plaintiff. The attorney may accept a corresponding reduction in the contingency fee. A defendant may want to settle to avoid additional litigation costs and the risk of a large verdict. A majority of lawsuits are resolved through settlements and dismissals.

In response to overcrowded courts, state legislatures have been enacting legislation to encourage settlements. A common theme is to encourage both plaintiffs and defendants to make reasonable monetary settlement offers. If a settlement offer is rejected by the other party and the case goes to trial, the statute imposes penalties if the monetary award is significantly different from the offer. Section 9-11-68(b), Official Code of Georgia Annotated (OCGA), shows one example of what state legislatures are doing.

> *OCGA § 9-11-68(b). Offers of settlement; damages for frivolous claims or defenses*
>
> *(b) (1) If a defendant makes an offer of settlement which is rejected by the plaintiff, the defendant shall be entitled to recover reasonable attorney's fees and expenses of litigation incurred by the defendant or on the defendant's behalf from the date of the rejection of the offer of settlement through the entry of judgment if the final judgment is one of no liability or the final judgment obtained by the plaintiff is less than 75 percent of such offer of settlement.*
>
> *(2) If a plaintiff makes an offer of settlement which is rejected by the defendant and the plaintiff recovers a final judgment in an amount greater than 125 percent of such offer of settlement, the plaintiff shall be entitled to recover reasonable attorney's fees and expenses of litigation incurred by the plaintiff or on the plaintiff's behalf from the date of the rejection of the offer of settlement through the entry of judgment.*
>
> *(c) Any offer made under this Code section shall remain open for 30 days unless sooner withdrawn by a writing served on the offeree prior to acceptance by the offeree. ...*

Under these provisions, a plaintiff who rejects a settlement offer and is awarded at least 25 percent less than a defendant's offer is obligated to pay additional costs and attorney's fees to the defendant. A defendant who rejects a settlement offer and subsequently is found liable, with the plaintiff being awarded more than 125 percent of the offer, is obligated to pay additional costs and attorney's fees to the plaintiff.

## Questions

1. What does OCGA § 9-11-68(b) mean for plaintiffs rejecting offers?
2. What does OCGA § 9-11-68(b) mean for defendants rejecting offers?
3. A defendant offers to settle for $100,000; the plaintiff refuses. The trial results in a $74,000 judgment for the plaintiff with $10,000 in expenses and $20,000 in attorney's fees after the rejection of the offer. How much does the plaintiff owe?

## Discussion Questions

1. Should state legislatures set caps for pain and suffering, and at what level? Explain your reasoning.
2. Should our law allow damage awards for intangible environmental damages founded upon descriptions lacking dollar amounts? Why or why not?

3. Are there environmental statutes that would benefit from the addition of authority for citizen suits? If so, which?
4. Should state legislatures adopt provisions allowing class action lawsuits for selected situations? Why or why not?

# CHAPTER TWELVE
## Insurance and Handling Risk

## Learning Objectives

- *Examine characteristics that suggest insurance would be beneficial.*
- *Describe the relationship between degree of risk and frequency of losses.*
- *Explain why insurance policies have deductibles.*
- *Illustrate the collateral source rule.*
- *Explain the need for physical loss to recover under an insurance policy.*

Insurance has long been a tool used by individuals to protect themselves against harmful events that cause some sort of physical loss. Insurance is defined as the pooling of fortuitous losses by a transfer of risk to insurers, who agree to indemnify and pay the insured for such losses. Everyone faces all kinds of risks, and depending on each person's personality, individuals respond differently to certain risks. Risk seekers are willing to accept more types of risks, while risk-averse individuals want to avoid risks at all costs. This is where insurance has value. Individuals can simply pay someone else to deal with a type of risk they want to avoid. Due to simple statistics, insurance companies can pool together large amounts of similar risks, and charge individuals a reasonable "premium" based on the type of risk being transferred.

The need for insurance coverage depends on risks associated with losses. Both the frequency and the severity of expected losses need to be considered. Risk managers attempt to categorize risks into four different pools. At each level, decisions can be made on which loss control measure to implement, if any. These refer to mechanisms to reduce the frequency or severity of a loss. For example, to reduce the severity of a loss, a sprinkler system in a building may be installed to reduce damages from fire. The following table provides an outline for determining how to manage risk.

### Risk Management Matrix

| Loss Frequency | Loss Severity | Risk Management Technique |
|---|---|---|
| Low | Low | Retain risk |
| High | Low | Loss prevention & retention |
| Low | High | Insure against loss |
| High | High | Avoid these situations |

The type of risk most feared by individuals is the low-frequency, high-severity variety. Although high-frequency, high-severity risk is worse, proper risk management tells individuals they should avoid such risks. This means not engaging in activities that would be accompanied by high-frequency, high-severity risks. Low-frequency, high-severity losses are problematic because over 95 percent of the time, an individual will not experience a loss. However, if that particular loss does occur, it is very harmful. Financially speaking, it's challenging and worrisome to plan for such events. This is where insurance is so valuable; individuals can purchase insurance to transfer that type of risk to an insurance company. If a loss occurs, the insured will be protected.

## Insurable Risks

Although any risk can be insured for the right price, not all risks meet the criteria of being "insurable." If the cost of insurance gets too high, for example, it may not make sense to pay for that coverage. One must remember that insurance companies are in the business of making a profit. Thus, in order to properly insure a risk, the risk must meet several criteria.

I.   Large Number of Homogeneous Exposure Units. The vast majority of insurance policies are provided for individual members of very large classes. Automobile insurance, for instance, covers millions of automobiles. The existence of a large number of homogeneous exposure units allows insurers to benefit from the so-called "law of large numbers," which explains that as the number of exposure units increases, the actual results are increasingly likely to become close to expected results. With a sufficiently large number of insured sharing a similar risk-exposure profile, the insurer can use past experience to accurately predict the risk faced by any individual.

II.  Definite Loss. The event that gives rise to the loss, at least in principle, must take place at a known time, in a known place, and from a known cause. Fire, automobile accidents, and worker injuries meet this criterion and so can be insured.

III. Accidental Loss. The event that constitutes the trigger of a claim should be fortuitous, or at least outside the control of the beneficiary of the insurance. The loss should be "pure," in the sense that it results from an event for which it only causes a loss to an insured. This means the insured cannot gain from the event. Events that contain speculative elements such as ordinary business risks are generally not considered insurable.

IV.  Economically Feasible Premium. If the likelihood of an insured event is so high—or the cost of the event so large—that the resulting premium is too large relative to the amount of protection offered, it is not likely that anyone will buy insurance. If premiums are too high, companies will simply accept the risk or avoid conducting such business activities.

V.   Calculable Loss. Persons must be able to estimate two elements: the probability of loss, and the resulting severity affecting cost. Probability of loss is generally an empirical exercise. Cost has more to do with the ability to make a reasonably definite and objective evaluation of the amount of the loss recoverable as a result of the claim.

VI.  Non-Catastrophic Losses. Only a small proportion of the insured group should be exposed to the risk of a loss at any one occasion, so that the insurer is not prone to too many claims simultaneously. If the same event can cause losses to numerous policyholders of the same insurer, the ability of that insurer to issue policies becomes constrained. Typically, insurers prefer to limit their exposure to a loss from a single event to some small portion of their capital base, on the order of 5 percent. The classic example is earthquake insurance, where the ability of an underwriter to issue a new policy depends on the number and size of the policies that it has already underwritten. Wind insurance in hurricane zones, particularly along coast lines, is another example of this phenomenon. Insurers want to avoid insuring events that could wipe out an entire group of insured. Such events would lead to the potential for debilitating costs for an insurer if the event were to occur.

## Insurance Issues

## 1. Moral Hazard

Moral hazard is an issue that is considered by insurers for all types of insurance policies. Moral hazard may be defined as anything done before or after a loss as a result of owning insurance that increases the frequency and severity of that loss. For example, drivers with car insurance who know they will be reimbursed if an accident occurs may drive more recklessly. Furthermore, if a car accident occurs, they may not take the same post-loss measures that they would if they did not have insurance. Moral hazard issues increase costs for insurers. In addition, they are hard to detect and properly manage. Insurers attempt to eliminate many of these problems through proper financial incentives. For example, by raising rates used to calculate premiums based on driving records and accident claims, drivers may be more cautious because they know an accident will result in higher insurance costs.

Moral hazard issues are present in pollution insurance. Insurance companies fear that if companies hold pollution insurance protection, it may make them less cautious about the actions they take with regard to the environment. For example, some companies may stop researching the impact some of their products have on the environment if they are under the impression that liability costs will be paid for by insurance companies.

## 2. Adverse Selection

Adverse selection is another worrisome issue for insurers. It refers to the phenomenon whereby those who most need insurance are the ones who will purchase it. Insurance is only able to function properly when certain frequencies and severities of risks can be measured. For product liability insurance, insurance companies know certain accident statistics and can break them down by product type and industry. However, the people who know their products could be dangerous are very likely to buy insurance, while companies who may know there is virtually no chance of injury from their product may elect to operate with no insurance. It is difficult for insurance companies to determine these issues because they lack the information the company possesses about the product. This can result in mostly high-risk individuals purchasing insurance that detracts from the calculation of an accurate insurance rate.

Insurance companies attempt to combat the problem of adverse selection through the use of deductibles. They allow the insured to choose what part of the loss they self-insure. High-risk individuals are likely to choose the lowest deductible possible because they expect losses to occur. This allows the insurer to charge those individuals a higher rate than the people who choose a higher deductible.

The adverse selection problem is a major issue for firms providing pollution insurance. Companies operating in the most dangerous industries such as chemical and petroleum extraction are those who most desire insurance. Thus, high-risk companies will seek to purchase insurance. However, small- to mid-size companies that could face potential pollution losses greater than the company's assets may feel the probability of a loss is so small that insurance is not needed. Because insurers know that companies that want pollution insurance are likely to experience losses, they either will refuse to

Fig. 12.1 Pollutants from sources such as powerplants pose difficulties for insurance coverage.

participate in the pollution insurance market or charge high premiums, which makes pollution insurance nearly impossible to obtain.

## 3. The Collateral Source Rule

The collateral source rule presents controversial policy issues regarding medical malpractice and tort law. The collateral source rule precludes an injured person from having damages reduced by monies received from another source. Other sources might include insurance proceeds, workers' compensation, and disability or Social Security benefits. Under the rule, juries are not supposed to know about other benefits or payouts to injured plaintiffs. Rather, juries determine from the evidence whether the defendants were negligent and, if so, what were the damages. With this information, the jury awards injured plaintiffs 100 percent of their damages, despite the fact that the same plaintiffs may have already been compensated for some or all of these damages by another source. The collateral source rule allows injured persons to collect more than 100 percent of their damages.

While the policy of not allowing wrongdoers to benefit from other payments is attractive, some legislatures have decided that a more weighty consideration is to preclude duplicative recoveries. Why should injured victims receive more than 100 percent of their damages, and why shouldn't juries learn about other payments covering damages? Given the high costs of medical malpractice claims, many states decided to alter the collateral source rule and allow setoffs for amounts received from other sources. The abrogation of the collateral source rule means that injurers only pay part of the damages inflicted whenever an injured victim qualifies for benefits under an insurance policy or some other payment.

## *Dees v. Logan*
### Georgia Supreme Court

*Who is suing?* _____

*Who is being sued?* _____

*For what?* _____

*What is the issue on appeal?* _____

We granted a writ of certiorari to the Court of Appeals to determine whether, under the provisions of an uninsured motorist policy, a damage award to the insured can be offset by workers' compensation and similar benefits paid to the insured. The short answer is "no."

Dees and his wife brought suit against Logan seeking damages for injuries suffered in an automobile collision. The jury awarded the Dees $130,000 for lost wages, $4,939 for reimbursement of COBRA payments, $10,000 for pain and suffering, and $5,000 for loss of consortium. The Dees' uninsured motorist carrier, State Farm Mutual Automobile Insurance Company (State Farm), argued that it could offset the jury's award by amounts Dees had already received in workers' compensation benefits ($83,200), social security disability benefits ($70,056), and a pretrial settlement with Logan's liability insurer ($25,000). State Farm pointed out that its uninsured motorist policy expressly provided that "any amount payable shall be reduced by any amount paid or payable to or for the insured: (a) under any workers' compensation, disability benefits or similar law." The trial court accepted State Farm's argument and ordered that the Dees recover nothing from State Farm or Logan. The Dees appealed, and the Court of Appeals affirmed holding that the trial court properly reduced the damage award by offsetting the benefits paid to Dees. In so doing, the Court of Appeals relied upon earlier decisions in which it ruled that non-duplication of benefits clauses in uninsured motorist policies were enforceable.

Georgia's uninsured motorist statute, Official Code of Georgia Annotated (OCGA) § 33-7-11, provides:

> *The endorsement or provisions of the policy providing the coverage required by this Code section may contain provisions which exclude any liability of the insurer for injury or destruction of property of the insured for which he has been compensated by other property or physical damage insurance.*

The plain meaning of this subsection is that an uninsured motorist carrier can setoff benefits which its insured may have received to compensate for property loss. This being so, we must conclude that the legislature did not intend to authorize an insurer to setoff benefits received for personal injury. That is because when a statute expressly mentions one of many things, the omitted things must be regarded as having been deliberately excluded.

When an uninsured motorist policy provision is in conflict with the clear intent of OCGA § 33-7-11, the policy provision is unenforceable and the statute controls. Exclusions in uninsured motorist endorsements cannot circumvent the clear mandate of the Georgia Uninsured Motorist Act by withholding the protection required. Inasmuch as the uninsured policy provision in this case permits a setoff for personal injury benefits, it is in conflict with the plain mandate of the Uninsured Motorist Act. It follows that the policy provision is void and unenforceable.

State Farm posits that, inasmuch as Dees is not entitled to a double recovery, he cannot be permitted to receive workers' compensation benefits or other similar benefits in addition to a recovery under his uninsured motorist policy. Again, we disagree. Dees is not recovering twice; and State Farm is not paying twice. On the contrary, Dees is merely recovering sums he is due from Logan, the owner of the uninsured motor vehicle, and benefits he is otherwise entitled to receive from other sources. In passing, we note that our holding is in accord with a majority of jurisdictions which have uninsured motorist statutes that do not expressly permit or prohibit reduction clauses and which hold that offsets for workers' compensation benefits are impermissible. Judgment reversed.

## Questions

1. Why did the insurance company argue for an offset by amounts recovered under workers' compensation benefits?
2. What happens if a provision of an insurance policy is in conflict with state law?
3. Does the court allow a double recovery for Dees?
4. Why might a state legislature preclude double recovery for property damages and allow double recovery for personal injuries?

# Pollution Insurance

The potential for pollution accidents are worrisome for a company or homeowner. The cleanup and restoration costs, along with the resulting liability stemming from an accident, can impose significantly high costs on an organization. Because these events don't occur often, but do have the threat of unbearable costs, they meet the low-frequency, high-severity definition of risk. Consequently, these are risks that most individuals would want to transfer away through the use of insurance.

However, looking at the characteristics of an insurable risk, it becomes clear that pollution-based risks are precarious to insure. Because the environment is constantly changing, new pollutants being discovered, and laws governing pollution always being altered, firms are challenged in developing standardized pollution insurance policy provisions. While there might be a large group of individuals who face pollution risks, each risk is unique and constantly changing. Thus, the "large homogeneous exposure units" criterion does not apply. Furthermore, because laws and environmental standards are fluid, it makes it impossible for insurance companies to accurately calculate the frequency and severity of potential losses, as monetary sanctions and cleanup requirements may increase. Hence, the "calculable losses" criterion is not present, so an insurer may elect not to offer any insurance for pollution.

Some types of pollution may occur over a long period of time, so their impact may not be known until some later date. This means it is infeasible to pinpoint a time, place, and cause of the loss. Thus, the "definite loss" criterion is not applicable. Furthermore, since the definition of a pollutant may change, there is the chance of an industry-wide problem. A chemical may be deemed a dangerous toxin as new information surfaces. If that chemical is widely used in an industry, losses could meet the "catastrophic" definition, where numerous companies face cleanup efforts all at once. Finally, because of the uncertainty and potential severity of certain pollution accidents, it is difficult for insurance companies to charge "economically feasible premiums." For small companies, pollution cleanup expenses can sometimes be greater than the entire worth of the company. Premiums may be too high to justify insuring against pollution damages.

While pollution insurance isn't as readily available as many other types of insurance, there are ways for organizations to obtain certain coverage. Below are several categories of common insurance coverage available in the industry.

## 1. Pollution Liability Policies

Under a standard pollution liability policy, an insurer covers claims from unknown pollution conditions at covered locations specified in the policy. Generally, these policies cover both on- and off-site pollution conditions and include claims for bodily injury, property damage, and cleanup costs. Often, business interruption and transportation claims will be covered. However, the costs of an ongoing cleanup or a known contamination event are not covered. Pollution legal liability policies can be modified to fit individual circumstances. Numerous terms and types of coverage are negotiable. However, for each contract, the question is its coverage. Insureds may be surprised that pollution insurance policies do not cover circumstances for which they thought they had purchased coverage.

## 2. Property Transfers

Similar to pollution legal liability policies, property transfer policies cover claims arising from a covered location for preexisting, unknown contamination and known contamination below reportable levels. In some cases, it covers known contamination at levels above regulatory limits, but permitted by a governmental body. Like pollution legal liability insurance, these policies cover bodily injury, property damage, and cleanup costs. Limits, deductibles, and exclusions are also similar to those found in pollution liability policies.

## 3. Cleanup Cost Cap or Stop Loss

These are very specific policies that protect insured against cost overruns for remediation of individual projects. Covered overruns may result from the discovery of additional amounts or newly discovered contaminants or from changes in regulatory requirements at a site. Coverage is limited to cleanup costs and claims for bodily injury. This means that property damage or other liabilities are not covered. Also commonly excluded are the costs of legal defense and governmental negotiations.

## 4. Brownfields Restoration and Development

Brownfields are former industrial or commercial sites where future use is complicated by the presence or potential presences of a hazardous substance. Insurers may insure properties with known contamination where remediation of pollution has occurred or will take place as part of a development or restoration plan. The policies combine pollution legal liability and cost-cap insurance and generally cover bodily injury, property damage, cleanup costs for unknown pollutants, and cost-cap coverage for cleanup.

## 5. Secured Creditors

Insurers will insure secured creditors of properties that may have losses. Coverage is generally limited to the lesser of either (a) the loan balance due with respect to property found to be contaminated; or (b) the cost to clean up the property. Coverage may include default on loans and third-party claims for bodily injury and property damage. However, unless specifically negotiated, the coverage will not apply to known contamination or in situations where the loan goes into default beyond the policy period.

## 6. Professional and Contractor Environmental Liability

Insurers can issue policies to cover environmental consultants and contractors who may be exposed to third-party claims, as well as liability to the client in the event an error causes cleanup costs to exceed the estimate. Bodily injury and property damage claims are usually covered. Contractors may be advised to keep these policies in place for a period of time after the work is completed.

## 7. Transporter Insurance

An insurance policy may be written to cover a transporter for off-site spills and liability for disposal of waste at a non-owned location. Coverage may extend to oil, asphalt, sand and gravel, construction material, chemicals, and other toxic materials. Bodily injury, property damage, and cleanup costs can be covered, but known conditions, completed operations, and deliberate acts are commonly excluded.

## 8. Storage Tank Pollution Liability

Properties with storage tank systems may want to purchase insurance to cover required corrective actions both on-site and off-site. Bodily injury and property damages are covered, and these policies can be used to meet Environmental Protection Agency and state financial responsibility requirements.

## 9. Closure and Post-Closure

Insurance may be designed as an alternative to bonds, letters of credit, and trust funds to cover regulated facilities with financial assurance obligations. No liability or associated defense coverage is included. They are useful for solid waste landfills, hazardous waste treatment, storage and disposal facilities, and some manufacturing and materials processing sites.

# Coverage under Policies

Property owners may desire to purchase pollution insurance as a safeguard against liability for some environmental damages. Under "occurrence-based" liability insurance policies, there may be coverage for insured events with details on the damages. The general industry rule is that premises' liability insurance contracts do not cover pollution: each contract would have a pollution exclusion clause. But even when parties enter into a contract for pollution coverage, there are difficulties. One is a disagreement on what is the "insured event." A second is whether an event resulting in damages involves a direct physical loss or damage. Thus, persons purchasing insurance need to think about what coverage they need and want, and ask their agent questions about whether certain types of events would be covered by the policy.

## 1. Insured Events

### *Whitney v. Vermont Mutual Insurance Company*
#### Supreme Court of Vermont

*Who is suing?* _____

*Who is being sued?* _____

*For what?* _____

*What is the issue on appeal?* _____

This case calls upon us to apply a "pollution exclusion" in an insurance policy. Plaintiffs Neil and Patricia Whitney assert that damage to their home and personal property resulting from the spraying within their home of a pesticide known as chlorpyrifos is covered by their homeowners policy. Defendant Vermont Mutual Insurance Company (Vermont Mutual) argues that the pollution exclusion in the policy bars the Whitneys' claim. The Rutland

Superior Court, granted the Whitneys summary judgment motion on the question of coverage, concluding that the exclusion in question was ambiguous, and construing the ambiguous provision in favor of coverage. We conclude that the property damage to the Whitneys' home is an excluded risk in the applicable policy and accordingly reverse.

The Whitneys' home is insured by a policy issued by Vermont Mutual. The Whitneys are foster parents and they noticed bed bugs in their home after a new foster child was placed with them by the Vermont Department for Children and Families (DCF). Shortly thereafter, Triple A Pest Control (Triple A) sprayed the Whitneys' home with the pesticide chlorpyrifos in order to eradicate the bed bugs. Triple A sprayed the house, corner to corner, wall to wall, and sprayed the Whitneys' personal effects within the home. When the Whitneys returned to their home after the spraying operation, the walls and surfaces of the home were visibly dripping with the pesticide.

Chlorpyrifos is a toxin that can cause "nausea, dizziness, confusion, and, in very high exposures, respiratory paralysis and death." The substance is banned for residential use by the Federal Environmental Protection Agency, and the spraying of the Whitneys' home with chlorpyrifos violated federal and state law. Concerned by the amount of chemicals sprayed within their home, the Whitneys contacted DCF, who referred them to the Vermont Department of Agriculture (the Department). When the Whitneys informed the Department's representative of the name of the applicator, the representative advised them to stay out of the house until it could be tested. Following testing about a week after the spraying, a representative of the Department advised the Whitneys to stay out of their home until further notice. The testing revealed high levels of chlorpyrifos. According to the EPA, a cleanup is required if testing reveals levels in excess of 0.006 micrograms per square centimeter. Swabs of the Whitneys' home revealed concentration levels of chlorpyrifos as high as 3.99 micrograms per square centimeter. As a result of the extremely high concentration levels, the Whitneys have been unable to inhabit their home.

Shortly after the Department's testing, the Whitneys filed a claim with Vermont Mutual. Coverage A of their homeowners policy insures against a "physical loss to property." Among the exclusions to the property damage coverage in Coverage A is a "pollution exclusion." The policy states that insurer does not insure for loss caused by:

> *discharge, dispersal, seepage, migration, release or escape of pollutants unless the discharge, dispersal, seepage, migration, release or escape is itself caused by a Peril Insured Against under Coverage C of this policy. Pollutants means any solid, liquid, gaseous, or thermal irritant or contaminant, including smoke, vapor, soot, fumes, acids, alkalis, chemicals and waste. Waste includes materials to be recycled, reconditioned or reclaimed.*

Vermont Mutual denied the Whitneys' claim, citing the pollution exclusion. The Whitneys filed suit against Vermont Mutual, seeking a declaratory judgment that the losses incurred by the spraying of chlorpyrifos within their home were covered by their homeowner's policy. On cross-motions for summary judgment on the question of coverage, the trial court ruled in the Whitneys['] favor. On appeal, Vermont Mutual argues that the trial court erred in finding the pollution exclusion ambiguous. In addition, Vermont Mutual argues that even if the pollution exclusion is ambiguous and we construe it to apply only to traditional environmental contamination, the intentional spraying of chlorpyrifos throughout the Whitneys' home qualifies as the kind of traditional environmental pollution that falls squarely within the scope of the policy's pollution exclusion.

The issue is whether the pollution-exclusion clause in the property damage coverage in Vermont Mutual's homeowners policy excludes the damage to the Whitneys' home resulting from the spraying of chlorpyrifos throughout their home. In the recent case of *Cincinnati Specialty Underwriters Insurance Co. v. Energy Wise Homes*, we observed that pollution exclusions are not presumed, as a class, to be ambiguous or to be limited in their application to traditional environmental pollution. They should be construed in the same way as any other insurance contract provision. Our goal in interpreting an insurance policy, like our goal in interpreting any contract, is to ascertain and carry out the parties' intentions. Therefore, we interpret policy language according to its "plain, ordinary and popular meaning."

Words or phrases in an insurance policy are ambiguous if they are fairly susceptible to more than one reasonable interpretation. If we determine that language within the policy is ambiguous, we construe the ambiguity against the insurer. The pollution exclusion in this case excludes from coverage any loss caused by "discharge, dispersal, seepage, immigration, release, or escape of pollutants." "Pollutants mean any solid, liquid, gaseous or thermal irritant or contaminant, including smoke, vapor, soot, fumes, acids, alkalis, chemicals and waste." That the dousing of the Whitneys' home with chlorpyrifos constitutes "discharge, dispersal, seepage, immigration, release, or escape" of the substance is clear. Whether chlorpyrifos, applied in this context, qualifies as a "pollutant" is the more contested question in this appeal.

The undisputed facts are that chlorpyrifos is: toxic to humans; can cause nausea, dizziness, confusion, and at very high exposures, respiratory paralysis and death; and is banned for residential use. Triple A's use of chlorpyrifos in the Whitneys' home violated EPA regulations, and federal and state law. The concentration levels of the substance in the Whitneys' home were consistently high relative to the EPA "action level" at which the EPA has determined that cleaning of housing units is required. As a result of the contamination, the Whitneys have been unable to live in their home. We do not find it hard to conclude that, in the context of this case, the terms "irritant," "contaminant," and "pollutant" plainly and unambiguously encompass the chlorpyrifos sprayed "corner to corner, wall to wall" throughout the Whitneys' home. As we have previously noted, "we cannot deny the insurer the benefit of unambiguous provisions inserted into the policy for its benefit."

For the above reasons, we reverse the trial court's award of summary judgment to the Whitneys, and direct the trial court to award summary judgment to Vermont Mutual. Reversed.

## Questions

1. What type of insurance policy is involved in this case?
2. Can the Whitneys sue Triple A, and if so, under what causes of action?
3. When should the expectations of the insured be considered?
4. What does this case suggest about many insurance contracts?
5. How can property owners protect themselves from service providers that engage in activities that damage property?

## 2. Physical Loss

### *Universal Image Productions, Inc. v. Federal Insurance Company*
US Court of Appeals for the Sixth Circuit, Cincinnati

*Who is suing?* _____

*Who is being sued?* _____

*For what?* _____

*What is the issue on appeal?* _____

In this action, plaintiff-appellant Universal Image Productions, Inc. (Universal) filed suit against defendant-appellee Federal Insurance Company (Federal), asserting that Federal wrongfully denied its claim of coverage under a property insurance policy. Following discovery, Federal moved for summary judgment, asserting that Universal's claim of mold and bacteria contamination did not constitute "direct physical loss or damage" as required under the policy. The district court granted the motion, and this appeal followed. We affirm.

Universal is a television post-production company specializing in editing, special effects, and computer graphics. Universal signed a lease to occupy space at a three-floor commercial building, and subsequently relocated operations to new space on the first floor. After heavy rainstorms, a strong odor was detected on the first floor of the building. Universal contacted Jon Datillo, a certified indoor air quality professional. Datillo confirmed the presence of water and a significant odor consistent with microbial contamination stemming from the subgrade duct system on the first floor. Based upon these observations, Datillo concluded that a significant microbial contamination likely existed in the ventilation system, requiring that the heating, ventilation, and air conditioning (HVAC) system be shut down and isolated to prevent the emission of microbial spores. Datillo recommended that the health of building occupants be monitored, that all floors be tested for air quality, and that the HVAC system and areas of water damage be tested and inspected.

Based upon the findings of Datillo, Universal's landlord shut down the HVAC system. Datillo thereafter returned to conduct mold and bacteria testing. These tests revealed a bacterial contamination in the building's ductwork and elevated bacteria in the air. Datillo also discovered the presence of *Stachybotrys* (black mold) and *Penicillium Aspergillus*. Datillo noted water and high moisture content in the walls throughout the building, causing mold and staining. Datillo, however, did not find any "notable airborne contamination" and did not find that evacuation of the building was necessary. Dan Maser, an expert hired by Universal's landlord, also conducted mold and bacteria testing, the results of which were nearly identical to those of Datillo. Maser did not recommend that Universal evacuate the building, but did recommend that it move its operations from the first floor to the third floor during remediation.

Once the HVAC system was shut down, Universal's business suffered severe disruptions. The diminished ventilation caused temperatures in the building to exceed 100 degrees, causing extreme discomfort. In addition, Universal was required to move all of its operations from the first floor to the third floor of the building. Finally, premature cleaning by the landlord caused duct debris and possible contaminant blowback. Nevertheless, Universal decided that it would vacate the premises. Universal provided notice to Federal (its insurer) of its alleged losses stemming from the mold and bacterial contamination. Specifically, Universal claimed damages by way of lost leasehold improvements, cleaning and moving expenses, and lost business income under its property insurance policy. Federal denied the claim, resulting in the present lawsuit.

Upon Federal's motion for summary judgment, the district court held that Universal was not entitled to coverage under its property insurance policy as a matter of law. Specifically, the court held that Universal had not suffered any "direct physical loss" as required by the policy. Following entry of final judgment, Universal filed this timely appeal. In applying Michigan law to insurance-coverage matters, we must give the words of an insurance policy their plain and ordinary meaning. If a term is ambiguous, the ambiguity is to be construed against the insurer. Summary judgment is appropriate if the applicable policy terms are unambiguous.

The insurance policy at issue contains the following coverage provision: "We will pay for direct physical loss or damage to building or personal property caused by or resulting from a peril not otherwise excluded." The word "building" is defined as: "a structure; building components; completed additions; additions to the structure under construction; and alterations and repairs to the structure." The policy further specifies that the word "building" does not mean "land, water or air, either inside or outside of a structure" or "any structure Universal does not own, occupy and is not legally or contractually required to insure." The phrase "personal property" is defined as:

> all Universal business personal property; business personal property in which Universal has an insurable interest; patterns, molds and dies; personal property of others; labor, materials and services furnished or arranged by Universal on personal property of others; sign fixtures, glass and other tenant's improvements and betterments; and glass in buildings Universal does not own if it is legally or contractually required to maintain such glass.

The phrase "personal property" is similarly defined to exclude "land, water or air, either inside or outside of a structure."

Left undefined by the insurance policy is the critical phrase "direct physical loss or damage." Federal contends that the mold and bacterial contamination experienced by Universal at the building does not constitute "direct physical loss or damage" because no tangible property insured by Universal was structurally damaged. In contrast, Universal contends that it did suffer "direct physical loss" because the mold, odor, and bacterial contamination rendered the building "uninhabitable" or substantially "unusable," forcing the evacuation of the building.

Universal did not experience any form of "tangible damage" to its insured property. All remediation efforts were paid for by Universal's landlord, and not a single piece of Universal's physical property was lost or damaged as a result of mold or bacterial contamination. Universal seeks coverage for cleaning and moving expenses, lost (undamaged) improvements attached to the building, as well as lost business income. These are not tangible, physical losses, but economic losses. Furthermore, even if Michigan were to adopt a more expansive definition of the phrase "direct physical loss or damage," Universal would still not be entitled to coverage. Several courts have held that "physical loss" occurs when real property becomes "uninhabitable" or substantially "unusable."

Based upon our detailed review of the record, we agree with the district court that Universal has failed to present a genuine issue of material fact regarding the uninhabitability or usability of the building. No expert recommended that Universal evacuate the building. Accordingly, there is no evidence in the record indicating that Universal was unable to remain in the building during remediation. Moreover, Universal cannot recover for alleged uninhabitability relating to air-quality issues. Indeed, the insurance policy excludes "air" from the definition of both "building" and "personal property." Certainly, there is evidence in the record indicating that working in the building during remediation was difficult. Through no fault of its own, Universal was forced to work in a hot and crowded space. However, Universal has not put forth any evidence indicating that such temporary conditions rendered the building "uninhabitable" or substantially "unusable."

In sum, while Universal certainly suffered a large inconvenience as a result of the mold and bacterial contamination of the building, the damages resulting therefrom are not covered by the insurance policy issued by Federal. Universal did not suffer any tangible damage to physical property, nor were the premises rendered uninhabitable or substantially unusable. Accordingly, we affirm the judgment of the district court.

## Questions

1. What was the coverage offered by Federal's insurance policy?
2. What is the meaning of the exclusion for "land, water, or air?"
3. Was Universal's personal property insured by Federal?
4. Why couldn't Universal collect any damages?
5. Can you think of some evidence that Universal's attorney failed to introduce that could have bolstered its claim for damages?

## Discussion Questions

1. What can you insure?
2. Who drafts the insurance policies available for sale?
3. When should you have insurance?
4. Should price be the determining factor of which company you buy insurance from?

## Image Credit

# Section Three

---

# Precluding Environmental Degradation

# CHAPTER THIRTEEN

## Water Law and Quality

### Learning Objectives

- *Summarize the constitutional provisions applying to water law and quality.*
- *Describe federal actions affecting the rights in the Tri-State Water Rights litigation.*
- *Explain the three major water doctrines.*
- *Distinguish water uses under the riparian doctrine.*
- *Defend the use of the prior appropriation doctrine for western states.*

H umans depend on water for sustenance, as well as for the production of food. Competition for scarce water supplies and for cleaner water have led to extensive governmental regulations addressing water issues. In the western part of the United States, governments replaced the riparian doctrine of water rights with appropriation doctrines. Demands for drinking water and for fishing, recreational pursuits, and irrigation water have led to controls on pollutants entering waters. While the most ubiquitous pollutant is sediment, greater threats are posed by heavy metals, toxic chemicals, pathogens, and excessive nutrients.

The regulation of water quality starts with the federal government. The US Constitution, statutes passed by Congress, and federal regulations apply throughout the country, and states must follow the proscriptions. However, states with their reserved powers are able to regulate other water issues. Each state has its own common law, state constitution, statutes, and regulations that govern water issues. Moreover, local governments are able to regulate matters of local concern affecting water resources.

Turning to the federal constitutional powers, the federal government has broad authority to regulate navigation, flood control, water projects for irrigation and power, river basin development, and pollution under the Commerce Clause. Any water agreement between states must be approved by Congress under the Compact Clause (Constitution, Art. 1, § 10, cl. 3). Every treaty with Canada, Mexico, and an Indian tribe concerning water is handled by the federal government. The federal government also governs coastal waters seaward from mean low tide.

The major federal law governing water quality is the Clean Water Act (CWA). Today, this act refers to a collection of federal statutes governing drinking water and water quality. Numerous other laws also regulate our country's water resources, including the Marine Protection, Research, and Sanctuaries Act and the Endangered Species Act.

## Competition for Water Resources

In the southeastern United States, competition for water exists, despite its considerable rainfall. With the growth of Atlanta and its suburbs, considerable amounts of drinking water are removed from the Chattahoochee River in north Georgia. Alabama and Florida contend that Georgia is removing too much water, and a series of lawsuits has sought to resolve the disputes over the water resources of the Chattahoochee and other rivers. The following case details the complicated regulatory situation.

### In Re: MDL-1824 Tri-State Water Rights Litigation
US Court of Appeals for the Eleventh Circuit, Atlanta

*Who is suing?* _____

*Who is being sued?* _____

*For what?* _____

*What is the issue on appeal?* _____

The Georgia Parties, Gwinnett County, Georgia, and the U.S. Army Corps of Engineers (Corps), appeal from the Middle District Court of Florida's grant of summary judgment in this consolidated suit. The appeal arises from more than 20 years of litigation involving numerous parties including the states of Alabama and Florida, and Southeastern Federal Power Customers, Inc. (SeFPC), a consortium of companies that purchase power from the federal government. All of the underlying cases relate to the Corps' authority to operate the Buford Dam and Lake Lanier, the reservoir it created, for local water supply. In its order, the Florida district court found that the Corps' current operation of the Buford Project (Buford Dam and Lake Lanier collectively) exceeded the Corps' statutory authority and ordered the Corps to drastically reduce the quantity of water that it made available for water supply. The court's summary judgment order also affirmed the Corps' rejection of Georgia's 2000 request for additional water supply allocations to meet the needs of the localities through 2030.

The Georgia Parties argue that the district court erred by concluding that the Corps lacked authority to allocate substantial quantities of storage in Lake Lanier to water supply on the basis of the legislation that authorized the creation of the Buford Project, the 1946 Rivers and Harbors Act (RHA). Although not in agreement with the Georgia Parties, the Corps argues that the district court underestimated its authority to accommodate the water supply needs of the Atlanta area. The Georgia Parties and the Corps both assert that the district court erred by misinterpreting the scope of the Corps' authority under the 1958 Water Supply Act (WSA). The Georgia Parties and the Corps urge this Court to remand the case to the agency to make a final determination of its water supply authority. We find that the district court and the Corps erred in concluding that water supply was not an authorized purpose of the Buford Project under the RHA. The Corps' denial of Georgia's 2000 water-supply request must be remanded to the Corps for reconsideration. Finally, the Corps shall have one year to make a final determination of its authority to operate the Buford Project under the RHA and WSA.

Buford Dam sits on the Chattahoochee River, approximately forty miles upstream of Atlanta. The river flows southwest into the Florida Panhandle, where it combines with the Flint River to form the Apalachicola River. The Chattahoochee, Flint, and Apalachicola Rivers together are referred to as the ACF Basin. In 1946, the Corps, in its "Newman Report," recommended certain amendments and revisions to the original plan for the ACF system, including combining several of the hydroelectric sites near Atlanta into one large reservoir at Buford to increase power generation and to better regulate flows downstream. The report concluded that the Buford Project would "greatly increase the minimum flow in the river at Atlanta," which would safeguard the city's water supply during dry periods. The Report expected that any decrease in power value would be marginal and outweighed by the benefits of an "assured" water supply for the City of Atlanta.

The 1946 RHA stated that the Buford Project would be prosecuted in accordance with the report of the Chief of Engineers. Because that report incorporated the Newman Report in full, the Newman Report became part of the authorizing legislation for the project. The Corps released its "Definite Project Report" for the project in 1949. The report provided a detailed discussion of the plans for the Buford Project and its operations. The report referred to flood control, hydroelectric power, navigation, and an increased water supply for Atlanta as the primary purposes of the Buford project.

Buford Dam was constructed from 1950 to 1957, creating the reservoir known today as Lake Sidney Lanier. The Southeastern Power Administration (SEPA), the federal government agency from which SeFPC purchases the power generated at the dam, paid approximately $30 million of the $47 million of construction costs. The creation of Lake Lanier inundated the water intake structures of the cities of Buford and Gainesville, and the Corps signed relocation agreements with the two municipalities authorizing water withdrawals directly from the reservoir. Although no storage was specifically allocated for water supply, the fact that the dam operated during "off-peak" hours, to the detriment of power generation, demonstrated that downstream water supply was a consideration. In accordance with the recommendations of the Newman Report, the Corps maintained the necessary minimum river flow at Atlanta by making off-peak releases of 600 cubic feet per second during these hours of the week.

In 1956, Congress passed a law that granted the Corps authority to enter into a contract with Gwinnett County for the allocation of 11,200 acre-feet of storage for regulated water supply. In 1958, Congress passed the WSA. The policy of the WSA indicates that Congress aimed only to expand water supply allocations, not contract them by limiting previous authorizations. In the case of Buford, the WSA's grant of authority for water supply constitutes a supplement to any authority granted by the 1946 RHA. In 1959, the Corps issued its Reservoir Regulation Manual for Buford Dam (Buford Manual) which remains in effect today. The manual states that the project will be run to maximize releases of water during peak hours but will also utilize off-peak releases in order to maintain a minimum flow of 650 cubic feet per second at Atlanta.

In June, 1990, Alabama filed suit against the Corps in the Northern District of Alabama to challenge a section of the draft Corps' Post-Authorization Change Notification (PAC) Report and the continued withdrawal of water from the Buford Project by the Georgia Parties. This suit is the first of the four currently on appeal. In 1997, after the completion of a comprehensive study, the parties entered into the Apalachicola-Chattahoochee-Flint River Basin Compact (ACF Compact), which was ratified by Congress and the three states. The ACF Compact included a provision allowing continued withdrawals. The Compact created an "ACF Basin Commission" charged with establishing an allocation formula for apportioning the surface waters of the ACF Basin among the states of Alabama, Florida, and Georgia. Under the Compact, existing water supply contracts would be honored, and water-supply providers could increase their withdrawals "to satisfy reasonable increases in the demand" for water.

In December 2000, SeFPC filed suit against the Corps in the United States District Court for the District of Columbia (D.C. district court), the second of the four suits currently on appeal. SeFPC alleged that the Corps had wrongfully diverted water from hydropower generation to water supply, thereby causing SeFPC's members to pay unfairly high rates for their power. In January 2003, SeFPC, the Corps, and the Georgia Parties agreed to a settlement in the case, but the D.C. Circuit Court held that the settlement agreement exceeded the Corps' authority under the WSA. The Judicial Panel on Multidistrict Litigation transferred the case to the Middle District of Florida.

Meanwhile, in 2000, the State of Georgia submitted a formal request to the Corps to modify its operation of the Buford Project in order to meet the Georgia Parties' water supply needs through 2030. In February 2001, nine months after the request was sent to the Corps and without a response from the Corps, the State of Georgia filed suit in the United States District Court for the Northern District of Georgia seeking to compel the Corps to grant its request, beginning the third of the four underlying cases. The case was consolidated into the multidistrict litigation in the Middle District of Florida.

In January 2008, the City of Apalachicola sued the Corps in the federal district court for the Northern District of Florida. This is the last of the four cases being considered as part of this appeal. This case was also consolidated into the multidistrict litigation.

The Middle District of Florida court granted partial summary judgment to the plaintiffs in Alabama, Apalachicola, and SeFPC and to the Corps in Georgia, and it denied summary judgment to the Georgia Parties. The court's order concluded that the Corps had exceeded its authority in its "de facto" reallocation of storage to accommodate current water supply withdrawals. The court concluded that the Corps' current operations exceeded the WSA because they seriously affected the authorized purpose of hydropower generation. Because the Georgia request represented an even larger water supply storage allocation than the current operations, the court also found that it exceeded the Corps' authority.

Under the Administrative Procedures Act, reviewing courts must set aside agency action that is arbitrary, capricious, an abuse of discretion, or otherwise not in accordance with law. The denial of Georgia's request was based on a clear error of law: the Corps' misinterpretation of the RHA. The clear Congressional intent in the 1946 RHA was that water supply was to be an authorized purpose. The Corps never considered its authority under the RHA to substantially increase its provision of water supply and reallocate storage therefore, authority which we hold today was granted by the RHA. And the Corps never considered its WSA authority to provide water supply as an addition to (or as supplementing) its RHA authority.

Several other factors also indicate that the Corps' rejection of the water supply request should be remanded for further consideration. First, the Corps' analysis on the effects of the Georgia request was incomplete. Because the Corps' authority to grant the request may be dependent on the precise size and effect of the request, it is crucial that the Corps complete its evaluation of the request. Second, it is also apparent that the Corps' views regarding its authority to allocate storage in Lake Lanier to water supply are evolving and that it has not come to a final, determinative decision regarding the issues underlying this authority. Finally, because the other matters in this appeal must be remanded to the Corps, it is sensible and efficient for the agency to consider the overlapping issues that are common to Georgia and the other cases together as part of a comprehensive decision about the Corps' future water supply operations. Our holding—that water supply is an authorized purpose under the RHA, that the Corps does have some authority under the RHA to balance as among the authorized uses and increase the water supply purpose at the expense of the power purpose and to reallocate storage therefore, and that the Corps' authority under the WSA is in addition to its authority under the RHA—constitutes a clarification of the legal environment which will aid the Corps in its analysis on remand.

On remand, the Corps should consider several important factors with respect to the Newman Report (i.e., the RHA). First, the Corps should take into consideration that water supply for the Atlanta metropolitan area was an authorized purpose of the Buford Project as well as hydroelectric power, flood control, and navigation. Second, Congress contemplated that the Corps would be authorized to calibrate operations to balance between the water supply use and the power use. Third, because Congress explicitly provided that the "estimated present needs" of the Atlanta area for water supply be satisfied at the expense of "maximum power value," we know that the water supply use is not subordinate to the power use. Fourth, from the Newman Report, we know that Congress contemplated that water supply may have to be increased over time as the Atlanta area grows.

However, the authorizing legislation is ambiguous with respect to the extent of the Corps' balancing authority—i.e., the extent of the Corps' authority under the RHA to provide water supply for the Atlanta area. We conclude that the Corps should evaluate precisely what this balance should be. Once the Corps has determined the extent of its authority under the RHA, it should then determine its authority pursuant to the WSA. The authority under the WSA will be in addition to the Corps' authority under the RHA and the 1956 Act.

## Questions

1. Why are the Georgia parties appealing?
2. What is the significance of the 1946 Rivers and Harbors Act?
3. What is the significance of the "Newman" report?
4. What is the significance of the 1958 WSA?
5. What is the significance of the ACF Compact?
6. Why was the DC settlement allocating 240,858 acre-feet of water found invalid?
7. Why was the decision by the Middle District of Florida overturned?
8. With the 11th Circuit's remand, which parties celebrated?
9. How much discretion does the Corps have in setting storage reallocation?

In February 2017, the special master appointed by the US Supreme Court rejected Florida's claims about excessive water usage in Georgia. The Supreme Court will take this advice to rule on the issues.

# Major Water Doctrines under State Law

State law governs the use of water resources among property owners and water users. Two major water-rights doctrines have emerged: the riparian doctrine and the prior appropriation doctrine. As riparian states experience shortages of water during droughts, they are enacting legislation that acts to allocate water resources. Thus, the riparian doctrine is being subjected to a mixed combination of riparian and appropriation principles.

# 1. The Riparian Doctrine

A riparian doctrine adopted from English common law governs water usage in most of the eastern United States. Under the riparian doctrine, water usage is part of land ownership and applies to those landowners who are adjacent to surface waters. Surface water usage is divided into two major categories: natural uses and artificial uses. Riparian water users may use unlimited quantities of water for natural uses that include water for drinking, household uses, animals, and limited gardening. For other uses of water such as irrigation (often called artificial uses), a riparian water user is limited to reasonable quantities of water. A state defines reasonableness on a case-by-case basis. Some states are adopting permitting systems for water usage during droughts, and these statutes supersede common-law riparian rights. Groundwater, water percolating below the surface of the earth, is subject to a separate set of rules. The following case shows a trial court having difficulty in understanding the tenets of the riparian doctrine.

*Pierce v. Riley*
Court of Appeals of Michigan

*Who is suing?* _____

*Who is being sued?* _____

*For what?* _____

*What is the issue on appeal?* _____

This is the fourth time the matter has come before this Court. Plaintiffs are owners of property on Stony Lake in Oceana County. They originally filed suit in circuit court seeking to enjoin defendants, also owners of land abutting Stony Lake, from granting right of way easements for lake access to nonriparian owners in a development called Holiday Shores. The trial court dismissed plaintiffs' complaint, but this Court, on appeal, remanded for further consideration.

On remand, the trial court again dismissed plaintiffs' complaint. This Court reversed that decision in *Pierce v. Riley* (*Stony Lake II*), and enjoined defendants from granting riparian rights to nonriparian owners. Defendants' proposed use of the lot as the site of a dredged channel was deemed unreasonable. Plaintiffs then requested, at the trial court level, that the dredged area in the riparian lot be filled and the docks removed. The trial court refused the request, plaintiffs appealed. In *Pierce v. Riley* (*Stony Lake III*), this Court ordered the filling of the channel. The Supreme Court reversed the Court of Appeals (*Stony Lake III*) and ordered the circuit court to hold the cause in abeyance pending findings of fact and a decision by the Department of Natural Resources (DNR) on an application by defendants to build a canal. The DNR approved the application, and thus, we have arrived at *Stony Lake IV*.

The core of the present controversy is the Supreme Court's Delphic order. We do not construe that order as overruling either *Stony Lake I* or *Stony Lake II*. The use of the lot as described in *Stony Lake II* is still unreasonable and *Stony Lake II* remains the law of the case. Defendants applied for leave to appeal the decision in *Stony Lake II*,

Fig. 13.1 People owning property on lakes may want to preclude others from using the lakes.

an application which was denied by the Supreme Court. A conclusion reached in an earlier appeal to the Michigan Supreme Court becomes the law of the case and is not subject to review on appeal from a subsequent trial. It is the well-settled rule that courts will not review former decisions made by the same court in the same cause, and on the same facts.

The Inland Lakes and Streams Act, pursuant to which the DNR makes its findings, states that one of its purposes is to protect riparian rights and the public trust in inland lakes and streams. In protecting the public trust, the Legislature was keeping watch over the environmental impact of various operations on inland lakes and streams. The business acumen of defendants cannot preclude this Court from protecting the interests for which the Legislature had regard nor can it preclude plaintiffs from exercising their rights as riparian owners. The Act explicitly states that it shall not modify the rights and responsibilities of any riparian owner to the use of his or her riparian water. Accordingly, the DNR's approval of the marina does not end the matter.

The original use contemplated by defendants called for the granting of easements to 90 nonriparian lot owners to and through the riparian lot, #91, in which a channel was built. In *Stony Lake II*, this Court found and it is the law of the case that such use is unreasonable, since the number of families having access to the lake would have increased 66% and the number of families per surface acre of lake would have increased from about 0.5 to 0.89.

Reasonableness remains the criterion for use of water by riparian owners. When there are several owners to an inland lake, such proprietors and their lessees and licensees may use the surface of the whole lake for boating, swimming, fishing and other similar riparian rights, so far as they do not interfere with the reasonable use of the waters by other riparian owners. In determining whether a use is reasonable we must consider what the use is for; its extent, duration, necessity and its application; the nature and size of the stream, and the several uses to which it is put; the extent of the injuries to the one proprietor, and the benefit to the other; and all other factors which may bear upon the reasonableness of the use.

The Inland Lakes and Streams Act specifies that nothing in the act limits the right of a riparian owner to institute proceedings in any circuit court of the state against any person when necessary to protect his or her riparian rights. The only effective relief in this case is the refilling and restoration of the channel. Refilling the channel is the only way in which all riparian owners will be able to make a reasonable use of the lake without interfering with the rights of others. Providing residents of Holiday Shores with a means of ready access places an undue burden on the lake which unreasonably interferes with the rights of other riparian owners. We are not unaware that use of the channel is no longer proposed, but is now reality. Defendants chose to proceed with the development at their own risk while the issue was still in litigation, so have imposed the economic burden on themselves that it would be inappropriate for this Court to take it into account. We therefore order defendants to fill the channel in compliance with a permit issued by the Department of Natural Resources. The judgment of the trial court is reversed.

## Questions

1. What rights does riparian law grant to property owners abutting a small lake?
2. What might have contributed to the trial court's incorrect assessment of the rights of the riparian owners abutting the lake?
3. Did the Inland Lakes and Streams Act change riparian law? If it did, how so?
4. What do you think about the actions of the defendants in building the canal prior to the resolution of the dispute?
5. Is this court interpreting the law or the facts?
6. Why was the DNR's approval of the marina and canal not relevant to the resolution of this dispute?

## 2. The Prior Appropriation Doctrine

Most states west of the Mississippi River have decided that the riparian doctrine does not foster the wise use of available water resources, so each state government has adopted an appropriation doctrine. The state legal provisions supersede the riparian doctrine and establish a system of seniority or priority usage called a prior appropriation doctrine. Whoever makes the first use of water and records this use continues to have seniority for using the water. This means that rights to water are not connected to the ownership of land.

Under an appropriation doctrine, a water user needs to make "beneficial use" of the water. If a water user fails to continue to use the water, the nonuse may result in loss of this right under a doctrine of abandonment. Moreover, the appropriation doctrine allows use outside the basin of origin, which generally is not available under the riparian doctrine. The appropriation doctrine allows market exchanges in water rights so that water goes to the highest and best use. A person with a priority right to an amount of water can sell it to another user. Although the economic transfer of water is possible, in many areas, agricultural uses continue due to their early claims. This means that the lack of water may impede the development of new residential and recreational water uses. The following case shows how a person may lose water rights due to the lack of beneficial use of waters allocated.

### Delta Canal Co. v. Frank Vincent Family Ranch, LC
#### Utah Supreme Court

*Who is suing?* _____

*Who is being sued?* _____

*For what?* _____

*What is the issue on appeal?* _____

Appellants Delta Canal Company and others (collectively, Irrigation Companies) and Appellee Frank Vincent Family Ranch, LC (Vincent) are water-rights holders on the Sevier River system. The Irrigation Companies are nonprofit Utah corporations that distribute water to their shareholders for irrigation of agricultural land. They filed a complaint in district court alleging that Vincent's water right had been partially forfeited and partially abandoned. The district court granted summary judgment to Vincent. We reverse and remand.

The water right in question was awarded to the Samuel McIntyre Investment Company (McIntyre) in 1936 when a district court issued a final decree, referred to as the "Cox Decree." The Cox Decree awarded McIntyre twenty-two cubic feet of water per second from March 1 through October 1 of each year. Vincent purchased this water right in 1998 when it also purchased the McIntyre farm. Vincent has used the farm and water right to grow crops, such as corn, hay, and alfalfa, and to run a commercial bird-hunting operation.

The Irrigation Companies allege that during the twenty-year limitations period preceding the filing of their complaint in 2008, Vincent and its predecessor forfeited and abandoned a portion of the water right. They allege that from 1988 to 1998, McIntyre irrigated only 830 of its 1,051.5 acres, and that after 1998, Vincent cultivated fewer than 900 of the 1,051.5 acres. Vincent contends that it was unable to cultivate all 1,051.5 acres because in times of water shortages, the Sevier River Commissioner reduced its diversion right. Vincent further defends on the grounds that it irrigated many acres of natural habitat for commercial bird hunting.

We seek insight into the legislature's purpose for the Forfeiture Statute in the neighboring Beneficial Use Statute, which provides that "beneficial use shall be the basis, the measure and the limit of all rights to the use of water in this state." "Beneficial use" is not statutorily defined in many western states, including Utah. But beneficial use has two different components: the type of use and the amount of use. Over time, the types of use considered to be beneficial have expanded to encompass not only economically beneficial uses, but also uses that promote conservation, recreation, and other values deemed to be socially desirable.

The touchstone of the second requirement of beneficial use is reasonableness: the amount of water used must be reasonable. Usage of water in accordance with "the general custom of the locality" is usually reasonable, so long as the custom does not involve unnecessary waste. An appropriator who diverts water in excess of the appropriator's actual requirements and allows the excess to go to waste acquires no right to the excess. The same is true for water diverted in excess of reasonable requirements and used inefficiently. A particular use must not only be of benefit to the appropriator, but it must also be a reasonable and economical use of the water in view of other present and future demands upon the source of supply.

In Utah, all water users must pay careful attention to the manner of use, and courts, when appropriate, should exercise their power to order improved methods of conveying, measuring and diverting water so as to assure the greatest possible use of the natural resource. These requirements of beneficial use—beneficial purpose and reasonable amount—are ongoing requirements. If an appropriator ceases to beneficially use a water right, the wasted or unused water is made available to other appropriators. In Utah, the process for making such water available to other appropriators is governed by the Forfeiture Statute.

Vincent would have us hold that under the Forfeiture Statute, a water right can be fully maintained through partial use. This rule would be inconsistent with the concept of beneficial use. We interpret the Beneficial Use Statute and the Forfeiture Statute in harmony with one another. If beneficial use is to be the basis, the measure and the limit of water rights in Utah, as required by the Beneficial Use Statute, then partial forfeiture must be available. We hold that the only plausible reading of the Forfeiture Statute, when viewed in conjunction with the Beneficial Use Statute, is that a water right may be forfeited either in whole or in part.

The Irrigation Companies allege that Vincent abandoned part of its water right. The district court treated the abandonment claim as a claim under the Forfeiture Statute, which states that forfeiture occurs when an appropriator "abandons or ceases to use" a water right. The district court's summary judgment for Vincent on the abandonment claim was improper as abandonment of a water right is not a statutory claim. Our jurisprudence has treated abandonment as a common-law claim, independent of the Forfeiture Statute. While upon the one hand, abandonment is the relinquishment of the right by the owner with the intention to forsake and desert it, forfeiture upon the other hand, is the involuntary or forced loss of the right, caused by the failure of the appropriator or owner to do or perform some act required by the statute.

We have recognized that abandonment is a separate and distinct concept from that of forfeiture in that an abandonment requires a definite intent to relinquish the right to use and ownership of such water right and does not require any particular period of time, but the forfeiture herein provided for requires that the appropriator cease to use the water for a period of five years before it is complete. We reverse the grant of summary judgment on the abandonment claim and remand for the claim to be considered under our common-law precedents. Unlike forfeiture, abandonment has no time element. Instead, it has an intent requirement. To succeed in this claim, the Irrigation Companies must show that Vincent or its predecessor intentionally relinquished a portion of the water right.

The authoritative description of Vincent's water right is found in the Cox Decree, issued in 1936 at the conclusion of a general adjudication of the Sevier River system. The Cox Decree specifies only the flow component of Vincent's water right: twenty-two cubic feet per second. However, the proposed determination drawn up in preparation for the 1936 general adjudication of the Sevier River system indicated that Vincent's predecessor annually used 5,000 acre feet of water. Because the Cox Decree does not indicate that this amount was disputed or altered, we agree with the district court that it is reasonable to infer that the volume component of Vincent's water right is 5,000 acre feet. Thus, Vincent's water right consists of a maximum rate of diversion of twenty-two cubic feet per second and a total volume allowance of 5,000 acre feet.

Forfeiture under Utah Code § 73-1-4(2) occurs when an appropriator fails to use material amounts of a water allowance during five or seven consecutive years without securing an extension of time from the state engineer. If during five consecutive irrigation seasons, an appropriator has failed to use material amounts of its volume allowance, a forfeiture has occurred. The volume component of the water right should be reduced by the unused amount. The number of acres irrigated is not determinative in a forfeiture analysis, though it may be relevant insofar as it indicates whether water usage is beneficial. Farmers may reduce the total acres irrigated to grow a more water-intensive crop, or vice versa, so long as they beneficially use their full entitlement. The focus of a forfeiture analysis should be on volume. Thus, if Vincent and its predecessor used substantially all of their allotment of 5,000 acre feet, they have not forfeited their water right.

The district court held that genuine issues of material fact precluded summary judgment on the questions of (1) how much water Vincent used on its bird hunting grounds and (2) whether such use was beneficial. We do not disturb this ruling but wish to reiterate that "watering indigenous vegetation generally is not a beneficial use." An appropriator (Vincent) has the burden to show that under the individual facts and circumstances of the appropriator's situation, watering a natural habitat is beneficial. Triers of fact should be wary of hindsight justifications for waste and of fanciful uses whose primary purpose is to protect a water right from forfeiture. A water right is maintained only to the extent it is used efficiently and for a proper purpose. Summary judgment to Vincent was improperly granted in this case. We remand for further proceedings.

## Questions

1. Why doesn't the riparian doctrine apply in Utah?
2. Where did Vincent obtain his rights to water from the Sevier River system?
3. Why doesn't Vincent's partial use of allocated waters prevent a forfeiture of water rights?
4. What does the Forfeiture Statute address that is different from the Beneficial Use Statute?
5. Why does the court employ both the Forfeiture Statute and the Beneficial Use Statute in determining Vincent's water rights?
6. What is the problem for Vincent in claiming that some of the allocated water was used on bird hunting grounds?
7. Did Vincent make beneficial use of his total water allocation?

## 3. Other State Regulations Affecting Water

Continuing disputes for water have led riparian states to adopt laws delineating rights in surface and ground waters. Thus, these states have a "mixed combination" of riparian and appropriation provisions. States may also have regulations restricting the drainage of wetlands or programs for the acquisition of conservation easements of wetlands. Some states have established setback distances from water bodies for various activities so that vegetation in the setback area can diminish sediments and pollutants from entering surface waters.

Turning to a mixed combination of riparian and statutory law, provisions from Georgia may be used to show how the state legislature responded to issues involving water quantities. With the Georgia Water Quality Control Act adopted in 1964, the state sought to use the state's water resources prudently for the maximum benefit of the people to restore and maintain a reasonable degree of purity and an adequate supply. Additional goals were to require reasonable usage of the waters, reasonable treatment of wastes prior to their discharge, and to provide protection from overuse, pollution, and other damaging activities.

The Georgia legislation requires permits for the alteration of surface waters, including withdrawals above statutory levels, diversions of water, or impoundments (Official Code of Georgia Annotated § 12-5-31). The state legislature also enacted legislation to deal with competing water uses and shortages. The Board of Natural Resources was directed to establish a reasonable system of classification for application in situations involving competing uses for a supply of available surface waters. In the event that two or more competing applicants or users qualify equally, the Director of the Department of Natural Resources is authorized to grant permits to applicants or modify the existing permits of users for use of specified quantities of surface waters on a prorated or other reasonable basis in those situations where such action is feasible.

The Georgia legislature also provided for emergency water shortage situations. Whenever it appears to the director from facts shown by affidavits of residents of the affected area that an emergency period of water shortage exists so as to jeopardize the health or safety of the citizens or to threaten serious harm to the water resources, the director may impose restrictions by emergency order on one or more permits previously issued, as may be necessary to protect citizens or water resources. Restrictions may be imposed based upon any reasonable system of classification established by the Board of Natural Resources through rule or regulation. During emergency periods of water shortage, the director shall give first priority to providing water for human consumption and second priority to farm use.

## Discussion Questions

1. Given water shortages, should states in the eastern part of the country consider adopting a prior appropriation doctrine? Why?
2. Water is consumed by several distinct categories of users: industrial, commercial, residential, agricultural, recreational, and conservation. Should greater consideration be given to the merits of water use under a state's prior appropriation doctrine, and if so, what?
3. In times of drought, should a state preclude local governments from devising rules on water usage? If so, why?

# CHAPTER FOURTEEN

## The Clean Water Act and Recycling Animal Waste

### Learning Objectives

- *Examine water pollution and recycling nutrients from animal waste.*
- *Analyze which animal production facilities should be regulated.*
- *Describe how most pollutants from large animal production facilities enter surface waters.*
- *Explain how animal producers minimize their discharges of water pollutants.*
- *Critique the federal provisions under the Clean Water Act governing animal waste.*

The Clean Water Act (CWA) employs federal National Pollutant Discharge Elimination System (NPDES) permits to reduce pollutants entering waters of the United States. Large concentrated animal feeding operations (CAFOs) are point sources of pollutants under the CWA and so need an NPDES permit if they have a discharge. Because permits allow the discharge of pollutants into surface waters, an evaluation of the justifications for such pollutants shows the government devising regulations under which polluting activities are balanced with economic production.

The Environmental Protection Agency (EPA), animal producers, and environmental groups have clashed on proposals to regulate CAFOs. The regulations disclose a set of controls that operates to stop egregious pollution while facilitating reductions in the cost of producing food products from animals. The provisions also incorporate the recycling of phosphorus and nitrogen from animal manure to fields for the production of crops. This chapter delineates the issues and how the government has responded to this pollution problem.

## Problems with Too Many Nutrients

Animal production is accompanied by the generation of manure and waste by-products that can result in pollution. With concentrations of animals at facilities and in regions, the risk of pollution from animal production has increased. When animals were raised on many farms and their manure was used as fertilizer, streams and water bodies usually were not overwhelmed by the animal waste pollutants. With concentrations of animals, there is a greater potential for pollution. Given transportation costs and economic considerations, animal feeding operations (AFOs) often dispose of manure as quickly and cheaply as possible close to the facility where it was generated. Disposal is generally accomplished by land application in which machinery carries the manure from where it is produced (or stored) to deposit it on nearby fields and pastures. Particulates, nitrogen, phosphorus, and pathogens are introduced into the environment with the application of manure to land, and rains can carry these components into streams and waterbodies.

The overapplication of manure and fertilizer leads to excess nutrient enrichment of waterbodies. The nutrients cause increased algae growth causing eutrophication, which reduces the dissolved oxygen in the water. Algae and dead algae block sunlight required by other vegetative species, causing both vegetation and fish to die off. Nitrogen carried into waterbodies indirectly reduces marine diversity and contributes to global warming. In some areas of the United States, costly purification systems are being installed to protect humans from excessive amounts of nitrogen. The reason for large amounts of nitrogen in soils is that the overapplication of manure and fertilizer is common. Plants need nitrogen for optimal growth and for the production of food crops. To assure that plants have sufficient quantities of nitrogen, persons growing plants overapply it. This includes applications of fertilizer products by home gardeners and suburbanites desiring green lawns. With a well-defined industry providing fertilizer products, it is more economical to overapply nitrogen fertilizer than to suffer reduced yields due to insufficient nutrients.

Phosphorus also contributes to the eutrophication of water bodies. Since it is cheaper to treat the cause of eutrophication than its effects, governments are seeking to reduce the phosphorus entering water bodies, including phosphorus from AFOs. While soil testing and a phosphorus index provide information on quantities of phosphorus, correlations to water pollution are nebulous. Phosphorus loss is a hydrological problem, as soils and sites have dissimilar potentials for transferring phosphorus into waters. This means that efforts controlling runoff and soil erosion through management practices can be more important in reducing phosphorus loss than manipulating production practices to achieve desired soil test results.

For the Gulf of Mexico, the nutrient-laden waters of the Mississippi River basin have created seasonally depleted oxygen levels in an area the size of New Jersey. The oxygen depletion—known as hypoxia—renders the area uninhabitable for many aquatic species and threatens commercial and recreational fisheries. One cause for the increased hypoxic zone is the threefold increase in the annual amounts of nitrate in river waters since 1950. Studies have found that agricultural activities are the largest contributors of nitrogen, with approximately 15 percent of the nitrogen flux coming from animal operations. The hypoxia problem suggests that greater efforts are needed to reduce the amounts of nitrogen from manure entering the waters of the Mississippi.

## Federal Regulation of CAFOs

Governments have recognized that AFOs and CAFOs may contribute to water pollution. To determine whether a facility constitutes an AFO, we look for the confinement of domestic animals. For facilities that keep animals in pens or cages, the answer is obvious: they are AFOs. For facilities that have animals in barns or limited encumbered areas, we must look further. To earn the AFO designation, the animal-production facility must confine and feed animals for a total of forty-five days or more during any twelve-month period. In addition, the animals must prevent vegetative forage growth from surviving the normal growing season over a portion of the confined area. Feedlots and dairies are AFOs. Most livestock farms with animals enclosed and fed until they are ready for sale are AFOs. Stockyards, auction barns, pens, corrals, roundup areas, and wintering facilities may be AFOs. Ranches with thousands of cattle that graze in pastures or on the range are not AFOs, as the animals are not confined in a limited area.

Whenever a facility is an AFO, it is examined further to determine whether it should be classified as a CAFO. Facilities with a sufficient number of a species of animal are classified as CAFOs. Classification as a CAFO means that the operation is subject to the federal National Pollutant Discharge Elimination System (NPDES) permit provisions of the CWA. Under federal law, a CAFO with discharges of pollutants needs a federal NPDES permit or a similar permit issued by a state agency authorized to issue state permits. Non-CAFOs are not required to have federal permits, although a state may impose its own permit requirements.

Since not all types of animals are the same, the EPA determined threshold numbers of different animal species to be used in designating "Large" and "Medium" CAFOs. Medium CAFOs delineate numbers for major animal species that are less than Large CAFOs and involve a discharge of pollutants. The federal regulations allow authorized governmental officials to designate a small CAFO if the operation is impairing water quality. The following have been set as animal thresholds for Large CAFOs:

- *700 dairy cows*
- *1,000 cattle*

- *2,500 swine (over 55 pounds)*
- *10,000 swine (under 55 pounds)*
- *30,000 poultry—liquid system*
- *125,000 broilers—nonliquid system*
- *82,000 laying hens—nonliquid system.*

# Mandatory Permits

In 2003, the EPA adopted revised CAFO regulations to augment governmental oversight of potential sources of pollutants. The revised regulations established further requirements to safeguard water quality and were amended in 2008 and 2012 to expand the scope of federal control over CAFOs. Every AFO that meets the CAFO requirements and that has a discharge of pollutants is obligated to have an NPDES or similar state permit. Approximately 13,000 CAFOs in our country need permits, either from the federal government or a state with authority to issue the permits.

While state agencies have been hesitant to engage in enforcement activities that burden farmers, their failure to take action against existing problems may be counterproductive. By failing to stop existing pollution under current regulations, regulators are allowing streams, rivers, and lakes to become polluted. Those polluted waters that fail to meet established water quality standards need to be listed under the Clean Water Act. A total maximum daily load (TMDL) program needs to be developed. Thus, the lack of sufficient regulatory oversight of pollution from CAFOs may lead to additional expenses in meeting the TMDL requirements. Furthermore, failure to control CAFO pollution encourages the public and legislators to request even more stringent regulations.

Under NPDES permits, each CAFO is governed by conditions to ensure attainment of applicable state-established water quality standards. Where states have not attained water quality standards, regulators can implement response actions. Also important under the federal permit guidelines is the fact that a state can adopt more stringent controls on discharges into the waters of the state than required by the Clean Water Act. About one-half of our states have permit programs that incorporate some other state permit, license, or authorization program for CAFOs.

A major method to address animal waste pollution is to require CAFOs to develop and implement nutrient management plans. While comprehensive nutrient management plans are obligatory for CAFOs, AFO operators have also developed such plans to build upon the ethic of land stewardship and sustainability. The development and implementation of a nutrient management plan are the responsibilities of the operator. Technical assistance for developing comprehensive plans is available from federal agencies, including the Natural Resources Conservation Service, Cooperative Extension Service agents and specialists, soil and water conservation districts, and land grant universities. Operators can also receive assistance from private consultants, integrators, industry associations, and qualified vendors. The USDA's Natural Resources Conservation Service Field Office Technical Guide is the primary technical reference for the development of comprehensive nutrient management plans.

The federal regulations require every CAFO to secure a permit delineating a nutrient management plan. States can employ their own individualized comprehensive management plan requirements as long as they meet federal requirements. Every nutrient management plan must be reviewed by the permitting authority and be available for public inspection.

## Effluent Limitations Guidelines

In addition to the NPDES permit requirements, CAFOs with manure, litter, and/or process wastewater discharges are also governed by federal effluent limitations guidelines that delineate additional requirements concerning nutrient management plans. Large CAFOs raising dairy cows, cattle, swine, poultry, and veal calves (see numbers of animals listed above) are required to develop and implement best management practices for the land application of manure, litter, and process wastewater. These practices consist of a nutrient management plan, waste application rates, manure and soil sampling, inspection for leaks from liquid storage structures, and setbacks. Other provisions delineate distinctive technological requirements for CAFO production areas, CAFO land application areas, and for new sources. While the effluent limitations guidelines for land application requirements only apply to some Large CAFOs, other CAFOs need to comply with the provisions on land application discharges under their NPDES permits.

Large CAFOs need a nutrient management plan based upon a field-specific assessment of the potential for nitrogen and phosphorus transport from the field. Application rates for manure, litter, and process wastewater must minimize the movement of nitrogen and phosphorus from the field to surface waters. Annual analyses of manure are required for nitrogen and phosphorus content. Soils need to be analyzed at least once every five years for phosphorus content. With the utilization of best management practices, nutrients will be used by crops, rather than being carried into surface waters. Another significant provision delineates setback requirements for the applications of manure, litter, and process wastewater.

For most Large CAFOs, several additional measures are required. The owner or operator must perform weekly visual inspections of all storm water diversion devices, runoff diversion structures, animal waste storage structures, and devices channeling contaminated storm water to storage and containment structures. Daily inspections of water lines, including drinking water or cooling water lines, should be performed. For existing operations with liquid impoundments, depth markers are required to indicate the design volume and to clearly indicate the minimum capacity necessary to contain a twenty-five-year, twenty-four-hour rainfall event. If the owner or operator should find a deficiency as a result of a daily or weekly inspection, it should be remedied as soon as possible.

Most CAFOs (probably 90 percent) will dispose of animal waste through a land application method. The dispersal of manure on land is encouraged because it reuses the nitrogen and phosphorus for crop production. The federal NPDES permit requirements apply with respect to all animals in confinement at a CAFO and all manure, litter, and process wastewater generated by those animals or the production of those animals. This means that the federal regulations govern both production areas and lands used for the application of CAFO by-products.

# Agricultural Storm Water Discharges

The Clean Water Act provides that agricultural storm water discharges are exempted from coverage of its point-source regulations. Producers have maintained that this long-standing regulatory exemption means that runoff from the application of manure cannot be regulated under the CAFO regulations. The revised federal regulations resolve this issue by differentiating two types of land application discharges: agricultural storm water discharges that continue to qualify under the existing exemption and other discharges subject to the NPDES permit requirements.

Discharges occurring due to a rainfall event when manure, litter, or process wastewater was applied in accordance with site-specific nutrient management practices are agricultural storm water discharges. In these situations, the producer has applied the manure in a manner to ensure appropriate agricultural utilization of the nutrients as a production input. Such discharges were intended to be exempted from point-source pollution controls by the agricultural storm water discharge exemption. These discharges are allowed, although they may result in contaminants entering surface waters.

However, any discharge from a CAFO's land application area that occurs because manure and process wastewater were not applied in accordance with site-specific nutrient management practices to ensure appropriate agricultural employment of the nutrients is not an agricultural storm water discharge. Such a discharge would not be sanctioned by the CAFO's permit. Thus, whenever site-specific management practices to ensure appropriate agricultural utilization of the nutrients in manure, litter, and process wastewater are not used, subsequent discharges are not protected by the agricultural storm water exception. Moreover, any discharge occurring without a rain event is not an agricultural storm water discharge. Any CAFO with such a discharge is violating federal law.

# Recycling Animal Waste

The following two cases address challenges to federal regulations that address pollution from CAFOs. In both cases, farm groups challenged some provisions, while environmental groups challenged other provisions, and both sets of groups had some success with at least one argument. The first case, *Waterkeeper Alliance, Inc. v. Environmental Protection Agency*, illuminates the statutory requirement that only actual pollution is regulated. The second case, *National Pork Producers Council v. EPA*, presents a summary of the *Waterkeeper* case and answers various challenges to the 2008 CAFO Rule to describe the regulations that operate to preclude unacceptable pollution.

### *Waterkeeper Alliance, Inc. v. Environmental Protection Agency*
US Court of Appeals for the Second Circuit, New York

*Who is suing?* _____

*Who is being sued?* _____

*For what?* _____

*What is the issue on appeal?* _____

In this consolidated petition, we review various challenges to a regulation promulgated by the U.S. Environmental Protection Agency (EPA) under the Clean Water Act in order to abate and control the emission of water pollutants from concentrated animal feeding operations (CAFOs). While we deny many of the challenges here brought, we find that several aspects of the regulation violate the express terms of the Clean Water Act or are otherwise arbitrary and capricious under the Administrative Procedure Act. Accordingly, we grant the petitions in part and deny the petitions in part.

The Clean Water Act (Act) is a cornerstone of the federal effort to protect the environment. Designed to restore and maintain the chemical, physical, and biological integrity of the nation's waters, the Act is the principal legislative source of EPA's authority—and responsibility—to abate and control water pollution. The Act formally prohibits the discharge of a pollutant by any person from any point source to navigable waters except when authorized by a permit issued under the National Pollutant Discharge Elimination System (NPDES). This means that EPA primarily advances the Act's objectives, including the ambitious goal that water pollution be not only reduced, but eliminated, through the use of NPDES permits that, while authorizing some water pollution, place important restrictions on the quality and character of discharges that limit pollution.

NPDES permits are issued either by EPA, itself, or by the states in a federally approved permitting system. Regardless of the issuer, every NPDES permit is statutorily required to set forth, at the very least, effluent limitations, that is, certain restrictions on the quantities, rates, and concentrations of chemical, physical, biological, and other constituents which are discharged from point sources into navigable waters. The specific effluent limitations contained in each individual NPDES permit are dictated by the terms of more general effluent limitation guidelines, which are separately promulgated by EPA.

We are asked to review the permitting requirements and effluent limitation guidelines promulgated by EPA in its attempt to regulate the emission of water pollutants from CAFOs. CAFOs are the largest of the nation's 238,000 or so animal feeding operations—agricultural enterprises where animals are kept and raised in confinement. CAFOs are large-scale industrial operations that raise extraordinary numbers of livestock. Economically, these CAFOs generate billions of dollars of revenue every year. EPA has focused on the industry because CAFOs also generate millions of tons of manure every year, and when improperly managed, this manure can pose substantial risks to the environment and public health.

Animal waste includes a number of potentially harmful pollutants. According to EPA, the pollutants associated with CAFO waste principally include: (1) nutrients such as nitrogen and phosphorus; (2) organic matter; (3) solids, including the manure itself and other elements mixed with it such as spilled feed, bedding and litter materials, hair, feathers and animal corpses; (4) pathogens (disease-causing organisms such as bacteria and viruses); (5) salts; (6) trace elements such as arsenic; (7) odorous/volatile compounds such as carbon dioxide, methane, hydrogen sulfide, and ammonia; (8) antibiotics; and (9) pesticides and hormones.

These pollutants can infiltrate the surface waters in a variety of ways including spills and other dry-weather discharges, overflows from storage lagoons, and discharge to the air coupled with subsequent redeposition on the landscape. Perhaps the most common way by which pollutants reach the surface waters is through improper land application. Land application, the predominant means by which CAFOs dispose of animal waste, is a process by which manure, litter, and other process wastewaters are spread onto fields controlled by CAFOs. As all parties here agree, when properly land-applied, manure, litter, and other process wastewaters can act as a fertilizer, because land application of CAFO waste fosters the reuse of the nitrogen, phosphorus, and potassium in these wastes for crop growth. However, when waste is excessively or improperly land-applied, the nutrients contained in the waste become pollutants that can and often do run off into adjacent waterways or leach into soil and ground water.

In light of these environmental threats, EPA first promulgated regulations for CAFOs in 1974 and 1976. After having been sued, in 1989, for failing to publish a plan to revise existing effluent limitations for the industry, EPA proposed to revise and update the first set of CAFO regulations. The new rule adopted in 2003 aimed to address not only inadequate compliance with existing policy, but also the changes that have occurred in the animal production industries. The Farm Petitioners challenge the permitting scheme established by the CAFO Rule. They contend that EPA has exceeded its statutory jurisdiction by requiring all CAFOs to either apply for NPDES permits or otherwise demonstrate that they have no potential to discharge. We agree and grant their petition in this regard.

The Clean Water Act authorizes EPA to regulate, through the NPDES permitting system, only the discharge of pollutants. The Act generally provides that except as in compliance with all applicable effluent limitations and permit restrictions, the discharge of any pollutant by any person shall be unlawful. Consistent with this prohibition, the Act authorizes EPA to promulgate effluent limitations for, and issue permits incorporating those effluent limitations for, the discharge of pollutants. Section 1311 provides that effluent limitations shall be applied to all point sources of discharge of pollutants. Section 1342 then gives NPDES authorities the power to issue permits authorizing the discharge of any pollutant or combination of pollutants. In other words, unless there is a discharge of any pollutant, there is no violation of the Act, and point sources are, accordingly, neither statutorily obligated to comply with EPA regulations for point source discharges, nor are they statutorily obligated to seek or obtain an NPDES permit.

Congress left little room for doubt about the meaning of the term "discharge of any pollutant." The Act expressly defines the term to mean "(A) any addition of any pollutant to navigable waters from any point source, or (B) any addition of any pollutant to the waters of the contiguous zone or the ocean from any point source other than a vessel or other floating craft." Thus, in the absence of an actual addition of any pollutant to navigable waters from any point, there is no point source discharge, no statutory violation, no statutory obligation of point sources to comply with EPA regulations for point source discharges, and no statutory obligation of point sources to seek or obtain an NPDES permit in the first instance.

The CAFO Rule violates this statutory scheme. It imposes obligations on all CAFOs regardless of whether or not they have, in fact, added any pollutants to the navigable waters (i.e., discharged any pollutants). After all, the Rule demands that every CAFO owner or operator either apply for a permit, and comply with the effluent limitations contained in the permit, or affirmatively demonstrate that no permit is needed because there is "no potential to discharge." In EPA's view, such demands are appropriate because all CAFOs have the potential to discharge pollutants. While we appreciate the policy considerations underlying EPA's approach in the CAFO Rule, however, we are without authority to permit it because it contravenes the regulatory scheme enacted by Congress; the Clean Water Act gives EPA jurisdiction to regulate and control only actual discharges, not potential discharges, and certainly not point sources themselves.

For the foregoing reasons, we hereby vacate those provisions of the CAFO Rule that: (1) allow permitting authorities to issue permits without reviewing the terms of the nutrient management plans; (2) allow permitting authorities to issue permits that do not include the terms of the nutrient management plans and that do not provide for adequate public participation; and (3) require CAFOs to apply for NPDES permits or otherwise demonstrate that they have no potential to discharge.

## Questions

1. What is the meaning of granting the petitions in part and denying the petitions in part?
2. What federal permit is required for CAFOs?
3. Why has the EPA focused on CAFOs?
4. What is the most common way that pollutants from CAFOs enter surface waters?
5. Must all CAFOs secure a permit?

6. What did the court pronounce about nutrient management plans? This will be further explained in the *National Pork Producers Council* case.

### *National Pork Producers Council v. EPA*
US Court of Appeals for the Fifth Circuit, New Orleans

*Who is suing?* _____

*Who is being sued?* _____

*For what?* _____

*What is the issue on appeal?* _____

In 2003, the Environmental Protection Agency (EPA) revised its regulations, implementing the Clean Water Act's (CWA or the Act) oversight of Concentrated Animal Feeding Operations (CAFOs). Several parties challenged the 2003 revisions (hereinafter the 2003 Rule), and the Second Circuit reviewed the challenges in *Waterkeeper Alliance, Inc. v. Environmental Protection Agency*. In 2008, EPA, responding to *Waterkeeper*, revised its regulations (hereinafter the 2008 Rule). Subsequently, the Farm Petitioners filed petitions for review of the 2008 Rule with this court. Subsequently, the Environmental Intervenors filed a motion to intervene in support of EPA's position.

At issue here is EPA's regulation of animal feeding operations (AFOs). Because these facilities house hundreds and sometimes thousands of animals in confined spaces, they produce millions of tons of animal manure every year. The management of this manure involves the collection, storage, and eventual use of the manure's nutrients as fertilizer. Following its collection, the manure is typically transported to an on-farm storage or treatment system. Treated manure effluent or dry litter (chicken waste) is typically applied to cropland as fertilizer. This fertilizing process is called land application. Because the improper management of this waste can pose a significant

Fig. 14.1 Wastes from animal operations may be flushed into lagoons.

hazard to the environment, EPA focuses much of its attention on regulating certain AFOs that meet EPA's definition of a CAFO.

In 1948, Congress enacted the Federal Water Pollution Control Act (FWPCA). FWPCA encouraged states to enact uniform laws to combat water pollution, recognizing that water pollution control was primarily the responsibility of state and local governments. In 1972, FWPCA was amended with an obligation to obtain and comply with a federally-mandated National Pollutant Discharge Elimination System (NPDES) permit program. These amendments also transformed FWPCA into what is known today as the CWA.

The NPDES permit program allows EPA to issue a permit for the discharge of any pollutant, or combination of pollutants. To be clear, the CWA prohibits the discharge of pollutants into navigable waters. However, if a facility requests a permit, it can discharge within certain parameters called effluent limitations and will be deemed a point source. Accordingly, the point source will be regulated pursuant to the NPDES permit issued by EPA or one of 46 States authorized to issue permits. Relevant here, the definition of point source excludes "agricultural stormwater discharges." This occurs, for example, when rainwater comes in contact with manure and flows into navigable waters. If a CAFO discharges without a permit, it is strictly liable for discharging without a permit and subject to severe civil and criminal penalties. For example, monetary sanctions can accrue at a rate of up to $50,000 per violation, per day, for criminally negligent violations, or up to $100,000 per violation, per day, for repeated, knowing violations. Criminal violators may be subject to imprisonment.

EPA enacted the first set of CAFO regulations in 1976. Since that time, the substance of these regulations has changed only twice, in 2003 and 2008. The 1976 regulations specified that CAFOs that wanted to discharge were required to have a permit primarily based on the number of animals housed in the facility. All large CAFOs, those with 1,000 or more animals, were required to have an NPDES permit to discharge pollutants. Medium CAFOs, those with 300 to 1,000 animals, were required to have a permit if they emitted certain discharges. Finally, most small CAFOs, those with 300 animals or less, generally were not required to have a permit. Under this regulatory scheme, if a discharging CAFO was required to have a permit, but did not have one, it would be subject to civil or criminal liability.

The 1976 regulatory scheme was in place for almost thirty years. However, after being sued for failing to revise the effluent limitations for CAFO operations, EPA revised its regulations to address not only inadequate compliance with existing policy, but also the changes that have occurred in the animal production industries. Subsequently, in the 2003 Rule, EPA shifted from a regulatory framework that explained what type of CAFO must have a permit to a broader regulatory framework that explained what type of CAFO must apply for a permit. Under the 2003 Rule, all CAFOs were required to apply for an NPDES permit whether or not they discharged.

In *Waterkeeper*, the Environmental Petitioners (Waterkeeper Alliance, Inc., Sierra Club, Natural Resources Defense Council, Inc., and the American Littoral Society) and the Farm Petitioners (American Farm Bureau Federation, National Chicken Council, and the National Pork Producers Council), many of whom are petitioners or intervenors in the present matter, challenged the 2003 Rule on several grounds. Specifically, the petitioners challenged the 2003 Rule's duty to apply and the type of discharges subject to regulation. The court held that EPA cannot require CAFOs to apply for a permit based on a "potential to discharge."

The Environmental Petitioners argued that the 2003 Rule was unlawful because (1) it empowers NPDES authorities to issue permits to CAFOs in the absence of any meaningful review of the nutrient management plans (NMPs) those CAFOs have developed; and (2) it fails to require that the terms of the NMPs be included in the NPDES permits. The Second Circuit agreed and held that by failing to provide for EPA review of the NMPs, the 2003 Rule violated the statutory commandments that the permitting agency must assure compliance with applicable effluent or discharge limitations.

The parties also disputed whether the terms of the NMPs, themselves, constitute effluent limitations that must be included in the NPDES permits. The Second Circuit held that because the 2003 Rule failed to require that the terms of NMPs be included in NPDES permits, the 2003 Rule violated the CWA. The court explained that the CWA defined effluent limitation as any restriction established by a State or the Administrator on quantities, rates, and concentrations of chemical, physical, biological, and other constituents which are discharged from point sources. Thus, because the requirement to develop an NMP constitutes a restriction on land application discharges only to the extent that the NMP actually imposes restrictions on land application discharges, the CWA's definition of effluent limitations encompassed an NMP.

In 2008, EPA published its 2008 CAFO Rule that clarifies the "duty to apply" liability scheme. It reiterates that CAFOs "propose to discharge" if they are designed, constructed, operated, or maintained such that a discharge would occur. Furthermore, each CAFO operator is required to make an objective case-by-case assessment of whether it discharges or proposes to discharge, considering, among other things, climate, hydrology, topology, and the man-made aspects of the CAFO. It further clarifies that a CAFO can be held liable for failing to apply for a permit, in addition to being held liable for the discharge itself. The 2008 Rule also reiterates that certification is voluntary, but if a CAFO does not certify, in an enforcement proceeding for failing to apply for a permit, the CAFO would have the burden of proving that it did not propose to discharge. Finally, with regard to NMPs, the 2008 Rule restates that NMPs are an enforceable part of an NPDES permit and clarifies that the terms of NMPs would remain the same as the terms articulated in the 2003 Rule.

On appeal, the Farm Petitioners primarily challenge EPA's "duty to apply" for an NPDES permit and imposition of liability for failing to apply for a permit. The duty-to-apply liability scheme has three parts. To begin, the 2008 Rule requires CAFOs that discharge or propose to discharge to apply for an NPDES permit—the duty to apply. If a CAFO discharges and does not have a permit, the CAFO will not only be liable for discharging without a permit, but also prosecuted for failing to apply for a permit—failure to apply liability. However, a CAFO can circumvent this liability if the CAFO operator can establish that the CAFO was designed, constructed, operated, and maintained in a manner such that the CAFO will not discharge. The Farm Petitioners argue that certain parts of the liability scheme are in excess of EPA's statutory authority.

In *Waterkeeper*, the Second Circuit's decision is clear: without a discharge, EPA has no authority and there can be no duty to apply for a permit. Cases leave no doubt that there must be an actual discharge into navigable waters to trigger the CWA's requirements and EPA's authority. Accordingly, we conclude that EPA's requirement that CAFOs that "propose" to discharge apply for an NPDES permit is *ultra vires* and cannot be upheld.

Although the CWA forecloses EPA's regulation of a CAFO before there is a discharge, the question remains: Can EPA require discharging CAFOs to apply for an NPDES permit? The primary purpose of the NPDES permitting scheme is to control pollution through the regulation of discharges into navigable waters. Therefore, it would be counter to congressional intent for the court to hold that requiring a discharging CAFO to obtain a permit is an unreasonable construction of the Act. In fact, the text of the Act indicates that a discharging CAFO must have a permit. The CWA explains that discharging without a permit is unlawful, and punishes such discharge with civil and criminal penalties. This has been the well-established statutory mandate since 1972. It logically follows that, at base, a discharging CAFO has a duty to apply for a permit. In summary, we conclude that EPA cannot impose a duty to apply for a permit on a CAFO that "proposes to discharge" or any CAFO before there is an actual discharge. However, it is within EPA's province, as contemplated by the CWA, to impose a duty to apply on CAFOs that are discharging.

The 2008 Rule provides that a CAFO can be held liable for failing to apply for a permit. The Farm Petitioners contend that EPA does not have the authority to create this liability. We agree. Here, the CWA is clear about when EPA can issue compliance orders, bring a civil suit for an injunction or penalties, or bring criminal charges for penalties. Specifically, 33 U.S.C. § 1319 allows EPA to impose liability if it finds that any person is in violation of any condition or limitation which implements violations of: the discharge prohibition, certain water-quality based effluent limitations, national standards of performance for new sources, toxic and pretreatment effluent standards, EPA's information-gathering authority, provisions permitting the discharge of specific aquaculture pollutants, any permit condition or limitation, and provisions governing the disposal or use of sewer sludge. Notably absent from this list is liability for failing to apply for an NPDES permit.

An agency's authority is limited to what has been authorized by Congress. Here, the "duty to apply," as it applies to CAFOs that have not discharged, and the imposition of failure to apply liability is an attempt by EPA to create from whole cloth new liability provisions. The CWA simply does not authorize this type of supplementation to its comprehensive liability scheme. Nor has Congress been compelled, since the creation of the NPDES permit program, to make any changes to the CWA, requiring a non-discharging CAFO to apply for an NPDES permit or imposing failure to apply liability.

We hereby vacate those provisions of the 2008 Rule that require CAFOs that propose to discharge to apply for an NPDES permit, but we uphold the provisions of the 2008 Rule that impose a duty to apply on CAFOs that are discharging.

## Questions

1. Do most individual CAFO owners and operators secure federal NPDES permits or state permits?
2. Are fines for violating a permit significant?
3. Why were new regulations adopted in 2003?
4. What was the major shift in coverage between the 1976 and 2003 provisions?
5. Why are NMPs important?
6. What is the problem with not reviewing an NMP under the 2003 CAFO Rule?
7. Why can't the EPA regulate proposed discharges?
8. Why did the court find there was no duty for failing to apply for a permit?

As the result of the 2011 *National Pork Producers Council* case, the EPA revised its CAFO regulations in 2012 that currently govern water pollution from CAFOs. While farm groups feel the regulations are too demanding, environmental groups continue to push for more stringent requirements that would keep more pollutants out of our country's federal waters. Yet the thrust of the regulations governing CAFOs continues to recognize that the use of animal manure as a fertilizer for growing crops is important. Thus, the regulations continue to allow for the land application of manure, even though it is known that rain events will cause some pollutants to enter surface waters as agricultural storm water discharges.

## Discussion Questions

1. Should Congress amend the CWA and allow the EPA to regulate proposed discharges? Why or why not?
2. Are the federal CAFO regulations sufficient to protect our country's water resources?
3. How should water runoff from streets and parking lots be regulated under the CWA, and are there sufficient safeguards minimizing pollutant discharges from these areas?

## Image Credit

# CHAPTER FIFTEEN
## Preventing Damages from Waste

## Learning Objectives

- *Recommend legal requirements for assigning responsibilities for damages from waste disposal.*
- *Define the provisions of the two major laws governing hazardous wastes.*
- *Describe public and private efforts to prevent damages from wastes.*
- *Identify how governments know the locations of hazardous wastes.*
- *Classify three types of environmental audit programs.*

Federal, state, and local governments have long been active in regulating waste to safeguard people and the environment. Under the Commerce Clause, the federal government has the authority to regulate waste. The Environmental Protection Agency (EPA) deals with the federal proscriptions and delegates to states the authority to oversee many of the waste requirements. Over the years, federal waste statutes have become more detailed. The first major federal law to specifically address solid waste was the Solid Waste Disposal Act of 1965. The act was amended and incorporated into the Resource Conservation and Recovery Act (RCRA). After exposure of people to hazardous waste at Love Canal in Niagara Falls, New York, Congress passed the Comprehensive Environmental Response, Compensation, and Liability Act (CERCLA). Subsequent amendments have strengthened these laws to reduce exposure to waste, foster the reduction of waste, and remedy existing sites containing wastes.

Waste laws in general seek to reduce the risks posed by situations and materials. While scientific uncertainty means that the identification and categorization of risks are challenging, governmental agencies have tackled these issues to devise regulations that are important in protecting humans from carcinogens and in protecting the environment. One only has to read about some of the tragedies of contamination occurring today in developing countries to realize how important our statutes and regulations are in protecting people from dangers and damages.

# Resource Conservation and Recovery Act

With the adoption of the RCRA, Congress declared it to be national policy to reduce the generation of hazardous waste. Waste that is nevertheless generated should be treated, stored, or disposed of so as to minimize the present and future threat to human health and the environment. Specifically, the objectives of the act are to promote the protection of health and environment and to conserve valuable material and energy resources. RCRA addresses hazardous waste management and defines hazardous waste as special types of solid waste. Solid waste includes garbage, refuse, sludge, and other discarded material, including solid, liquid, semisolid, or contained gaseous material from industrial, commercial, mining, and agricultural activities. Hazardous waste is divided into listed waste, characteristic waste, universal waste, and mixed waste.

## 1. Tracking Hazardous Waste

RCRA delineates several terms and categories for the regulation of hazardous waste. The act regulates hazardous waste generators by dividing them into categories based on the amount of waste they produce each month. Each large and small quantity generator of waste is assigned an EPA identification number that facilitates tracking the waste. Hazardous waste treatment, storage, and disposal facilities (TSDF) are required to secure permits.

Regulations prescribe a manifest system to track the location of waste. The Uniform Hazardous Waste Manifest (EPA Form 8700-22) allows all parties involved in hazardous waste management (e.g., generators, transporters, TSDFs, EPA, state agencies) to track the movement of hazardous waste from the generator's site to the site where the waste will be treated, stored, or disposed. Furthermore, a manifest requires certification that (i) the generator has a waste minimization program in place at its facility to reduce the volume and toxicity of hazardous waste, to the degree economically practicable; and (ii) the treatment, storage, or disposal method chosen by the generator is the most practicable method currently available that minimizes the risk to human health and the environment.

Transporters of hazardous waste moving waste from one site to another by highway, rail, water, or air are also regulated and must obtain an EPA identification number. Before hazardous waste can be transported, the transporter must sign and date the manifest. This enables the transporter to formally acknowledge the acceptance of hazardous waste from the generator. The transporter must then deliver the hazardous waste shipment to the next transporter, the designated facility, or the alternate facility listed on the manifest. RCRA's "cradle-to-grave" regulation ends at a TSDF that follows the generator and transporter in the chain of waste management activities.

All TSDF owners and operators must obtain site-specific EPA identification numbers. Before an owner or operator treats, stores, or disposes of any hazardous waste, there must be a detailed chemical and physical analysis of a representative sample of the waste. This information may be supplied either through sampling and laboratory analysis or through acceptable knowledge. All owners and operators of TSDFs must demonstrate that they have sufficient funds to pay for the cleanup of any accidental releases of hazardous constituents during the active life of their facilities, compensate any third parties for any resulting bodily injury or property damage, and to provide for the post-closure care of their facilities.

## 2. Additional Oversight

Security provisions for TSDFs are intended to prevent accidental entry and minimize the possibility of unauthorized entry of people or livestock. Facility owners are required to visually inspect the facility for malfunction, deterioration, operator errors, and discharges. Inspection provisions are carried out according to a written inspection schedule that is developed and followed by the owner or operator and kept at the facility. When a hazardous waste management unit stops receiving waste at the end of its active life, it must be cleaned up, closed, and monitored and maintained in accordance with the RCRA closure and post-closure care requirements.

RCRA allows governments to act whenever waste materials are improperly stored, treated, or disposed. Corrective action requirements facilitate the cleanup of releases of hazardous waste or hazardous waste constituents that threaten human health or the environment. Another provision of RCRA provides protection against imminent hazards. This provision authorizes suit against any person who has contributed or who is contributing to the past or present handling, storage, treatment, transportation, or disposal of any solid or hazardous waste that may present an imminent and substantial endangerment to health or the environment. Courts may issue mandatory cleanup orders.

## 3. Waste Minimization under RCRA

As noted, the manifest system delineates a waste minimization provision. Regulators and industries are working to reduce the amount, toxicity, and persistence of waste that is generated. Three methods of minimizing waste are delineated.

- *"Source reduction" is the most desirable method of waste minimization. This is an activity that reduces or eliminates the generation of waste at its source.*
- *"Recycling" is a second approach for waste minimization. When a waste material is used for another purpose, treated, and reused in the same process or reclaimed for another process, it recycles materials and eliminates waste.*
- *"Treatment" is a third minimization method. This may involve elementary neutralization, or chemical, physical, or biological methods for treating hazardous materials.*

The following case details some of the regulatory efforts concerning recycling efforts. The encouragement of recycling is important, and regulations foster this by exempting recycling facilities from RCRA permitting requirements. The controversy in this litigation concerns qualification as a recycling facility.

### United States v. Rineco Chemical Industries, Inc.
US District Court for the Eastern District of Arkansas

*Who is suing?* _____

*Who is being sued?* _____

*For what?* _____

*What is the issue on appeal?* _____

The United States brings this civil action against Rineco Chemical Industries, Inc. (Rineco) under the Resource Conservation and Recovery Act (RCRA). The United States seeks injunctive relief and civil penalties against Rineco for violations of RCRA Sections 3005(a) and 3010, and Arkansas Pollution Control and Ecology Commission (APCEC) Regulation No. 23. The state regulation incorporates federal regulations approved by the Environmental Protection Agency (EPA) pursuant to RCRA that are part of the federally-enforceable state hazardous waste program. Now before the court are cross-motions of the parties for summary judgment. For the reasons that follow, the court grants the United States' motion for summary judgment and denies Rineco's motion for summary judgment.

RCRA is a comprehensive environmental statute that governs the treatment, storage, and disposal of solid waste. RCRA's primary purpose is to reduce the generation of hazardous waste and to ensure the proper treatment, storage, and disposal of that waste which is nonetheless generated so as to minimize the present and future threat to human health and the environment. RCRA's Subtitle C establishes a "cradle-to-grave" regulatory system for the treatment, storage and disposal of hazardous wastes through a combination of national standards established by EPA regulations and a permit program. Permits are generally required under RCRA for any facility that engages in the treatment, storage, or disposal of hazardous waste. Section 3005(a) of RCRA establishes a case-by-case permitting process. Pursuant to Section 3005(a), EPA promulgated regulation 40 C.F.R. § 270.1(b) that prohibits treatment, storage, or disposal of hazardous waste by any person who has not applied for or received a RCRA permit.

Pursuant to RCRA subsection 3006(b), EPA may authorize a state to administer and enforce its own hazardous waste program. When a state obtains such authorization, the state hazardous waste program operates in lieu of the federal program. During the time Arkansas has been authorized to administer the RCRA hazardous waste program, facilities in that state have been regulated under the provisions of APCEC Regulation No. 23, which was adopted and incorporated verbatim from the federal RCRA regulations. Despite having authorized a state to act, EPA frequently files its own enforcement actions against suspected environmental violators, even after the commencement of a state-initiated enforcement action (a process known as overfiling).

Rineco owns and operates a facility in Benton, Arkansas that is engaged in the generation, treatment, and storage of hazardous waste. Rineco is the largest single-site hazardous waste fuel blending facility in the United States and receives more than 400 different types of listed and characteristic solid phase and liquid phase hazardous wastes at its facility from a large number of generators of hazardous waste. Rineco applied for and obtained a permit to operate a hazardous waste management facility at its Benton facility. Located at this facility is a Thermal Metal Wash Recycling Unit (TMW). The operation of the TMW, which does not have a RCRA permit, is at the center of the United States' claims in this action. The United States claims the primary purpose of the TMW is to convert a chemical soup of hazardous waste streams into hazardous waste derived fuel for sale to boiler and industrial furnaces, an activity it claims requires a RCRA permit. Rineco, however, claims the TMW is designed to recycle metal from hazardous and non-hazardous materials, an activity it claims is exempt from regulation and does not require a RCRA permit.

Based on two inspections and documentation provided by Rineco, EPA determined that the TMW is a thermal treatment device that applies heat (over 1000 degrees Fahrenheit) to vaporize hydrocarbons and water and thereby change the physical and chemical composition of the hazardous waste fed into the unit, by separating the waste into six waste streams after treatment in the unit: water, oil, char, metal, vapor, and inerts. EPA states that the metal is discharged via a conveyor to dump trucks for possible sale and that the char is transferred to the hydropulper where it is mixed, along with the liquid waste, into fuel for sale to boiler and industrial furnaces, including cement kilns. The United States argues that the TMW, far from being designed for recycling metal, is an integral part of a fuel blending activity. Rineco states that the TMW is a relatively simple device designed to recycle metal from hazardous and non-hazardous materials.

Two months after EPA's first inspection, the Arkansas Department of Environmental Quality determined that the TMW unit does not require a hazardous waste management permit pursuant to the APCEC Regulation No. 23. EPA, however, states that a substantial percentage of oil and char resulting from the treatment process in the TMW is blended into hazardous waste derived fuel and that this activity requires a RCRA permit. EPA states Rineco's RCRA Permit No. 28H-M001 does not include the treatment, storage, or disposal activities connected with the TMW, and that it has asked Rineco to apply for a modification of its RCRA permit to include such activities but that Rineco has not done so.

The United States moves for summary judgment on each of the claims asserted in its original complaint, asserting that Rineco is not engaged in a recycling activity in the TMW and cannot qualify for the recycling exemption because when waste materials are abandoned by disposal, burning or incineration, they are not recycled. The Court agrees with the United States that the TMW is not eligible for the recycling exemption because substantial hazardous wastes that are treated in the TMW are destroyed by thermal treatment and not recycled in the TMW. With respect to such activity, the materials being burned in incinerators or other thermal treatment devices, other than boilers and industrial furnaces, are considered to be abandoned by being burned or incinerated under APCEC Regulation No. 23 § 261.2(a)(1)(ii), whether or not energy or material recovery also occurs. This is waste destruction subject to regulation. If energy or material recovery occurs, it is ancillary to the purpose of the unit—to destroy wastes by means of thermal treatment—and so does not alter the regulatory status of the device or the activity.

It is undisputed that vapors, a portion of inputs to the TMW, are volatilized by the high temperature, vented to the thermal oxidation unit, and destroyed through burning and incineration. In addition, the presence of substantial char shows that the destruction of organic materials takes place in the TMW. Accordingly, the exemption for the recycling process does not apply. For the foregoing reasons, the Court grants summary judgment to the United States on its First Claim for Relief under RCRA.

## Questions

1. Why didn't the court agree with Rineco that the TMW was a recycling facility?
2. Is there an inconsistency in the decision of the Arkansas agency in finding that no permit was needed and EPA's decision that the fuel-blending facility needs a permit?
3. Why is the TMW facility not eligible for the recycling exemption?
4. Where did Arkansas obtain the text for APCEC Regulation No. 23 § 261.2(a)(1)?
5. Is the EPA being too demanding in subjecting Rineco to additional permitting requirements?

Fig. 15.1 Abandoned ships may create environmental problems.

# Comprehensive Environmental Response, Compensation, and Liability Act

In adopting CERCLA, Congress passed a strong law allowing the government to take action for the cleanup of contaminated properties. The law allows for the cleanup of hazardous substances previously deposited, provides emergency assistance for cleanup actions, collects funds for emergencies, embodies retroactive liability for potentially responsible parties, establishes a system of priorities for cleaning up hazardous sites, and encourages private cleanup efforts.

CERCLA section 106 abatement actions allows the president to determine whether there may be an imminent and substantial endangerment to the public health or welfare or the environment because of an actual or threatened release of a hazardous substance from a facility, and the president may require the attorney general of the United States to secure such relief as may be necessary to abate such danger or threat. The president may also take other action necessary to protect public health and welfare and the environment. This allows action to be taken for threatened problems and allows injunctive relief.

CERCLA liability delineates a strict liability regime for the cleanup of contaminated sites and other expenses. However, this excludes personal injury damages. Persons suffering personal injuries must use tort law for the recovery of their damages. CERCLA places liability on persons who are potentially responsible parties (PRPs). A "person" is defined to include an individual; firm; corporation; association; partnership; consortium; joint venture; commercial entity; US government; state; political subdivision of a state; municipality; commission; or interstate body. Persons who may be PRPs include:

- *Current owners and operators of a vessel or facility*
- *Past owner or operator of hazardous substances when disposal occurred*
- *Operator managing and controlling day-to-day activities*
- *Person arranging for disposal of hazardous substances*
- *Person accepting hazardous substances for transport*
- *Active participant in the management of a facility*
- *Lending institution that takes charge*
- *Independent contractors who are carriers if in control of the hazardous substance.*

A facility includes building; structure; installation; equipment; pipe or pipeline; well; pit; pond; lagoon; impoundment; ditch; landfill; storage container; motor vehicle; rolling stock; aircraft; sites; but excludes consumer products.

However, CERCLA enumerates a very limited number of exceptions that enables a few persons to escape liability in qualifying situations. State and local governments, if acquiring property due to bankruptcy, foreclosure, tax delinquencies, or abandonment of real estate, are not PRPs. Security interest owners, mortgagees, and secured parties that do not participate in the management or exercise any control over the contaminated property are not PRPs. Qualifying common carriers and contract carriers (excluding independent contractors) also do not incur liability under CERCLA. The law also provides in § 107(b) a defense under which persons are not liable for recoverable costs and damages for an act of God, an act of war, or an act or omission of a third party meeting stringent qualifications.

Under CERCLA, any person releasing a hazardous substance must notify the National Response Center of the release. Failure to report leads to the individual liability of owners or operators. The EPA CERCLA Site Database—CERCLIS: Comprehensive Environmental Response, Compensation, and Liability Information System—lists releases. Required cleanup actions under CERCLA can be very expensive. These costs may lead a firm to contest the CERCLA provisions, as shown by the following case.

### *General Electric v. Jackson*
US Court of Appeals for the District of Columbia Circuit, Washington

*Who is suing?* _____

*Who is being sued?* _____

*For what?* _____

*What is the issue on appeal?* _____

In this case, appellant General Electric challenges the constitutionality of a statutory scheme that authorizes the Environmental Protection Agency (EPA) to issue orders, known as unilateral administrative orders (UAOs), directing companies and others to clean up hazardous waste for which they are responsible. Appellant argues that the statute violates the Due Process Clause because EPA issues UAOs without a hearing before a neutral decisionmaker. We disagree. To the extent the UAO regime implicates constitutionally protected property interests by imposing compliance costs and threatening fines and punitive damages, it satisfies due process because UAO recipients may obtain a pre-deprivation hearing by refusing to comply and forcing EPA to sue in federal court. We therefore affirm the district court's grant of summary judgment to EPA.

Congress enacted CERCLA in response to the serious environmental and health risks posed by industrial pollution. CERCLA seeks to promote prompt cleanup of hazardous waste sites and to ensure that responsible parties foot the bill. Although CERCLA speaks in terms of the President, the President has delegated his UAO authority to EPA, so throughout this opinion we shall refer only to EPA. Under CERCLA, EPA may conduct two types of "response actions": (1) removal actions are short-term remedies designed to cleanup, monitor, assess, and evaluate the release or threatened release of hazardous substances, while (2) remedial actions are longer-term, more permanent remedies to minimize the release of hazardous substances so that they do not migrate to cause substantial danger to present or future public health or welfare or the environment. CERCLA imposes strict liability on several classes of responsible parties, including current and former facility owners and operators, as well as parties that arrange for the transport, treatment, or disposal of hazardous substances.

When EPA determines that an environmental cleanup is necessary at a contaminated site, CERCLA gives the agency four options: (1) it may negotiate a settlement with potentially responsible parties (PRPs); (2) it may conduct the cleanup with "Superfund" money and then seek reimbursement from PRPs by filing suit; (3) it may file an abatement action in federal district court to compel PRPs to conduct the cleanup; or (4) it may issue a UAO instructing PRPs to clean the site. This last option is the focus of this case. To use its UAO authority, EPA must first determine that there may be an imminent and substantial endangerment to the public health or welfare or the environment because of an actual or threatened release of a hazardous substance from a facility. If EPA makes such a determination, it must then compile an administrative record and select a response action.

Once EPA issues a UAO, the recipient PRP has two choices. It may comply and complete the cleanup. Alternatively, the PRP may refuse to comply with the UAO, in which case EPA may either bring an action in federal district court to enforce the UAO or clean the site itself. In either proceeding, if the court concludes that the PRP "willfully" failed to comply with an order "without sufficient cause," it "may" (but need not) impose fines, which are currently set at $37,500 per day. If EPA itself undertakes the cleanup and the district court finds that the PRP "failed without sufficient cause" to comply with the UAO, the court may impose punitive damages of up to three times the amount of any costs the agency incurs. Central to this case, these two options—comply and seek reimbursement, or refuse to comply and wait for EPA to bring an enforcement or cost recovery action—are exclusive. CERCLA section 113(h) bars PRPs from obtaining immediate judicial review of a UAO.

Over the years, appellant GE has received at least 68 UAOs. In addition, GE is currently participating in response actions at 79 active CERCLA sites where UAOs may issue. GE filed suit in the United States District Court challenging CERCLA's UAO regime alleging that the statute violates the Fifth Amendment to the United States Constitution because it deprives persons of their fundamental right to liberty and property without constitutionally adequate procedural safeguards. According to GE, the unilateral orders regime imposes a classic and unconstitutional Hobson's choice: because refusing to comply risks severe punishment, i.e., fines and treble damages, UAO recipients' only real option is to comply before having any opportunity to be heard on the legality and rationality of the underlying order. GE sought a declaratory judgment that the provisions of CERCLA relating to unilateral administrative orders are unconstitutional.

The district court granted EPA's motion for summary judgment on GE's facial due process challenge. The district court held that the statute provides constitutionally sufficient process because by refusing to comply with a UAO, a PRP can force EPA to bring a court action in which the PRP can challenge the order. To prevail on this appeal, GE must establish either that no set of circumstances exists under which CERCLA's UAO provisions would be valid, or that those provisions lack any plainly legitimate sweep.

The Fifth Amendment to the United States Constitution provides that "No person shall be deprived of life, liberty, or property, without due process of law." The first inquiry in every due process challenge is whether the plaintiff has been deprived of a protected interest in liberty or property. The parties agree that the costs of compliance and the monetary fines and damages associated with noncompliance qualify as protected property interests. They disagree, however, as to whether judicial review is available before any deprivation occurs.

EPA contends that CERCLA gives PRPs the right to pre-deprivation judicial review: by refusing to comply with a UAO, a PRP can force EPA to file suit in federal court, where the PRP can challenge the order's validity before spending a single dollar on compliance costs, damages, or fines. GE responds that noncompliance—and thus pre-deprivation judicial review—is but a theoretical option. According to GE, daily fines and treble damages are so severe that they intimidate PRPs from exercising the purported option of electing not to comply with a UAO so as to test an order's validity via judicial review. PRPs are thus forced to comply and spend substantial sums prior to any hearing before a neutral decisionmaker.

The Supreme Court has made clear, however, that statutes imposing fines—even "enormous" fines—on noncomplying parties may satisfy due process if such fines are subject to a "good faith" or "reasonable grounds" defense. CERCLA offers noncomplying PRPs several levels of protection: a PRP faces daily fines and treble damages only if a federal court finds (1) that the UAO was proper; (2) that the PRP "willfully" failed to comply "without sufficient cause"; and (3) that, in the court's discretion, fines and treble damages are appropriate. Although the PRP must prove that it is not liable by a preponderance of the evidence, EPA's liability determination warrants no judicial deference. As to the second, CERCLA's "willfulness" and "sufficient cause" requirements are quite similar to the good faith and reasonable grounds defenses the Supreme Court has found sufficient to satisfy due process. Moreover, PRPs receive added protection from the fact that the district court has authority to decide not to impose fines even if it concludes that a recipient without sufficient cause, willfully violated, or failed or refused to comply with a UAO.

Given these safeguards, we have no basis for concluding that the necessary effect and result of CERCLA must be to preclude a resort to the courts for the purpose of testing a UAO's validity. We fully understand that the financial consequences of UAOs can be substantial. We also understand that other administrative enforcement schemes that address matters of public health and safety may provide greater process than does CERCLA. Because our judicial task is limited to determining whether CERCLA's UAO provisions violate the Fifth Amendment, we affirm the decisions of the district court.

## Questions

1.  What prompted GE to expend so much money challenging CERCLA?
2.  What are the two options for response actions?
3.  What is the major difference between the two options?
4.  What are the choices for a PRP after receiving a UAO?
5.  Why aren't CERCLA's penalties violative of due process?

# State Regulation of Waste

State legislatures have recognized the need to regulate the creation, storage, treatment, and disposal of hazardous waste to protect public health through the enactment of state hazardous waste management acts. Each act institutes a comprehensive, statewide program for managing hazardous waste, administered by a state agency that has been granted powers to adopt, change, and repeal rules and regulations to implement and enforce the act's provisions. Furthermore, a state may require the listing of hazardous sites. For example, a Georgia law requires listing sites if either of two conditions is met: (1) the state director determines that a release exceeds the "Reportable Quantity" score; or (2) the director determines a release "poses a danger to human health and the environment." After a property owner provides notice of a release, the state will determine whether the release involved a "reportable quantity," as defined in the regulations.

Some states have enacted disclosure laws requiring that contamination be noted in the property's deed or recorded in county or local land records. Another issue involves liens claimed by the EPA. Under CERCLA, EPA liens have priority against purchasers and the holders of other liens on the property from the time they are recorded in the appropriate county courthouse. In general, state environmental liens have similar priority, although in a few states, there are environmental "superliens." Superliens may take priority over preexisting liens and interests, and may encumber other property owned by the person from whom collection is sought.

Due to the requirement under federal law to reduce waste, states have enacted a variety of specific laws addressing various types of waste.

I.  Landfill Plans. Federal regulations set forth requirements for the startup, shutdown, and malfunctions at landfills, and the administration of these requirements is usually managed by authorized states. Owners or operators of landfills need to develop and implement a written startup, shutdown, and malfunction plan. For such a landfill plan, the primary concern is with malfunction of the landfill gas collection and control system and associated monitoring equipment. Each operation must have air pollution control practices for minimizing emissions to the levels required by the relevant standards.

II.  Tire Disposal Restrictions. States and local governments may impose restrictions on scrap tires originating in or which may ultimately be disposed of in its area of jurisdiction. These restrictions may include: (1) a ban on the disposal of scrap tires at solid waste disposal facilities within its control; and (2) a requirement that scrap tires be recycled, shredded, chopped, or otherwise processed in an environmentally sound manner prior to disposal at solid waste disposal facilities. The disposal of tires is generally accompanied by a fee imposed upon the retail sale of all new replacement tires.

III.  Yard Trimmings Disposal Restrictions. Municipal governments and solid waste management authorities are able to impose restrictions on yard trimmings which are generated in or may ultimately be disposed of in its area of jurisdiction. These restrictions may: (1) require that yard trimmings not be placed in or mixed with municipal solid waste; (2) ban the disposal of yard trimmings at municipal solid waste disposal facilities having liners and leachate collection systems; (3) require yard trimmings be sorted and stored for collection in such a manner as to facilitate collection, composting, or other handling; and (4) require that yard trimmings be sorted and stockpiled or chipped, composted, used as mulch, or otherwise beneficially reused or recycled to the maximum extent feasible.

IV.  Underground Storage Tanks. Section 9002 of the federal Solid Waste Disposal Act requires states to have an agency oversee provisions on underground storage tanks. Under federal law, owners of such tanks must notify the state agency of the tank.

V. Lead Acid Vehicle Batteries. Due to the toxicity of acid and lead in car batteries, states adopted provisions saying that no person may place a used lead acid vehicle battery in mixed municipal solid waste or discard or otherwise dispose of a lead acid vehicle battery, except by delivery to a battery retailer or wholesaler, to a secondary lead smelter, or to a collection or recovered materials processing facility that accepts lead acid vehicle batteries.

VI. Abandoned Methamphetamine Production Areas. Another environmental problem involves abandoned production areas used to make methamphetamine, commonly sold as crank, crystal, ice, speed, glass, and tweak. Clandestine methamphetamine labs often contain hazardous substances left over from the production of the drug. Landlords, property owners, and business operators may become obligated to clean up wastes remaining from former meth laboratories.

# Environmental Auditing

Current public awareness of environmental pollution and legislative responses to contamination incidents mean that violations of statutory and regulatory provisions can lead to criminal and civil liability. Financial liability, uncertainties, and the cost of environmental impairment insurance have put environmental compliance on the agendas of management. Managers need to reflect upon what they should be doing to protect themselves and their businesses. Responsible managers seek assurance on the elimination of environmental risks. This may include a system to detect environmental risks and verify compliance with applicable internal and external controls. The vehicle used to attain these goals is environmental auditing.

Environmental auditing offers several specific benefits. First, it is a type of risk management that reduces the probability of legal actions against a company and its officers. Second, with an audit, corporate officers are less likely to be sued or to face issues of liability for environmental problems. Third, the audit may lower insurance premiums or affect the ability to obtain environmental impairment insurance. Fourth, audits tend to facilitate better relations with environmental agencies. Finally, audits help integrate environmental expenditures with corporate planning.

Less direct benefits could include the absence of unfavorable publicity, improved operating performance, and speedier permit issuance. A successful auditing program must be tailored to the needs of a specific organization. The program a business should choose depends upon such factors as the particular objectives, available resources, company structure, environmental impacts, past history and compliance, and the desirability of confidentiality. Three types of audits have been noted for controlling different risks.

# 1. Compliance Audits

Environmental compliance auditing is the process of determining whether all or selected levels of an organization are in compliance with environmental regulatory requirements. It does not replace environmental awareness or protection programs; rather, it measures their effectiveness. Stated in a different manner, environmental auditing is a systematic and objective review by a regulated entity of facility operations and practices related to meeting environmental requirements. Audits can be designed to verify compliance with environmental requirements, evaluate the effectiveness of environmental management systems already in place, or assess risks from regulated or unregulated materials and practices. Compliance audits are not required by federal law, although the Environmental Protection Agency may require audits as part of enforcement actions. Federal and state regulations do not prescribe standards on what an environmental audit must contain.

# 2. Transactional (Acquisition) Audits

If a property owner, operator, or purchaser is dealing with property that has some type of association with hazardous or toxic substances, or unusual amounts of pesticides, an assessment of the property is justified. Property sellers may need an environmental audit to verify the absence of contamination on the property. Property buyers may want an audit as part of their acquisition review to determine whether contamination exists or how past contamination was addressed. Property buyers should conduct a physical assessment of property to identify potential liabilities under CERCLA, RCRA, the Toxic Substances Control Act, and other federal and state laws. The assessment should commence as early in the acquisition process as possible.

The location, previous uses, and nature of the property will determine how much effort to expend in the review. Guidelines for acquisitions prepared by various publishers provide detailed lists of things that should be checked when dealing with properties that may involve major environmental problems. In addition to a site visit and report on the site history, an acquisition review should consider the following:

- *Search of local health department records for violations.*
- *Check with environmental authorities on past violations or problems.*
- *Verification of the location of fuel or other storage tanks and tests for leakage.*
- *Review of permits, registrations, and record-keeping documentation.*
- *Require tests if evidence of hazardous waste is found.*
- *Review of the title insurance company report to discern presence of problems.*
- *Check of neighboring properties.*
- *Note the availability of permission to transfer permits or registrations.*

If extensive testing or the drilling of test borings is desired, an agreement with the seller will be necessary to protect each party's interests. Buyers of real property should have a clear provision in the sales contract that requires the seller to clean up existing hazardous substance contamination or that allows the buyer to terminate the sales contract without a penalty if cleanup costs are excessive. Due to the possible high costs of environmental violations, sellers may want to include a precautionary provision that establishes a maximum amount that the seller is obligated to spend to cure the environmental violations. If curing costs more than the stated amount, the purchaser must choose between terminating the contract or taking the property with a liquidated payment.

Due to the possibility of the discovery of environmental violations between the signing of the sales contract and closing, a provision should assign responsibility for such. Generally, sellers will be responsible for curing such violations, assuming that the contract assigns responsibility to the seller to remedy violations. The contract also should state that the seller will not undertake or permit others to undertake any activities that might result in environmental problems between the date of the contract and closing.

## 3. Pollution Prevention Audits

Pollution prevention audits are used to identify opportunities to reduce waste and pollution. Firms may use in-house expertise or hire a consulting company to perform an audit that identifies possibilities for eliminating the need to use hazardous substances, how to reuse hazardous substances to reduce waste, and how to treat substances to reduce amounts of wastes being discarded.

# Discussion Questions

1. What are the most important factors that the EPA should consider when working with your community on preventing damages from waste, and why?
2. What are you and your neighbors doing to reduce amounts of waste? Are the efforts sufficient? Why or why not?
3. How can your local government best convey information to citizens that would advance local recycling efforts?
4. How can the EPA leverage its partnerships with manufacturers and recyclers to encourage the use of certified recyclers who use the best Environmental Sound Management practices and create domestic jobs?
5. How can the EPA help consumers increase their donations of used electronics to third-party-certified electronics recyclers?

# CHAPTER SIXTEEN
## Addressing Air Quality

### Learning Objectives

- *Recite the NAAQS pollutants.*
- *Explain why GHGs are air pollutants.*
- *Synthesize problems and damages from air pollution.*
- *Explain how society can force polluters to pay for pollution damages.*

t is a known fact that poor air quality adversely affects the health of animals, humans, and plants. Air pollution is defined as the contamination of the air by the discharge of harmful substances. This pollution causes a variety of ailments, ranging from mild skin and eye irritation to lung and respiratory sickness, birth defects, cancer, brain damage, and premature death. Trees and animals are susceptible to the same pollutants, and their growth and survival may be impeded. Furthermore, air pollution has led to a decrease in ozone levels in the upper atmosphere. Without the protective ozone layer, humans are more susceptible to skin cancer and cataracts. Air pollutants also destroy stone structures, including buildings, statuary, and monuments.

Activities that place pollutants into the air may be regulated by governments to prevent unreasonable damages. The first air pollution controls were by state and local governments. Cities such as Chicago and New York enacted ordinances to regulate smokestacks and boilers in an attempt to clean up the air. In the 1950s and 1960s, Congress enacted various legislation addressing air pollution. All of the efforts failed to achieve significant gains in air quality.

Fig. 16.1 Clean air and frigatebirds offer a splendid sight.

The first powerful piece of legislative action concerning controlling air pollution was the Clean Air Act of 1970 (CAA). Congress was dissatisfied with the inability of the government to control air pollution, and there was growing concern about air quality throughout the nation. The CAA created a partnership between state and federal governments in which states control monitoring and limiting air pollution, while the EPA is in charge of establishing standards, conducting research, providing assistance, and enforcing standards when states fail to preclude egregious polluting activities. The CAA deals with stationary sources (factories) by establishing limitations on hazardous air pollutants, national ambient air quality standards, and the prevention of significant deterioration. It also governs mobile sources, acid rain, and ozone protection. Major sources of air pollution need permits, governments have air quality monitoring requirements, and citizens are able to bring lawsuits to enforce the act.

Despite several decades of concern, as many as 90 million Americans live in areas where air pollution is above recommended levels, including the residents of Atlanta. Controlling pollutants is expensive, and governments worried about federal, state, and local economies have not been diligent in adopting and enforcing pollution controls. Some presidents attempted to reduce air quality controls, with the most notable being the George W. Bush administration attempting to administratively revise the new source review rules in 2004 to allow more pollutants to be released into the air.

Federal controls over air pollution are cumulative provisions adopted over the years for which administration and enforcement are often delegated to states. The foundation is the delineation of six criteria pollutants and the establishment of air standards for these pollutants. The country is divided into air quality regions, and states adopt state implementation plans (SIPs) to address how each region will meet air quality standards. For regions that do not meet standards for criteria pollutants, nonattainment program provisions apply. Other specific programs address the most pressing air quality problems.

# Criteria Pollutants

The EPA is required to determine which pollutants are harmful to human life and to set safe air quality levels for criteria pollutants. Pollutants are recognized because they are primarily harmful to human health, especially children and the elderly. Pollutants are also recognized because they affect visibility, buildings, plants, and animals. The EPA identified six criteria pollutants to be regulated.

## 1. Sulfur Dioxide

Sulfur dioxide ($SO_2$) is a gas formed by the burning of fuels containing sulfur, usually fossil fuels. Half of all the sulfur dioxide put into the atmosphere each year is from human activity. Other sources of sulfur dioxide include volcanoes, sea spray, and decaying organic matter. Sulfur dioxide is a health risk to humans, with the biggest health risk being damage to the lungs and respiratory tract. Buildings and vegetation are also harmed by sulfur dioxide.

## 2. Nitrogen Oxides

Nitric oxide (NO) and nitrogen dioxide ($NO_2$) are the two forms of nitrogen oxides (NOx) that are considered relevant to humans. Cars, power plants, and industrial plants emit approximately half of all nitrogen oxides every year. The other half comes from lightning and decomposing matter. The negative effects of nitrogen oxides include lung and respiratory damage, acid rain, destruction of the ozone layer, and smog.

## 3. Carbon Monoxide

Carbon monoxide (CO) is largely produced by natural resources. Only 40 percent of carbon monoxide is produced by human sources, including improperly tuned cars, wood-burning stoves, incinerators, and other industry. Carbon monoxide is considered the least harmful of pollutants to humans, but it can cause impaired vision, dizziness, and decreased attention. The main negative effects of carbon monoxide are the greenhouse effect and the creation of ground-level ozone.

## 4. Ozone

Ozone ($O_3$) is a pollutant at ground level, unlike its high-altitude relative, the ozone layer, which protects us from solar radiation. Unlike other pollutants, ozone is not directly emitted by humans. Ozone is formed when nitrogen oxide reacts with oxygen and sunlight. This reaction is enhanced in urban areas, where hydrocarbons are plentiful. Ozone's health effects include eye irritation, asthma, lung tissue damage, and reduced ability to fight infections. Ozone is also the main ingredient in smog, and it can harm vegetation.

## 5. Particulate Matter

Particulate matter, or particulates, are solid or liquid materials suspended in the air. Particulates are formed during the transformation of gaseous emissions from steel mills, power plants, smelters, diesel engines, construction, demolition, and many other industrial activities. A major natural source of particulate matter is pollen. The main natural environmental impact from particulates is decreased visibility. Health problems related to particulates include lung damage, respiratory illness, and, in some cases, cancer. Small particles are actually more damaging to the body than large particles because small particles can get past the body's natural defenses.

## 6. Lead

Lead is primarily produced by airplanes that burn leaded fuel and metal processing. Lead emissions used to be much higher than they are today. In 1970, it was estimated that 220 metric tons were introduced into the atmosphere, mostly by automobile. By 1998, that number had dropped to four metric tons. The decrease is due to the banning of leaded gas for most vehicles. The detrimental health effects of lead include neurological damage and kidney damage. The body does not do a good job of cleansing itself of lead, so it accumulates in blood and soft tissue. Lead can also cause seizures and retardation if a person is exposed to a large amount. The United States allows small planes to use leaded gasoline, which contribute half of the lead pollution in our air.

# Controls under the National Ambient Air Quality Standards

For each criteria pollutant, the EPA has established one or more National Ambient Air Quality Standards (NAAQS). Federal laws and regulations establish a comprehensive system of controls to reduce air pollution. The following are the important components in implementing our air quality controls.

## 1. Air Quality Regions

To keep track of criteria pollutant levels, the EPA has divided the United States into 247 regions, in which air quality is monitored and controlled. Criteria pollutants are reevaluated every five years, and the NAAQS are changed accordingly. For each region, there are maximum allowable concentrations for industry pollutants for outside air; primary standards to protect human health with a wide margin of safety; secondary standards for the general welfare of the entire environment; and maximum concentrations prescribed for time periods.

## 2. Nonattainment Program

If a region fails to meet NAAQS, that region is said to be in nonattainment. Nonattainment is the result of a region failing to meet standards for just one of the criteria pollutants. The vast majority of these areas are nonattainment because they fail to meet ground-level ozone standards (ozone has been the hardest of the criteria pollutants to control). Nonattainment regions have from three to twenty years to meet NAAQS, depending on how bad the air pollution is and how hard it will be to meet NAAQS. This involves stricter emission limitation standards for stationary sources, and new and modified major sources must install the most stringent control technology available.

## 3. Prevention of Significant Deterioration (PSD) Program

If air quality is better than that established by the NAAQS, the Prevention of Significant Deterioration (PSD) Program applies. A permit needs to be obtained before a pollutant-emitting source can be constructed.

## 4. State Implementation Plans

State Implementation Plans (SIPs) have been developed by each state in order to meet NAAQS. The states are free to regulate by any means they see fit, as long as NAAQS are met in each region. The EPA can cut off funding for highways within a state if an approvable SIP is not implemented by the state.

## 5. Permit Programs

Under a permit program, all producers of pollutants must apply for a permit in order to operate. The permit sets five-year limits on the amount of criteria pollutants a producer can omit during the life of the permit. Permits are issued by state and local governments. As long as producers stay within the limits of their permits, they are not in violation of the CAA.

## 6. Automobile Inspection Programs

Nonattainment regions with populations of 200,000 or more are required to have automobile inspection and maintenance programs. These programs require annual emissions testing before an automobile can be registered.

# New Source Review Permits

A New Source Review (NSR) permit is a construction permit given to a large source that is either building a new facility or significantly modifying an existing facility and emitting large amounts of certain air pollutants. There are two types of NSR permits: Nonattainment Area permits and Prevention of Significant Deterioration permits. The type of permit a source needs depends on its location and the pollutants it will emit. In most cases, a state or local government agency issues NSR permits. The EPA will only issue an NSR permit if the state, local, or tribal permitting authority has no approved NSR program of their own. A region's main role in the NSR permitting process is to oversee the issuance of NSR permits by the permitting authorities and review the NSR permits for national and regional consistency, as well as adherence to the Clean Air Act.

When the Clean Air Act was amended in 1977 to establish stricter pollution limits for power plants, all power plants in operation or under construction before 1977 were exempted from meeting the new standards. These plants were grandfathered in because it was believed they would be retired over the next several decades and replaced by plants meeting the improved standards. The 1977 amendments also provided that if an old plant was modified and pollution increased as a result of that modification, the plant lost its grandfathered status and would have to meet modern pollution standards. It turns out, however, that few of the grandfathered plants were taken out of service over the next 30 years. Nor has the pollution-control equipment at the vast majority of these plants been upgraded to meet modern pollution standards. Instead, utilities have invested in what they call "life extension projects," spending tens of millions of dollars to keep their grandfathered plants running without upgrading pollution controls.

# Environmental Effects of Air Pollution

## 1. Acid Rain

Acid rain (precipitation with deposition of acids) has long been recognized as a pollution problem. Acid rain occurs when sulfur dioxide or nitric oxides in the atmosphere react with sunlight and water vapor to form sulfuric and nitric acids. The acids then form into droplets and fall to the earth as acid rain. Rain is considered to be acid rain when it has a pH of less than 5, while normal rain has a pH of ~5.6. Sulfur dioxide from tall smokestacks is the main culprit behind acid rain. Most acid rain in the United States is caused by industry and power plants in states other than where the acid rain is falling. This long-reaching problem is even worse in Canada, where the United States "exports" much of its acid rain. The worst effect of acid rain is the destruction of aquatic life. Aquatic species in lakes perished when the pH of the lake water dropped below 5. Another noticeable effect of acid rain is the destruction of stone buildings and monuments.

## 2. Destruction of the Ozone Layer

The depletion of the ozone layer is a second major air pollution problem. The ozone layer protects life on earth from harmful ultraviolet radiation. It is slowly being eaten away by air pollution, with chlorofluorocarbons (CFCs) being a major culprit. CFCs were first used 80 years ago as propellants, coolants, and sterilizers. CFCs have destroyed enough of the ozone layer that there are places on earth, such as Antarctica, where it is unsafe to be outside because of dangerous levels of UV radiation. In 1987, the Montreal Protocol on Substances That Deplete the Ozone Layer was adopted to protect global ozone.

The United States ratified the Montreal Protocol and amended the CWA to provide additional protection to the ozone layer by ending the production of chemicals that adversely affect this layer. Regulations also addressed the recycling of refrigerants and halon fire extinguishing agents, identifying safe and effective alternatives to ozone-depleting substances, banning the release of ozone-depleting refrigerants during the service, maintenance, and disposal of air conditioners and other refrigeration equipment, and requiring that manufacturers label products either containing or made with the most harmful ozone-depleting substances. The seasonal hole in the ozone layer over Antarctica fluctuates but is below its peak recorded in 2006.

## 3. Regulation of $CO_2$

Global warming continues to be a major environmental concern, with air pollutants prescribed as the cause. As sunlight enters the earth, it is transformed into heat radiation. Carbon dioxide ($CO_2$) emissions in the atmosphere from human activities capture heat from the sun and keep the earth warm. The long-term effects of global warming are unclear, but popular theories include the melting of the polar ice caps, causing ocean levels to rise and higher water temperatures that contribute to increased rates of violent weather. Concern with global warming led a group of states and others to claim that the EPA abdicated its responsibility under the Clean Air Act to regulate the emissions of four greenhouse gases, including carbon dioxide. The resulting opinion by the US Supreme Court found that the EPA had not complied with the CAA in failing to evaluate the need to regulate greenhouse gases.

*Massachusetts v. Environmental Protection Agency*
United States Supreme Court

*Who is suing?* _____

*Who is being sued?* _____

*For what?* _____

*What is the issue on appeal?* _____

A well-documented rise in global temperatures has coincided with a significant increase in the concentration of carbon dioxide in the atmosphere. Respected scientists believe the two trends are related. For when carbon dioxide is released into the atmosphere, it acts like the ceiling of a greenhouse, trapping solar energy and retarding the escape of reflected heat. It is therefore a species—the most important species—of a "greenhouse gas."

Calling global warming "the most pressing environmental challenge of our time," a group of States, local governments, and private organizations alleged in a petition for certiorari that the Environmental Protection Agency (EPA) has abdicated its responsibility under the Clean Air Act to regulate the emissions of four greenhouse gases, including carbon dioxide. Specifically, petitioners asked us to answer two questions concerning the meaning of § 202(a)(1) of the Act: whether EPA has the statutory authority to regulate greenhouse gas emissions from new motor vehicles; and if so, whether its stated reasons for refusing to do so are consistent with the statute.

In response, EPA, supported by 10 intervening States and six trade associations, correctly argued that we may not address those two questions unless at least one petitioner has standing to invoke our jurisdiction under Article III of the Constitution. Notwithstanding the serious character of that jurisdictional argument and the absence of any conflicting decisions construing § 202(a)(1), the unusual importance of the underlying issue persuaded us to grant the writ. Section 202(a)(1) of the Clean Air Act, provides:

> *The EPA Administrator shall by regulation prescribe (and from time to time revise) in accordance with the provisions of this section, standards applicable to the emission of any air pollutant from any class or classes of new motor vehicles or new motor vehicle engines, which in his judgment cause, or contribute to, air pollution which may reasonably be anticipated to endanger public health or welfare. ...*

The Act defines "air pollutant" to include any air pollution agent or combination of such agents, including any physical, chemical, biological, radioactive substance or matter which is emitted into or otherwise enters the ambient air. "Welfare" is also defined broadly: among other things, it includes effects on weather and climate. When Congress enacted these provisions, the study of climate change was in its infancy. On October 20, 1999, a group of 19 private organizations filed a rulemaking petition asking EPA to regulate greenhouse gas emissions from new motor vehicles under § 202 of the Clean Air Act. Fifteen months after the petition's submission, EPA requested public comment on all the issues raised in the petition, adding a "particular" request for comments on any scientific, technical, legal, economic or other aspect of these issues that may be relevant to EPA's consideration of this petition.

In September 8, 2003, EPA entered an order denying the rulemaking petition. The Agency concluded that it lacked statutory authority over greenhouse gases, observing that Congress was well aware of the global climate change issue when it last comprehensively amended the Clean Air Act in 1990, yet it declined to adopt a proposed amendment establishing binding emissions limitations. Congress instead chose to authorize further investigation into climate change. Petitioners sought review of EPA's order in the United States Court of Appeals for the District of Columbia Circuit and the court denied the petition.

Article III of the Constitution limits federal-court jurisdiction to "Cases" and "Controversies." Those two words confine the business of federal courts to questions presented in an adversary context and in a form historically viewed as capable of resolution through the judicial process. It is therefore familiar learning that no justiciable "controversy" exists when parties seek adjudication of a political question, or when the question sought to be adjudicated has been mooted by subsequent developments. This case suffers from none of these defects.

EPA maintains that because greenhouse gas emissions inflict widespread harm, the doctrine of standing presents an insuperable jurisdictional obstacle. We do not agree. At bottom, "the gist of the question of standing" is whether petitioners have such a personal stake in the outcome of the controversy as to assure that concrete adverseness which sharpens the presentation of issues upon which the court so largely depends for illumination. EPA's steadfast refusal to regulate greenhouse gas emissions presents a risk of harm to Massachusetts that is both "actual" and "imminent." There is, moreover, a "substantial likelihood that the judicial relief requested" will prompt EPA to take steps to reduce that risk. The harms associated with climate change are serious and well recognized.

That these climate-change risks are "widely shared" does not minimize Massachusetts' interest in the outcome of this litigation. Where a harm is concrete, though widely shared, the Court has found injury in fact. According to petitioners' unchallenged affidavits, global sea levels rose somewhere between 10 and 20 centimeters over the 20th century as a result of global warming. These rising seas have already begun to swallow Massachusetts' coastal land. Because the Commonwealth "owns a substantial portion of the state's coastal property," it has alleged a particularized injury in its capacity as a landowner.

EPA does not dispute the existence of a causal connection between manmade greenhouse gas emissions and global warming. At a minimum, therefore, EPA's refusal to regulate such emissions "contributes" to Massachusetts' injuries. EPA nevertheless maintains that its decision not to regulate greenhouse gas emissions from new motor vehicles contributes so insignificantly to petitioners' injuries that the Agency cannot be hauled into federal court to answer for them. A plaintiff satisfies the redressability requirement when he shows that a favorable decision will relieve a discrete injury to himself. He need not show that a favorable decision will relieve his every injury. We therefore hold that petitioners have standing to challenge EPA's denial of their rulemaking petition.

On the merits, the first question is whether § 202(a)(1) of the Clean Air Act authorizes EPA to regulate greenhouse gas emissions from new motor vehicles in the event that it forms a "judgment" that such emissions contribute to climate change. We have little trouble concluding that it does. In relevant part, § 202(a)(1) provides that EPA shall by regulation prescribe standards applicable to the emission of any air pollutant from any class or classes of new motor vehicles or new motor vehicle engines, which in the Administrator's judgment cause, or contribute to, air pollution which may reasonably be anticipated to endanger public health or welfare. Because EPA believes that Congress did not intend it to regulate substances that contribute to climate change, the agency maintains that carbon dioxide is not an "air pollutant" within the meaning of the provision.

The statutory text forecloses EPA's reading. The Clean Air Act's sweeping definition of air pollutant includes any air pollution agent or combination of such agents, including any physical, chemical substance or matter which is emitted into or otherwise enters the ambient air. On its face, the definition embraces all airborne compounds of whatever stripe, and underscores that intent through the repeated use of the word "any." Carbon dioxide, methane, nitrous oxide, and hydrofluorocarbons are without a doubt physical and chemical substances which are emitted into the ambient air. The statute is unambiguous.

If EPA makes a finding of endangerment, the Clean Air Act requires the Agency to regulate emissions of the deleterious pollutant from new motor vehicles. EPA no doubt has significant latitude as to the manner, timing, content, and coordination of its regulations with those of other agencies. But once EPA has responded to a petition for rulemaking, its reasons for action or inaction must conform to the authorizing statute. Under the clear terms of the Clean Air Act, EPA can avoid taking further action only if it determines that greenhouse gases do not contribute to climate change or if it provides some reasonable explanation as to why it cannot or will not exercise its discretion to determine whether they do. To the extent that this constrains agency discretion to pursue other priorities of the Administrator or the President, this is the congressional design.

EPA has refused to comply with this clear statutory command. Instead, it has offered a laundry list of reasons not to regulate. Yet, EPA cannot avoid its statutory obligation by noting the uncertainty surrounding various features of climate change and concluding that it would therefore be better not to regulate at this time. If the scientific uncertainty is so profound that it precludes EPA from making a reasoned judgment as to whether greenhouse gases contribute to global warming, EPA must say so. That EPA would prefer not to regulate greenhouse gases because of some residual uncertainty is irrelevant. The statutory question is whether sufficient information exists to make an endangerment finding.

In short, EPA has offered no reasoned explanation for its refusal to decide whether greenhouse gases cause or contribute to climate change. Its action was therefore arbitrary, capricious, or otherwise not in accordance with law. We need not and do not reach the question whether on remand EPA must make an endangerment finding, or whether policy concerns can inform EPA's actions in the event that it makes such a finding. We hold only that EPA must ground its reasons for action or inaction in the statute. The judgment of the Court of Appeals is reversed, and the case is remanded for further proceedings consistent with this opinion. It is so ordered.

## Questions

1. What two questions did the petitioners present to the Supreme Court?
2. Why did the EPA decline the rule-making petition in 2003?
3. Why did the Court find that the petitioners had standing under Article III to maintain the lawsuit?
4. Why did the EPA claim that greenhouse gases were not air pollutants?
5. Can the EPA decline to regulate greenhouse gases?
6. If Congress disagrees with the Supreme Court, can it do anything to change the need to regulate $CO_2$?

## 4. Seeking Damages from $CO_2$

With the decision in *Massachusetts v. Environmental Protection Agency*, various groups decided more action was needed to reduce carbon dioxide emissions. They filed a common-law nuisance claim against carbon-dioxide emitters and pursued their claim to the Supreme Court. The Court ruled that Congress delegated to the EPA the decision on whether and how to regulate carbon dioxide emissions from power plants that displaced federal common law.

### *American Electric Power Company, Inc. v. Connecticut*
United States Supreme Court

*Who is suing?* _____

*Who is being sued?* _____

*For what?* _____

*What is the issue on appeal?* _____

We address in this opinion the question whether the plaintiffs (several States, the city of New York, and three private land trusts) can maintain federal common law public nuisance claims against carbon-dioxide emitters (four private power companies and the federal Tennessee Valley Authority). As relief, the plaintiffs ask for a decree setting carbon-dioxide emissions for each defendant at an initial cap, to be further reduced annually. The Clean Air Act and the Environmental Protection Agency action the Act authorizes, we hold, displace the claims the plaintiffs seek to pursue.

In *Massachusetts v. EPA* (2007), this Court held that the Clean Air Act authorizes federal regulation of emissions of carbon dioxide and other greenhouse gases. Naturally present in the atmosphere and also emitted by human activities, greenhouse gases are so named because they trap heat that would otherwise escape from the Earth's atmosphere, and thus form the greenhouse effect that helps keep the Earth warm enough for life. *Massachusetts* held that the Environmental Protection Agency (EPA) had misread the Clean Air Act when it denied a rulemaking petition seeking controls on greenhouse gas emissions from new motor vehicles. Greenhouse gases, we determined, qualify as "air pollutants" within the meaning of the governing Clean Air Act provision; they are therefore within EPA's regulatory ken. Because EPA had authority to set greenhouse gas emission standards and had offered no reasoned explanation for failing to do so, we concluded that the agency had not acted in accordance with law when it denied the requested rulemaking.

Responding to our decision in *Massachusetts*, EPA undertook greenhouse gas regulation. In December 2009, the agency concluded that greenhouse gas emissions from motor vehicles cause, or contribute to, air pollution which may reasonably be anticipated to endanger public health or welfare, the Act's regulatory trigger. The agency observed that atmospheric greenhouse gas concentrations are now at elevated and essentially unprecedented levels, almost entirely due to anthropogenic emissions; mean global temperatures, the agency continued, demonstrate an unambiguous warming trend over the last 100 years, and particularly over the past 30 years. Acknowledging that not all scientists agreed on the causes and consequences of the rise in global temperatures, EPA concluded that "compelling" evidence supported the attribution of observed climate change to anthropogenic emissions of greenhouse gases. Consequent dangers of greenhouse gas emissions, EPA determined, included increases in heat-related deaths; coastal inundation and erosion caused by melting icecaps and rising sea levels; more frequent and intense hurricanes, floods, and other extreme weather events that cause death and destroy infrastructure; drought due to reductions in mountain snowpack and shifting precipitation patterns; destruction of ecosystems supporting animals and plants; and potentially significant disruptions of food production.

EPA and the Department of Transportation subsequently issued a joint final rule regulating emissions from light-duty vehicles, and initiated a joint rulemaking covering medium- and heavy-duty vehicles. EPA also began phasing in requirements that new or modified major greenhouse gas emitting facilities use the "best available control technology." Finally, EPA commenced a rulemaking to set limits on greenhouse gas emissions from new, modified, and existing fossil-fuel fired power plants. Pursuant to a settlement finalized in March 2011, EPA has committed to issuing a proposed rule by July 2011, and a final rule by May 2012.

The lawsuits we consider here began well before EPA initiated the efforts to regulate greenhouse gases just described. In July 2004, two groups of plaintiffs filed separate complaints in the Southern District of New York against the same five major electric power companies. The first group of plaintiffs included eight States and New York City, the second joined three nonprofit land trusts; both groups are respondents here. The defendants, now petitioners, are four private companies and the Tennessee Valley Authority, a federally owned corporation that operates fossil-fuel fired power plants in several States. According to the complaints, the defendants are the five largest emitters of carbon dioxide in the United States. Their collective annual emissions of 650 million tons constitute 25 percent of emissions from the domestic electric power sector, 10 percent of emissions from all domestic human activities, and 2.5 percent of all anthropogenic emissions worldwide.

By contributing to global warming, the plaintiffs asserted, the defendants' carbon-dioxide emissions created a substantial and unreasonable interference with public rights, in violation of the federal common law of interstate nuisance, or, in the alternative, of state tort law. The States and New York City alleged that public lands, infrastructure, and health were at risk from climate change. The trusts urged that climate change would destroy habitats for animals and rare species of trees and plants on land the trusts owned and conserved. All plaintiffs sought injunctive relief requiring each defendant to cap its carbon dioxide emissions and then reduce them by a specified percentage each year for at least a decade. The Second Circuit held that all plaintiffs had stated a claim under the federal common law of nuisance.

There is no federal general common law, *Erie R. Co. v. Tompkins*, famously recognized. In the wake of *Erie*, however, a keener understanding developed. *Erie* left to the states what ought to be left to them, and thus required federal courts to follow state decisions on matters of substantive law appropriately cognizable by the states. *Erie* also sparked the emergence of a federal decisional law in areas of national concern. The "new" federal common law addresses subjects within national legislative power where Congress has so directed or where the basic scheme of the Constitution so demands. Environmental protection is undoubtedly an area within national legislative power, one in which federal courts may fill in statutory interstices, and, if necessary, even fashion federal law. As the Court stated in *Illinois v. Milwaukee* (1972): "When we deal with air and water in their ambient or interstate aspects, there is a federal common law."

We hold that the Clean Air Act and EPA actions it authorizes displace any federal common law right to seek abatement of carbon-dioxide emissions from fossil-fuel fired power plants. *Massachusetts* made plain that emissions of carbon dioxide qualify as air pollution subject to regulation under the Act. And we think it equally plain that the Act "speaks directly" to emissions of carbon dioxide from the defendants' plants.

Section 111 of the Act directs EPA Administrator to list categories of stationary sources that in her judgment cause, or contribute significantly to, air pollution which may reasonably be anticipated to endanger public health or welfare. Once EPA lists a category, the agency must establish standards of performance for emission of pollutants from new or modified sources within that category. And, most relevant here, § 111 then requires regulation of existing sources within the same category. For existing sources, EPA issues emissions guidelines; in compliance with those guidelines and subject to federal oversight, the States then issue performance standards for stationary sources within their jurisdiction.

The Act provides multiple avenues for enforcement. If States (or EPA) fail to enforce emissions limits against regulated sources, the Act permits "any person" to bring a civil enforcement action in federal court. If EPA does not set emissions limits for a particular pollutant or source of pollution, States and private parties may petition for a rulemaking on the matter, and EPA's response will be reviewable in federal court. The Act itself thus provides a means to seek limits on emissions of carbon dioxide. We see no room for a parallel track. The plaintiffs argue, as the Second Circuit held, that federal common law is not displaced until EPA actually exercises its regulatory authority, i.e., until it sets standards governing emissions from the defendants' plants. We disagree. The critical point is that Congress delegated to EPA the decision whether and how to regulate carbon-dioxide emissions from power plants; the delegation is what displaces federal common law.

Federal courts can review agency action (or a final rule declining to take action) to ensure compliance with the statute Congress enacted. As we have noted, the Clean Air Act directs EPA to establish emissions standards for categories of stationary sources that, in the Administrator's judgment, cause, or contribute significantly to, air pollution which may reasonably be anticipated to endanger public health or welfare. EPA may not decline to regulate carbon-dioxide emissions from power plants if refusal to act would be arbitrary, capricious, an abuse of discretion, or otherwise not in accordance with law. If the plaintiffs in this case are dissatisfied with the outcome of EPA's forthcoming rulemaking, their recourse under federal law is to seek Court of Appeals review, and, ultimately, to petition for certiorari in this Court.

Indeed, this prescribed order of decision-making—the first decider under the Act is the expert administrative agency, the second, federal judges—is yet another reason to resist setting emissions standards by judicial decree under federal tort law. The appropriate amount of regulation in any particular greenhouse gas-producing sector cannot be prescribed in a vacuum: as with other questions of national or international policy, informed assessment of competing interests is required. Along with the environmental benefit potentially achievable, our Nation's energy needs and the possibility of economic disruption must weigh in the balance.

The Clean Air Act entrusts such complex balancing to EPA in the first instance, in combination with state regulators. Each "standard of performance" EPA sets must take into account the cost of achieving emissions reduction and any nonair quality health and environmental impact and energy requirements. EPA may distinguish among classes, types, and sizes of stationary sources in apportioning responsibility for emissions reductions. And the agency may waive compliance with emission limits to permit a facility to test drive an "innovative technological system" that has not yet been adequately demonstrated. The Act envisions extensive cooperation between federal and state authorities, generally permitting each State to take the first cut at determining how best to achieve EPA emissions standards within its domain. It is altogether fitting that Congress designated an expert agency, here, EPA, as best suited to serve as primary regulator of greenhouse gas emissions. The expert agency is surely better equipped to do the job than individual district judges issuing ad hoc, case-by-case injunctions.

The plaintiffs also sought relief under state law, in particular, the law of each State where the defendants operate power plants. The Second Circuit did not reach the state law claims because it held that federal common law governed. None of the parties have briefed preemption or otherwise addressed the availability of a claim under state nuisance law. We therefore leave the matter open for consideration on remand. For the reasons stated, we reverse the judgment of the Second Circuit and remand the case for further proceedings consistent with this opinion.

# Questions

1. Can the EPA regulate carbon dioxide? Why or why not?
2. How does *Massachusetts v. EPA* affect this case?
3. How does the Court interpret the issue of whether there is federal common law?
4. What should Connecticut do now?
5. How can society get polluters to pay for damages from carbon dioxide?

# Discussion Questions

1. What courses of action would you recommend for large cities that want to improve their air quality?
2. There may be inequalities in the exposure to air pollution and related health risk. In your area of the country, who is disproportionally disadvantaged by existing air pollution, and why? Which government might address this problem? How?
3. Is your state doing more than the minimum for reducing air pollution? What else needs to be done?
4. Do you think cars should be banned from certain areas of large cities? If so, why?

# CHAPTER SEVENTEEN
## Energy and Hydrocarbon Development

## Learning Objectives

- *Appraise the different sources that provide energy.*
- *Identify environmental problems with oil and gas development.*
- *Explain how liability for damages works under an indemnity contract.*
- *Critique provisions addressing landowners' rights concerning the payment of royalties for extracted oil and gas resources.*
- *Describe requirements for obtaining governmental records under an open-records law.*

The development of energy resources has long been an important environmental topic due to the externalities associated with extraction activities and land use. Activities such as mining for coal and drilling for petroleum reserves have left scarred landscapes and poisoned waters. Tons of pollutants have also fouled the air, exacerbating health problems for millions of people. Although governments have enacted numerous laws and regulations to address the problems associated with energy extraction and production, problems remain, demonstrated by events associated with horizontal drilling and hydraulic fracturing (fracking) for natural gas. The United States also lacks a comprehensive energy policy, meaning that some of our efforts are counterproductive.

To discuss energy law, the beginning might be the demand for sources of energy. Per capita, Americans use exorbitant quantities of energy, as our society has adopted a lifestyle dependent on the automobile, affordable, cheap housing, and energy-hogging appliances. By failing to meaningfully develop public transportation and by favoring new development, we are dependent upon individual vehicular transport that consumes copious amounts of gasoline and requires the development of an expensive highway system.

Housing and development policies in the United States have also fostered energy usage. Many people live in suburbs or areas from which they commute significant distances in their own vehicles for work and other activities. Children are driven to specialized activities in different locations in communities. In order to provide more affordable housing, builders decline to incorporate energy-efficient materials and features in buildings because they are more expensive. Due to relatively cheap energy, buildings are not energy efficient, and considerable quantities of energy are needed to heat and cool buildings. We also believe in large houses, and many people live alone. These facets of our society also contribute to greater energy consumption.

## A Problem of Consumption and Externalities

Many Americans feel they have a right to use energy and that there are unlimited energy resources. If fossil fuels become scarce, we believe we will find new technology that provides energy. Rather than offering meaningful encouragement for conservation, our policies allow activities connected to energy resources to place costs on surrounding property owners, people, and the government. We continue to directly and indirectly subsidize energy resources to keep energy prices low. We allow energy development to pollute water and air resources. Inadequate regulations on coal mining mean streams are still being polluted by waste from mining activities. Oil and gas drilling firms placing pollutants into the air are not responsible for the health costs that result from their carcinogens. We also spend large amounts of money to maintain a military presence in areas that are vital to securing petroleum supplies.

Congress has been presented with ideas to tax externalities associated with energy. President Carter's proposal to tax gasoline was defeated; President Clinton's Btu energy tax plan was unable to gain momentum; and President Obama did not receive support for a cap-and-trade program. Congress continues to reject legislation that would help institute policies that require consumers to pay the true price of energy.

Oil continues to be a major part of our energy portfolio. Our huge demand for oil, coupled with the depletion of reserves in Texas and Oklahoma, means we are very dependent on oil imports. While we continue to discuss the development of reserves in Alaska and the continental shelf, environmental issues and costs serve to delay drilling in these areas. Even with production from these areas, we would remain dependent on oil from foreign sources.

Coal is the most plentiful fossil fuel source in the United States. However, the use of coal for electricity generation is accompanied by the release of sulfur dioxide and nitrous oxide emissions that contribute to acid rain. Coal mining is also accompanied by water and air pollution. Thus, coal usage has deleterious environmental effects. With marked increases in natural gas production due to horizontal drilling and hydraulic fracturing, power plants have converted from coal to natural gas. Compared to coal, gas is cheaper and a cleaner energy source. The decreased demand for coal has led to layoffs of persons working in the coal industry and depressed nearby towns.

Nuclear energy accounts for about 20 percent of the country's electricity. Many people feel that the industry has had poor cost projections, as most completed facilities went over budget. People are also concerned about the disposal of nuclear waste. Thus, no new nuclear power plant was built in the country for more than twenty years. In 2016, a new plant in Tennessee commenced providing power. Four other plants are projected to come into production in Georgia and South Carolina. Finally, the United States continues to use hydropower, solar energy, wind, and biomass. However, due to costs and environmental effects, these sources remain minor contributors of energy in our country, accounting to approximately 10 percent of our energy needs.

## Liability for Environmental Damages

One of the leading questions with energy production is who will pay when an accident injures other people. The Deepwater Horizon Oil Spill in the Gulf of Mexico in 2010 killed 11 people and was accompanied by the spreading of more than 2 million gallons of toxic dispersants into the Gulf. It was estimated that more than 82,000 birds, about 6,000 sea turtles, nearly 26,000 marine mammals, and an unknown number of fish and invertebrates may have been harmed by the spill and its aftermath. This environmental disaster also has had severe repercussions for business in coastal areas. While a court-supervised settlement program was adopted, behind the scenes, firms applied to the judiciary to determine who was obligated to pay for damages. The following lawsuit highlights the importance of insurance contract provisions and coverage for environmental damages.

### *In re: Oil Spill by the Oil Rig "Deepwater Horizon" in the Gulf of Mexico*
US District Court, E. D. Louisiana

*Who is suing?* _____

*Who is being sued?* _____

*For what?* _____

*What is the issue on appeal?* _____

Halliburton Energy Services, Inc. (Halliburton) and the BP entities (BP) have cross-moved for partial summary judgment on the issue of whether Halliburton is owed contractual indemnity from BP for certain claims. Halliburton asserts that the contract between it and BP (Contract) required BP to defend and indemnify Halliburton against any and all claims related to a blowout or uncontrolled well condition and relating to pollution and/or contamination from the reservoir. Thus, Halliburton seeks a ruling that it is entitled to indemnity, including payment of defense costs, from BP for third-party claims related to the Deepwater Horizon incident. BP's Cross-Motion seeks a ruling that, as a matter of law, it is not required to indemnify Halliburton for punitive damages, fines, or penalties. Additionally, BP opposes Halliburton's Motion on the grounds that Halliburton committed fraud, breached the contract, and/or materially increased risks to BP as indemnitor, and such acts discharge BP's indemnity obligations.

The Contract's indemnity clauses are contained in Section 2, Clause 19, which provide in pertinent part:

> *19.4 Pollution*
>
> *(a) … Company [BP] shall save, indemnify, release, defend and hold harmless Contractor [Halliburton] Group from and against any claim of whatsoever nature arising from pollution and/or contamination including without limitation such pollution or contamination from the reservoir or from the property or equipment of Company Group arising from or related to the performance of the contract.*
>
> *(b) … Contractor shall save, indemnify, release, defend and hold harmless Company Group and Service Company Group from and against any claim of whatsoever nature arising from pollution occurring on the premises of Contractor Group or originating from the property or equipment of Contractor Group located above the surface of the land or water arising from or relating to the performance of the Contract. …*
>
> *19.6 Other Company Responsibilities*
>
> *Subject to Clauses 19.1 and 19.4(b), … Company shall save, indemnify, release, defend and hold harmless Contractor Group against all claims, losses, damages, costs (including legal costs) expenses and liabilities resulting from: (a) loss or damage to any well or hole …; (b) blowout, fire, explosion, cratering, or any uncontrolled well condition …;*
>
> *19.7 Indemnities in their Entirety*
>
> *All exclusions, releases of liabilities and indemnities given under this Clause … shall apply irrespective of cause and notwithstanding the negligence or breach of duty (whether statutory or otherwise) of the indemnified Party or any other entity or party and shall apply whether or not the claim, liability, damage, or expense in question is:*
>
> *(a) predicated on sole, joint or concurrent fault, negligence (whether active, passive or gross), strict liability, statutory duty, contractual indemnity or otherwise at law, or*
>
> *(b) sought directly or indirectly by way of recovery, indemnification, or contribution by any person or entity against Company Group, Service Company Group, or Contractor Group as the case may be.*

This Court recently issued an Order and Reasons pertaining to similar contractual indemnity issues between Transocean and BP. The holdings in that Order resolve many of the issues presented here. Accordingly, for reasons stated in the Transocean Indemnity Order, the Court finds as follows:

- *Subject to the statements below, BP is required to indemnify Halliburton for third-party compensatory claims that arise from pollution or contamination that did not originate from the property or equipment of Halliburton located above the surface of the land or water, even if Halliburton's gross negligence caused the pollution.*
- *BP does not owe Halliburton indemnity to the extent Halliburton is held liable for punitive damages.*
- *BP does not owe Halliburton indemnity to the extent Halliburton is held liable for civil penalties under Section 311(b)(7) of the Clean Water Act (CWA).*
- *Whether Halliburton breached the contract, and whether that breach was of a type that would invalidate the indemnity clause, cannot be determined on summary judgment. Similarly, the Court cannot determine here whether an act was committed that materially increased the risk, or prejudiced the rights of BP as indemnitor, so as to invalidate the indemnity. The Court defers ruling on these issues.*
- *BP does not owe Halliburton the expenses of establishing its right to indemnity and BP is not obligated to fund Halliburton's defense at this time.*

A remaining issue that was not addressed in the Transocean Indemnity Order concerns fraud. BP alleges in its Cross Complaint and Third Party Complaint that Halliburton made fraudulent statements and fraudulently concealed material information concerning the cement tests it conducted and other matters, and that BP, relying on these statements, allowed Halliburton to pour the unstable cement slurry that led to the uncontrollable well and blowout. BP asserts that the language of the indemnity does not extend to fraud, nor would public policy permit such indemnification, given that fraud involves willful misconduct exceeding gross negligence. Halliburton denies that it committed fraud, but also argues that BP's allegations are merely breach of contract claims cloaked as fraud. Halliburton also argues that, in any respect, Clause 19.7 is broad enough to include fraud.

The Court agrees that fraud could void an indemnity clause on public policy grounds, given that it necessarily includes intentional wrongdoing. The Court is also mindful that mere failure to perform contractual obligations as promised does not constitute fraud but is instead breach of contract. Consequently, there are material issues of fact that preclude summary judgment on this issue. The Court defers ruling on this issue. Accordingly, it is ordered that Halliburton's and BP's Cross-Motions for Partial Summary Judgment are granted in part and denied in part.

## Questions

1. Who offered what under the indemnity agreement?
2. Is BP liable for Halliburton's gross negligence? Why?
3. Can BP incur liability for Halliburton's punitive damages? Why?
4. Why does BP feel that Halliburton engaged in fraud, which should defeat indemnity?
5. Who seemed to want this contract the most?

# Fracturing for Shale Gas

As part of an effort to reduce dependence on foreign energy sources, governments support and encourage domestic energy development. With the commercial use of horizontal drilling and hydraulic fracturing, new quantities of shale gas are being produced from reserves that lie deep underground. Shale gas accounts for approximately 30 percent of the country's natural gas usage, and extraction activities are very important to state and local economies. By drilling wells and injecting large quantities of water mixed with specially formulated chemical mixtures and granular material at high pressures, rocks that store petroleum resources are cracked open, allowing their contents to flow to the surface.

Fig. 17.1 Drilling for hydrocarbons may create environmental problems.

Yet some feel that the rush to produce shale gas exposed the public to risks of health and environmental problems. Toxic substances in flowback and produced waters (wastewater) accompanying fracturing have contaminated land and water resources. Improper surface well casings, blowouts, accidents, spills, and other mishaps resulting in the migration of fracturing chemicals have been alleged to be connected to human injuries. Individuals and communities are concerned that accidental releases of toxic substances will contaminate their drinking water sources, and that governments may not adequately enforce existing environmental regulations.

Controversies about risks and environmental degradation accompanying the development and operation of shale gas challenge legislators and regulators. Risks of damages from shale gas production activities have led regional agencies—as well as federal, state, and local governments—to adopt provisions that provide additional oversight. Many are concerned that energy production allows producers to place negative externalities and damages on neighbors, communities, and future generations. Due to a number of exceptions to federal environmental laws, states have had to take an active role in overseeing fracturing and shale gas production. State oversight includes requirements for well operators to make timely reports and inspections.

## 1. Federal Exceptions

Exceptions in five major federal laws for various aspects of shale gas production have meant that existing federal oversight is inadequate in protecting humans and the environment. The first exception is set forth in the Energy Policy Act of 2005, whereby underground injections accompanying fracking are not regulated by the Safe Drinking Water Act. Under this exception, the federal government does not provide sufficient oversight for toxic substances that are used to fracture wells. A second exception is related to water pollution during shale gas production that could cause contamination of surface waters by wastewater or other materials. Shale gas producers have been granted an exception from the National Pollutant Discharge Elimination System permit requirements of the Clean Water Act.

The third exception is a provision that exempts "drilling fluids, produced waters, and other wastes associated with the exploration, development, or production" of oil and gas from the definition of "hazardous wastes" regulated under the Resource Conservation and Recovery Act. Despite the possibility that a mishap could cause toxic petroleum materials to be discharged, there is no cradle-to-grave regulation of these wastes. The fourth exception regarding shale gas production involves the reporting requirements of the Comprehensive Environmental Response, Compensation and Liability Act (CERCLA). This act exempts natural gas, natural gas liquids, liquefied natural gas, or synthetic gas usable for fuel from hazardous substances that set in motion CERCLA's reporting requirements.

Shale gas production has also secured an exception from the federal Emergency Planning and Community Right-to-Know Act, so that oil and gas operators do not need to report annual releases of toxic chemicals, except for cases where a sufficient quantity of a hazardous substance is released. The absence of a federal disclosure requirement allows drilling operators to use hazardous chemicals in close proximity to people and communities without sufficient information for use by responders to emergencies or people exposed to toxic chemicals. In the absence of sufficient federal protection from hazards and risks that accompany shale gas production, individual states have had to decide how to address the risks of human health problems and environmental degradation accompanying shale gas production.

## 2. Reliance on State Regulations

As might be expected, states have addressed shale gas production quite differently. Americans in states such as Texas familiar with gas extraction welcomed the development of shale gas production under existing governmental oversight. Where energy exploration has not been as prevalent such as in Illinois and New York, states proceed more cautiously. Populations in these states have major concerns about potential health and environmental damages.

The state-by-state regulation of environmental issues accompanying shale gas production suggests that full consideration of the cumulative impact of extraction activities on downstream areas may not receive adequate attention. Individual states may neglect the successive, incremental, and combined effects of drilling activities within their jurisdiction that affect other areas. In the absence of accurate accountings of cumulative impacts, effective science will not be captured in a state's policy making, so that regional sustainability and ecological integrity will suffer. Concerns exist that there may be future health problems that are not being addressed. Moreover, data suggest that states have shirked enforcement responsibilities for violations of regulatory provisions by drilling companies, allowing spills to adversely affect people and the environment.

## 3. Landowner Compensation

Private property ownership in the United States entails ownership of mineral rights. In some cases, the mineral rights have been split from surface rights so that there are different owners. But whoever owns the mineral rights is able to contract with a private firm that wants to develop the minerals. In arranging for contracts for oil and gas leases, the firms write the contracts, and the owners of the oil and gas resources have little say about what is in the contract. Numerous disputes have arisen concerning the use of leased properties, releases of pollutants, and the payment of royalties. As might be expected, the oil and gas leases are generally favorable to the interests of the firms writing the leases. Moreover, states support the development of oil and gas reserves. Their laws tend to be biased in favor of drilling firms and others developing the resources. The following case discloses that the common law contract remedy of canceling a contract due to a breach of contract does not apply to oil and gas leases.

*Armstrong v. Chesapeake Exploration*
Court of Appeals of Ohio, Fifth Appellate District

*Who is suing?* _____

*Who is being sued?* _____

*For what?* _____

*What is the issue on appeal?* _____

Plaintiffs-Appellants Myron and Nikki Armstrong became the owners of approximately 61 acres of real property located in Tuscarawas County, Ohio (Property). When the Armstrongs acquired the Property, it was encumbered by an oil and gas lease (Lease) entered by and between the Edwards as lessors and Stocker & Sitler Leasehold Corporation as lessee. Under the terms of the Lease, the owner of the Armstrong Property was required to notify the lessor of any change in ownership of the property. Additionally, among other things, the express terms of the Lease required that a 1/8 royalty be paid by the lessee for all oil and/or gas produced from the unitized property.

Following the execution of the Lease, the Armstrong Property was unitized with surrounding property to create a drilling unit. An oil and/or gas well was drilled on one of the properties within the drilling unit; however, no oil and/or gas well has ever been drilled on the Armstrong Property. Prior to Appellants obtaining ownership of the Armstrong Property, the Lease was assigned to Appellee Belden & Blake. According to Appellants, upon purchase [of] the Property, they promptly provided notice of the change in ownership as required under the terms of the Lease. Appellants maintain that Appellees have failed to pay any of the required royalty payments due and owing to Appellants throughout their entire ownership of the Armstrong Property.

Appellants filed an action seeking the cancellation of the oil and gas lease for breach of its express terms. Appellees, filed a Motion to Dismiss for failure to state a claim upon which relief could be granted. The trial court granted Appellees' Motion to Dismiss. Appellants appeal, contending that the trial court erred in granting Appellees' motion to dismiss. We disagree. This case involves the interpretation of a written contract. The rights and remedies of the parties to an oil or gas lease must be determined by the terms of the written instrument, and the terms of the contract with the law applicable to such terms must govern the rights and remedies of the parties.

The oil and gas lease in this case does not contain an express provision empowering the lessor or royalty owner to declare a forfeiture thereof for the nonpayment of oil and gas royalties from production. Absent specific language in the lease, nonpayment of royalties is not grounds for cancellation of an oil and gas lease. In a recent case involving the issue of forfeiture of an oil and gas lease for failure to pay minimum royalty payments, the Fourth District Court of Appeals stated:

> *We explained the distinction between leases with forfeiture clauses and those*
> *without in an earlier case. A principal argument advanced by appellants in*

> *asserting summary judgment was improper is that the failure to pay royalties, absent a forfeiture clause in the lease so providing, gives rise only to an action for damages and not cancellation. This, indeed, is the general rule. The majority view is failure to pay royalty or for injury to the land as provided by the lease will not give the lessors sufficient grounds to declare a forfeiture, unless by the express terms of the lease they are given that right and power.*

We find no error in the trial court's dismissal of Appellants' Complaint. Appellants' sole Assignment of Error is overruled. The judgment of the Court of Common Pleas is affirmed.

## Questions

1. Why did the Armstrongs feel the lease should be canceled?
2. With respect to oil and gas leases, what is unitization?
3. How does the court's interpretation of contract law affect the result?
4. What do the Armstrongs need to do to recover their royalty payments?
5. What error was made by the Armstrongs' counsel?

## 4. Public Disclosure of Fracking Chemicals

Shale gas production involves the use of chemicals and the release of flowback and production waters. In overseeing risks that accompany shale gas extraction, states have adopted reporting requirements for operators under which proprietary information and trade secrets need not be disclosed. Despite the presence of toxic substances in fracturing fluids and wastes in communities, information about fracturing fluids may be kept secret at individual drilling sites. Flowback fluids and waste from fracturing may contain additional toxins, including arsenic, selenium, radionuclides, and other inorganics. A mishap or accident involving shale gas production might expose persons to a hazard that causes serious damages.

Information on what chemicals were used is vital in determining whether concentrations of released chemicals from fractured wells cause health problems to individuals and their offspring. The information is important for governments in adopting policies to keep people and the environment safe. The disclosure of fracturing chemicals is also needed by emergency personnel responding to releases and by persons who are exposed to releases. The nondisclosure of fracturing chemicals may be contrasted with the required disclosure of similar potentially harmful chemicals in household cleaners that are required to be labeled. Additional disclosure requirements might also have long-term benefits for the industry by facilitating environmental safety, encouraging the development of more environmentally friendly fracturing fluids, and encouraging the reuse of produced waters.

Energy production involves accidents. Although governments have enacted laws and regulations in response to many of the issues, citizens still have difficulty finding information to make considered choices on avoiding potential exposure to pollutants for oil and gas development. Governments are often eager to assist firms that make major contributions to a state's economy, and thereby have not been forthright in learning whether there will be long-term damages from hydrocarbon development activities. The following case concerns the discovery of information on water supplies potentially damaged by drilling in Pennsylvania, and the state agency's refusal to disclose information.

### *Commonwealth of Pennsylvania v. Legere*
Pennsylvania Commonwealth Court

*Who is suing?* _____

*Who is being sued?* _____

*For what?* _____

*What is the issue on appeal?* _____

The Pennsylvania Department of Environmental Protection (DEP) petitions for review of an Office of Open Records' (OOR) final determination, ordering DEP to release all responsive records requested by Laura Legere and The Times-Tribune (collectively Legere) under the Pennsylvania Right-to-Know Law (RTKL) within thirty days. DEP raises five issues for this Court's review: (1) whether the OOR erred when it concluded that Legere's request was sufficiently specific; (2) whether the OOR should have considered the burden on DEP to locate and produce the records when determining whether Legere's request was sufficiently specific; (3) whether the OOR erred in directing DEP to produce the records when DEP had produced evidence that it conducted a good faith search; (4) whether Section 705 of the RTKL excuses DEP's obligation to produce the records; and (5) whether DEP provided sufficient evidentiary support to assert RTKL exemptions. We affirm.

Legere submitted requests under the RTKL to three DEP regional offices, seeking:

> *All Act 223, Section 208 determination letters issued by the DEP since January 1 as well as the orders issued by DEP to well operators in relation to those determination letters, as described in Section 208 of the Oil and Gas Act. If DEP finds that the pollution or diminution was caused by the drilling, alteration or operation activities or if it presumes the well operator responsible for pollution ..., then it shall issue such orders to the well operator as are necessary to assure compliance with subsection (a).*

On October 13, 2011, DEP's regional offices partially granted the requests, providing access to some responsive records and denied the remainder of the requests, stating in part:

*Your request is denied in part because it is not sufficiently specific. Your request for Section 208 determination letters issued since January 1, and the orders issued by DEP to well operators in relation to those determination letters, fails to provide specific names, geographic locations, well or permit numbers, and/or complaint numbers. Absent this specific information, we have no systematic way to search for the records that you request. Namely, our files are not maintained in such a fashion that allows us to look for all Section 208 determination letters and corresponding orders without having the specific information identified above. Consequently, we are unable to determine if other responsive records exist for the time period that you have requested. Additionally, some of the records that might potentially be included in your request may also be exempt under the RTKL. Furthermore, records may also be exempt as privileged under the attorney-client privilege or attorney-client work product.*

Legere appealed the three responses to the OOR. The OOR consolidated the appeals and permitted both parties to supplement the record. On November 17, DEP submitted a position statement and three notarized affidavits. On December 5, the OOR issued its final determination, finding: (1) that Legere's request was sufficiently specific; and (2) that DEP failed to establish that any exemption(s) or privilege protects the responsive records. Accordingly, the OOR ordered DEP to provide all responsive records to Legere within thirty days. DEP appealed to this Court.

DEP first argues that the OOR erred when it concluded that Legere's request was sufficiently specific under Section 703 of the RTKL. We disagree. Section 703 of the RTKL provides in pertinent part: "A written request should identify or describe the records sought with sufficient specificity to enable the agency to ascertain which records are being requested." DEP asserts that Legere's request is overbroad. However, specific types of documents have been requested, documents that are created by DEP pursuant to statute. Legere has requested a clearly-defined universe of documents. There are no judgments to be made as to whether the documents are "related" to the request. The documents either are or are not Section 208 determination letters. The documents either are or are not orders issued by DEP arising from Section 208 determination letters. Legere's request was clearly sufficiently specific, given that DEP provided some of the responsive records.

DEP next argues that the OOR should have considered the burden on DEP when determining whether Legere's request was insufficiently specific, that responding to Legere's request would be extremely burdensome and, thus, her request should be deemed overbroad. We disagree.

The fact that a request is burdensome does not deem it overbroad, although it may be considered as a factor in such a determination. In the instant matter, Legere's request is not overbroad, but instead seeks a clearly delineated group of documents. The fact that DEP does not catalogue or otherwise organize Section 208 determination letters or corresponding orders in a way that permits them to be easily located does not render the request insufficiently specific.

DEP next argues that Section 901 of the RTKL merely requires it to conduct a good faith search for the documents requested, and that the OOR erred when it disregarded DEP's affidavits and ordered DEP to produce the requested documents. We disagree. Section 901 of the RTKL requires an agency to make a good faith effort to determine if the record requested is a public record and whether the agency has possession, custody or control of the identified record, and to respond as promptly as possible under the circumstances existing at the time of the request. However, here the issue is where within DEP those determination letters and orders may be found. DEP's affidavits indicate that it used various methods to attempt to locate the Section 208 determination letters and orders. Those steps did not include an actual physical search of its files. Because the requested Section 208 determination letters and related orders do exist, and are within the possession of DEP, absent an exemption, they must be produced. Accordingly, we conclude that the OOR did not err when it ordered the records to be produced. For the aforementioned reasons, the OOR's order is affirmed.

## Questions

1. Why did the court feel that a request for Section 208 determination letters was specific?
2. Does the administrative burden imposed by a request address specificity?
3. Why did the court conclude DEP had not conducted a good faith search for the requested records?
4. What caused the court to conclude that DEP failed to offer evidence supporting the claims for exemption?
5. Do you think the Pennsylvania DEP was typical of state agencies overseeing gas drilling?

# Using Biofuels to Produce Energy

In the wake of concern about dependency on foreign oil and other sources of energy, biofuels are expected to become more important as energy sources. Brazil has been the pioneer in the use of biofuel, becoming completely energy independent and demonstrating to the world the potential benefits of substituting biofuels for fossil fuels. The United States in recent years has developed a strong biofuel industry based on corn. The European Union and countries around the world are rapidly developing their own biofuel potentials.

However, the production of alternative energy sources may be accompanied with problems. The use of crops for biofuel productions may jeopardize food supplies or result in increased food prices. Experts feel that the prices of sugar, corn, rapeseed oil, palm oil, and soybeans have already increased due to their use as biofuels. Accompanying the need for more food is the possibility of clearing forested areas for cropland. With the loss of forested areas from burning, more carbon may enter the atmosphere. In some areas, the introduction of monocultures, which detract from biodiversity, is another concern.

The Energy Policy Act of 2005 includes the first federal mandate that liquid biofuels be purchased by motorists. Subsequent encouragement was given to biofuels that replace gasoline and diesel fuels to prevent the release of carbon stored over geologic time periods. Renewable fuels are divided into "additional renewable fuel" and "advanced biofuel." Additional renewable fuels are those produced from renewable biomass. Advanced biofuels are qualified to those that have at least 50 percent less than baseline life-cycle greenhouse gas (GHG) emissions. Advanced biofuels do not include ethanol derived from cornstarch. This means that the legislation for biofuels differentiates between biofuels to offer more support for biofuels that more markedly reduce GHG emissions. The regulations set forth requirements for the EPA to administer a renewable fuel program, with distinct production volumes for additional renewable fuel and advanced biofuel. Thus, there are changing provisions that provide tax credits, favorable loans, and subsidy programs concerning the encouragement of the production and refining of biofuel.

These legislative provisions on biofuels arguably represent a successful lobbying effort by agricultural interest groups. Because the production of corn and soybean feedstock uses fossil fuels, biofuels may do little to reduce GHGs. It is generally believed that corn ethanol generates a modest positive energy return. Moreover, negative externalities may offset the benefits of biofuel production. Corn production is accompanied by the use of nitrogen fertilizer and pesticides that may end up in water supplies. Corn uses a lot of water, and production areas relying on irrigation may be lowering their water tables. Ethanol must be blended with gasoline and cannot be pumped through existing gas pipelines. Thus, ethanol is shipped to locations by barge, train, or truck, blended with gasoline, and sold. It requires investments in an infrastructure developed using fossil fuels that again detracts from its ability to reduce GHG omissions.

Another issue involves the US protectionist approach to biofuel policies. The United States has adopted various limitations on the importation of ethanol from other countries, most notably Brazil and nations in the Caribbean, which can produce ethanol from sugarcane more cheaply than US producers. These provisions have changed over time.

Corn and sugarcane are not the only sources of ethanol; it can also be produced from trees, forest residues, and agricultural residues not specifically grown for food. Nonfood inputs would allow marginal lands to be used for feedstock production that would not adversely affect food production. Moreover, cellulosic ethanol requires fewer pesticides and less fertilizer than corn-based ethanol, and offers the potential for a significant net energy balance. To convert these cellulosic biomass sources to ethanol involves significant pretreatment or mechanical separation that increases the costs of production. It is believed that cellulosic ethanol could be produced using less nonrenewable energy than corn-based ethanol. If hybrid poplar or switchgrass is gasified to produce electricity, rather than being used to produce ethanol, the net energy obtained is doubled because the process of converting switchgrass to gas—and then producing electricity—is much more efficient than converting switchgrass to ethanol.

There is not a single renewable energy source that can replace fossil energy. Thus, most support a national strategy with multiple sources of energy. Diversification is the key. We need to invest in new technologies that increase energy efficiency, including gasoline and diesel hybrids. The United States must become more conservation minded in constructing and retrofitting buildings and developing public transportation.

## Discussion Questions

1. With respect to coal, what do current developments portend for coal's future use?
2. What do downward projections for natural gas prices mean for US energy policy?
3. How would you provide incentives for renewable sources of fuels, and why?
4. Are the provisions of our building codes concerning insulation and windows sufficient?
5. Governments may impose severance taxes or impact fees on extracted hydrocarbons. What are the reasons for selecting a tax or a fee? What are the merits of each option?
6. Why might one conclude that US state governments have underinvested in good management practices governing shale gas development?

## Image Credit

# CHAPTER EIGHTEEN
## The Regulation of Pesticides

## Learning Objectives

- *Describe how the EPA regulates pesticides.*
- *Define liability for causing pesticide spray drift to damage another's property.*
- *Summarize a manufacturer's liability for damages to users of a pesticide.*
- *Explain what a registrant of a new pesticide must show concerning potential damages to humans or the environment.*

## Regulating Pesticide Usage

Food production relies heavily on the use of pesticides for growing crops and raising animals. Pesticides are also used extensively to control pests carrying disease organisms, such as mosquitoes carrying West Nile virus. Data suggest that approximately 7.7 billion pounds of pesticides are used each year in the world. In the United States, agricultural uses of pesticides account for nearly 80 percent of pesticides applied. Most pesticides are carcinogens, and their widespread usage raises concern about the possibility of negative effects on people and the environment. Given dangers posed by pesticides, Congress enacted the Federal Insecticide, Fungicide, and Rodenticide Act (FIFRA) to oversee the manufacture, distribution, and use of pesticides. Under FIFRA, the Environmental Protection Agency (EPA) is responsible for overseeing the registration, labeling, and use of pesticides.

A major objective of FIFRA is to protect public health and the environment. Pesticide registration is a scientific and administrative procedure through which the EPA examines the ingredients of the pesticide, the particular site or crop on which it is to be used, the amount and frequency of its use, and storage and disposal practices. Applications delineate the intended target crop, claims of pesticide effects, and scientific data supporting the claims. Separate registration is required for different crops, pests, and dosage levels. While the initial provisions of FIFRA were primarily implemented in order to monitor the efficacy of pesticides, subsequent provisions increased the prominence of environmental and health concerns. Regulations adopted pursuant to FIFRA set forth limitations that deny registration of unsafe or unproven pesticides.

Furthermore, FIFRA addresses applications of pesticides that may adversely affect the environment. Only pesticides that can be used in accordance with widespread and commonly recognized practices without causing "unreasonable adverse effects on the environment" are allowed. Unreasonable adverse effects on the environment are further defined to address risks to man and the environment. Adverse effects consider economic, social, and environmental costs and benefits of the use of a pesticide. Thereby, FIFRA sets forth a cost-benefit analysis for analyzing the risks that accompany the use of pesticides to deny registration to those that pose too many dangers to humans or the environment. The cost-benefit analysis offers a quantitative approach to addressing risk, but controversies exist on how to evaluate ecological values, community values, and normative considerations. In declining to fully consider these costs, cost-benefit analyses may be biased in favor of pesticide manufacturers.

Regulations under FIFRA govern the authorized use of pesticides pursuant to their registration and label. Any application beyond those authorized by the label violates

Fig. 18.1 Crop scouting for pests, including weeds and insects, can help reduce pesticide usage.

FIFRA. FIFRA regulations also enunciate directions for the use of pesticides to minimize unreasonable adverse effects on the environment. Pesticide applications deviating from dosage levels, concentrations, timing, or other specifics violate label instructions and so are contrary to federal law. However, applications of pesticides on land and in water are not monitored by any governmental official, and sometimes pesticides are misapplied, causing injuries. The EPA estimates that 10,000–20,000 physician-diagnosed pesticide poisonings occur each year among US agricultural workers.

Under FIFRA, states have adopted regulations addressing the misbranding of pesticides and pesticide-related devices in an effort to prohibit misuse that could lead to health or environmental damages. The term "misbranded" applies to any pesticide or device with false or misleading labeling that is an imitation or is distributed under another pesticide's name, or fails to include required information in a conspicuous and understandable fashion. Misbranding also applies to any pesticide labeling that fails to include required information. Furthermore, if the pesticide contains substances that are highly toxic to people, it must be labeled clearly and explicitly with certain requirements, such as containing the word *poison* in red lettering.

Pesticides must be registered under FIFRA, and multiple-year registration is available. Often, a pesticide applicant must also comply with state regulations. Generally, three distinct licensure requirements are enumerated: pesticide contractor's licenses, certified private applicators' licenses, and certified commercial pesticide applicators' licenses. Persons applying pesticides to the land of another must obtain a contractor's license. Applicants for a contractor's license must provide pertinent information such as name, address, and information on their pesticide-applying equipment. Applicators' licenses are required for individuals buying, using, or supervising the use of any pesticide as a private applicator, unless the individual is licensed as a certified private applicator or is acting under the direct supervision of someone who is. Applicants for a private applicator's license shall demonstrate competency to apply restricted-use pesticides. Persons are not allowed to purchase or use any pesticide as a commercial applicator, unless that person is properly licensed. Exemptions exist for farmers applying general-use pesticides for themselves or for farmer neighbors. Veterinarians and experimental research personnel may also be exempt from the licensure provisions.

Persons who discard pesticides are no longer using them for their intended purpose, so disposal must conform to requirements governing waste disposal. Because most pesticides are toxic, their disposal must comply with the federal Resource Conservation and Recovery Act's hazardous waste regulations. Given many sources of small quantities of pesticide waste, relaxed regulations are prescribed in Part 273 of the Code of Federal Regulations for their disposal. Stocks of unused pesticide products collected and managed as part of a waste pesticide collection program do not have to meet the paperwork normally required of generators disposing of hazardous waste. Nearly every state has become involved in collection efforts to remove unwanted pesticides from storage and to dispose of them safely.

# Preemption of State Law

A significant issue associated with actions to recover damages from pesticide usage involves federal preemption. FIFRA preempts some state causes of action to limit recoveries of persons suffering damages associated with pesticide usage. The following case highlights the complexities of federal preemption over actions based on state law.

### *Bates v. Dow Agrosciences LLC*
United States Supreme Court

*Who is suing?* _____

*Who is being sued?* _____

*For what?* _____

*What is the issue on appeal?* _____

Petitioners are 29 Texas peanut farmers who allege that their crops were severely damaged by the application of respondent's newly marketed pesticide named "Strongarm." The question presented is whether the Federal Insecticide, Fungicide, and Rodenticide Act (FIFRA) preempts their state-law claims for damages.

Pursuant to its authority under FIFRA, the Environmental Protection Agency (EPA) conditionally registered Strongarm thereby granting respondent (Dow) permission to sell this pesticide—a weed killer—in the United States. According to petitioners—whose version of the facts we assume to be true at this stage—Dow knew, or should have known, that Strongarm would stunt the growth of peanuts in soils with pH levels of 7.0 or greater. Nevertheless, Strongarm's label stated, "Use of Strongarm is recommended in all areas where peanuts are grown," and Dow's agents made equivalent representations in their sales pitches to petitioners. When petitioners applied Strongarm on their farms—whose soils have pH levels of 7.2 or higher, as is typical in western Texas—the pesticide severely damaged their peanut crops while failing to control the growth of weeds. The farmers reported these problems to Dow.

Meanwhile, Dow reregistered its Strongarm label with EPA a year after petitioners' crops were damaged. EPA approved a "supplemental" label that was for distribution and use only in the states of New Mexico, Oklahoma and Texas, the three States in which peanut farmers experienced crop damage. This new label contained the following warning: "Do not apply Strongarm to soils with a pH of 7.2 or greater."

After unsuccessful negotiations with Dow, petitioners gave Dow notice of their intent to bring suit as required by the Texas Deceptive Trade Practices-Consumer Protection Act (Texas DTPA). In response, Dow filed a declaratory judgment action in Federal District Court, asserting that petitioners' claims were expressly or impliedly preempted by FIFRA. Petitioners, in turn, brought counterclaims, including tort claims sounding in strict liability and negligence. They also alleged fraud, breach of warranty, and violation of the Texas DTPA. The District Court granted Dow's motion for summary judgment.

The Court of Appeals affirmed. It read FIFRA's § 136v(b) to preempt any state-law claim in which a judgment against Dow would induce it to alter its product label. The court held that because petitioners' fraud, warranty, and deceptive trade practices claims focused on oral statements by Dow's agents that did not differ from statements made on the product's label, success on those claims would give Dow a "strong incentive" to change its label. Those claims were thus preempted. The court also found that petitioners' strict liability claim alleging defective design was essentially a "disguised" failure-to-warn claim and therefore preempted. We vacate the court's judgment.

Under FIFRA, a manufacturer seeking to register a pesticide must submit a proposed label to EPA as well as certain supporting data. The agency will register the pesticide if it determines that the pesticide is efficacious; that it will not cause unreasonable adverse effects on humans and the environment; and that its label complies with the statute's prohibition on misbranding. A pesticide is "misbranded" if its label contains a statement that is "false or misleading in any particular," including a "false or misleading statement" concerning the efficacy of the pesticide. A pesticide is also misbranded if its label does not contain adequate instructions for use, or if its label omits necessary warnings or cautionary statements. Because it is unlawful under the statute to sell a pesticide that is registered but nevertheless misbranded, manufacturers have a continuing obligation to adhere to FIFRA's labeling requirements.

In 1978, Congress amended FIFRA in response to EPA's concern that its evaluation of pesticide efficacy during the registration process diverted too many resources from its task of assessing the environmental and health dangers posed by pesticides. Congress addressed this problem by authorizing EPA to waive data requirements pertaining to efficacy. This general waiver was in place at the time of Strongarm's registration; thus, EPA never passed on the accuracy of the statement in Strongarm's original label recommending the product's use "in all areas where peanuts are grown."

In *Wisconsin Public Intervenor v. Mortier*, we considered a claim that § 136v(b) preempted a small town's ordinance requiring a special permit for the aerial application of pesticides. Although the ordinance imposed restrictions not required by FIFRA or any EPA regulation, we unanimously rejected the preemption claim. In our opinion we noted that FIFRA was not a sufficiently comprehensive statute to justify an inference that Congress had occupied the field to the exclusion of the States. States have ample authority to review pesticide labels to ensure that they comply with both federal and state labeling requirements.

The prohibitions in § 136v(b) apply only to "requirements." An occurrence that merely motivates an optional decision does not qualify as a requirement. The Court of Appeals was therefore quite wrong when it assumed that any event, such as a jury verdict, that might "induce" a pesticide manufacturer to change its label should be viewed as a requirement. The Court of Appeals did, however, correctly hold that the term "requirements" in § 136v(b) reaches beyond positive enactments, such as statutes and regulations, to embrace common-law duties.

For a particular state rule to be preempted, it must satisfy two conditions. First, it must be a requirement "for labeling or packaging"; rules governing the design of a product, for example, are not preempted. Second, it must impose a labeling or packaging requirement that is "in addition to or different from those required under this subchapter." A state regulation requiring the word "poison" to appear in red letters, for instance, would not be preempted if an EPA regulation imposed the same requirement.

It is perfectly clear that many of the common-law rules upon which petitioners rely do not satisfy the "requirement" condition. Rules that require manufacturers to design reasonably safe products, to use due care in conducting appropriate testing of their products, to market products free of manufacturing defects, and to honor their express warranties or other contractual commitments plainly do not qualify as requirements for "labeling or packaging." Dow's express warranty was located on Strongarm's label. The label stated: "Dow AgroSciences warrants that this product conforms to the chemical description on the label and is reasonably fit for the purposes stated on the label." Because this common-law rule does not require the manufacturer to make an express warranty, the rule does not impose a requirement "for labeling or packaging."

Unlike their other claims, petitioners' fraud and negligent-failure-to-warn claims are premised on common-law rules that qualify as "requirements for labeling or packaging." These rules set a standard for a product's labeling that the Strongarm label is alleged to have violated by containing false statements and inadequate warnings. Section 136v(b) prohibits only state-law labeling and packaging requirements that are "in addition to or different from" the labeling and packaging requirements under FIFRA. Thus, a state-law labeling requirement is not preempted by § 136v(b) if it is equivalent to, and fully consistent with, FIFRA's misbranding provisions. Petitioners argue that their claims based on fraud and failure to warn are not preempted because these common-law duties are equivalent to FIFRA's requirements that a pesticide label not contain "false or misleading" statements, or inadequate instructions or warnings. We agree with petitioners.

In sum, under our interpretation, § 136v(b) retains a narrow, but still important, role. In the main, it preempts competing state labeling standards—imagine 50 different labeling regimes prescribing the color, font size, and wording of warnings—that would create significant inefficiencies for manufacturers. The provision also preempts any statutory or common-law rule that would impose a labeling requirement that diverges from those set out in FIFRA and its implementing regulations. It does not, however, preempt any state rules that are fully consistent with federal requirements.

Having settled on our interpretation of § 136v(b), it still remains to be decided whether that provision preempts petitioners' fraud and failure-to-warn claims. Because we have not received sufficient briefing on this issue, which involves questions of Texas law, we remand it to the Court of Appeals. We emphasize that a state-law labeling requirement must in fact be equivalent to a requirement under FIFRA in order to survive preemption. The judgment of the Court of Appeals is vacated, and the case is remanded for further proceedings consistent with this opinion.

## Questions

1. What is misbranding under FIFRA?
2. Why does FIFRA contain a preemption clause?
3. What is the legal significance of the change of label that said: "Do not apply Strongarm to soils with a pH of 7.2 or greater?"
4. Why does the court discuss *Wisconsin Public Intervenor v. Mortier*?
5. Why isn't defective design preempted?
6. What was Dow's express warranty?
7. Why might petitioners' fraud and failure-to-warn claims not be preempted by FIFRA?

# Pesticide Drift

Increasing demands for food production, consumer support for organic food, and outbreaks of mosquito-borne diseases have been accompanied by controversies involving the use of pesticides and spray drift. Spray drift is the physical movement of pesticide particles through the air from a target site to a non–target site and includes dust drift. When spray drift damages a neighboring property, the issue is whether misuse of the pesticide should give rise to liability. For example, spray drift can result in financial losses when an organic crop is disqualified from being marketed under an organic certification program and the producer's land must be withdrawn from organic production.

Agricultural production decisions involving changes in pesticide use—including the adoption of organic practices—require consideration of risks associated with damages from airborne pesticide particulates. Spray drift transported to neighboring properties can cause injuries to persons, land, water, crops, and the environment. While people have the right to use pesticides on their private properties in compliance with the law, there are limitations under American jurisprudence on causing injuries or damages to neighboring properties. However, recovering damages accompanying the misuse of pesticides is challenging. Persons claiming damages must meet the requirements of a recognized legal cause of action. Due to the demanding proof of showing a connection between the use of pesticides and specific injury to crops, property owners suffering damages from a neighbor's use of pesticides may find it expensive and difficult to secure recompense.

Five major causes of action may be identified for claims against applicators of pesticides causing damages to crops: strict liability, trespass, negligence, violation of governmental declarations, and nuisance. However, accompanying these causes of action are defenses that preclude recoveries in many cases. With low or medium rates of success at securing damages under each cause of action, it may be difficult for claimants with injuries to establish a foundation for recovering damages. Yet injured plaintiffs continue to file drift cases and may allege damages against third parties such as occurred in the following case.

### *Bader Farms, Inc. v. Monsanto Co.*
US District Court, Eastern District of Missouri

*Who is suing?* _____

*Who is being sued?* _____

*For what?* _____

*What is the issue on appeal?* _____

Plaintiffs are engaged in a massive peach growing business in Dunklin County, Missouri. Defendant is well known for its development of genetically engineered (GE) seeds in addition to its development of herbicides. At issue in this case is the commercial release and sale of two of defendant's GE seeds, Roundup Ready 2 Xtend soybeans (Xtend soybeans) and Bollgard II XtendFlex cotton seeds (Xtend cotton). The seeds were subject to federal regulation by the Animal and Plant Health Inspection Service and following an investigation of their safety, they were deregulated, which allowed them to be sold. Xtend cotton seeds were first sold in 2015, and Xtend soybean seeds were first sold in 2016.

The sales occurred, however, before the Environmental Protection Agency approved the seeds' corresponding weed-killing herbicide, XtendiMax, for commercial release. Plaintiffs allege that defendant violated standard industry practice and committed a number of tortious acts by releasing its new GE seeds without such an existing, approved herbicide on the market as a "complete crop system." The foreseeable result of this negligent act, plaintiffs contend, was that third-party farmers were enticed to spray dicamba—a generic herbicide—onto their new GE seed crops to curb inevitable weed growth, ignoring product warning labels for the GE seeds as well as prohibitions under federal and state law. Further, because dicamba "drifts" onto surrounding properties, the spraying and drift of dicamba caused millions of dollars in damage to plaintiffs' peach orchards.

The Xtend seeds are unusual because they are resistant to the herbicide dicamba, so that dicamba will not harm the Xtend seed crops. Dicamba has been manufactured and marketed since 1967 by several companies, but not Monsanto. Before 2015, dicamba was not often used by American farmers in-crop because it is a "highly volatile" herbicide that "is prone to drift" onto surrounding properties. Dicamba is toxic to all broadleaf plants such as fruits, nuts, vegetables, and notably, cotton and soybeans that are not genetically engineered to withstand it.

Apparently, defendant's new dicamba technology, XtendiMax, will not share the same drift problems as old dicamba. If applied correctly, XtendiMax will kill broadleaf weeds on the fields of dicamba-resistant crops and will not drift onto the property of neighboring landowners. Plaintiffs allege that defendant invested over a billion dollars into the development of XtendiMax because of the rise of "super weeds" that are resistant to Roundup, another Monsanto herbicide. Roundup, which contains glyphosate, is a non-selective herbicide, meaning it can kill most plants. Dicamba can be used in conjunction with Roundup, and together, these two herbicides will kill most weeds, increasing the yield of the farmer's crops.

Plaintiffs acknowledge that, at all relevant times of this lawsuit, it was a violation of state and federal law to use old dicamba on the seeds and the use of dicamba on the seeds was expressly prohibited by product use labels on the bags containing the GE seeds. Plaintiffs also concede that the defendant did not manufacture, distribute, sell, or apply the dicamba sprayed by the third-party farmers on their crops that drifted onto plaintiff's property. Nonetheless, plaintiffs claim they were harmed by defendant's release of the Xtend seeds because it was foreseeable that third-party farmers who purchased the seeds would illegally spray older formulations of dicamba onto their own crops to kill weeds, and that dicamba drifted onto plaintiff's property, causing millions of dollars of damages.

To prevail, plaintiffs must establish that defendant's actions proximately caused plaintiffs' injury. Proximate causation is found when the defect in a product is the cause or act of which the injury was the natural and probable consequence. When negligence appears merely to have brought about a condition of affairs or a situation in which another and entirely independent and efficient agency intervenes to cause the injury, the latter is deemed the direct and proximate cause and the former only the indirect or remote cause.

In the case at hand, even if Monsanto was negligent in its release of the GE seeds without a corresponding herbicide, it appears that its conduct was simply too attenuated to establish proximate cause. Instead, plaintiffs' injuries stem directly from an intervening and superseding cause—the unforeseeable independent acts by the third-party farmers who unlawfully sprayed dicamba on their crops. Again, this is not a case in which a plaintiff's use or a third-party's use of a defendant's defective product caused damage to plaintiff, because Monsanto did not manufacture, sell or apply the dicamba. And it is not as if plaintiffs otherwise have no remedy, because obviously they have a cause of action against the farmers, themselves, for unlawfully applying dicamba.

To the extent that the third-party farmers' unlawful conduct was at all foreseeable because dicamba was an available herbicide and the new GE seeds were dicamba-resistant, that foreseeability was wholly negated by the GE seeds' product warning labels, prominently highlighted on all bags of cotton and soybeans sold. Not only do the labels expressly forbid in bold print the application of dicamba to the GE seed crops, they also make clear that to do so is a violation of federal and state law. In view of these warnings and prohibitions, it was not foreseeable that the farmers would resort to the unlawful use of dicamba.

In fact, however, the adequacy of a warning, like proximate cause itself, may be determined as a matter of law if the facts and circumstances warrant it. It is this Court's opinion that the warning was adequate as a matter of law, at least for the purpose of negating plaintiffs' claim that the release of GE seeds was the proximate cause of the damage to plaintiffs' orchards. This Court will treat the defendant's motion to dismiss as a motion for summary judgment. The parties are granted an additional 21 days to present any other material that is pertinent to the adequacy of the warning labels including additional briefing on the issue.

## Questions

1. Why is the defendant being sued when the damage arose from the use of a pesticide it did not manufacture?
2. What appears to be the major cause of action against the defendant?
3. Why did the defendant release its Xtend soybeans prior to the release of the accompanying XtendiMax?
4. Why didn't the plaintiffs sue the persons who wrongfully sprayed with dicamba?
5. Should seed and pesticide manufacturers have more responsibility in precluding potential damages from spray drift? Why or why not?

# Regulation of Pesticides Deposited in Surface Waters

A contemporary issue is whether the use of pesticides accompanied by the deposition of some residues into surface waters may be regulated by the water quality control provisions of the Clean Water Act (CWA). These deposits may occur during aerial applications of pesticides to control agricultural and forest pests, as well as disease-carrying mosquitoes. Under the CWA, a National Pollutant Discharge Elimination System (NPDES) program mandates a permitting system to reduce pollutants entering surface water. This program requires persons discharging pollutants from point sources to apply for an NPDES permit. Each permit sets forth conditions and requirements for allowable discharges to minimize amounts of pollutants entering surface waters.

In the *National Cotton Council of America v. EPA* (2009) lawsuit, a federal court of appeals found that pesticides deposited into navigable water were discharges of pollutants. Because the discharges were pollutants coming from a point source, they needed to be authorized under an NPDES permit. EPA developed a new Pesticide General Permit in 2011 to regulate deposits of pesticides into surface waters, which requires an estimated 365,000 NPDES permits by pesticide applicators, whose applications deposit pesticides in navigable waters due to the Pesticide General Permit. Given the costs associated with securing an NPDES permit, interest groups representing agricultural and public health applicators objected to the Pesticide General Permit. They felt that the costs of securing NPDES permits for registered pesticides were unnecessary. Interest groups advanced a proposed federal law that says the permitting provisions of the CWA do not apply for applications of pesticides registered under FIFRA.

A cursory analysis of the permitting provisions of the CWA supports a finding that they are needed to protect drinking water supplies so that pesticide residues do not adversely affect human health. While FIFRA includes detailed rules covering a variety of issues, the act includes minimal instruction regarding pesticide use in relation to water. None of the FIFRA provisions suggest that the act was intended to preempt other federal legislation addressing pollution, health, and environmental issues.

# Protecting Honeybees

A class of pesticides known as neonicotinoids has created controversy due to their possible damage to beneficial insects, especially honeybees. Some studies have concluded that usage does not affect bees, while other research maintains the high toxicity of these pesticides is adversely affecting bee populations. Subsequently, the use of pesticides containing sulfoxaflor has been scrutinized for their association with adverse effects on honeybees. Neonicotinoids and sulfoxaflor kill insects when they come into contact with the pesticide and when they ingest a plant that has absorbed the pesticide.

A new pesticide can only be used by agricultural producers if it is registered. As previously noted, registration considers environmental damage that may accompany the usage of the pesticide. In the following case, a court found that the EPA had approved the use of sulfoxaflor without adequate testing and so vacated its unconditional registration. Subsequently, agricultural producers have asked the EPA for emergency exemptions so that sulfoxaflor may be used in limited situations.

### *Pollinator Stewardship Council v. U.S. EPA*
US Court of Appeals for the Ninth Circuit, San Francisco

*Who is suing?* _____

*Who is being sued?* _____

*For what?* _____

*What is the issue on appeal?* _____

The Federal Insecticide, Fungicide, and Rodenticide Act (FIFRA) prohibits the sale of pesticides that lack approval and registration by the Environmental Protection Agency (EPA). The EPA may deny an application for registration when necessary to prevent unreasonable adverse effects on the environment. This case is a challenge to the EPA's approval of insecticides containing sulfoxaflor, which initial studies showed were highly toxic to honey bees. Bees are essential to pollinate important crops and in recent years have been dying at alarming rates. Petitioners are commercial bee keepers and bee keeping organizations.

The EPA initially proposed to conditionally register sulfoxaflor and requested additional studies to address gaps in the data regarding the pesticide's effects on bees.

A few months later, however, the EPA unconditionally registered the insecticides with certain mitigation measures and a lowering of the maximum application rate. It did so without obtaining any further studies. Because the EPA's decision to unconditionally register sulfoxaflor was based on flawed and limited data, we conclude that the unconditional approval was not supported by substantial evidence. We therefore vacate the EPA's registration of sulfoxaflor and remand.

FIFRA uses a cost-benefit analysis to ensure that there is no unreasonable risk created for people or the environment from a pesticide. Specifically, FIFRA allows the EPA to deny an application for registration of a pesticide to prevent "unreasonable adverse effects." Unreasonable adverse effects is defined as any unreasonable risk to man or the environment, taking into account the economic, social, and environmental costs and benefits of the use of the pesticide.

In order to register a new pesticide, a manufacturer must submit an application for registration, describing how the pesticide will be used, the claims made of its benefits, the ingredients, and a description of all tests and studies done and the results thereof, concerning the product's health, safety, and environmental effects. The EPA may either "unconditionally" register a pesticide, or "conditionally" register it. The EPA conditionally registers a pesticide when there is insufficient data to evaluate the environmental effects of a new pesticide, permitting the pesticide to be used for a period reasonably sufficient for the generation and submission of required data. Unconditional registration necessarily requires sufficient data to evaluate the environmental risks.

In 2010, Respondent-Intervenor Dow Agrosciences LLC applied for approval of sulfoxaflor. Sulfoxaflor is a new insecticide that targets a range of insects. It acts on the same receptor in insects as does the class of insecticides referred to as neonicotinoids, but its mechanism is distinct from other neonicotinoids. All neonicotinoids kill insects by interfering with their central nervous system, causing tremors, paralysis, and death. Neonicotinoids, including sulfoxaflor, are "systemic" insecticides, which means that they are sprayed onto plants, which then absorb the chemicals and distribute them throughout the plant, into the tissues, pollen, and nectar. Sulfoxaflor and other systemic insecticides therefore kill insects in two different ways: insects die when they come into contact with the pesticide, as when they are sprayed with it, and also when they ingest the plant which has absorbed the pesticide.

Dow asked the EPA to approve sulfoxaflor for use on a variety of different crops. The maximum rate of application that Dow proposed varied depending on the crop, with the highest rate being 0.133 pounds of active ingredient per acre per application. As part of its registration application, Dow submitted studies and data about the effects of sulfoxaflor on various species, including bees. Because of the gaps in data, the EPA declined to give unconditional approval to sulfoxaflor. It proposed instead to conditionally register sulfoxaflor while it collected additional data. As part of its proposed conditional registration, announced in January 2013, the EPA decided to lower the maximum single application rate of sulfoxaflor from 0.133 pounds of active ingredient per acre to 0.09 pounds of active ingredient per acre. The EPA also proposed some other mitigation measures. To address the insufficiency of data, the EPA's proposed conditional registration required Dow to conduct and submit the results of additional tests, specifically a Tier 2 semi-field study for assessing impacts on honey bee colony strength and brood development and an additional residue study to address the nature and magnitude of sulfoxaflor residues on a pollinator-attractive crop (e.g., canola).

Although the EPA announced its decision to propose conditional registration of sulfoxaflor in January 2013, pending receipt of additional data, less than seven months later, on May 6, the EPA decided, to "unconditionally" register sulfoxaflor. It did so even though the record reveals that Dow never completed the requested additional studies. The EPA justified its new unconditional registration decision by the addition of various mitigation measures: lower maximum application rate of 0.09 pounds of active ingredient per acre, longer minimum intervals between applications, and certain crop-specific restrictions on spraying before or during bloom.

The EPA acknowledged that it had classified sulfoxaflor as "very highly toxic" to bees. And it acknowledged that the existing studies were inconclusive as to risks to brood development and colony strength. Although the EPA argued that all of the studies provided relevant data, as noted, only two of the six semi-field studies studied the effects of sulfoxaflor at 0.09 pounds of active ingredient per acre (the application rate that the EPA ultimately unconditionally approved). The EPA nevertheless concluded that while there exists "potential hazard to bees from exposure to sulfoxaflor," that hazard will be appropriately mitigated by "reduced application rates, increased minimum application intervals, and the pollinator-related labeling mitigation." After the EPA announced its final decision to unconditionally register sulfoxaflor, petitioners filed a petition for review with this court, claiming that the EPA's decision was not supported by substantial evidence in the record as a whole.

The EPA's regulations require the EPA to review all relevant data in its possession and to determine that no additional data are necessary to make determinations of no unreasonable adverse effects. The regulations also require "field testing for pollinators" to be submitted as part of an application for registration if data from other sources indicates a risk to honey bees. All parties agree that, because some data indicated a potential risk of adverse effects on honey bee colonies, Dow was required to submit pollinator field testing. What data Dow submitted did not support approval of sulfoxaflor at either the proposed maximum rate of 0.133 pounds of active ingredient per acre or the reduced maximum rate of 0.09 pounds of active ingredient. The record reveals a number of deficiencies in Dow's submitted semi-field studies. All of the studies suffered from an additional significant flaw: they provided inconclusive or insufficient data on the effects of sulfoxaflor on brood development and long-term colony health.

In addition, all of the semi-field studies provided limited information about longer term effects on colony strength. The studies that did not have valid controls measured colony strength before and after application and did not discern a measurable decline in colony strength; however, these studies measured colony health over a relatively short time period. In addition to needing studies on brood development and long-term colony strength, it is clear that the EPA was lacking sufficient data on the impact of sulfoxaflor generally even at the reduced application rate of 0.09 pounds of active ingredient per acre. On the basis of the studies submitted, the EPA lacked substantial evidence to support its conclusions that application of sulfoxaflor at a rate of 0.09 pounds per acre would not have an unreasonable adverse effect on the environment. Without sufficient data, the EPA has no real idea whether sulfoxaflor will cause unreasonable adverse effects on bees, as prohibited by FIFRA. Accordingly, the EPA's decision to register sulfoxaflor was not supported by substantial evidence. We therefore vacate the EPA's unconditional registration of sulfoxaflor and remand for the EPA to obtain further studies and data regarding the effects of sulfoxaflor on bees, as required by EPA regulations.

## Questions

1. Why does the EPA allow conditional registration of pesticides?
2. If there are environmental risks accompanying the use of a pesticide, can the EPA still approve an application for registration? Why?
3. Why did the court decide the EPA could not unconditionally approve the registration of sulfoxaflor in 2013?
4. What was the flaw noted in Dow's submitted semi-field studies?
5. Why did the court find that Dow's measurements of colony health were insufficient?

# The Use of Glyphosate

Considerable concern is being voiced about the use of glyphosate in the production of agricultural foodstuffs. Glyphosate is a phosphonomethyl amino acid herbicide registered to control weeds in various agricultural and nonagricultural settings. It is probably the most heavily used herbicide in the world, and is often known under the trade name "Roundup."

Numerous groups have analyzed environmental and human safety data concerning glyphosate usage and have reached different conclusions. The World Health Organization's International Agency for Research on Cancer determined that glyphosate was a probable carcinogen. However, both the US EPA and the European Food Safety Authority concluded that glyphosate is unlikely to pose a carcinogenic hazard to humans. Moreover, a review of four independent panels that analyzed the carcinogenic potential of glyphosate concluded it was not genotoxic.

However, these studies may not be the last word on the safety of glyphosate. The EPA expects to conclude a complete human health study in 2017. Other researchers feel that the safety standards for glyphosate-based herbicides are outdated and fail to provide assurances that public health is being protected. They urge more biomonitoring for glyphosate and its metabolites, epidemiological studies of groups at risk, and evaluations of herbicide mixtures. It is conceivable that a future study could find a carcinogenic connection between glyphosate and human health.

## Discussion Questions

1.  Do you feel the current regulations of pesticides are adequate to protect human health? Why or why not?
2.  Do you feel the current regulations of pesticides are adequate to protect the health of beneficial insects such as honeybees? Why or why not?
3.  Should the EPA develop a third category of pesticides to add to existing "general use" and "restricted use" pesticides? Why or why not?
4.  Do you feel enough is being done to protect people and property from spray drift? Why or why not?
5.  You feel you are being exposed to too many pesticides. What actions would you take, and why?

## Image Credit

# Section Four

---

# Safeguarding Environmental Quality

# CHAPTER NINETEEN
## Zoning and Land Use

## Learning Objectives

- *Explain how zoning concepts affect environmental quality.*
- *Relate public opinion to changes in zoning.*
- *Explain the relationships of federal, state, and local regulations on land use.*
- *Critique the shortcomings of zoning.*
- *Illustrate qualifications for variances from a zoning ordinance.*

Persons owning property need to be aware of the legal aspects of land-use controls and zoning issues. Governments enact land-use plans and zoning ordinances to provide for the health, safety, welfare, and morals of their citizens. Communities undertake the adoption of land-use planning and zoning due to perceived benefits. Planning and zoning allow communities to control the timing and type of development that occurs within their jurisdiction. Zoning places compatible uses together that enhance real estate values, especially in residential subdivisions. Zoning is important for augmenting safety and limiting risks. It allows for the planning of transportation circulation, controlling amounts of traffic, and decreasing costs for public utilities. Amenities that often accompany zoning include parks and the protection of existing open space.

Communities adopt a comprehensive zoning plan and a corresponding zoning ordinance that govern land uses within the community's jurisdiction. If conditions change, the local government or property owners can request rezoning to change the comprehensive plan. Each state has separate rules for requests to rezone property. These have developed under legislative dictates and judicial decisions. Buildings and property uses in existence prior to adoption of an ordinance that do not meet the requirements of a newly established zone are exempted from compliance. They are considered to be "nonconforming uses" and are allowed to continue, despite the fact that they are not permitted under the ordinance. But if a building is destroyed by fire or the nonconforming use is not continued, the facts present difficult questions. Courts may be asked to rule whether a nonconforming use has ended due to the circumstances of the case.

In adopting zoning provisions and amendments, public notice and hearing requirements apply. The failure of a local government to comply with all public notice requirements will invalidate an ordinance or amendment adopted, even if no prejudice is actually shown. Public notice must contain an adequate description of the property affected, an understandable statement of the action to be considered, and a clear statement about procedures available for interested citizens to comment on the zoning. Required notice requirements for public hearings must be carefully followed. Before a governing body adopts a zoning ordinance or amendment to an ordinance, it may be required to read the title of the ordinance at a public hearing to apprise the public of the scheduled action.

## Relation to the Police Power

A zoning ordinance must have a substantial relation to the promotion of public health, safety, or general welfare, including morals. The constitutional requirement of due process includes a minimum of four separate standards.

I.   The regulations must be designed to promote some public interest that was authorized under the state's police power.

II.  There must be an actual and substantial relationship between the restrictions and a legitimate governmental goal.

III. Even if the regulations advance some such public interest, if excessive hardship to individuals outweighs the public benefits, the restrictions may be invalidated as unreasonable.

IV.  Since the zoning power of local governments is derived from the police power of the state, such regulations must be primarily supportive of a public interest, rather than private interest, or they will be declared arbitrary and void.

In regulating land, governments limit property owners' uses of their properties. If a zoning ordinance completely prevents a property owner from using his property by ruling out all practical uses, the ordinance will be invalid. The question is whether the

Fig. 19.1 Unusual buildings may add character to an area.

government's limits go too far and result in an unconstitutional "taking" under the Fifth Amendment's just compensation clause. Courts have found that local governments must pay compensation when a regulation causes a physical invasion of private property, leaving the owner unable to use it. This is in contrast with the regulation of the use of property, which is allowed pursuant to a government's police powers.

## Zoning Concepts

Four zoning concepts may be highlighted to provide a better understanding on how local governments employ zoning to oversee the use of land. "Contract zoning" shows that communities can extract funds or property from developers in authorizing new development projects that affect the community. A request for a rezoning of a small parcel identifies "spot zoning" as illegal. Cases on variances and special permits help show how local governments manage zoning requests involving special circumstances.

### 1. Contract Zoning

Impermissible contract zoning may result when local government commits itself to rezone property in return for consideration (i.e., money or property) from a private developer. Local governments must limit dealings with proposed developers to professional communication of information about the proposal and related facts to avoid the appearance of impropriety. While local governments may require donations from rezoning applicants, contract zoning is illegal if it fails to adhere to stated legislative criteria.

### *Golder v. City of Saco*
Supreme Judicial Court of Maine

*Who is suing?* _____

*Who is being sued?* _____

*For what?* _____

*What is the issue on appeal?* _____

This appeal arises from the City of Saco's approval of a contract zoning agreement for property purchased by Estates at Bay View, LLC. Joel Golder and other nearby property owners (Neighbors) filed a five-count complaint challenging the legality of the contract zoning agreement and the Saco Planning Board's subsequent approval of a subdivision and site plan for the property. The Neighbors now appeal from a judgment granting the City's motion to dismiss three of the counts, granting summary judgment in favor of the City and Bay View on one of the counts, and affirming the decision of the Saco Planning Board on the final count. We affirm.

Estates at Bay View, LLC entered into a purchase and sale agreement for property in Saco, at the corner of Bay View Road and Seaside Avenue. The property consists of 9.42 acres of land and, at the time of purchase, was occupied by a five-story, 41,800-square-foot inn with several outbuildings, which were nonconforming buildings and uses for the zone. At its eastern border, the property includes a beach that the public has used for many years. Bay View approached the Saco Planning Board with an application for a contract zone agreement (CZA) seeking certain zoning amendments to permit the development of a proposed residential subdivision on the property. In particular, the application sought to reduce the minimum lot size for the lots in the subdivision to allow for a greater density of development. The Planning Board and City Council conducted public hearings and approved the CZA, with several amendments.

The CZA approved by the City permitted the development of a fourteen-lot subdivision with lot sizes smaller than the 7,500 square feet required by the otherwise applicable zoning district. In addition, the CZA listed several conditions for approval that related to the public's beach access, including the conveyance to the City and improvement of a separate parcel of property across Seaside Avenue; the contribution of $100,000 from Bay View to the City towards construction of a sidewalk to the beach; improvements to the City's existing parking lot across from the proposed development; construction of a public restroom facility on the subdivision property, with an associated easement to the City; and the conveyance to the City of the beach property to the east of the existing sand dune fence for public use.

The Neighbors all own residential property on the northern side of Bay View Road across the street from the proposed development. After the City approved the CZA and the Planning Board approved Bay View's subdivision and site plan, the Neighbors filed a five-count complaint alleging that the City's approval of the CZA violated Maine Revised Statutes § 4352(8), the provision for contract zoning in the zoning enabling statute. The Superior Court granted summary judgment in favor of the City and Bay View. The court noted that the parties had narrowed the issue to whether the rezoning "Only includes conditions and restrictions that relate to the physical development or operation of the property," pursuant to § 4352(8). Observing that the Legislature has given municipalities substantial freedom in determining whether there should be contract zoning at all and what form any agreement might take, the court concluded that, given the historic use and operation of the property as public beach access, the conditions and restrictions all "relate to" the physical development of the property or its operation.

In a subsequent decision, the court granted the City's motion to dismiss three of the four remaining counts and entered judgment in favor of the City and Bay View on the final count, concluding that the subdivision plan approved by the Planning Board was in compliance with the intended effect of the CZA. Because we find no merit in the Neighbors' arguments regarding their other claims, we address only the grant of summary judgment in favor of the City with respect to the § 4352(8) issue. We reiterate here a fundamental point: zoning is a legislative act. When addressing whether a zoning action is consistent with a city's comprehensive plan, the test for the court's review of the city council's rezoning action is whether from the evidence before it the city council could have determined that the rezoning was in basic harmony with the comprehensive plan.

When this Court considers whether a zoning amendment is consistent with a statutory requirement, the record is limited to the record before the municipality's legislative body, deference is given to the judgment of the legislative body, and the challenger bears the burden of proving that the amendment is inconsistent. Section 4352(8) permits municipalities to implement zoning ordinances that include provisions for conditional or contract zoning so long as the requirements of that statutory section are met. The City's ordinance permits contract zoning pursuant to § 4352(8). The Saco City Council is ultimately responsible for approving the contract zoning amendment. In addition to certain procedural requirements, § 4352(8) requires that all contract zoning:

- *Be consistent with the growth management program adopted under this chapter;*
- *Establish rezoned areas that are consistent with the existing and permitted uses within the original zones; and*
- *Only include conditions and restrictions that relate to the physical development or operation of the property.*

The Neighbors contend that certain provisions in the CZA were not sufficiently related to the physical development or operation of the property being rezoned to meet the requirements of § 4352(8), and therefore the court erred in granting summary judgment. The Neighbors assert that § 4352(8) should be read to prohibit contract zoning agreements containing provisions affecting property beyond the boundaries of the property being rezoned. We decline to adopt the narrow reading of § 4352(8) suggested by the Neighbors. Here, it is self-evident that the City could rationally conclude that the CZA's provisions regarding the public parking improvements and beach access were related to the development and operation of the property. It was entirely appropriate for the City to consider the impacts of development on an area's existing use, particularly with respect to an area such as this: one with a history of public beach access, public parking, and public restrooms. All of the provisions in the CZA relate to property in the immediate vicinity of the development and serve to ensure that development of the parcel will be in harmony with the public's access to the beach and continued health and safety. In the present case, the relationship between the off-site conditions in the CZA and the physical development and operation of the property is self-evident from the record. Judgment affirmed as to all counts.

## Questions

1.  What is the problem with contract zoning?
2.  Does this case involve the city's zoning ordinance or something else?
3.  Can a local government demand the donation of property to itself for a public use when approving a rezoning?
4.  What did Estates at Bay View, LLC gain due to its payment of $100,000?
5.  Why didn't the neighbors want the fourteen-lot subdivision?

## 2. Spot Zoning

One restriction on rezoning is that "spot zoning" is invalid. Spot zoning occurs when a zoning ordinance singles out and reclassifies a relatively small tract of land, often owned by one person, which is surrounded by a larger, uniformly zoned area. The smaller area would not be in conformance with the comprehensive plan due to its location in a different zone. The following case shows how a city failed to follow zoning rules and neighboring property owners were successful in invalidating the city's rezoning. Because any evidence supporting a city's decision to rezone is sufficient, it is difficult for persons to successfully challenge an ordinance that rezones property.

### *Collins v. Mayor and Council of the City of Gautier*
Court of Appeals of Mississippi

*Who is suing?* _____

*Who is being sued?* _____

*For what?* _____

*What is the issue on appeal?* _____

This appeal arises from a decision of the Mayor and the City Council of Gautier, Mississippi (collectively, the City or city council) to rezone a 13.5-acre lot from R-1, single-family residential, to R-2, multi-family residential, at the developer's request. Silver Girl, LLC, the owner and developer, wishes to construct condominiums on the subject property. Jimmy and Felicia Collins, owners of property adjacent to the subject property, opposed the rezoning and filed an appeal with the circuit court. The circuit court affirmed the City's decision, and the Collinses now appeal to this Court arguing that the city council's decision was arbitrary and capricious. Finding that there was no substantial evidence to support the rezoning and that the rezoning constituted illegal "spot zoning," we reverse.

The City uses a two-tiered process for changing its zoning ordinances. First, a planning commission reviews rezoning requests and makes recommendations to the city council. Afterwards, the city council accepts or rejects the planning commission's recommendations. Silver Girl, LLC filed an application seeking to rezone the subject property from R-1 single-family residential to R-2 multi-family residential. Documents submitted in support of the application show a proposal to construct a 120-unit condominium development. Prior to the planning commission's hearing, the director of the City's community services department issued a written report recommending that the application be denied, citing concerns that the subject property would be an "island" surrounded by land zoned R-1. The report ultimately concluded, however, that an argument could be made for or against rezoning.

The planning commission conducted a public hearing on the rezoning request. After hearing testimony and arguments, the commission denied the request, finding that the developer had not shown that the character of the neighborhood had changed. The developer appealed the commission's decision to the city council, which held a public hearing on the matter. At the hearing, the developer offered additional arguments and evidence. Several citizens appeared at the hearing and offered arguments and evidence against the rezoning request. The opponents also presented a petition signed by fifty-one residents opposing the rezoning. Ultimately, the city council unanimously passed an ordinance granting the rezoning request. The ordinance specifically found a substantial change in the neighborhood and a public need for rezoning. The Collinses appealed the city council's decision and the appellate court affirmed the decision. Aggrieved by that decision, the Collinses appeal arguing: (1) there was not substantial evidence in the record of a change in the character of the neighborhood or a public need sufficient to justify rezoning; and (2) the rezoning ordinance constituted illegal "spot zoning."

The order of the governing body may not be set aside unless it is clearly shown to be arbitrary, capricious, discriminatory, or is illegal, or without a substantial evidentiary basis. The action of the Board of Supervisors in enacting or amending an ordinance, or its action of rezoning, carries a presumption of validity, casting the burden of proof upon the individual or other entity asserting its invalidity. On appeal we cannot substitute our judgment as to the wisdom or soundness of the Board's action. Our task on appeal is to determine whether the circuit court erred in its judicial review of whether the local authority's decision to rezone was arbitrary and capricious and unsupported by substantial evidence.

The courts presume that comprehensive zoning ordinances adopted by municipal authorities are well planned and designed to be permanent. Therefore, before property is reclassified, an applicant seeking rezoning must prove by clear and convincing evidence either that: (1) there was a mistake in the original zoning, or (2) the character of the neighborhood has changed to such an extent as to justify rezoning and that a public need exists for rezoning. No mistake in the original zoning has been alleged. In its ordinance, the city council approved the rezoning as it expressly found a change in the character of the neighborhood and the existence of a public need for rezoning the subject property to R-2. However, the city council did not make detailed or specific findings; it stated only that its finding was "based on the evidence presented." The city council was entitled to rely upon the entire record before it: information obtained at the hearings, hearsay evidence, and the council's own common knowledge and the familiarity with the ordinance area are all valid bases for its findings.

On appeal, the City points to the record and hearings as well as the documents that were submitted in support of the developer's application for rezoning. We find no change in the character of the neighborhood. We find that the evidence presented was insufficient to support the change in zoning. The principal evidence presented to justify the rezoning was summarized in a document prepared by the developer for the city council hearing about developments built on land zoned for such uses and consistent with existing uses in a different area of the City. Thus, each of these "changes" was in accordance with the original zoning plan. We must agree with the Collinses that the record reflects that the areas in which the condominiums and new apartment complex were being built were already zoned R-2 or C-2. The use of property in accordance with an original zoning plan is not a material change of conditions which authorizes rezoning. We reverse the circuit court's judgment and render the zoning change invalid as there was not substantial evidence to support a finding of a change in the character of the neighborhood.

In a related issue, the Collinses assert that the City's decision represents a prime example of "spot zoning." Again, we agree. The supreme court has defined "spot zoning" as a zoning amendment reclassifying one or more tracts or lots for a use prohibited by the original zoning ordinance and out of harmony therewith. A zoning ordinance is illegal "spot zoning" where it is not in harmony with the comprehensive or well-considered land use plan of a municipality and is designed to favor someone. There is no question that this reclassification would create an island of R-2 zoned property in the midst of R-1 zoned property. Both before and after the rezoning, the property does not abut any area zoned R-2.

We have already found that no substantial evidence of a change in the neighborhood was presented which justified the rezoning. Further, this reclassification clearly favored the developer over the adjacent landowners; accordingly, we find that it constituted invalid "spot zoning." Accordingly, we reverse the judgment of the circuit court and render the zoning reclassification invalid.

## Questions

1. Can a city council pass an ordinance granting a rezoning request when most people appear to be opposed to it?
2. Who has to show that an ordinance rezoning property is invalid?
3. What is the burden of proof necessary to overturn a rezoning decision?
4. Why was it required that there be a change in the character of the neighborhood to justify rezoning?
5. Can a court acknowledge superior evidence and use it to enter a different judgment from the governing body?
6. What is the problem with spot zoning?
7. Is the burden for reversing a local governmental zoning decision in Mississippi the same (or similar to) the burden in Maine (see the *Golder* case above)?

## 3. Variances

A variance is a permit granted by a government to a property owner to avoid unnecessary hardship. A variance allows the property owner to use property in some way that conflicts with the provisions of the existing zoning classification. Two major categories of variances exist; (1) area variances (i.e., a lot too small for

Fig. 19.2 A posted notice prior to issuing a variance may be required by law.

zoned setbacks) and (2) use variances (i.e., a structure not fit for a zoned use). The following case illustrates a situation where a property owner failed to qualify for a variance.

### *Schultz v. Village of Mantua*
Court of Appeals of Ohio

*Who is suing?* _____

*Who is being sued?* _____

*For what?* _____

*What is the issue on appeal?* _____

Vernard E. Schultz appeals from a decision of the Portage County Court, affirming the Village of Mantua Board of Zoning Appeals' (BZA) denial of two requested zoning variances. Mr. Schultz sought variances for buildings he erected on his property which failed to conform with setback and square-footage requirements delineated in the Village of Mantua Zoning Code (Zoning Code). Because we find that the BZA's denial of the variances was supported by substantive, reliable and probative evidence, and that the trial court did not abuse its discretion in affirming the BZA's determination, we affirm the judgment of the Portage County Court.

Mr. Schultz owns an "L" shaped piece of property in the downtown district of Mantua. He acquired the property and has made substantial improvements and developments to the property. Scott and Christina Vyhnal, intervenors in this matter, purchased the residential property adjacent to the eastern border of Mr. Schultz' property. Mr. Schultz applied for a zoning permit from the Mantua Village Zoning Inspector (Zoning Inspector) to build a 32 by 40-foot garage to be attached to the back of an already existing 12 by 24-foot garage. This application, which was approved by the Zoning Inspector, indicated that the building would be 16 feet tall and consist of only one story. The addition would add 1280 square feet of floor area. A drawing of the proposed garage addition indicated that the new structure would have a 12-foot setback from the Vyhnals' property, as well as a 12-foot setback from the northern border of the property.

Mr. Schultz spoke with the Zoning Inspector about altering the proposed new garage addition's roof to a pitched roof. Mr. Schultz also wished to add a 12 by 24-foot addition to the older garage's roof, to go "up not out." He memorialized this in a new zoning application. During construction of the 12 by 24-foot pitched roof, Mr. Schultz was informed by the builders that, for a small charge, a second floor could easily be added. Mr. Schultz had the Zoning Inspector come to the property to discuss this change, and was told he had to stay within the Village's height requirements. Mr. Schultz then had the builder go forward with construction of the second floor. While doing so, it appears Mr. Schultz also had the building extended outward, westerly toward the Vyhnals' property line, and the building's height rose from 16 feet to 35 feet. This extension was contrary to the zoning permit, and effectively eliminated any setback between Mr. Schultz' property and the Vyhnals'.

Shortly thereafter, Mr. Schultz received written notice from the Zoning Inspector that he was in violation of the Zoning Code and the Village of Mantua solicitor sent Mr. Schultz a formal "Notice of Violation." Mr. Schultz applied for a retroactive zoning permit for the newly constructed second floor and westward expansion. The Zoning Inspector denied the application. Mr. Schultz then filed an appeal with the BZA. A hearing was held before the BZA. The Vyhnals made specific objections as to each of the desired variances. They pointed out that the Zoning Code required commercial properties to have a setback of at least 20 feet from abutting residential properties in a side-yard and 30 feet for rear yards, but that no setback existed between the garage and their property. The Vyhnals argued that:

*(1) Mr. Shultz's property can be put to beneficial use without the variances; (2) the variances requested are substantial, given that they request permission to maintain two to three times the allowable square footage of buildings on the property, and to maintain no setback whatsoever between the Schultz property and the Vyhnal property; (3) they will suffer substantial detriment because their enjoyment of the property has been diminished due to the garage's interference with light, air and sunshine, and the value of their property is decreased; (4) the variances would adversely affect delivery of governmental services and create a potential fire hazard; (5) Mr. Schultz purchased the property with full knowledge of the zoning restrictions, and created the violations himself; and (6) granting of the variances would fail to protect and enhance the character and value of residences.*

The Vyhnals also argued that substantial justice would not be accomplished by granting the variances because it would be tantamount to spot zoning, and would empower residents to make additions first and seek permission later.

The BZA denied Mr. Schultz' application. He subsequently filed an appeal in the Portage County Court. The trial court considered whether substantive, reliable and probative evidence existed in the administrative record to support the BZA's denial of the requested variances. The court found the BZA's denial to be rooted in substantive, reliable and probative evidence. The court stated:

*In each case the variances are substantial, have negatively changed the character of the immediate neighborhood, and will limit governmental fire protection services to Appellant's building and the adjoining residence. It is plain that approval of either variance will not preserve the spirit and intent of the zoning regulations. Further, Appellant had feasible alternatives in continuing his business in the 32 x 40 garage or constructing his enlarged business buildings elsewhere. Finally, Appellant created this situation through unapproved expansion of his building. As Appellant has created his own hardship, neither substantial justice nor equity allows approval of these variances.*

Mr. Schultz now appeals from the decision of the trial court, bringing the following assignments of error: (1) The trial court erred in failing to fully apply and consider the practical difficulties test; and (2) The trial court erred in failing to properly weigh competing interests of Schultz against that of the community to achieve substantial justice.

Ohio Revised Code § 2506.04 grants a court of appeals reviewing the decisions of administrative agencies limited powers to review the judgment of the lower only on questions of law. The appellate standard of review of such "questions of law" is whether the court of common pleas abused its discretion. Mr. Schultz effectively asks us to reweigh the evidence. This we may not do. A court of appeals must affirm the trial court's judgment unless the decision is not supported by a preponderance of reliable, probative and substantial evidence, and, in making such a determination, the court of appeals applies an abuse-of-discretion standard. Whether the trial court abused its discretion is within the ambit of "questions of law" for appellate review.

Mr. Schultz sought an area variance (as opposed to a use variance). The standard for granting an area variance is whether the party seeking the variance faces practical difficulties in the use of his property if not provided with the variance. We cannot say the trial court abused its discretion in finding substantive, reliable and probative evidence to support the BZA's denial of the variance applications. The trial court was obligated to defer to the determination of the BZA, so long as it was not unconstitutional, illegal, arbitrary, capricious, unreasonable, or unsupported by the preponderance of substantial, reliable and probative evidence. Because we find the trial court did not abuse its discretion in affirming the BZA's denial of Mr. Schultz' applications for area variances, we affirm the judgment of the Portage County Court.

## Questions

1. What construction was not authorized by permits?
2. Did the village object to the violations in a timely manner?
3. What should be the neighbors' role in a violation?
4. What is the role of a trial court for an appeal from the BZA's denial of a variance?
5. What is the role of an appellate court reviewing the ruling of the trial court that upheld the BZA's denial of a variance?
6. What action by Mr. Schultz comes next?

## 4. Special Permits

Special permits may be required by an ordinance to allow a governmental body to grant permission upon an applicant meeting certain conditions. These permits may also be referred to as "special exceptions" or "conditional use permits." A special permit does not encompass the power to make exceptions to an ordinance, but rather encompasses the power to authorize specific exceptional uses under stated conditions.

If the request for a special use permit is found to be within an ordinance, does not violate its intent, and safeguards the interests of the community, the governmental body must grant the permit.

## Conservation Easements

A conservation easement is a voluntary legal agreement that permanently restricts specified activities on a piece of property to protect conservation values such as open space, forest ecosystems, wildlife habitat, biodiversity, agricultural lands, and water quality. The conservation easement is granted by the property owner to a conservation organization or government agency. Easements involve deed restrictions that landowners voluntarily place on their properties to protect environmental resources. Each restriction stays with the property and is binding on all future owners. Conservation easements thereby constitute legal documents that keep property in private ownership and use, while ensuring that important natural values are protected forever.

The process starts with careful thought by landowners about long-term conservation goals for their properties. If the owners believe a conservation easement might be appropriate, they should contact a nonprofit land trust or government agency qualified to receive and manage conservation easements. That organization will send someone to look at the property and discuss conservation goals with the landowners to determine whether it would be eligible for a conservation easement under the land trust's criteria. By establishing a conservation easement, the landowner and land trust will become partners in conservation.

Based on a mutually agreeable conservation plan, a deed of conservation easement will be drafted. Another document called a baseline report is generally prepared. It describes the property's physical characteristics and conservation values as they exist at the time the easement is established. Maps and surveys of the property and its natural resources may be needed for the baseline report. In consultation with the landowner, the land trust also prepares a monitoring plan so it can ensure the easement terms are honored in the future. Thereby, conservation easements are tailored to the needs of each property owner.

Conservation easements are typically sold for their fair-market value, donated, or sold as a bargain sale (lower than the fair-market value) to a qualified conservation organization or a public agency. The agency, or "grantee," receives the right to monitor and enforce the restrictions set forth in the easement. Although the landowner, or "grantor," relinquishes the right to develop the land, that right is not conveyed to the grantee. The grantee simply acquires the right to prevent the landowner from developing the land, while the actual right to develop the land is extinguished. The agencies involved in conservation easement acquisitions are often nonprofit groups and land trusts. The government has no role in the administration of a conservation easement donated to a nonprofit land trust. No new regulations or governmental rules are imposed by establishing a conservation easement.

Property owners (grantors) retain title to their property and generally are not limited in their right to enter, conduct permitted business operations, lease, mortgage, bequeath, sell, restrict public access, or demand compensation for rights transferred. This allows the landowner to live on their property, to sell it, or to pass it on to heirs. The property continues to contribute to the local tax base. Some easements may specify certain conservation standards that must be met, while others may permit building lots for qualifying persons. This means the grantor's use of the property continues, subject to the restrictions agreed to in the conservation easement. Timber rights, water rights, mineral rights, and development rights are the grantor's property rights that may be used or sold. Thereby, a conservation easement allows a landowner to exercise the right not to develop.

A grantor's estate taxes may be significantly lower as a result of reduced property value. The reduced taxes would enable heirs to hold on to family land, instead of selling it to pay inheritance taxes. Furthermore, the donation of a perpetual conservation easement to a land trust can be treated as a charitable gift on the landowner's federal and state income tax returns. The conservation easement must run in perpetuity in order to receive tax benefits. Other limitations related to tax advantages may apply, so that a person considering a conservation easement should contact a knowledgeable tax adviser or attorney.

## Smart Growth

Urban sprawl is an issue that continues to receive attention due to its costs on society. Sprawl may be defined as "unplanned, uncontrolled, and uncoordinated single-use development that does not provide for an attractive and functional mix of uses and/ or is not functionally related to surrounding land uses and which variously appears as low density, ribbon or strip, scattered, leapfrog, or isolated development." The costs involve needed expansions of public and private services and the loss of productive farmland.

"Smart growth" (also called "growth management") and similar initiatives have been proposed in communities across the nation to help communities develop in a more environmentally friendly manner. Growth management involves the implementation of government regulations that control the type, location, quality, scale, rate, sequence, or timing of development. The prohibitions contained in a traditional zoning ordinance are a form of growth management, but the term implies a much greater involvement of local government in development decisions. Sophisticated growth management systems are closely tied to comprehensive land use plans and specific development policies. State and local governments are adopting smart growth statutes and ordinances that explicitly list the protection of open space and farmland as a key goal of their development efforts.

Most would agree that smart growth has failed to live up to its hype. Growth management advocates have underestimated the "not in my back yard" opposition. Unforeseen circumstances and unintended consequences have dampened support for growth management. Regional and state interests are unlikely to be heeded by local zoning authorities responding to local concerns. Good ideas can be difficult to implement given local desires to spur development and growth to create jobs and new tax revenues. Given the high value Americans place on private property rights, it is unlikely that the benefits of growth management will be realized, as local governments will not adopt the necessary ordinances and laws to implement creative urban and suburban growth parameters.

## Land Use Governance for Climate Change

Another issue is the ability of local governments, especially those in coastal areas, to address the anticipated problems that will accompany weather events connected to climate change. With the rise of sea levels, storms will erode coastal areas, submerge some lands, and result in more frequent flooding. For areas inland, extreme precipitation events will adversely affect areas in which flood waters collect or are channeled. In 2017, the nation learned about unnatural rainfall in California that threatened reservoirs and flooded residential areas. Another weather-related problem has been the lack of rain and drought conditions that have exacerbated wildfires.

Many communities are not prepared to respond to these weather events. Existing development was commissioned with little regard to increases in sea levels or stream flows. Housing developments were allowed in areas without adequately considering the risk of a wildfire. Entrenched business interests and interest groups often succeed in convincing local authorities to approve development with short-term financial profits, even though there are substantial risks of future flooding or fire. Creating jobs and tax revenues are more important than adapting for likely climatic events.

Moreover, many climate impacts are not exclusively local but rather necessitate a larger jurisdictional role to manage adaptation responses. For example, communities along a river cannot control land use development in upstream areas that exacerbates flooding. Communities may face drinking water shortages due to reduced surface water flows or lower groundwater levels outside of their jurisdiction. Additional state and local adaptation programs are needed to help communities prepare for climate events that could damage property and cause hardships due to flooding, wildfires, air contamination, or the spread of disease.

## Discussion Questions

1. Who should make zoning decisions, and under what authority? Why?
2. What does the law say about the future use of existing property uses that do not conform to an adopted zoning plan?
3. If your property is unsuitable for uses permitted by the zoning ordinance, what should you do?
4. Your property has a unique physical feature precluding development in compliance with the zoning ordinance. What should you do, and why?
5. Assuming you like your neighbors and community, why might you not want your property zoned?

# CHAPTER TWENTY
## Natural Resources

## Learning Objectives

- *Recognize the federal government's roles in managing forest resources.*
- *Explain sources of authority for agency rules over natural resources.*
- *Describe the meaning of third-party certification provisions for forestry production.*
- *Recite how property owners can challenge agency mistakes.*

Governmental policies on the management of federal lands, natural resources, and forests are subjects of lively debate in most countries of the world. Governments want to develop and use natural resources, but also serve as trustees of public resources and the guardians of resources for future generations. While earlier chapters dealing with water, air, and waste have identified federal provisions that are important in protecting people and the environment, this chapter provides a more detailed accounting on the stewardship and preservation of public resources and forests.

## Federal Lands

The Bureau of Land Management under the Department of the Interior manages non-forest public lands. The US Department of Agriculture's Forest Service (USFS) is directed to manage the country's forest resources, consisting of over 190 million acres of federal forest and rangelands in forty-four states. These lands possess resources and values of major economic, social, and environmental importance to the nation. They are managed for multiple uses, on a sustained-yield basis, using sound ecological principles and the best available science. Public benefits include cleaner water, wood and paper products, a high-quality environment for outdoor recreation, energy and minerals, wilderness preservation, forage for grazing livestock, and abundant fish and wildlife.

A key federal law in protecting natural resources is the Federal Land Policy and Management Act of 1976 (FLPMA). FLPMA requires that public lands be managed under principles of multiple use in accordance with land use plans developed by the Bureau of Land Management (BLM). Mineral resources are specifically listed among resource values included within the term "multiple use." Further, FLPMA requires that public lands be managed in a way that recognizes the nation's need for domestic sources of minerals, including implementation of the Mining and Minerals Policy Act of 1970. All lands that the United States acquired from other nations or from Indian tribes—and which have not been sold off or set aside as national forests, national parks, military reservations, and so forth—are managed by the BLM. Most of the public lands managed by BLM are located in twelve western states, including Alaska.

The BLM's land use plans are termed resource management plans. Each plan inventories resources within geographic management areas and determines whether areas are open or closed to certain land uses and the terms and conditions applicable

Fig. 20.1 Yosemite National Park.

to such uses. Plans must achieve a balance between multiple use and sustained yield. The secretary of agriculture and the secretary of the interior jointly determine the value of grazing on the lands under FLPMA in eleven western States. To assure long-term stability and use of BLM lands by the livestock industry, FLPMA authorizes ten-year grazing permits and requires two-year notices of cancellation.

# Federal Management Decisions

Federal officials administering federal laws and regulations have responsibilities in protecting the country's natural resources. Given the requirements of the National Environmental Policy Act (NEPA), they often must divulge considerable information in an environmental assessment or an environmental impact statement. Furthermore, under citizen suit provisions of several environmental statutes, federal agencies can be sued if they neglect their responsibilities. With business interests and environmental groups holding different interpretations of what is required under federal law, agencies find themselves defending their actions in lawsuits. The following case is an example where the US Forest Service was overzealous in imposing a requirement of an environmental impact statement on owners of mineral rights in a national forest.

### *Minard Run Oil Company v. United States Forest Service*
US Court of Appeals for the Third Circuit, Philadelphia

*Who is suing?* _____

*Who is being sued?* _____

*For what?* _____

*What is the issue on appeal?* _____

This appeal concerns a dispute between the U.S. Forest Service (the Service) and owners of mineral rights in the Allegheny National Forest. Although the Service manages the surface of the Allegheny National Forest for the United States, mineral rights in most of the Forest are privately owned. Mineral rights owners are entitled to reasonable use of the surface to drill for oil or gas. From 1980 until recently, the Service and mineral owners had managed drilling in the Allegheny National Forest through a cooperative process under which the Service would issue owners a Notice to Proceed (NTP). However, as a result of a Settlement Agreement with environmental groups, the Service dramatically changed its policy and decided to postpone the issuance of NTPs until a multi-year, forest-wide Environmental Impact Study (EIS) under the National Environmental Policy Act (NEPA) is completed.

Minard Run Oil Company and related businesses affected by this new policy sought to enjoin the Service from implementing the policy, which would halt new drilling in the Allegheny National Forest. After holding a hearing and carefully considering the evidence, the District Court issued a preliminary injunction against the Service requiring it to return to its prior, cooperative process for issuing NTPs. The Service and others appeal the preliminary injunction, contending that the District Court lacked jurisdiction and erred in issuing a preliminary injunction. We affirm in all respects the District Court's opinion.

NEPA requires federal agencies to file an EIS before taking "major federal actions significantly affecting the quality of the human environment." Until recently, the Service took the position that issuance of an NTP to a mineral rights owner was not a "major federal action" requiring environmental analysis under NEPA because the Service's rights as surface owner were so limited. When interacting with mineral rights owners in the Allegheny National Forest, the Service viewed itself as a resource management agency negotiating use of jointly owned land, not as a regulatory agency issuing permits. In 2007, an attorney in the Service's Office of General Counsel authored a memorandum concluding that the issuance of an NTP is a "major federal action" subject to NEPA.

The plaintiffs' complaint alleged that the Service had imposed a de facto drilling ban in the Allegheny National Forest until a forest-wide EIS is completed and that this ban exceeded the authority of the Service and was contrary to NEPA and the Administrative Procedure Act (APA). Additionally, plaintiffs allege that the EIS will probably not be completed for several years. As a result, mineral rights owners will be prevented from exercising their property rights during this period, resulting in damage to the owners, related businesses, and the local community. At a hearing on the preliminary injunction motion, plaintiffs presented the testimony of several business owners, who testified that they were prevented from drilling new wells, causing significant losses to their businesses and harm to the community. Plaintiffs also presented testimony from several former Forest Rangers who estimated that the EIS would probably require at least several years to complete.

The District Court found the Settlement Agreement represented a fundamental "sea change" in the Service's policy; therefore, it constituted final agency action subject to review under the APA. The effect of this policy was a "drilling ban," which precluded new drilling in the Allegheny National Forest until the Service completed a forest-wide EIS. The Service had instituted the drilling ban without following the APA's notice and comment procedures, and the ban was not justified under NEPA because the issuing of an NTP was not a major federal action. The District Court then enjoined the Service from requiring the preparation of a NEPA document as a precondition to the exercise of private oil and gas rights in the Allegheny National Forest, and required the Service to return to the cooperative framework for processing NTPs that had been in place prior to the settlement agreement.

To obtain a preliminary injunction, a plaintiff must show: (1) a likelihood of success on the merits; (2) that it will suffer irreparable harm if the injunction is denied; (3) that granting preliminary relief will not result in even greater harm to the nonmoving party; and (4) that the public interest favors such relief. We review the court's ultimate decision to issue an injunction for abuse of discretion. The District Court found that appellees were likely to prevail on the merits of two claims: (a) that issuance of an

NTP is not a major federal action for which prior NEPA analysis is required, and (b) the Settlement Agreement was not preceded by notice and comment procedures as required by the APA.

The merit of appellees' first claim turns on whether the issuance of an NTP is a major federal action which under NEPA must be preceded by an appropriate environmental analysis. We have identified three types of agency action that typically constitute "major federal action": first, where the agency itself undertook a project; second, where the agency supported a project by contract, grant, loan, or other financial assistance; and third, where the agency enabled the project by lease, license, permit, or other entitlement for use. But federal approval of a private party's project, where that approval is not required for the project to go forward, does not constitute a major federal action. The District Court properly concluded that issuance of an NTP is not a "major federal action" under NEPA and an EIS need not be completed prior to issuing an NTP.

The District Court found that the Service's moratorium on new drilling irreparably harmed appellees because it infringed their property rights and threatened bankruptcy or closure for some businesses. Under Pennsylvania law, oil and gas resources are subject to the "rule of capture," which permits an owner to extract oil and gas even when extraction depletes a single oil or gas reservoir lying beneath adjoining lands. The adjoining owner's only remedy against such drainage is to "go and do likewise." The Service's moratorium on new drilling deprives mineral owners in the Allegheny National Forest of this remedy and will cause them to lose oil and gas to other landowners drilling on private lands adjoining the Forest, which are not subject to the moratorium. Therefore, the moratorium also causes irreparable injury to mineral rights owners by depriving them of the unique oil and gas extraction opportunities afforded them by their mineral rights.

Granting the injunction would vindicate the public's interests in aiding the local economy, protecting the property rights of mineral rights owners, and ensuring public participation in agency rulemaking as required by the APA. On the record before it, the District Court therefore did not err in finding that the balance of the equities and the public interest favored injunctive relief. We affirm the preliminary injunction entered by the District Court against appellants.

## Questions

1. What prompted the Forest Service to change its policy issuance of NTPs?
2. Why were plaintiffs upset with this policy change?
3. What is required for an injunction, and how did plaintiffs establish their case?
4. Why didn't an NTP require an EIS?
5. What irreparable harm was sufficient for qualifying for injunctive relief?
6. How were plaintiffs impacted by delays in permission to drill?

# Freedom of Information Requests

Under the federal Freedom of Information Act (FOIA) enacted in 1967, persons are able to gain access to federal records. Most agencies have an online FOIA request form that can be used for this purpose and any person can submit a written request to an agency's FOIA office reasonably describing the records sought. The agency needs to release the requested information in a timely fashion but does not need to release information that falls under one of nine exemptions which protect interests such as personal privacy, national security, and law enforcement. The following case enumerates a judicial evaluation of an FOIA request involving an assertion by the government that certain materials did not need to be disclosed due to an exception.

### *Natural Resources Defense Council v. United States Department of Interior*
US District Court, Southern District of New York

*Who is suing?* _____

*Who is being sued?* _____

*For what?* _____

*What is the issue on appeal?* _____

This opinion resolves a dispute between the Natural Resources Defense Council (NRDC), and the U.S. Department of Interior and Bureau of Land Management (BLM) (collectively, the Government). Under the Freedom of Information Act (FOIA), the NRDC sought to obtain records of coal-mining leases previously awarded by the Government to private mining companies in the Powder River Basin in Montana and Wyoming. The Government produced the requested documents but redacted them extensively pursuant to FOIA Exemptions. As to some of the redactions pursuant to Exemption 5, which reflected the BLM's qualitative reasoning in connection with its decisions as to coal-mining lease awards, the Court requested additional briefing addressing whether the redacted material, if disclosed, would significantly harm the Government's commercial interests. For the following reasons, the Court now grants summary judgment for the Government as to this point.

The Mineral Leasing Act authorizes the Secretary of the Interior to lease public lands for coal-mining operations. Under the Act, BLM cannot accept less than fair market value for the sale of a coal lease. Before every lease sale, BLM estimates the fair market value of the coal lease in a document called an "appraisal report." The appraisal report incorporates information from three other BLM-prepared reports: an economic report, an engineering report, and a geologic report. BLM's estimate of fair market value is kept confidential. Following a competitive bidding process, BLM awards the lease to the company that submitted the highest bid as long as the bid meets or exceeds BLM's confidential estimate of fair market value. In lease sales where there is only one bid, BLM's confidential estimate of fair market value effectively supplies the sole price competition for the applicant.

To determine whether BLM has complied with the Mineral Leasing Act, NRDC submitted an FOIA request seeking (1) all information and analysis documents used to appraise each of the Powder River Basin tracts that BLM had leased since 1990, and (2) any Interior Department guidance, handbooks, manuals or similar documents with information on estimating the value of coal tracts. The Government produced the requested handbooks and manuals. As to the requested reports and computer models, the Government produced versions with extensive redactions. The Government invoked Exemption 5 in support of its redactions. NRDC objected to all redactions and withholdings.

Exemption 5 protects inter-agency or intra-agency memorandums or letters which would not be available by law to a party other than an agency in litigation with the agency. Exemption 5 encompasses traditional discovery privileges, and incorporates a qualified privilege for confidential commercial information. The privilege thus exists to prevent the Government from being placed at a competitive disadvantage. The Court granted the Government's motion for summary judgment under Exemption 5 as to (1) the Government's pricing model and (2) its fair market value estimates. The Court reasoned that disclosure of that information would effectively enable a coal company to derive the number it must beat in order to lease the next tract for mining.

As to the Government's "qualitative reasoning process," the Court directed the Government to submit supplemental declarations concretely explaining why the qualitative statements that have been withheld would, if revealed, work "significant harm." Summary judgment is warranted on the basis of agency affidavits when the affidavits describe the justifications for nondisclosure with reasonably specific detail, demonstrate that the information withheld logically falls within the claimed exemption, and are not controverted by either contrary evidence in the record nor by evidence of agency bad faith.

The Perlewitz Declaration, submitted by the Government in support of its renewed motion for summary judgment, establishes that disclosure of the withheld qualitative information in BLM's appraisal reports and supporting documents would significantly harm the Government's monetary functions or commercial interests by allowing bidders to approximate the Government's confidential floor price with substantially greater accuracy. First, the declaration clearly explains that BLM uses a common qualitative methodology to estimate the fair market value of each tract of land. Disclosure of fully unredacted reports would reveal the factors that BLM considers at each stage of the valuation process, how its appraisers evaluate those factors, and the weight each factor is given. Disclosure of this information would allow bidders to more closely predict BLM's fair market value estimate.

Second, the Perlewitz Declaration clarifies that some of the salient information is identical for every fair market value estimate. Because this data remains static across reports, at least for some period of time, disclosure would provide bidders with the exact information BLM will use to estimate fair market value for future lease sales. In addition, BLM redacted the specific publications, reports, articles, subscriptions, and databases referenced and used, and the identity of the commercial software used. With that information, bidders could determine how BLM would value the tracts in future lease sales.

The Perlewitz Declaration demonstrates that the qualitative and quantitative data are inextricably intertwined. The appraisers consider both quantitative and qualitative factors in the course of a unified analysis. Access to qualitative narratives in unredacted reports would allow prospective bidders to determine at least some of the numeric figures BLM uses to reach its fair market value estimates. Even if the Government redacted BLM's numeric estimate of the recoverable coal in a particular tract, that figure is a direct result of BLM's geologic models. The engineering report briefly describes the mining cost model BLM uses and how, using the cost model, BLM generates input for the discounted cash flow model. The reports also contain the results of BLM's economic valuation, just one step removed from the confidential floor price itself.

The Court's earlier opinion explained why disclosure of BLM's pricing model and fair market value estimates would harm the Government's commercial interests. The Court then considered the possibility of distinguishing between qualitative and quantitative information. The Perlewitz Declaration makes clear that disclosure of the qualitative information would be independently harmful and, in any event, that such information is not "reasonably segregable." The Government's justification for withholding the redacted information is, therefore, "logical or plausible." Accordingly, the Court grants the Government's motion for summary judgment as to FOIA Exemption 5.

## Questions

1. What is an FOIA request?
2. Why did the Government redact certain text in materials provided to the NRDC?
3. What is the Perlewitz Declaration? Why did the Government submit it to the court?
4. Why was the Government able to redact its qualitative reasoning process?
5. If another FOIA request for a governmental qualitative reasoning process involves a process that is separate from the quantitative information, how might a court analyze the government's redaction of qualitative materials? Why?

# Protecting Our Forests

With the federal government's vast holdings of forest lands, various policies on all facets of the management, harvesting, and use of these lands invoke considerable interest. The topics include sustainable forest management, trade issues, economic growth in underdeveloped areas, land tenure and rights, national security, biodiversity, and land use. Reflected in the dialogue of these issues is a range of perspectives on how values and benefits should be used, conserved, and protected. Congress has enacted several significant legislative directives that provide direction to the federal responses to forestry issues. In addition, the certification of forest products, with its potential for assisting in the sustainable management of forestry resources, is important for both public and private forests.

## 1. Forest Management Act of 1897

The Forest Management Act of 1897, also known as the Organic Act, clarifies the role of the forest reserves: to protect the forests so that citizens may have a reliable supply of water and timber. The act established a system of relative values for determining whether an area should become, or be retained within, a reserve, continued the practice of allowing local residents to use the timber, stone, and water on the reserves, opened forests for mining, and authorized the sale of dead and mature timber after appraisal, advertisement, and sale.

## 2. Multiple-Use, Sustained-Yield Act of 1960

Congress passed the Multiple-Use, Sustained-Yield Act (MUSYA) in 1960. This act provides that the national forests shall be administered for outdoor recreation, range, timber, watershed, and wildlife and fish purposes in a manner supplemental to the purposes established by the Organic Act of 1897. Courts have acknowledged that under these statutes, as well as under general principles of public land preservation, a fundamental mission of land stewardship requires that we sustain viable populations of all native vertebrates. However, in the public rangeland context, the multiuse concept often gives way to the interests of the livestock industry. MUSYA has been interpreted as providing only minimal limitations on USFS discretion.

## 3. Forest and Rangeland Renewable Resources Planning Act of 1974

Following the passage of MUSYA, the public and the Congress became increasingly concerned over excessive clear-cutting on national forests. This concern led Congress to enact the Forest and Rangeland Renewable Resources Planning Act in 1974. The Act requires long-range planning on a nationwide basis, and the secretary of agriculture is required to make an assessment of the availability and demand for renewable resources and formulate a renewable resource program specifying objectives and output goals. The Act allows for clear-cutting practices if it can be justified to meet objectives of land and resources management plans.

## 4. National Forest Management Act of 1976

The National Forest Management Act (NFMA) sets forth a detailed and participatory forest and rangeland planning process. Both procedural and substantive standards are imposed upon USFS management decisions, providing less discretion in decision making than had existed prior to the passage of the act. The NFMA details requirements for land and resources management plans (LRMPs) that guide the management of our National Forests and Grasslands. LRMPs have been prepared for each National Forest and Grassland in compliance with NFMA. For LRMPs currently being developed, the USFS has a status report on its NFMA page. USFS line officers implement or revise these plans by issuing thousands of resource management decisions each year. These decisions are accompanied by environmental impact statements (EISs), environmental assessments, or categorical exclusions and may be subject to administrative appeal.

NFMA includes provisions that were intended to resolve the controversy over clear-cutting. The government is directed to ensure that clear-cutting, seed tree cutting, shelterwood cutting, and other cuts designed to regenerate an even-aged stand of timber will be used as a cutting method on National Forest System lands only according to listed provisions. Clear-cutting may only be used if it is the optimum method to meet the objectives of the LRMP. Before the chosen cutting method may be implemented, an interdisciplinary review must be completed, and the potential environmental, biological, aesthetic, engineering, and economic impacts on each advertised sale arena must be assessed. Further, the timber sale must be consistent with the multiple use of the general area.

## 5. Healthy Forests Restoration Act of 2003

US forests and rangelands face a high risk of catastrophic fire. Years of natural fuel buildup, coupled with drought and insect and disease damage, make our forests vulnerable to environmentally destructive fires. In 2003, Congress passed a new law to change decades of federal forest policy. The law encouraged efforts to thin increasingly fuel-rich forests on federal lands to make wildfires less dangerous, particularly in developed areas. It increased money for fire prevention, reduced environmental reviews, and limited appeals. A majority of the efforts on forest thinning are in areas near towns. More than 8 million acres of the at-risk land are in California, where deadly fires often threaten homes.

# Reconciling Various Federal Statutes

Given that multiple laws have been adopted over two centuries with quite different objectives, it is not surprising that conflicts develop and courts must decide which provisions take precedence. The following case discloses a conflict over water rights. The plaintiffs were unhappy that the federal government reduced amounts of water available for agricultural irrigation to protect endangered fish.

### *County of Okanogan v. National Marine Fisheries Service*
US Court of Appeals for the Ninth Circuit, San Francisco

*Who is suing?* _____

*Who is being sued?* _____

*For what?* _____

*What is the issue on appeal?* _____

Appellants, plaintiffs below, challenge a decision by the United States Forest Service requiring reduced use of water from ditches in time of low flow, intended to protect certain endangered species of fish. The district court granted summary judgment in favor of the federal defendants. We affirm. Plaintiffs use water from the Skyline Irrigation Ditch and the Early Winters Ditch. These ditches traverse the Okanogan National Forest (set aside in 1897) in the state of Washington and divert water to plaintiffs for agricultural and other purposes.

The Skyline Irrigation Ditch can be traced to 1903 when the Secretary of Interior issued a permit to construct and maintain a ditch to take water from the Chewuch River subject to revocation by the Secretary of the Interior, in his discretion, at any time, notwithstanding the period for which this agreement is approved may not have then expired. The record traces the Early Winters Ditch to 1910, when the Forest Service granted a special use permit for the ditch, stating that the permittee shall comply with all the laws and regulations governing National Forests and that the permit shall terminate at the discretion of the Forester. All of the subsequent permits for the two ditches contained similar conditions. These permits also stated that they do not convey any legal interest in water rights as defined by applicable state Law.

Under the Endangered Species Act (ESA), the National Marine Fisheries Service (NMFS) listed the steelhead trout and Chinook salmon as endangered species, and the Fish and Wildlife Service (FWS) listed the bull trout as a threatened species. The 1998 special use permittees were sent notices stating that it may be necessary to amend your permit to include conditions which may be required by the NMFS or the FWS.

Under ESA regulations, an agency is required to consult with either the FWS or the NMFS (the consulting agencies) whenever a federal action "may affect" a threatened or endangered species. The Forest Service initiated formal consultation with the NMFS and FWS. In 2000, NMFS issued biological opinions for the two ditches. It concluded that a proposed plan for the Early Winters Ditch that included using wells in lieu of surface water diversions during low flow conditions was not likely to jeopardize the steelhead and chinook. However, with respect to the Skyline Irrigation Ditch, the NMFS concluded that proposed modifications to the headgate and the fish screen were insufficient, and that the action as proposed was likely to jeopardize the continued existence of both steelhead and spring Chinook salmon and result in the destruction or adverse modification of designated critical habitat.

Agency action can be found not to violate the ESA if "reasonable and prudent alternatives" are implemented, and can be approved subject to the implementation of "reasonable and prudent measures." As to the Skyline Irrigation Ditch, the biological opinion found that measures were necessary to "increase the amount of water in the Chewuch River during low flow periods." The Forest Service therefore amended the Skyline Irrigation Ditch special use permit, requiring that instream flows on the river be measured and that diversions to the ditch be limited to maintain certain instream flows. As to the Early Winters Ditch, the biological opinion found that the proposed plan was acceptable under the ESA provided that reasonable and prudent measures were taken including the maintenance of a minimum instream flow for the creek.

The appellants brought this suit for a declaratory judgment, alleging that the actions of the NMFS, the FWS, and the Forest Service concerning the renewals of the special use permits for the two ditches were unconstitutional and exceeded the agencies' statutory authority. The appellants argue that the Forest Service does not have the authority to condition the use of the rights-of-way in a national forest on the maintenance of instream flows because such restrictions deny them their vested water rights under state law. The ditch rights-of-way granted over federal land, from their inception, were subject to termination at the discretion of the federal government through its designated agent. The more recent permits expressly state that they do not convey water rights and are subject to amendment. We are of the view that the Forest Service had the authority to restrict the use of the rights-of-way to protect the endangered fish. The permits themselves, from their inception, provided the government with unqualified discretion to restrict or terminate the rights-of-way.

The Federal Land Policy and Management Act of 1976 (FLPMA) authorizes the Secretaries of the Interior and Agriculture to grant, issue, or renew rights-of-way over public lands for ditches for the transportation of water. Such rights-of-way require compliance with applicable water quality standards established by or pursuant to applicable Federal or State law. In addition, the National Forest Management Act requires the Forest Service to specify guidelines for land management plans that provide for watershed, wildlife, and fish and provide for diversity of plant and animal communities. The Organic Act provides that no national forest shall be established, except to improve and protect the forest within the boundaries, or for the purpose of securing favorable conditions of water flows. The Multiple Use Sustained-Yield Act of 1960 provides that it is the policy of the Congress that the national forests are established and shall be administered for outdoor recreation, range, timber, watershed, and wildlife and fish purposes. These statutes give the Forest Service authority to maintain certain levels of flow in the rivers and streams within the boundaries of the Okanogan National Forest to protect endangered fish species.

The FLPMA specifically authorizes the Forest Service to restrict such rights-of-way to protect fish and wildlife and maintain water quality standards under federal law, without any requirement that the Forest Service defer to state water law. The pending case is not a controversy over water rights, but over rights-of-way through lands of the United States, which is a different matter, and is so treated in the right-of-way acts before mentioned. We agree with the district court that the placement of restrictions in the right-of-way permits was within the authority of the Forest Service. Affirmed.

## Questions

1. Why were the appellants unhappy?
2. Where did the appellants obtain their rights to water? Were there any noted limitations on the rights?
3. What laws were considered by the court?
4. Which federal law was most important for the court's conclusion?

# Sustainable Forest Management Certification Standards

Forestry imports and exports are important in meeting the world's demand for paper and timber products. To assure continued sources of wood products, harvests need to be well-managed to minimize impact on the environment and local communities. One key to the conservation of forests worldwide is a rapid transition toward forestry practices that maintain or restore the health and integrity of forest ecosystems. Sustainable forest management, coupled with increased productivity and continued efficiency improvements in manufacturing, can move the forest industry toward meeting future needs.

The immediate challenge is to combat illegal harvest, poor practices, and overexploitation in some areas that threaten the future of forests and tarnish the entire industry. Forest management certification offers an effective tool for achieving these goals. With today's growing emphasis on corporate responsibility and consumer demands for environmental and social accountability, forest management certification provides a global solution for businesses and consumers. It offers a balance between economic needs and conservation objectives, featuring a market-based—rather than a regulatory—solution for improving forest practices.

Forest management certification provides an independent third-party assurance that a forestry operation meets standards set by a certification program. Companies apply voluntarily, and governments have no direct role in the process. Forests are evaluated according to previously defined standards and certified as well managed by a qualified independent auditor. A well-managed forest satisfies standards for environmentally, socially, and economically responsible management. These standards ensure the long-term health and productivity of forests for timber production, wildlife habitat, and water quality, while also providing social benefits such as stable and lasting community employment.

Wood products from those forests are then labeled so that consumers can identify them as coming from well-managed sources. Consumer demand for certified forest products is a powerful incentive for forest managers to adopt more ecologically sound practices and for retailers and manufacturers to seek wood from certified forests. In combination with other strategies, including more efficient wood use and the designation of forest reserves, certification becomes a method to assist in the protection of our forest heritage.

Today, two major forest management certification systems vie for consumers' attention around the world: (1) the Forest Stewardship Council (FSC); and (2) the Sustainable Forestry Initiative (SFI) standard of the American Forest & Paper Association. Independent certification programs encourage the management of forests to consider environmental, social, and economic issues. Forest certification enables consumers to make informed choices when selecting wood and other forest products.

## 1. Forest Stewardship Council

The Forest Stewardship Council (FSC) is an international nonprofit organization headquartered in Bonn, Germany, that offers forest certification on an international basis. The FSC was founded in 1993 by representatives from environmental and conservation groups, the timber industry, the forestry profession, indigenous peoples' organizations, community forestry groups, and forest product certification organizations. Although it is international in scope, the FSC also supports the development of national and regional standards that are consistent with the international values and requirements adopted by the scheme.

The FSC has developed a set of ten principles and 56 criteria that address legal aspects, indigenous rights, labor rights, multiple benefits, and environmental impacts surrounding forest management. Although the principles and criteria are applicable to all forest ecological types throughout the world, the FSC encourages national working groups to adapt these principles and criteria to local ecological, economic, and social conditions to create regional or national standards. The accreditation process is based on FSC-developed procedures and standards to evaluate whether certification bodies can provide an independent and competent evaluation service. Certified entities must undergo a full evaluation to renew their certificates every ten years.

Products originating from forests certified by FSC-accredited certification bodies are eligible to carry the FSC logo if the chain of custody (tracking of the timber from the forest to the shop) has been checked. FSC-accredited certifiers have certified 31,746 companies who manage 479 million acres of forests globally. Of these, 4,200 companies are chain-of-custody codified in the United States, covering more than 35 million acres. In the green building context, the Leadership in Energy & Environmental Design (LEED) program uses FSC-certified wood.

## 2. Sustainable Forestry Initiative

In 1994, the American Forest & Paper Association developed a sustainable forestry initiative (SFI) standard. It currently is based on nine principles that address economic, environmental, cultural, and legal issues. The initiative seeks to document their members' commitment in the United States and Canada to a high level of sustainable forestry. While SFI certifies significant acreages in North America, allegations that it allows clear-cutting, practices adverse to indigenous communities, and the cutting of old-growth forests raise questions about the practices condoned by the SFI standard.

## 3. Legitimacy of Forest Certification Programs

Given that certification systems have very little coercive capacity, how do they achieve legitimacy? A voluntary legal system has legitimacy when it can elicit compliance with its rules or decisions from people who disagree with the substance of those rules or decisions. The certification movement has made considerable progress in recent years. Industries appear to be moving in the right direction, and with each new agreement adopting a more progressive view, the future of the world's forests becomes greener. The process of international privatization of regulation of forestry practices through certification is achieved through a growing reliance on markets and market-based strategies as mechanisms to foster compliance. Market-based mechanisms—such as tradable pollution permits and independent certification—are replacing or supplementing command-and-control methods in an effort to manage environmental impacts. These regulations appeal to consumers who, looking for the appropriate certifying mark, will prefer environmentally friendly goods to unfriendly ones.

# Discussion Questions

1. Should the federal government transfer some of its federal lands to state governments in the western part of the United States? Why or why not?
2. Who should foot the costs of fighting fires in California? Explain your reasoning.
3. Given limited segments of undammed rivers in Tennessee, should some of the dams be removed to provide more natural rivers for recreational purposes? Explain your reasoning.
4. Can industry-sponsored certification standards for sustainably managed forests provide the same guarantees as provided by an independent certifier? Why or why not?

# CHAPTER TWENTY-ONE

## Wetlands and the National Environmental Policy Act

---

## Learning Objectives

- *Describe the major permit that applies to wetlands.*
- *Explain why swampbuster has been credited with preserving wetlands.*
- *Summarize the requirements to lessen denigration of the environment by federal agencies.*
- *Describe when a federal agency is required to prepare an EIS.*

Federal legislation on the separate issues of wetlands and environmental policy has been enacted to protect our environmental resources. While wetlands are regulated under the Clean Water Act (CWA), they are also the subject of other legislation. Moreover, the definition of what a wetland is remains controversial. Congress enacted the National Environmental Policy Act (NEPA) in 1969, and this law became effective in 1970. The law requires the federal government to consider environmental issues in its actions. Most states have followed with state environmental policy acts applying to state governmental actions.

## Wetlands

It is estimated that over half of the wetlands that existed in the continental United States two centuries ago have been destroyed, and wetlands continue to disappear at a disturbing rate. Some of the major causes of wetland conversion include draining for agricultural and forestry production, draining and filling for urban and residential development, and dredging and filling for navigation. Concern about the loss of wetlands is based mainly upon the benefits of improved water quality, water waste removal, nutrient retention, sediment removal, fish and wildlife habitat, flood protection, erosion control, and groundwater recharge. Two major federal laws provide jurisdiction for the federal government over wetlands: Section 404 of the CWA and the swampbuster provisions of the 1985 Farm Bill.

The wetlands debate focuses mostly on the effectiveness, equity, and costs of wetland protection. Specifically, are remaining wetland resources adequately protected by existing policies and laws while protecting the rights of landowners? If not, what legislative actions would be appropriate? Addressing these issues is complicated because there are many different kinds of wetlands, many laws are involved, and some believe protection efforts need to be enhanced—while others believe they are already too extensive and inflexible.

Federal laws affect wetlands in a variety of ways. Some laws have directly or indirectly encouraged destruction of wetland areas such as selected provisions in the federal tax code, public works legislation, and farm commodity programs. As the value of wetlands has been recognized, many of these laws have been amended to reduce or neutralize adverse effects on wetland resources. In addition, a growing number of laws encourage wetlands protection. The protective provisions, however, do not add up to a fully consistent or comprehensive national approach.

The first issue is the definition of a wetland. A wetland is a swamp, marsh, bog, or any area that is covered or saturated with water at a frequency and duration sufficient to support plants that live in saturated soil. Wetlands are defined under regulations of the CWA and other laws. Wetlands may not include nonaquatic areas that have aquatic vegetation or areas that were transformed into dry land prior to applicable regulations. Property owners who are uncertain whether they have a plot for development that is a wetland should consult with the Natural Resources Conservation Service (NRCS), the Army Corps of Engineers, or an approved county list of hydric soil map units.

## 1. Wetlands and the Clean Water Act

The major protection for wetlands arises from Section 404 of the CWA. Its intent is to protect water and adjacent wetland areas from adverse environmental effects due to discharges of dredged or fill material. A "dredge-and-fill" permit, also known as a Section 404 permit, is required from the Army Corps of Engineers to discharge dredged or fill materials in waters including wetlands, although exceptions do exist. The district engineer of each Corps district determines the regulatory jurisdiction over wetlands.

Discharge of dredged or fill material from normal farming, silviculture, and ranching activities such as plowing, seeding, and cultivating is not prohibited by the CWA regulations. Minor drainage is also allowed without a permit, pursuant to the discharge

Fig. 21.1 Natural materials may also diminish water quality.

of dredged or fill materials incidental to effecting the removal of excess soil moisture from upland croplands. In the same manner, discharge of dredged or fill material from harvesting for the production of food, fiber, and forest products is also not prohibited. Furthermore, the construction of a farm pond or the maintenance of a drainage ditch does not require a permit. But, the construction of a new drainage ditch is subject to the Section 404 permit procedure.

## 2. Wetlands under the Swampbuster Provisions

The second law is the swampbuster provisions introduced by the 1985 Farm Bill and expanded by the 1990 Farm Bill. The secretary of agriculture, through the NRCS of the US Department of Agriculture, administers these provisions. The swampbuster provisions are not directly related to Section 404 of the CWA; rather, swampbuster was enacted to ensure that federal farm programs do not serve as a reason or motivation for draining additional wetlands and to improve water quality. The NRCS identifies wetlands and publishes hydric soil maps. The law uses the date of December 23, 1985, to determine whether a wetland was converted in violation of the swampbuster provisions. Wetlands converted prior to this date may be in violation of Section 404 of the CWA, but may not be violative of swampbuster. Wetlands converted after this date may be in violation of both acts.

Swampbuster is a disincentive program, rather than a regulatory program. Wetlands converted to agricultural uses in violation of the swampbuster provisions can cause the farmer to be disqualified from additional federal programs. Farmers may lose their eligibility for federal price and income support programs, including loans from the

Farmers Home Administration, disaster payments, federal crop insurance, and farm storage facility loans.

The definition of wetlands under swampbuster includes three components: soils, plants, and hydrology. The Army Corps of Engineers (Corps) applies a wetland delineation manual in making about 25,000 jurisdictional determinations each year. The purpose of the manual is to provide field-level consistency among the agencies that have roles in wetlands protection: the Corps, the EPA, NRCS, and the Fish and Wildlife Service. Other laws may impact the use or destruction of the wetlands.

## 3. Jurisdiction over Wetlands after *Rapanos v. United States*

In 2006, the US Supreme Court addressed the issue of whether three wetland areas were subject to Section 404 of the CWA in *Rapanos v. United States*. The CWA makes it unlawful to discharge dredged or fill material into "navigable waters" without a permit and defines "navigable waters" as the waters of the United States, including the territorial seas. The Army Corps of Engineers, which issues permits for the discharge of dredged or fill material into navigable waters, interprets the waters of the United States expansively to include not only traditional navigable waters, but also other defined waters, tributaries of such waters, and wetlands "adjacent" to such waters and tributaries. Adjacent wetlands include those bordering, contiguous to, or neighboring waters of the United States, even when they are separated from such waters by man-made dikes and the like.

The United States brought civil enforcement proceedings against the *Rapanos* petitioners, who had backfilled three wetland areas without a permit. The district court found federal jurisdiction over the wetlands because they were adjacent to "waters of the United States" and held petitioners liable for CWA violations. Affirming, the Sixth Circuit Court of Appeals found federal jurisdiction based on the sites' hydrologic connections to the nearby ditches or drains, or to more remote navigable waters. The Supreme Court reversed the lower court judgments, but was split on a rationale for the reversals—the vote was 4-4-1. Thus, the issue of what are "waters of the United States" is not totally clear.

The question is whether the wetlands qualified as waters of the United States. There was agreement by all the justices in the *Rapanos* decision that the CWA intended to define the term "navigable waters" more broadly than that traditional meaning, but disagreement as to how much. The district and circuit courts found the Corps of Engineers had jurisdiction over the wetlands at issue because the wetlands were hydrologically connected to navigable waters via a drain and ditch, even though it was not clear whether either of these structures always contained water. The reversal of the lower court decisions by the Supreme Court clarifies that a mere "hydrological connection" between a wetland and traditionally navigable water—while necessary as a minimum to confer jurisdiction—may by itself be insufficient. In particular, the ability of the Corps or the EPA to assert jurisdiction over waters where there is no continual surface water connection to navigable water is in question.

As the Supreme Court lacked a majority opinion in its ruling, the concurring opinion by Justice Kennedy has been interpreted as controlling the interpretation of the CWA to define the scope of federal jurisdiction more broadly than the four justices in the plurality, but more narrowly than the four dissenting justices. To be waters of the United States, a wetland must possess a significant nexus to waters that are or were navigable in fact. This nexus can be established in one of two ways: (1) by adjacency, where wetlands are physically adjacent to and connected with traditionally navigable waters; or (2) by ecological interconnection, where wetlands either alone or in combination with similarly situated lands in the region significantly affect the chemical, physical, and biological integrity of traditionally navigable waters.

Given this similarity between the reasoning of the plurality in *Rapanos* and Justice Kennedy, the opinion has had considerable significance. Previously, almost any (or even no) connection between a wetland and navigable water was enough to establish federal jurisdiction over the wetland. With five justices requiring some physical connection between the wetland and the navigable water in order to support jurisdiction, and with disagreement only as to whether a substantial ecological connection can substitute for the permanence of the physical connection, that era may be over.

In 2013, the EPA issued a proposal to clarify the definition of waters of the United States (WOTUS). The proposal sparked considerable controversy from farm groups, and it was not adopted.

## Questions

1. In *Rapanos*, why was a Section 404 permit required?
2. What did the *Rapanos* district and circuit courts decide?
3. In *Rapanos*, what was the jurisdictional issue?
4. In *Rapanos*, what did the Supreme Court decide?
5. Between environmentalists and business interests, who should be more pleased with the *Rapanos* decision?

# The National Environmental Policy Act

NEPA is a broad "stop-and-think" law that requires federal agencies to consider environmental consequences and disclose information to the public before embarking on new actions. Because NEPA does not enumerate environmental standards, it does not mandate mechanisms that operate to prevent environmental damages. However, by requiring agencies to consider environmental consequences of proposed actions and to produce publicly reviewable documents, it has achieved some success in curtailing federal projects that would be especially inimical to environmental quality.

NEPA acknowledges that citizens have the right to enjoy a healthful environment and that the federal government should consider that right in their decision-making processes. While governments might be expected to always consider healthful environments for their citizens, the economics and politics of governmental projects often relegate environmental quality to an inferior position. NEPA requires the federal government to consider environmental quality, yet does not force an agency to make a particular decision. Instead, it only requires government agencies to take the environment into account in the decision-making process. In some cases, this is done through an "environmental assessment" (EA), while in other cases, an "environmental impact statement" (EIS) is required. But regardless of the document required, NEPA does not require an agency to base its decisions upon the gathered information so that projects can be approved, despite their adverse impact upon the environment.

## 1. Environmental Assessments

NEPA's main function is to require federal agencies to take the environment into account before making certain decisions that may adversely affect the environment. This begins with an EA. By conducting an assessment of the environmental consequences and preparing a concise public document, federal agencies evaluate the significance of a proposed federal action's impact on the environment. An EA briefly provides sufficient evidence and analysis for determining whether there exists a need to prepare further documentation on a proposed federal project. After preparing the EA, there are two choices: (1) to prepare an EIS if there are significant impacts; or (2) make a "finding of no significant impacts" (FONSI). If the EA finds that a proposed project will have a significant environmental impact, the agency must prepare an EIS.

EAs are not as costly and time consuming as an EIS. Between four hundred and five hundred EISs are made by environmental agencies each year. If an agency performs research and decides that an action or project will not significantly impact the human environment, then a FONSI is proclaimed, and an EIS is not necessary. If, in the course of preparing an EA, an agency discovers that the proposed activity will result in a significant impact on the environment, the agency may change its proposal in order to avoid causing significant impact, and thus avoid the trouble of preparing an EIS. Generally, this requires the filing of both an EA and a FONSI.

An agency may adopt supplemental procedures to identify projects that do not individually or cumulatively have a significant effect on the human environment. These may be enumerated so that the entire category of actions do not require an EIS. Hence, the agency would declare a categorical exclusion.

## 2. Environmental Impact Statements

An EIS is a detailed analysis that serves to ensure that the policies and goals defined in NEPA are infused into the ongoing programs and actions of the federal agency. The EIS should provide a discussion of significant environmental impacts and reasonable alternatives (including a "no action" alternative). In this manner, an agency's action can minimize adverse impacts or enhance the quality of the human environment. The EIS requirement of NEPA has had a huge impact on the way the federal government conducts business because EISs have to be released to the public for comment. Projects that are bad for the environment are no longer hidden from the public. Public pressure—or even the threat of public pressure—can stop projects before they get off the drawing board.

When deciding whether or not to file an EIS, agencies make a decision based on three criteria:

I.   Is the activity a federal activity? Even private projects can be subject to an EIS if the government is involved in any way. Examples include loans from government financiers or licenses given by federal agencies.

II.  The activity must be major. This usually means an activity requires a lot of resources. There are no set dollar guidelines to follow for assessing whether an activity is major or not.

III. Significant impact is the hardest to define of the three criteria. By examining the context and intensity of an activity, an agency can gauge its impact.

Significant impact is defined to mean an agency must analyze the context and intensity of a proposal to determine whether an EIS is needed. The context of significant impact involves examining the short- and long-term effects of an activity on many different levels of government and society.

A notice of intent (NOI) is published by an agency in the *Federal Register* when the agency decides to prepare an EIS outlining the proposal, alternatives, and gives a contact individual at the agency. If more than one agency is involved, a lead agency will take primary responsibility for preparing the EIS, with cooperating agencies assisting because of their special expertise or legal responsibilities. NEPA requires an interdisciplinary team of people from lead and cooperating agencies for researching and writing the EIS.

An EIS needs to contain a description of the proposal of action and the purpose and need for the proposed action. The parts of the environment that could be significantly impacted by the proposed action and benefits and risks of each alternative will be identified. The EIS will list reasonable alternatives to the proposed action that should be given, with a preferred alternative identified. An EIS will describe the no-action alternative that identifies the benefits and risks of doing nothing, compared to taking action. The EIS should also delineate the cumulative impacts of the action that analyze the effects of the proposed action on other projects, both in the present and the future.

The following case considers a situation where the US Coast Guard failed to consider NEPA in adopting regulations for a bay area.

### *United States v. Coalition for Buzzards Bay*
US Court of Appeals for the First Circuit, Boston

*Who is suing?* _____

*Who is being sued?* _____

*For what?* _____

*What is the issue on appeal?* _____

Buzzards Bay comprises an inlet flowing landward from the Atlantic Ocean that is thirty miles long and a major channel of maritime commerce in southeastern Massachusetts. The combined environmental and commercial significance of the bay has sparked a pitched battle between federal and state sovereigns over the nature of preventative measures needed to safeguard against the risk of oil spills. The overarching question before us involves the Coast Guard's authority to promulgate regulations that preempt state environmental law with respect to tank vessels. We hold that, during the rulemaking process, the Coast Guard failed to comply with its obligations under the National Environmental Policy Act (NEPA). We reverse the district court's entry of summary judgment in favor of the Coast Guard, vacate the injunction against the enforcement of state law issued below, and remand for further proceedings.

In 2003, a vessel struck an outcropping of rocks spilling an estimated 98,000 gallons of oil into Buzzards Bay. Spurred by this incident, the state legislature enacted the Massachusetts Oil Spill Prevention Act (MOSPA). The federal government saw this as a threat to its power to regulate commercial shipping on Buzzards Bay and sued to abrogate certain provisions of the MOSPA. The suit asserted that the challenged provisions of the state statutory scheme were preempted by the Ports and Waterways Safety Act, as amended by the Port and Tanker Safety Act. The district court granted an injunction. With the case pending before the district court, the Coast Guard promulgated a final rule relating to navigation in Buzzards Bay (the 2007 Rule) to preempt the challenged provisions of the MOSPA. As part of the rulemaking process that culminated in the issuance of the 2007 Rule, the Coast Guard eschewed the preparation of either an environmental impact statement (EIS) or an environmental assessment (EA). It determined instead that its proposed action fell within a categorical exclusion that obviated any such analysis. The Commonwealth alleged that the Coast Guard, in the process of promulgating the 2007 Rule, had violated both the Administrative Procedure Act and NEPA.

The district court found a NEPA violation, but concluded that this violation was "essentially harmless" because the substance of the Coast Guard's actual rulemaking analysis was the functional equivalent of what an environmental impact statement would have generated. The court found preemption appropriate, entered a declaratory judgment for the Coast Guard, and permanently enjoined enforcement of the controverted portions of the state statute. We may set aside agency action if that action is arbitrary, capricious, an abuse of discretion, or otherwise not in accordance with law.

NEPA is our basic national charter for protection of the environment. It has dual objectives. First, it places upon an agency the obligation to consider every significant aspect of the environmental impact of a proposed action. Second, it ensures that the agency will inform the public that it has indeed considered environmental concerns in its decisionmaking process. Though significant, NEPA's requirements are procedural in nature. So long as the environmental effects of a proposed action have been adequately identified and studied, the agency is free to weigh those effects and decide—within the limits fixed by the Administrative Procedure Act—that other values overbalance environmental costs. Seen in this light, the role of judicial review is simply to insure that the agency has taken a hard look at environmental consequences.

NEPA's general requirement that federal agencies prepare either an EIS or an EA in anticipation of any major action is not absolute. An affected agency is charged in the first instance with determining if a proposed action is one which ordinarily requires an EIS, or which is exempted from environmental review because it comes within a categorical exclusion. A categorical exclusion is meant to encompass a category of actions which do not individually or cumulatively have a significant effect on the human environment and which have been found to have no such effect in procedures adopted by a Federal agency in implementation of these regulations. Such actions normally do not require the preparation of either an EIS or an EA.

If a proposed agency action is not one that ordinarily would require an EIS, but nevertheless is not exempted from environmental review, the agency must prepare an EA. That EA is intended to serve as the foundation upon which the agency will make its determination about whether it is necessary to prepare an EIS. While an EA is not as extensive as an EIS, it nonetheless must include discussion of the environmental impacts of the proposed action and alternatives. The Coast Guard has adopted supplemental procedures and codified them in Commandant Instruction M16475.1D. These supplemental procedures describe thirty-five categorical exclusions (CEs). When promulgating the 2007 Rule, the Coast Guard asserted the applicability of its exclusions. The Coast Guard has enumerated in its supplemental procedures various considerations to guide its assessment of whether a particular action, though nominally covered by a CE, involves "extraordinary circumstances" and, thus, requires the preparation of either an EIS or an EA. In effect, this constitutes a list of exceptions to the exclusions.

The Coast Guard has identified ten extraordinary circumstances exceptions which, if applicable, may trump a CE and require it to prepare an EIS or an EA. By the same token, the Coast Guard may not rely upon a CE if its proposed action triggers any of the extraordinary circumstances exceptions limned in an incorporated Department of Transportation (DOT) order. The incorporated order requires the preparation of an EIS or an EA for agency actions that are likely to involve any of four additional extraordinary circumstances. In its notice of proposed rulemaking, the Coast Guard explicitly cited Commandant Instruction M16475.1D—its own set of procedures, which incorporate the DOT order. It described this matrix as the document that would guide the Coast Guard in complying with NEPA. We hold that NEPA determination in this case must give full effect to the content of Commandant Instruction M16475.1D.

This brings us to the question of whether the Coast Guard, in relying on a CE as a means of sidestepping any meaningful environmental analysis, acted arbitrarily. In arguing for an affirmative answer to this question, the Commonwealth focuses on the extraordinary circumstances exceptions that, in its view, prevented the agency from relying on a CE. These extraordinary circumstances relate to those likely to be highly controversial in terms of scientific validity or public opinion. The Coast Guard was bound to determine whether further analysis was required based on the potential environmental effects of the proposed action. Careful perscrutation of the record in this case persuades us that the Coast Guard's bareboned negative response—a simple "no"—to the prompt asking whether the proposed action was likely to be highly controversial was arbitrary and capricious.

The record in this case belies the Coast Guard's conclusory determination that its proposed action was not likely to be highly controversial within the meaning of its own procedures and guidelines. During the rulemaking process, the Coast Guard received a plethora of worried comments from local officials, state legislators, and other representatives of state government. The public officials' comments were supplemented by submissions from private groups and individuals who believed that protections beyond those described in the proposed rule were needed to prevent environmental damage to Buzzards Bay. Given these realities, we conclude, as did the district court, that the Coast Guard's eschewal of any meaningful environmental inquiry was arbitrary and capricious.

We add that NEPA's framework is designed in part to stimulate public participation in the rulemaking process. It would be Kafkaesque to deem the very comments submitted by the public, in and of themselves, a competent proxy for the NEPA determination that is meant to prompt and inform such comments. The administrative record, viewed as a whole, does not show that the Coast Guard ever analyzed, or even adequately studied, the environmental impact of its proposed action. Consequently, its failure to prepare either an EIS or an EA was not harmless. We reverse the entry of summary judgment, vacate the injunction, and return the case to the district court with instructions to remand it to the Coast Guard for further proceedings consistent with this opinion.

## Questions

1. Can states normally enact restrictions that go further than requirements in federal law?
2. What does the court suggest about the potential for non–EA materials to satisfy NEPA's requirements?
3. Can a federal agency normally adopt regulations that preempt state action?
4. What was the meaning of the DOT order?
5. What was the significance of Commandant Instruction M16475.1D?

## 3. Council on Environmental Quality

NEPA includes the Council on Environmental Quality (CEQ). The CEQ is an advisory committee that coordinates federal environmental efforts and works closely with agencies and other White House offices in the development of environmental policies and initiatives. Its duties include (i) advising the president on the environment; (ii) gathering and analyzing environmental data; (iii) evaluating federal programs in light of the goals established in the Act; (iv) developing and promoting national policies to improve environmental quality; and (v) conducting studies, surveys, research, and analyses relating to ecosystems and environmental quality.

## 4. Categorical Exclusions

As already noted in the *Buzzards Bay* lawsuit, categorical exclusions under which categories of actions not individually or cumulatively having a significant effect on the human environment do not require further examination. For categorical exclusions, neither an environmental assessment nor an environmental impact statement is required. The following case considers a NEPA challenge to the National Park Service's claim that it relied on a categorical exclusion.

### *Wilderness Watch v. Mainella*
US Court of Appeals for the Eleventh Circuit, Atlanta

*Who is suing?* _____

*Who is being sued?* _____

*For what?* _____

*What is the issue on appeal?* _____

Wilderness Watch appeals the grant of summary judgment to the National Park Service on its complaint seeking to enjoin the Park Service's practice of using motor vehicles to transport visitors across the designated wilderness area on Cumberland Island, Georgia. Wilderness Watch asserts that this practice violates the Wilderness Act, and also that the Park Service made the decision to transport tourists without conducting the investigation and analysis of potential environmental impact required by the National Environmental Policy Act (NEPA). Finally, Wilderness Watch claims that the Park Service established an advisory committee without the public notice and participation required by the Federal Advisory Committee Act, rendering the agreement signed following those meetings invalid and unenforceable. The Administrative Procedure Act, which governs review of agency action, permits courts to set aside agency action when it is arbitrary, capricious, an abuse of discretion, or otherwise not in accordance with law.

Congress passed the 1964 Wilderness Act in order to preserve and protect certain lands "in their natural condition" and thus secure for present and future generations the benefits of wilderness. Congress therefore directed that designated wilderness areas shall be administered for the use and enjoyment of the American people in such manner as will leave them unimpaired for future use and enjoyment as wilderness, and so as to provide for the protection of these areas, the preservation of their wilderness character, and for the gathering and dissemination of information regarding their use and enjoyment as wilderness.

Cumberland Island, which features some of the last remaining undeveloped land on the barrier islands along the Atlantic coast of the United States, was declared by Congress to be a National Seashore in 1972. Ten years later, Congress designated as wilderness or potential wilderness some 19,000 acres, including most of the northern three-fifths of the island. Under the aegis of the Secretary of the Interior, the Park Service thus became responsible for administering the wilderness area in accordance with the applicable provisions of the Wilderness Act. Today, visitors to Cumberland Island must leave their vehicles on the mainland and travel to the island by boat. In addition to wilderness area, Park Service land includes several buildings and facilities on the southern end of the island as well as two historical areas on the northern and western coasts: "Plum Orchard," just outside the wilderness boundary, and the "Settlement," located in potential wilderness area. Historically, these two locations have been reached via the "Main Road," a one-lane dirt road that has also been designated as part of the wilderness and potential wilderness areas.

Once federal land has been designated as wilderness, the Wilderness Act places severe restrictions on commercial activities, roads, motorized vehicles, motorized transport, and structures within the area, subject to very narrow exceptions and existing private rights. The statute permits the use of motor vehicles and transport only as necessary to meet minimum requirements for the administration of the area for the purpose of this chapter. Following the wilderness designation, the Park Service continued to use the existing one-lane dirt road to access the historical areas. Motorized transportation on Cumberland Island became a controversial issue in the 1990s, as the federal government sought to obtain remaining private tracts on the island and various groups called for greater public access to and support of the historical sites.

In February 1999, the Park Service agreed to provide regular public access to Plum Orchard and the Settlement via Park Service motor vehicles until boat service could be established. The Park Service acquired a fifteen-person van in order to accommodate larger numbers of visitors. The Park Service offered trips to Plum Orchard three times per week and to the Settlement once per month. Wilderness Watch objects to this arrangement, arguing that the Wilderness Act restricts motorized vehicle use within wilderness areas to the minimum necessary for an agency to meet its administrative needs for the purpose of the Wilderness Act and not for any other purpose. This dispute thus requires us to interpret the limitations imposed on motor vehicle use under the Wilderness Act, in particular the requirement that motor vehicle use be restricted to the level necessary to meet minimum requirements for the administration of the area.

Wilderness Watch also argues that, regardless of whether the Wilderness Act permitted these tours, the agency should have evaluated the environmental impact of its proposal through the written review procedures required by NEPA. Both parties agree that the Park Service did not document any formal NEPA review before its decision.

The Park Service argues that its action qualified for a categorical exclusion from NEPA review, thus relieving the agency from the need to conduct any formal, written review. Wilderness Watch argues that the Park Service cannot invoke a categorical exclusion because there is no evidence that the agency determined that the exclusion applied at the time it agreed to transport visitors.

After reviewing the record, we cannot find any indication that the Park Service considered the application of the categorical exclusion prior to its decision, nor does the agency direct our attention to any such evidence. Rather, the Park Service argues that forcing an agency to formally document reliance on a categorical exclusion would defeat the purpose of the exclusion: to streamline procedures and reduce paperwork and delay. We disagree. Documentation of reliance on a categorical exclusion need not be detailed or lengthy. It need only be long enough to indicate to a reviewing court that the agency indeed considered whether or not a categorical exclusion applied and concluded that it did. In most instances, a short statement that a categorical exclusion has been invoked will suffice to assure a reviewing court that environmental effects have been considered.

NEPA imposes procedural requirements before decisions are made in order to ensure that those decisions take environmental consequences into account. Permitting an agency to avoid a NEPA violation through a subsequent, conclusory statement that it would not have reached a different result even with the proper analysis would significantly undermine the statutory scheme. In the absence of evidence that an agency seriously considered environmental impacts prior to making its decision, violations of NEPA cannot be considered harmless.

We recognize the difficult position of the Park Service in this case. Faced with competing demands from different constituencies in both Congress and the general public, the agency attempted to find a compromise that would satisfy all interested parties and potentially stave off legislative changes to the status of the Cumberland Island wilderness area. Although this goal is laudable, the statute limits motor vehicle use and transport to what is "necessary to meet minimum requirements for the administration of the area." The compromise on public transportation reached in this case cannot be squared with the language of the Wilderness Act. Reversed.

## Questions

1. Why couldn't the Park Service use more vehicles on Cumberland Island?
2. What vehicular access is allowed?
3. Why was there a legislative proposal to remove wilderness designation for the island?
4. What is a categorical exclusion from a NEPA review?
5. What is the problem with allowing categorical exclusions?
6. What is the problem with not requiring formal documentation of reliance on a categorical exclusion?

# State Environmental Policy Acts

Many states have adopted state environmental policy acts governing the disclosure of environmental effects of proposed state projects. In passing a state act, legislatures often note a number of criteria.

I.   The protection and preservation of the state's diverse environment is necessary for the maintenance of the public health and welfare and the continued viability of the economy of the state and is a matter of the highest public priority.

II.  State agencies should conduct their affairs with an awareness that they are stewards of the air, land, water, plants, animals, and environmental, historical, and cultural resources.

III. Environmental evaluation should be a part of the decision-making processes of the state.

IV.  Environmental effects reports can facilitate the fullest practicable provision of timely public information, understanding, and participation in the decision-making processes of the state.

State environmental policy acts often include proposed governmental actions by any department, board, bureau, commission, authority, or other agency of the state. Actions undertaken by a municipality or county are also included under the Act if more than a given percentage of the total cost of the project is funded by a grant of a state government agency. A proposed governmental action may include (i) any proposed land-disturbing activity by a state government agency or funded by a grant from a state government agency; (ii) any proposed sale or exchange of more than five acres of state-owned land; or (iii) any proposed harvesting of five acres or more of trees over two inches in diameter at breast height. A state act often excludes specified agricultural practices; forestry land management practices; emergency measures undertaken in response to an immediate threat to public health or safety; and activities in which government agency participation is ministerial in nature, involving no exercise of discretion on the part of the government agency.

In general, any covered proposed governmental action by a state government agency must be assessed by the responsible official of that agency to determine whether or not the proposed action may significantly adversely affect the quality of the environment. If the official reaches a determination that the proposed governmental action is one that may significantly adversely affect the quality of the environment, the government agency responsible for the project shall prepare further documentation. This would be similar to the information required by an EIS and would include public involvement.

# Discussion Questions

1. What wetland areas should be regulated as "waters of the United States?" Why?
2. What effects might a retrenchment of regulations governing wetlands have on the environment and the economy?
3. What benefits and costs might be expected if Congress weakens or repeals NEPA?
4. What should be required under NEPA for federal projects regarding the issue of climate change?
5. Should the federal government be able to implement a new right-of-way vegetation-maintenance policy for removing trees less than ten feet tall in highway rights-of-way without conducting the environmental review required by NEPA?

# CHAPTER TWENTY-TWO
## Sustainability

## Learning Objectives

- *Explain the meaning of sustainable development as set forth in the United Nations' sustainable development goals.*
- *Critique our country's use of energy from a viewpoint of wanting to be more sustainable.*
- *Discuss who might be opposed to renewable energy portfolio standards and why.*
- *Identify three food production technologies that reduce the use of resources.*
- *Describe an extended producer responsibility program.*

Varied definitions of sustainability make it difficult to summarize its meaning. Americans tend to think about using less energy, lowering greenhouse gas emissions, and recycling. However, for most of the world, sustainability is viewed as sustainable development. This concept surfaced at the World Charter for Nature in 1982, was pursued in the Brundtland Report of 1987, and elaborated upon in the 1992 Earth Summit and the 2012 United Nations (UN) Conference on Sustainable Development. The influential Brundtland Report offers a definition of sustainable development that captures the fundamentals most often related to this term.

> ***Sustainable development:*** *Development that meets the needs of the present without compromising the ability of future generations to meet their own needs.*

This definition has been interpreted as having three prongs. First, sustainability involves environmental impacts, and this component often receives the most attention. Persons who strongly support environmental quality may place a great deal of emphasis on development that minimizes potential environmental damage. They employ tools such as environmental footprint analysis, exposure assessment, integrated assessment modeling, life-cycle assessment, resilience analysis, risk assessment, chemical alternatives assessment, and sustainability impact assessment to discern how to select superior sustainable development options.

Second, sustainable development takes into account the economic impacts of development. It might be expected that these will vary from country to country. While developed countries may have the resources to refrain from certain activities that are inimical to future generations, poorer countries may choose to allow activities needed to relieve current health and social issues even though they do not optimally provide for future generations. Economic tools include benefit-cost analysis, eco-efficiency analysis, ecosystem service valuation, and green accountings.

The third prong involves the social impact of development. This considers responsibility, justice, equity, and the social consequences of development activities. Social equity tools include collaborative problem solving, environmental justice analysis, health impact assessment, segmentation analysis, social impact analysis, and social network analysis.

To consider sustainability efforts and objectives, it is useful to look at international efforts to identify the concerns. A legitimate starting point is the 2015 UN Conference on Sustainable Development held in New York and its listing of seventeen sustainable development goals (SDGs). The identification of SDGs provides a backdrop for examining sustainability issues in the United States.

# UN Conference on Sustainable Development

With the gathering of 193 Member States of the United Nations General Assembly in 2015, they debated, formulated, and adopted seventeen measurable SDGs. Given the efforts that went into the development and adoption of the SDGs and their breadth, they offer a compelling delineation of goals to support sustainable development. They are repeated in full below.

> *Goal 1. End poverty in all its forms everywhere.*
>
> *Goal 2. End hunger, achieve food security and improved nutrition and promote sustainable agriculture.*
>
> *Goal 3. Ensure healthy lives and promote well-being for all at all ages.*
>
> *Goal 4. Ensure inclusive and equitable quality education and promote lifelong learning opportunities for all.*

*Goal 5. Achieve gender equality and empower all women and girls.*

*Goal 6. Ensure availability and sustainable management of water and sanitation for all.*

*Goal 7. Ensure access to affordable, reliable, sustainable and modern energy for all.*

*Goal 8. Promote sustained, inclusive and sustainable economic growth, full and productive employment and decent work for all.*

*Goal 9. Build resilient infrastructure, promote inclusive and sustainable industrialization and foster innovation.*

*Goal 10. Reduce inequality within and among countries.*

*Goal 11. Make cities and human settlements inclusive, safe, resilient and sustainable.*

*Goal 12. Ensure sustainable consumption and production patterns.*

*Goal 13. Take urgent action to combat climate change and its impacts.*

*Goal 14. Conserve and sustainably use the oceans, seas and marine resources for sustainable development.*

*Goal 15. Protect, restore and promote sustainable use of terrestrial ecosystems, sustainably manage forests, combat desertification, and halt and reverse land degradation and halt biodiversity loss.*

*Goal 16. Promote peaceful and inclusive societies for sustainable development, provide access to justice for all and build effective, accountable and inclusive institutions at all levels.*

*Goal 17. Strengthen the means of implementation and revitalize the global partnership for sustainable development.*

Rather strikingly, the SDGs do not mention the environment or environmental protection. Rather, they establish sustainability as a concept that focuses on goals of ending poverty and ensuring that all people enjoy peace and prosperity. The SDGs also embody sharing responsibilities and respecting national policies and priorities.

Despite the positive foundation set forth by the SDGs, there is no framework for policy reforms and societal change to facilitate the achievement of their objectives. Further efforts at developing and building indicators to assess the relative contribution of each of the SDGs might offer implementation strategies for nations to pursue in their efforts to move toward sustainable development.

## Sustainability in the United States

In the United States, sustainability has different meanings for different people. However, we tend to focus on three issues: energy consumption, food production related to releases of greenhouse gases, and recycling. Many of us realize that our country uses a lot of energy, and most of it involves the use of fossil fuels. Our usage is related to SDG numbers 7 and 13: it detracts from sustainable development. Moreover, developed countries are urged to reduce consumption to free energy resources of petroleum, natural gas, and coal for lesser developed countries. This may be achieved through efforts to use renewable energy sources to meet energy needs.

Everyone consumes food every day; purchasing food products and meals are frequent events. Many people reflect upon sustainability and health concerns when they make their purchases of food. Thoughts about food production also extend to its relationship to healthy lives, sustainable consumption, food security, land degradation, and climate change. Such reflections are related to several of the SDGs noted by the UN.

We are also cognizant of recycling efforts. Yet most Americans view recycling as pertaining to a few items, including glass, cans, paper, cell phones, and tires. Recycling needs to be expanded to cover more of the wastes that are being deposited in landfills. Expanding recycling to "extended producer responsibility" programs offers opportunities to engage in additional recycling efforts that support sustainability.

# US Energy Usage

A few statistics on energy usage in the United States highlight our need to do more to conserve energy resources for future generations. A comparison of the consumption of energy by various countries through the release of $CO_2$ captures the inequalities of energy usage. The United States releases more than 17 metric tons of $CO_2$ per capita (person), compared to 8 metric tons by Europeans and 6 metric tons by the Chinese.

The largest sources of energy in the United States are petroleum (36 percent), followed by natural gas (29 percent), and coal (16 percent). Approximately 10 percent of our energy comes from renewable sources, with biomass supplying nearly one-half of this amount. Nearly 40 percent of the country's energy consumption is used to make electric power, followed by 28 percent being used for transportation. Electricity usage in the United States is about 7,000 kilowatts per capita, while usage in the European Union is about 3,200. The ability of Europeans to use 45 percent less electricity raises questions about actions that the United States might take to reduce its enormous energy consumption. Figures on greenhouse gas emissions show a similar story. Despite similar standards of living, the European Union releases 37 percent fewer hydrofluorocarbons, perfluorocarbons, and sulfur hexafluoride than the United States.

While Americans generally support new technologies, we have been slow to support energy conservation and renewable sources of energy. Part of this reluctance seems to be related to a desire to boost our economy by supporting the petroleum industry, including numerous tax breaks for various efforts at developing new sources of hydrocarbons. Three lawsuits show various aspects of resistance to developing renewable energy resources.

## 1. Opposition by Fossil Fuel Companies

In some states, citizens desiring the use of renewable energy have championed efforts mandating that a percentage of electricity come from renewable sources. Renewable portfolio standards have been adopted by state legislatures. California adopted an initiative that requires 33 percent of the state's electricity come from renewable sources by 2020, while Colorado's latest program requires 30 percent. Fossil fuel companies and their supporters do not encourage such mandates.

### *Energy and Environment Legal Institute v. Epel*
US Court of Appeals for the Tenth Circuit, Denver

*Who is suing?* _____

*Who is being sued?* _____

*For what?* _____

*What is the issue on appeal?* _____

The Energy and Environment Legal Institute (EELI) brought this lawsuit against Joshua Epel in his official capacity as Chairman of the Colorado Public Utilities Commission. State law requires electricity generators to ensure that 20% of the electricity they sell to Colorado consumers comes from renewable sources. Colorado consumers receive their electricity from an interconnected grid serving eleven states and portions of Canada and Mexico. Because electricity can go anywhere on the grid and come from anywhere on the grid, and because Colorado is a net importer of electricity, Colorado's renewable energy mandate effectively means some out-of-state coal producers, like an EELI member, will lose business with out-of-state utilities who feed their power onto the grid. And this harm to out-of-state coal producers, EELI says, amounts to a violation of the dormant commerce clause of the U.S. Constitution. The district court disagreed with EELI's assessment and so must we.

The Constitution's Commerce Clause extends to Congress the power to regulate Commerce among the several states. Most everyone accepts that this language grants Congress authority to pass laws concerning interstate commerce and to direct courts to disregard state laws that impede its own. Yet some see even more than that here. For many years, the Supreme Court has read the clause as embodying a sort of judicial free trade policy. Employing what's sometimes called "dormant" or "negative" commerce clause jurisprudence, judges have claimed the authority to strike down state laws that unduly interfere with interstate commerce.

Dormant commerce clause cases are said to come in three varieties. The farthest reaching of these may be associated with *Pike v. Bruce Church, Inc.* (1970). There the Court read the Commerce Clause as allowing judges to strike down state laws burdening interstate commerce when they find insufficient offsetting local benefits. Whether because of the difficulties associated with applying such an unwieldy test or for some other reason, the Court has devised two firmer rules applicable to discrete subsets of cases. The first might be associated with cases like *City of Philadelphia v.*

*New Jersey* (1978), and applies to state laws that "clearly discriminate" against out-of-staters. The second finds its roots in *Baldwin v. G.A.F. Seelig, Inc.* (1935), and is said to apply to certain price control and price affirmation laws that control "extraterritorial" conduct—that is, conduct outside the state's borders. Laws of that sort are deemed almost *per se* invalid.

Before us in this case only the final, Baldwin, test is at issue. For reasons known only to it, EELI has appealed just the district court's disposition under *Baldwin*. *Baldwin's* extraterritoriality principle may be the least understood of the Court's three strands of dormant commerce clause jurisprudence. It is certainly the most dormant for, though the Supreme Court has cited *Baldwin* in passing a number of times, a majority has used its extraterritoriality principle to strike down state laws only three times. In all three cases, the Court thus faced (1) a price control or price affirmation regulation, (2) linking instate prices to those charged elsewhere, with (3) the effect of raising costs for out-of-state consumers or rival businesses.

A careful look at the holdings in the three leading cases suggests a concern with preventing discrimination against out-of-state rivals or consumers. Colorado's mandate isn't a price control statute, it doesn't link prices paid in Colorado with those paid out of state, and it does not discriminate against out-of-staters. While Colorado's mandate surely regulates the quality of a good sold to instate residents, it doesn't directly regulate price instate or anywhere for that matter. Without a regulation more blatantly regulating price and discriminating against out-of-state consumers or producers, *Baldwin's* near *per se* rule doesn't apply. To be sure, fossil fuel producers like EELI's members will be hurt. But as far as we know, all fossil fuel producers in the area served by the grid will be hurt equally and all renewable energy producers in the area will be helped equally.

EELI contends that cases require us to declare "automatically" unconstitutional any state regulation with the practical effect of controlling conduct beyond the boundaries of the State. But, as we've explained, the Court's holdings have not gone nearly so far and have turned instead on the presence of three factors not present here. In fact, the Supreme Court has emphasized as we do that the *Baldwin* line of cases concerns only price control or price affirmation statutes that involve tying the price of instate products to out-of-state prices. *Baldwin* is not applicable to a statute that does not dictate the price of a product and does not tie the price of its instate products to out-of-state prices. The judgment is affirmed.

## Questions

1. Why must 20 percent of the electricity sold in Colorado come from renewable sources?
2. Why did EELI initiate the lawsuit?
3. What is meant by the dormant Commerce Clause?
4. Why doesn't *Baldwin* apply to the facts of this case?

## 2. Opposition to Solar Energy

For solar energy, utilities are not happy with decisions forcing them to accept energy from persons installing solar panels on their homes and buildings. In Florida, utility companies and others advanced a constitutional amendment to prevent solar power from being subsidized by ratepayers. Subsequent to the following case, the amendment was defeated. It did not win a supermajority of 60 percent of the vote as required by the Florida constitution.

### *Advisory Opinion to the Attorney General ... Regarding Solar Energy Choice*
Supreme Court of Florida

*Who is suing?* _____

*Who is being sued?* _____

*For what?* _____

*What is the issue on appeal?* _____

The Attorney General of Florida has petitioned this Court for an advisory opinion as to the validity of a proposed citizen initiative amendment to the Florida Constitution titled "Rights of Electricity Consumers Regarding Solar Energy Choice." This Court's review of the proposed amendment is limited to whether the proposed amendment satisfies the single-subject requirement of article XI, section 3 of the Florida Constitution. We conclude that the proposed amendment embraces a single subject and matter directly connected therewith, and therefore complies with article XI.

The ballot summary for the proposed amendment states:

> *This amendment establishes a right under Florida's constitution for consumers to own or lease solar equipment installed on their property to generate electricity for their own use. State and local governments shall retain their abilities to protect consumer rights and public health, safety and welfare, and to ensure that consumers who do not choose to install solar are not required to subsidize the costs of backup power and electric grid access to those who do.*

This Court has traditionally applied a deferential standard of review to the validity of a citizen initiative petition and has been reluctant to interfere with the right of self-determination for all Florida's citizens to formulate their own organic law. This Court does not consider or address the merits or wisdom of the proposed amendment and must act with extreme care, caution, and restraint before it removes a constitutional amendment from the vote of the people. Accordingly, it is this Court's duty to uphold a proposal unless it can be shown to be clearly and conclusively defective.

Article XI, section 3 of the Florida Constitution establishes the general requirement that a proposed citizen imitative amendment "shall embrace but one subject and matter directly connected therewith." In evaluating whether a proposed amendment violates the single-subject requirement, the Court must determine whether it has a logical and natural oneness of purpose. The single-subject requirement applies to the citizen initiative method of amending the Florida Constitution because the citizen initiative process does not afford the same opportunity for public hearing and debate that accompanies other constitutional proposal and drafting processes.

We conclude that the initiative has a logical and natural oneness of purpose. The logical and natural oneness of purpose of the proposed amendment is to establish a constitutional right for electricity consumers to own or lease solar equipment installed on their property to generate electricity for their own use while simultaneously ensuring that State and local governments shall retain their abilities to protect consumer rights and public health, safety and welfare, and to ensure that consumers who do not choose to install solar are not required to subsidize the costs of backup power and electric grid access to those who do.

The opponents of the initiative contend that the proposed amendment violates the single-subject requirement by combining disjointed subjects into one initiative. We disagree. Provision (b) of the proposed amendment is directly related to provision (a). The subparts of this amendment have a natural relation and connection as component parts or aspects of a single dominant plan or scheme. Combining a constitutional right with the government's authority to regulate that right represents two sides of the same coin, and we have approved ballot initiatives that similarly have created constitutional rights and allowed the government to regulate the right. The components of the amendment are therefore naturally related and connected to the amendment's oneness of purpose.

Additionally, we conclude that the proposed amendment does not substantially alter or perform the functions of multiple branches of government. The opponents of the initiative contend that the proposed amendment violates the single-subject requirement by removing the ability of the State to delegate its regulatory powers to its political subdivisions and prohibiting the State from revoking any powers it delegated to local governments before the adoption of the proposed amendment. However, nothing within the proposed amendment implicitly or explicitly abrogates the power of preemption "retained" by the State under the amendment. We conclude that the initiative petition and ballot title and summary meet the legal requirements of article XI, section 3 of the Florida Constitution. Therefore, we approve the proposed amendment for placement on the ballot.

## Questions

1.  Why did the sponsor of this initiative amendment want a change in the state constitution?
2.  Did the court take a stand on whether they supported the initiative amendment? Why or why not?
3.  What two subjects were identified by the court as naturally related and connected?
4.  Why does the Florida constitution limit the citizen initiative process to one subject?

5.  What types of groups were opposed to the initiative amendment?

## 3. Opposition by Neighbors

For wind power, few people want a wind farm in their area. They feel windmills are noisy, and in some areas they destroy natural settings. Given citizen disapproval, local governmental officials may also raise objections in an attempt to preclude the development of wind energy.

### *In the Matter of the Application of Champaign Wind, L.L.C.*
Supreme Court of Ohio

*Who is suing?* _____

*Who is being sued?* _____

*For what?* _____

*What is the issue on appeal?* _____

Appellants, a collection of local governmental entities and residents, appeal a decision made by appellee the Ohio Power Siting Board (the board) that granted a certificate to intervening appellee, Champaign Wind, L.L.C. (Champaign Wind), to construct a wind-powered electric-generation facility, or wind farm. After reviewing the record and considering the parties' arguments, we hold that appellants have established neither that the board's order is unlawful or unreasonable. Accordingly, we affirm the board's order.

In 2012, we affirmed a board order that granted a certificate to construct the Buckeye Wind Farm in Champaign County. Here, Champaign Wind, a sister company of the Buckeye Wind Farm developer, filed an application to construct another wind farm in Champaign County. Champaign Wind labeled this wind farm "Buckeye Wind II." In its application, Champaign Wind proposed to build up to 56 wind turbines, along with access roads, underground and overhead electric cables, construction-staging areas, an operations-and-maintenance facility, a substation, and up to four meteorological towers, on 13,500 acres of private land leased from about 100 participating landowners. The parties conducted significant discovery. The board held a three-week hearing, issued a 103-page opinion approving Champaign Wind's application, and granted a certificate subject to 72 conditions approving the construction of Buckeye Wind II.

The board has exclusive authority to issue certificates of environmental compatibility and public need for constructing, operation, and maintenance of major utility facilities, such as the proposed wind farm at issue here. Under Ohio Revised Code (R.C.) 4906.10(A), the board shall not issue a certificate unless it finds that the proposed application meets eight substantive criteria.

The term "setback" refers to the distance between a turbine and a neighbor's residence or property line. On appeal, both the neighbors and the county assert that the setbacks the board approved for Buckeye Wind II are not sufficient to serve the public interest or to meet the other statutory criteria under R.C. 4906.10(A). The Ohio Administrative

Code provided minimum setbacks of 541 feet from a neighbor's property line and 919 feet from a neighbor's residence. The board found that all approved turbines for Buckeye Wind II adhered to these regulatory setback requirements. On appeal, the county argues that setbacks must be increased to conform to the turbine manufacturers' recommendations in their safety manuals. Whether the setbacks were sufficient to protect the public from potential blade throw was an evidentiary issue, and we have consistently refused to substitute our judgment for that of the commission on evidentiary matters. The Appellants have failed to establish that the board's interpretation of the safety manuals was unreasonable.

In approving Buckeye Wind II, the board set noise limits to ensure that turbine noise does not unreasonably annoy nonparticipating neighbors. The neighbors object to the board's evidentiary and substantive decisions regarding turbine-noise levels. The board adopted Champaign Wind's proposed nighttime noise limit based on a noise-assessment study by an acoustical engineer hired by Champaign Wind. On appeal, the neighbors argue that the board's decision was unreasonable and unlawful because an inappropriate metric was used to calculate the noise limit and the limit does not prevent adverse health effects to neighbors of the turbines. In the absence of any statutory guidance regarding how the board should set noise regulations for a wind farm, we defer to the board regarding the appropriate methodology for determining a noise limit. The board's decision was not against the manifest weight of the evidence.

The neighbors argue that noise limits should be measured at a neighbor's property line, rather than at the residential structure, so that neighbors can enjoy all of their property free from wind-turbine noise. Due to the absence of any statutory or regulatory guidance, this is another issue on which we must defer to the board. The board found that the inclusion of a noise-complaint resolution process will ensure that the proposed facility will not compromise property owners' use and enjoyment of their entire properties.

The county and the neighbors have not demonstrated that the board's decision was unreasonable or unlawful. The county and the neighbors were active participants at every stage of the board proceeding. The board issued a comprehensive opinion reviewing and addressing all of the parties' arguments. The county and the neighbors have not proven that it is necessary to reopen the record to engage in more discovery or to hear more evidence. Accordingly, we affirm the board's order.

## Questions

1. Why did the state of Ohio assign oversight for certifying wind farms to a state board?
2. Were the appellants simply against wind power?
3. Why weren't appellants denied due process during the approval process?
4. When can the board issue a certificate of environmental compatibility and public need to an applicant?

5. Why was the appellants' argument regarding setbacks insufficient to overturn the board's decision?
6. Why was the appellants' argument regarding noise limits insufficient to overturn the board's decision?

# Food Production

Sustainable development goal #2 addresses hunger, food security, nutrition, and sustainable agriculture and SDG #3 involves health. Many people think about health and sustainability issues when they purchase food products. Because food production technologies involve conflicts between health concerns and resource usage, there are different opinions on the merits of several food production technologies.

Technologies that decrease inputs needed to produce food, increase crop yields, and reduce food prices tend to support SDG #2. Various agricultural production practices can reduce the use of resources for food production and can foster sustainability. Conversely, practices that require increases in resources or inputs for producing food products may be negative. Some of the production technologies affect health. Six production technologies are highlighted to show how the production of food relates to resource consumption and health.

## 1. Genetically Engineered Crops

Producers in the United States are embracing genetically engineered (GE) crops. In 2013, it was estimated that 90 percent of corn, 93 percent of soybeans, and 90 percent of cotton grown in the United States were GE crops. The United States Department of Agriculture, EPA, and FDA play significant roles in the regulation of GE crops. The FDA believes that GE crops and their food products are as safe and nutritious as their traditional counterparts, so the agency does not require special labels for most GE foods. However, many consumers disagree with the FDA's findings and want products containing GE crops to be labeled to dampen GE crop production. They succeeded in convincing some state governments to enact legislation requiring the labeling of food products containing ingredients from GE crops.

In response to these state labeling requirements, Congress passed Public Law 114-216 in 2016 covering bioengineered foods that preempts state labeling. Under the new federal law, the USDA has two years to (1) establish a national mandatory bioengineered food disclosure standard with respect to any bioengineered food and any food that may be bioengineered; and (2) establish such requirements and procedures as the secretary determines necessary to carry out the standard.

Current knowledge leads to the conclusion that the production of GE crops supports sustainability. Herbicide-resistant GE crops mean producers do not need to mechanically cultivate crops to kill competing weeds and leads to increased yields per acre. GE crops that are resistant to certain insect pests reduce the need for insecticides with corresponding increases in production per acre. This means that GE crops diminish the total acreage needed for food production and tend to reduce food prices.

## 2. Hormones, Including rBST

US producers use several different hormones in the production of cattle. The added hormones increase the animal's muscle growth, allowing animals to gain weight more quickly with fewer feedstuffs. Due to financial benefits from administering hormones to cattle, an estimated 92 percent of feedlot cattle in the United States receive hormones. Another hormone being used is recombinant bovine somatotropin (rBST), a genetically engineered animal drug used to supplement bovine somatotropin (BST). Dairy farmers administer rBST to cows to increase milk production.

Some consumers object to the use of hormones because they are concerned about whether residues might still be present in the food products. The FDA has determined that meat products from animals treated with hormones and milk products from animals administered rBST are safe for human consumption. The use of hormones reduces the need for feedstuffs and lowers food prices. Thus, hormones used in animal production support sustainability by reducing the use of energy and land resources needed for the production of food products.

## 3. Antibiotics Used in Animal Production

Antimicrobial agents are being employed to inhibit infections caused by bacteria, viruses, and fungi. The agents have revolutionized human health services and animal production. However, an estimated 20 to 50 percent of human use of antibiotics is unnecessary or highly questionable. Another nonessential use of antibiotics involves the administration of nontherapeutic antibiotics to food animals. Nontherapeutic antibiotics are used to help animals gain weight faster and reduce the consumption of feedstuffs. Animal use of antibiotics may account for 60 percent of the antibiotics used in the United States.

While we want to employ antibiotics to thwart harmful bacteria, simultaneously we should consider efforts to reduce antibiotic usage to slacken the pace of the development of antibiotic-resistant bacteria. Antibiotic resistance is exacerbated by repeated exposure of bacteria to antimicrobial agents and by the long-term exposure to low doses. The problem of antibiotic resistance has led to a recommendation to ban nontherapeutic antibiotics in animal production. However, reductions in nontherapeutic uses will be accompanied by more sick animals and the need of more feedstuffs to produce desired meat products. A ban would be expected to slightly raise food prices.

## 4. Beta Agonists

The FDA approved the use of two beta agonists, ractopamine and zilpaterol hydrochloride, as feed additives for food animals. These veterinary drugs enhance animals' muscle growth, limit the amount of fat in meat products, and improve feed efficiency and carcass weight gain. The use of ractopamine has also been approved by the United Nations' Food and Agriculture Organization, the World Health Organization, and the Codex Alimentarius Commission. However, in the European Union, a panel of the European Food Safety Authority conducted a safety evaluation of ractopamine and came to a different conclusion. The Authority decided that no maximum residue limits could be established, as no conclusion could be rendered on the safety of ractopamine residues in meat products consumed by humans.

American and Canadian livestock producers are feeding their cattle and pigs beta agonists because of the economic advantages. By improving feed efficiency and stimulating muscle growth, producers using beta agonists have lower costs per hundredweight of salable animal products. Discontinuing the use of beta agonists would require more acreage to produce food for animals to secure the same amounts of meat products and slightly higher prices for meat products.

## 5. Organic Production

Some people are advancing organic production as supporting sustainability. In the United States, a certification process guarantees that products meet the federal standards set forth for organic products. From a sustainability viewpoint, it is not clear that organic production supports the SDGs set forth by the United Nations. Three issues are noteworthy: health, resources use, and price. Overall, organic products are no safer than nonorganic products because organic production practices allow disease-causing microbes or pathogens such as *Escherichia coli*, *Campylobacter*, *Listeria*, and *Salmonella* to become established. A study of chicken meat suggested that the likelihood of buying *Campylobacter*-contaminated broiler meat was three times higher for organic broilers than for conventional broilers.

Because organic production does not use inorganic fertilizers, pesticides, and other processed inputs, organic crop yields may average about 80 percent of conventional yields. Lower yields for some organic crops are due to the absence of sufficient nutrients in the soil. Another contributing factor is pest damage. Finally, the production of crops without herbicides requires other methods to control competition from weeds. Organic production thereby requires more acreage to grow the same amount of food; often, organic food products are more expensive, so organic production may not support SDG #2. Thus, while organic production may seem appealing, the world's need for food suggests that practices that increase yields on existing acreages may offer superior environmental solutions by allowing forests and fragile lands to escape cultivation.

## 6. Local Food Production

Buying locally produced food products is being touted as supporting sustainability. People advocating local production feel that the distance from production to consumers, called "food miles," can serve as a measure supporting sustainability because the transport of food over longer distances uses energy and releases greenhouse gases (GHGs). However, there is no direct relationship between the energy expended for food miles and the energy associated with providing a food product. Simply looking at food miles fails to respond to total energy consumption for a given product, as only 4 percent of food's life-cycle GHG emissions are incurred during delivery from the producer to the retailer.

Given the small amount of energy used for transport, energy requirements for agricultural production may have a greater effect on the amounts of carbon attributable to food products. If food can be produced in a more efficient manner in one area, it may reduce environmental damages in other areas that outweigh the carbon cost of transporting the food to market. The distance to market does not consider what mode of transportation is chosen or what type of fuel it uses. This means that data on food miles fails to sort out the carbon emissions per unit of food. Food miles also generally do not consider the distance that consumers drive to purchase food.

Research from New Zealand showed that when all of the energy and carbon emissions of production are considered, some of New Zealand's products are the better choice for consumers in Europe. Livestock in New Zealand can graze outside

Fig. 22.1 Local markets offer fresh plants and food.

year-round instead of eating feed containing grains, and do not require housing for extended periods. Even when the cost of transportation is fully included, the United Kingdom uses twice as much energy to produce milk products locally, as contrasted to products from New Zealand.

## Recycling and Extended Producer Responsibility Programs

Our federal government has declined to become involved in recycling efforts. Thus, it is up to state and local governments to advance recycling, and their support varies. Environmentally friendly states have adopted recycling programs that have markedly reduced waste in landfills. Other states, however, have limited recycling and are not inclined to add regulatory provisions that would encourage recycling. One study shows Americans recycling about 31 percent of things tossed out, while several countries in the European Union countries recycle more than 50 percent of their waste. Europe's advantage is that the European Union has actively promoted recycling through legislation with a target of 50 percent for every country in 2020.

Europe also incinerates more of its waste and generates electricity. In the United States, most waste is deposited into landfills. Many of these landfills capture methane gas as it is produced by the waste, and it is used to generate electricity. However, incineration results in a greater reduction of greenhouse gas releases. In fact, the EPA estimates that 20 percent of the methane emissions in the United States come from landfills. Our disposal of waste is harming the environment.

More recently, recycling has lost some of its economic impetus as the value of recycled materials has plummeted, and some programs are no longer profitable. Falling oil prices, a strong dollar, and weakened economies in Asia have negatively impacted prices of recyclables. Furthermore, our recycling stream has become more polluted with nonrecyclable items. Recycling facilities are having difficulties in separating different recyclables, contributing to the falling prices for recycled materials.

Another recycling effort involves extended producer responsibility (EPR) programs to generate economic incentives to recycle and eliminate waste. EPR programs are premised on the policy that producers-manufacturers should help finance the costs of recycling or safely disposing of products no longer wanted by consumers. By making firms more responsible for future waste, EPR promotes the internalization of environmental externalities. For some situations, EPR can support collaboration for sustainable supply chain objectives or stimulate social responsibility. Societies also benefit from EPR because meeting requirements set by a regulatory framework tends to level the playing field for all firms in the implementation of sustainability activities.

Several European countries have adopted extensive EPR programs, and they are an extension of the polluter-pays principle embodied in European legislation. While the person discarding an object may be the polluter, under EPR, the producer of the object also has a responsibility regarding the waste. Because the producer had a central role in designing, creating, and marketing the product, some responsibility for its disposal costs is assigned to this producer.

In the United States, governments have been slower to implement EPR. Although more than thirty states have adopted some type of program, many of these programs only cover a couple of items. But a few state legislatures are seeking ways to help municipalities reduce their costs of handling wastes in implementing mandatory EPR programs. One idea adopted in California, Illinois, and New York is to allow local governments to adopt EPR programs. Local programs should support more recycling efforts.

## Discussion Questions

1. Should your state adopt a renewable energy portfolio, or if it has one, should it increase its requirements? Why?
2. What type of program would you adopt to reduce the energy consumption of Americans, and why?
3. How do GE crops affect resource consumption?
4. Why do Europeans object to the use of beta agonists?
5. Does the Codex approval of ractopamine maximum residue levels affect world trade?
6. Are organic products safer than nonorganic products?
7. Why are some states declining to adopt EPR programs?

# CHAPTER TWENTY-THREE
## Preservation of Species and Culture

## Learning Objectives

- *Explain the federal government's responsibility for threatened and endangered species.*
- *Examine the meaning of the prohibition of taking an endangered species.*
- *Define the coverage of the Convention Concerning the Protection of the World Cultural and Natural Heritage.*
- *Critique the responses of the US Senate to international environmental conventions.*

## Endangered Species

In 1973, Congress adopted the Endangered Species Act (ESA), listing both endangered and threatened species. Endangered species are those in danger of extinction. Threatened species are likely to become endangered. For persons in the United States, it is illegal to "take" any endangered species of fish or wildlife. The act includes protection for critical habitats of endangered and threatened species of fish and wildlife. Protection is also offered to plants, but the protection is not as extensive. The act is administered by the US Fish and Wildlife Service (terrestrial species) and the National Marine Fisheries Service (marine species). For considering issues under the ESA, these two agencies may be called the "Services."

A key provision is the ESA's definition of "take." *Take* means to harass, harm, pursue, hunt, shoot, wound, kill, trap, capture, or collect, or to attempt to engage in any such conduct. The Fish and Wildlife Service defined the component term "harm" in such a way as to encompass any significant habitat modification that leads to an injury to an endangered species of wildlife. Habitat modification or degradation may constitute harm where it actually kills or injures wildlife by significantly impairing essential behavioral patterns, including breeding, feeding, or sheltering.

For activities and projects that are unlikely to jeopardize an endangered species or its habitat, but might result in some harm to a species, the Services may issue an incidental take permit. For an incidental take permit, the applicant must take reasonable and prudent measures to minimize the impact and report on funding for these measures, and show that the taking will not appreciably reduce the likelihood of the survival and recovery of the species.

Concerning species from abroad, the ESA shut down the trade of endangered species into the United States. To augment enforcement of the ESA, citizens, including environmental groups, are able to initiate citizen suits to prevent a take of a species and to enforce the habitat protection provisions.

## 1. Federal Habitat Protection

For the federal government, the ESA directs all federal agencies to use their authority to conserve threatened and endangered species and to ensure that their actions do not jeopardize listed species or destroy or adversely modify a critical habitat. These provisions apply to management of federal lands and any federal action that may affect listed species. This includes federal approval of private activities through the issuance of federal permits, licenses, or other actions. Federal agencies consult with the Services to ensure that their actions will not jeopardize the continued existence of any listed species.

If a listed species is present in an area, the federal agency must determine if its action may affect them. A "may affect determination" includes those actions that are not likely to adversely affect, as well as likely to adversely affect, listed species. If the federal agency determines that the action is not likely to adversely affect listed species—and this is supported by credible evidence—no further consultation is required. However, if an action is likely to adversely affect listed species, then the agency must request initiation of formal consultation with the Services. In some cases, this may lead to a decision that the planned action cannot take place.

Federal agencies also must confer with the Services on any agency action which is likely to jeopardize the continued existence of any species proposed for listing or result in the adverse modification of critical habitats proposed to be designated. When a species is proposed for listing as endangered or threatened under the ESA, consideration must be given to areas of habitat believed essential to the species' conservation; an area may be designated as an area of "critical habitat." As might be expected, the determination and designation of critical habitat is controversial. Critical habitat refers to specific geographic areas that are essential for the conservation of a threatened or endangered species and which may require special management considerations. The designation of an area as critical habitat means that federal agencies are required to consult with the Services on actions that might destroy or adversely modify critical habitat. However, critical habitat designation does not affect landowners from undertaking projects on private land that involve no federal funding or permit, so long as no endangered species is taken.

Even when there is no critical habitat designation, federal agencies must consult with the Services to ensure any action they carry out, fund, or authorize is not likely to jeopardize the continued existence of a listed species. The vast majority of human activities that require a consultation with the Services proceeds with little or no modification.

## 2. Private Landowners' Habitat Conservation Plans

Activities by private landowners, including development and homebuilding, may inadvertently take a listed species. Prior to any take, an "incidental take" permit authorizing a take is needed.

Any person engaged in an activity that will take a listed species needs to prepare and submit for approval a "conservation plan" detailing what the effects of the taking on the species will be and how those effects will be mitigated. These plans are called habitat conservation plans (HCPs). HCPs are central to resolving endangered species issues on nonfederal lands. The HCP process attempts to integrate development activities with endangered species conservation, provide a framework for broad-based conservation planning, and foster a climate of cooperation between the public and private sectors. HCPs provide a means of conserving endangered species habitats at existing sites, while meeting growing social and economic needs for development.

Persons entering HCPs want some assurance that their efforts will not lead to more onerous requirements for the protection of habitat or conservation of a species. The Fish and Wildlife Service thereby offers "safe harbor" agreements, under which a landowner agrees to contribute to the recovery of a threatened or endangered species in exchange for assurances that the Services will not require additional management activities by the landowner. Under a safe harbor agreement, a landowner may engage in some activities that result in an incidental take of the covered species.

Another policy is the adoption by the Services of a "no surprises" rule to guarantee to a landowner that whenever a habitat conservation plan is properly executed, the landowner will not experience further restrictions or costs without mutual consent. The Services may also enter "candidate conservation agreements," under which landowners protect declining species that are not yet listed in exchange for assurance that no additional measures will be required if species are listed.

## 3. Exemption from the ESA

After a controversy involving an endangered species that halted construction of the Tennessee Valley Authority's Tellico Dam, Congress enacted legislation in 1978 to create an Endangered Species Committee. The revised ESA allows exemptions from the strict requirements of the ESA so that desirable projects or activities may proceed, despite a "take" of an endangered species. The Endangered Species Committee became known as the "God Squad" because it is able to waive ESA protection of a species, thereby possibly sanctioning the species' demise. The governor of a state, a federal agency, or a permit or license applicant may apply for an exception to the ESA to allow an activity or project to proceed, despite adverse effects on a listed species. The person applying for an exception will need to show that there are no reasonable or prudent alternatives to the agency action, the benefits of the action outweigh the benefits of conserving the species or critical habitat, such action is in the public interest, and other requirements.

The following case shows some of the controversies and policies that accompany the efforts of the Services to protect listed species. The case discloses that government agencies are aware of obligations under the ESA, yet disagreements may occur regarding the extent and timing of requirements.

### *Defenders of Wildlife v. U.S. Department of the Navy*
US Court of Appeals for the Eleventh Circuit, Atlanta

*Who is suing?* _____

*Who is being sued?* _____

*For what?* _____

*What is the issue on appeal?* _____

Appellants, Defenders of Wildlife and others, appeal the district court's grant of summary judgment in favor of Appellees, the United States Department of the Navy (Navy) and others. In this appeal, Appellants challenge the Navy's decision to install and operate an instrumented Undersea Warfare Training Range (USWTR or range) fifty nautical miles offshore of the Florida/Georgia border in waters adjacent to the only known calving grounds of the endangered North Atlantic right whale. This action is predicated on alleged violations of the National Environmental Policy Act (NEPA), the Endangered Species Act (ESA), and the Administrative Procedure Act in analyzing and approving the USWTR. We affirm.

The Navy has used instrumented undersea ranges to train its personnel since the 1960s. These ranges allow shore-based operators to evaluate the performance of the participants and to provide feedback in both real time and later replays of the exercises. In 1996, the Navy published a Notice of Intent to build such a range somewhere in the Atlantic to more effectively train its personnel in shallow-water anti-submarine warfare. The Navy then began the process of complying with its statutory mandates, including the two environmental statutes relevant here, NEPA and the ESA. Appellants do not

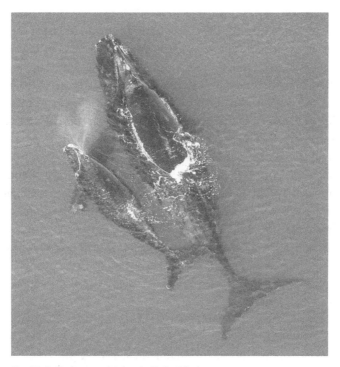

Fig. 23.1 Endangered Atlantic Right Whale.

challenge the substantive conclusions in the Navy's Environmental Impact Statement (EIS) in this appeal.

In addition to submitting its EIS pursuant to NEPA, the Navy also was required to comply with the ESA in planning for the USWTR. The ESA provides for the listing of species as threatened or endangered and the designation of their critical habitat. The Secretary of Commerce has responsibility for listed marine species (including marine mammals and sea turtles when in the marine environment) and administers the ESA through the National Marine Fisheries Service (NMFS), while the Secretary of the Interior is responsible for listed terrestrial species, inland fish species, and manatees, and administers the ESA through the U.S. Fish and Wildlife Service (FWS).

The ESA protects listed species in several ways. Section 9 establishes a prohibition on the "taking" of any member of a listed endangered or threatened species. Section 7 of the ESA directs federal agencies to insure that any action authorized, funded, or carried out by such agencies is not likely to jeopardize the continued existence of any endangered species or threatened species or destroy critical habitat. If the NMFS or the FWS concludes the action is likely to jeopardize the continued existence of listed species, it must suggest reasonable and prudent alternatives which can be taken by the federal agency to ensure that its action does not jeopardize the continued existence of the species.

In 1982, the ESA was amended to resolve the situation in which a federal agency has been advised that the proposed action will not violate Section 7(a)(2) of the Act (i.e., the prohibition on jeopardizing the continued existence of listed species) but will result in the taking of some species incidental to that action. In that situation, the NMFS's or the FWS's biological opinion must include an incidental take statement specifying the amount or extent of anticipated take. The incidental take statement must discuss reasonable and prudent measures necessary or appropriate to minimize the impact of the incidental take. The incidental take statement thus provides an exception to the ESA's take prohibition, as any take in compliance with the terms and conditions of an incidental take statement is lawful.

Where a proposed action is likely to result in a take of listed marine mammals, such as right whales in this case, the NMFS is prohibited from issuing an incidental take statement until the incidental take has first been authorized under the Marine Mammal Protection Act (MMPA). In relevant part, the MMPA generally prohibits the take of listed marine mammals but provides for several exceptions to the general take prohibition, including "incidental, but not intentional" take of "small numbers" of marine mammals by persons engaged in a specified activity during periods of not more than five consecutive years.

To comply with Section 7(a)(2) of the ESA, the Navy prepared a biological assessment and initiated formal consultation with the NMFS about the impacts to endangered species of installing and operating the USWTR. The NMFS then issued a biological opinion concluding that installation of the USWTR is not likely to adversely affect listed species, and that while expected operations on the USWTR are likely to adversely affect listed species, including some species of sea turtles and ESA-listed marine mammals such as right whales, expected operations are not likely to jeopardize their continued existence or destroy or adversely modify their critical habitat. Because USWTR operations are likely to adversely affect listed species and some take is expected to occur during operations, the Navy must obtain an incidental take statement from the NMFS prior to commencing operations on the USWTR in order to avoid potential take liability under Section 9 of the ESA.

However, the NMFS explained in the biological opinion that the document does not include an incidental take statement for the operations phase of the USWTR at this point because the ESA requires that the take of listed marine mammals must first be authorized under the MMPA before an incidental take statement may be issued, and any such MMPA take authorization issued in 2009, which is only effective for five year periods, would expire before operations ever commenced. Based on the Navy's final EIS and the NMFS's biological opinion, the Navy announced its decision to construct the USWTR at the Jacksonville site in a July 31, 2009 record of decision, stating that construction is expected to take at least five years to complete and thus operations are not anticipated to occur until at least 2014. The record of decision made a final decision only regarding a portion of the proposed action, a decision to move forward with installation of the USWTR. Because no take is expected to occur during range construction, and due to the anticipated four-to five-year period between now and completion of installation and the five-year limit on the period of NMFS' MMPA rulemaking, the record of decision explains that an MMPA rule related to training would likely expire before training could commence. As a result, the Navy authorized construction of the range, but it deferred authorization of operations on the range until closer in time to those operations occurring and until the requisite MMPA take authorization has been obtained, which could potentially impose conditions on activities.

Appellants filed this case challenging the Navy's record of decision and the NMFS's biological opinion as arbitrary and capricious under the Administrative Procedure Act because, they claimed, the agencies had failed to comply with various requirements of NEPA and the ESA. The parties filed cross motions for summary judgment on all claims. The district court held a hearing on the motions and denied Appellants' motion for summary judgment and granted summary judgment to all defendants, concluding that the Navy and the NMFS complied fully with NEPA, the ESA, and the Administrative Procedure Act. Appellants now appeal the district court's grant of summary judgment that the NMFS violated the ESA and the Administrative Procedure Act by failing to include in its biological opinion a required incidental take statement predicting, assessing the impact of, and taking measures to minimize the impact of incidental take of threatened and endangered species that is expected to occur in connection with operation of the USWTR.

The standard under the Administrative Procedure Act is whether the agency's action is arbitrary, capricious, an abuse of discretion, or otherwise not in accordance with law. The arbitrary and capricious standard is "exceedingly deferential." We are not authorized to substitute our judgment for the agency's as long as its conclusions are rational. The court's role is to ensure that the agency came to a rational conclusion, not to conduct its own investigation and substitute its own judgment for the administrative agency's decision.

Appellants claim that the biological opinion is arbitrary and capricious as it fails to include an incidental take statement for operations on the USWTR. However, the NMFS provided a valid reason for its failure to include an incidental take statement for operations in the biological opinion. Because an MMPA take authorization for listed marine mammal species, such as right whales in this case, must precede the NMFS's issuance of an incidental take statement, and because MMPA take authorizations are only effective for five year periods, the NMFS and the Navy rationally concluded that any MMPA take authorization pertaining to operations on the USWTR that the NMFS obtained at the time the biological opinion was issued in 2009 would expire long before the USWTR's operational date expected to be sometime between 2018 and 2023. To avoid redundant authorizations and wasting resources, the NMFS and the Navy chose to postpone the process of obtaining the MMPA take authorization and the resulting incidental take statement until the Navy reinitiates formal consultation with the NMFS on operations prior to authorizing training.

We find that it was not arbitrary or capricious for the NMFS to postpone the issuance of an incidental take statement for right whales in this situation. As an initial matter, no incidental take statement is required now, as the USWTR is still in the installation phase where no take of any listed species is expected. Moreover, an MMPA take authorization and corresponding incidental take statement, which will pertain solely to operations on the range, will serve no purpose while the USWTR is still in the installation phase and no operations are actually occurring.

We read the ESA as only requiring the incidental take statement to be included in the biological opinion if take of listed species is likely in the first place. Here, no take is likely because no take is expected from installation and because the Navy will not operate the range without first engaging in further environmental analysis with the NMFS. Under the facts of this case, the NMFS's decision to postpone the issuance of the incidental take statement for all listed species until closer in time to when the operations that warrant it actually occur was not inconsistent with the ESA's statutory scheme or otherwise arbitrary or capricious. The judgment of the district court is due to be affirmed on Appellants' ESA claims.

## Questions

1. How did the Navy divide its plans? What was the significance of the division?
2. Why did the Navy prepare an EIS?
3. Why wasn't an incidental take permit required for the Navy's installation of a training range?
4. What if a biological opinion shows that the Navy's installation would jeopardize the habitat of an endangered species?
5. When can a government agency destroy critical habitat for an endangered species?
6. What is the significance of an incidental take permit?
7. Can an action of the Navy take an endangered species?
8. Are the requirements of the ESA foisting too many costs on governments?

# Convention on International Trade in Endangered Species

The Convention on International Trade in Endangered Species of Wild Fauna and Flora (CITES) entered into force on July 1, 1975, and now has 183 parties. CITES provides a framework for countries to adopt domestic legislation to regulate international trade of wildlife and plant species in efforts to preserve those that are or might become endangered. The Convention regulates trade by assigning species in need of protection to one of three appendices of listed species, and trade is generally prohibited for all species listed in Appendix I. However, CITES has not been totally successful in preventing reductions in numbers of listed species that are in danger, with examples of rhinos and tigers. Due to the income-generating capacity of some protected species, quantities are being exported without determining whether such harvests are detrimental to the survival of the species.

Unlike the United States' Endangered Species Act, CITES does not control the conduct of individuals, only governments. There are no prohibitions of or sanctions on individuals engaging in actions that eliminate populations of a listed species. CITES does not require that any state or individual protect the habitat of listed species. The prohibitions of the treaty relate to governments allowing the importation or exportation without a CITES permit. Even with governmental restrictions, unsanctioned and illegal activities may result in the sale of, and export of products from, listed species.

Other limitations in preserving listed species under CITES are that preservation efforts require governments to interfere with human activities and, for various reasons, governments are unwilling to stop activities adversely affecting listed species. Some listed species are in areas where landowners want to change land uses to augment their incomes. In other areas, populations rely on listed species for food and sustenance. Finally, tourism may negatively affect listed species. Habitat destruction, pollution, invasive species, and overexploitation accompanying tourism are threatening some species.

# International Treaties

Countries around the world have recognized a need for environmental controls and the coordination of efforts to curtail environmental degradation. Since 1975, at least 13 international treaties have been ratified by many of the world's countries. The United States started out as a proponent of many of these treaties, but more recently has been hesitant to ratify treaties due to a number of reasons, most of them involving economics. Given new inventions, discoveries, and technological developments in the United States, many of our large corporations would prefer not to be bound by treaties that might detract from their economic interests. A review of treaties since 1975 discloses a troubling trend of the United States isolating itself from the world community by refusing to ratify widely accepted international commitments. Our country's isolation may become more severe with the Trump administration's rejection of the Trans-Pacific Partnership and the Transatlantic Trade and Investment Partnership.

For treaties, a country becomes a signatory when it declares its intention to make the terms of the treaty legally binding on itself. This simply means the country is agreeing it will try and adopt the treaty. Countries need to ratify a treaty in order to become parties.

1. **Convention on International Trade in Endangered Species**
   This treaty has been in force since 1975, and the United States is a party.
2. **Geneva Convention on Long-Range Transboundary Air Pollution**

This treaty has been in force since 1983; the United States is a party.

3.  **Bonn Convention on Conservation of Migratory Species**
    This treaty has been in force since 1983, with ninety-three signatories. The United States is not a party. Member states are required to prohibit the deliberate killing, hunting, fishing, and capturing of strictly protected animal species. States are also obliged to preserve the habitats or to remove obstacles which might jeopardize migratory routes.

4.  **Vienna Convention for the Protection of the Ozone Layer**
    This treaty has been in force since 1988, and the United States is a party.

5.  **Montreal Protocol to the Vienna Convention**
    This treaty has been in force since 1989; the United States is a party.

6.  **Basel Convention on Transboundary Movements of Hazardous Wastes and Disposal**
    This treaty has been in force since 1992, and the United States is not a party. The United States signed the Basel Convention, but has declined to ratify it. For this reason, the United States cannot participate in waste transfers with Basel parties without a separate and equivalent bilateral or multilateral agreement. The United States maintains a multilateral agreement with the members of the OECD governing transboundary movements of waste for recovery purposes. In addition, the United States has established two bilateral agreements—with Canada and Mexico—for importing and exporting hazardous waste.

7.  **Convention on Biological Diversity**
    This treaty has been in force since 1993; the United States is not a party. The United States is the only country to sign the treaty, but not ratify it. Ratification would put the United States in a better position to help strengthen the laws and policies of biodiverse regions and would give it a seat at the table for negotiations at upcoming conferences of the parties. The United States would also protect its own biodiversity by participating in international actions to protect the marine environment, control invasive species, mitigate and adapt to climate change, and coordinate enforcement efforts against biopiracy, poaching, and illegal habitat destruction.

8.  **UN Framework Convention on Climate Change (Rio Earth Summit)**
    This treaty, the UNCCC, has been in force since 1994, and the United States is a party.

9.  **Convention on the Law of the Sea**
    This treaty has been in force since 1994; the United States is not a party. The United States claims that the provisions of the treaty are not free-market friendly and argues that the International Seabed Authority established by the convention might become a bloated and expensive bureaucracy.

10. **Convention to Combat Desertification**
    This treaty has been in force since 1996, and the United States is a party.

11. **Rotterdam Convention: Hazardous Chemicals and Pesticides**

This treaty has been in force since 2004; the United States is not a party. The United States is concerned that passage would lead to additional chemicals being banned under the treaty.

12. **Kyoto Protocol to the Framework Convention on Climate Change**

    This treaty has been in force since 2005 after Russia signed it. The United States is not planning to become a party, as compliance could increase energy costs in reducing carbon dioxide emissions. The United States maintains that the convention fails to require sufficient efforts by important developing nations such as Indonesia, India, and China.

13. **Stockholm Convention on Persistent Organic Pollutants (POPs)**

    This treaty has been in force since 2004 and ratified by eighty-three countries, but the United States does not plan to be a party. The twelve POPs covered by the treaty are: aldrin, hexachlorobenzene, chlordane, Mirex, DDT, toxaphene, dieldrin, polychlorinated biphenyls (PCBs), endrin, heptachlor, dioxins, and furans. US ratification may require amending our existing Toxic Substances Control Act and the Federal Insecticide, Fungicide, and Rodenticide Act.

14. **Cartagena Protocol on Biosafety**

    This protocol has been approved by 132 countries, but not by the United States. The protocol aims to ensure the safe handling, transport, and use of living modified organisms resulting from modern biotechnology. Thereby, it aims to reduce adverse effects on biological diversity, taking also into account risks to human health.

15. **Paris Climate Change Agreement**

    This is not a treaty but rather an agreement that came into force on November 4, 2016. President Barack Obama joined Chinese president Xi Jinping in ratifying this agreement together in Hangzhou in 2016, but the agreement has not been ratified by the US Senate, so does not qualify for treaty status.

# World Heritage Sites

While efforts to protect species and the environment are important, many people want to also offer protection to natural and cultural areas of value so they can be held in trust for all mankind. In 1972, the United Nations Educational, Scientific and Cultural Organisation adopted the Convention Concerning the Protection of the World Cultural and Natural Heritage, which is commonly referred to as the World Heritage Convention, and this entered force in 1975. Under the convention, a World Heritage List was established to serve as a catalyst to enhance awareness for heritage preservation. To offer international support for World Heritage sites, an intergovernmental World Heritage Committee was established.

The convention delineates definitions for both cultural and natural heritage. Cultural heritage includes architectural works, sculpture, painting, inscriptions, cave dwellings, "and combinations of features, which are of outstanding universal value from the point of view of history, art or science." Natural features include geological and physiographical formations and areas constituting habitats of threatened species of animals and plants of outstanding universal value from the point of view of science or conservation; natural features of outstanding universal value from the aesthetic or scientific point of view; and natural sites or areas of outstanding universal value from the point of view of science, conservation, or natural beauty.

Countries are invited to nominate natural and cultural property sites to the World Heritage List. In 2017, 1,052 properties were entered on this list, of which 23 are in the United States. Properties listed on the World Heritage List must have adequate long-term legislative, regulatory, institutional, and/or traditional protection and management to ensure their safeguarding. In addition, concerns about the loss or denigration of cultural and natural heritage sites led to the compilation of a List of World Heritage in Danger for which assistance has been requested. Currently, 55 properties are listed.

## Indigenous Culture

In the discussion of World Heritage sites, we noted that cultural areas were an important part of the human environment. The initial international treaty to single out indigenous peoples as special subjects of human rights concern was the International Labor Organization Convention 107, adopted in 1957. Another important milestone in recognizing the connection of indigenous cultures with environmentalism was the United Nations Convention on Biological Diversity. Article 8 of this treaty noted that in situ conservation was related to the preservation of indigenous communities that have intimate and traditional relationships with biological resources. This recognizes that environmental protection in some cases is closely related to the preservation of indigenous cultures.

A more concrete statement for the preservation of indigenous cultures came in 2007 in the United Nations Declaration on the Rights of Indigenous Peoples (UNDRIP). Although not a treaty, this resolution is an instrument that sets out the rights of indigenous peoples to "maintain and strengthen their own institutions, cultures and traditions, and to pursue their development in keeping with their own needs and aspirations." The text recognizes that indigenous peoples have the right not to be subjected to forced assimilation or destruction of their culture and that countries should provide effective mechanisms for preventing the practice of their cultural values. Furthermore, the resolution recognized the rights of indigenous peoples to practice and revitalize their cultural traditions and customs, and to develop manifestations of their cultures, including sites, ceremonies, performing arts, and literature. Finally, UNDRIP recognizes the rights of indigenous peoples "to maintain, control, protect and develop their cultural heritage, traditional knowledge and traditional cultural expressions, as well as the manifestations of their sciences, technologies and cultures."

# Dolphin-Safe Tuna Challenge

In 1990, the United States enacted the Dolphin Protection Consumer Information Act that created a "Dolphin-Safe" label telling consumers that tuna were not caught using specified practices known to be harmful to dolphins. Mexico challenged the US legislative action through a World Trade Organization dispute, as authorized by the Technical Barriers to Trade Agreement and the General Agreement on Tariffs and Trade 1994, claiming the US legislation accorded Mexican tuna products less favorable treatment. The findings established the lack of access to the "dolphin-safe" label for Mexican tuna that had a detrimental impact on the competitive opportunities of Mexican tuna products in the US market.

The United States responded in 2013 by amending its legal provisions in an attempt to comply with the country's international commitments. However, a subsequent dispute settlement panel found that the United States had not brought its measure into compliance. An Appellate Body modified the panel's report, which was adopted by the Dispute Settlement Body. Due to the noncompliance of the United States, Mexico then requested concessions and the United States objected. The following is a portion of the dispute settlement decree entered in 2017.

### United States–Measures Concerning the Importation, Marketing and Sale of Tuna and Tuna Products
World Trade Organization WT/DS381/ARB, 25 April 2017

*Who is suing?* _____

*Who is being sued?* _____

*For what?* _____

*What is the issue on appeal?* _____

On 10 March 2016, Mexico requested authorization from the Dispute Settlement Body to suspend concessions to the United States in the amount of USD 472.3 million annually. The Dispute Settlement Body took note that the matter had been referred to arbitration as required by Article 22.6 of the Understanding on Rules and Procedures Governing the Settlement of Disputes. At the same meeting, the United States informed the Dispute Settlement Body that, on 22 March 2016, the US National Oceanic and Atmospheric Administration had issued a new rule modifying the dolphin safe labelling measure (the 2016 Rule). According to the United States, this Rule "directly addressed issues raised by both the Appellate Body and the compliance panel."

Our task is to determine whether the level of suspension of concessions requested by Mexico is equivalent to the level of nullification or impairment sustained by Mexico as a result of the United States' failure to bring the Tuna Measure into compliance. To discharge this mandate, we will first have to determine the level of nullification or impairment caused by the 2013 Tuna Measure (Tuna Measure), which was the measure existing at the time of the expiry of the reasonable period of time, and then compare that to the level of suspension of concessions proposed by Mexico.

Conceptually, the level of nullification or impairment caused by the United States' failure to comply with the Dispute Settlement Body recommendations and rulings represents the difference between the value of trade (if any) in Mexican tuna products that occurred despite the WTO-inconsistent US measure, typically calculated for one year, and the value of trade that would have occurred, over the course of one year, had the United States complied with the Dispute Settlement Body recommendations and rulings.

We have found that, following the adoption of the Tuna Measure, the volume of tuna exports from Mexico to the United States and US cannery purchases of yellowfin declined. We conclude that the assumption that the Tuna Measure restricted the supply of canned yellowfin from Mexico to the United States is reasonable.

The second assumption underlying Mexico's model is that US consumers have a preference for canned yellowfin, and that US retailers would sell Mexican canned yellowfin after the withdrawal of the Tuna Measure. Mexico maintains that, following the withdrawal of the Tuna Measure, Mexican producers would be able to inform US consumers about the real nature of their fishing methods. As a result of this, the misconception about setting on dolphins would be corrected and the US consumers' real preferences for yellowfin would be revealed to the market. In this situation, canned yellowfin produced from tuna caught by setting on dolphins would be supplied in the market as a product like canned yellowfin caught by other methods. Given this additional supply, the price of canned yellowfin would fall and its consumption in the US market would increase.

We consider reasonable Mexico's second assumption and assume that US retailers would sell Mexican canned yellowfin after the withdrawal of the Tuna Measure, except those that made statements to the contrary. We also note that the evidence on the record shows that the share of yellowfin in US cannery receipts was 34% in the period 1980–1989, prior to the adoption of the Tuna Measure. This, in our view, lends support to our finding that the second assumption is reasonable.

Under the counterfactual, we estimate the value for total exports in 2014 of canned tuna from Mexico to the United States (all of it being canned yellowfin) to be equal to USD 185.88 million. The value of Mexican canned tuna actually exported to the United States in 2014 was USD 22.65 million. Taking the difference between the total value of exports of canned tuna from Mexico to the United States under the counterfactual and the total value of actual exports in 2014, we find that Mexico's estimated trade loss in 2014 amounted to USD 163.23 million per annum. Therefore, in accordance with

Article 22.4 of the Understanding on Rules and Procedures Governing the Settlement of Disputes, Mexico may request authorization from the Dispute Settlement Body to suspend concessions or other obligations as indicated in document WT/DS381/29 at a level not exceeding USD 163.23 million per annum.

## Questions

1. What did the United States do to comply with the Technical Barriers to Trade Agreement?
2. Why is the expiry of the reasonable period of time significant?
3. What is a "counterfactual?"

# Discussion Questions

1. Do you feel the United States does a good job in protecting endangered species?
2. Is the US Endangered Species Act stronger or weaker than CITES? Explain your answer.
3. What is the problem with the United States not ratifying many international environmental agreements?
4. Has the United Nations done enough to preserve indigenous cultures? Explain your answer.

# Image Crdit

# CHAPTER TWENTY-FOUR

## Climate Change and Greenwashing

### Learning Objectives

- *Sketch the problems being created by climate change and international security.*
- *Describe how human activities contribute to climate change.*
- *Summarize why California has taken actions to address climate change.*
- *Explain actions to mitigate climate change.*
- *Illustrate the meaning of greenwashing.*

Some people argue that climate change is the most serious problem that society currently faces. Although the earth's climate has changed many times in the planet's history—usually due to natural factors such as volcanic eruptions and changes in the earth's orbit—beginning with the advent of the Industrial Revolution in the late eighteenth century, human activities have changed the composition of the atmosphere and climate. In the past thirty years, the rate of warming across the globe has been three times greater than the rate over the last one hundred years. Activities by humans are contributing to this unprecedented rate.

Different terminology arose to describe the changes in the Earth's atmosphere and climate. "Climate change" refers to any significant change in measures of climate for a long period of time, like temperature, rainfall, snow, or wind patterns. "Global warming" may be used interchangeably with "climate change," but the latter is more accurate in describing different trends of warming and cooling across the globe. Finally, "global change" refers to change in the global environment such as climate change, ozone depletion, or land-use change.

In 1988, the United Nations Environment Programme and the United Nations World Meteorological Organization created the International Panel on Climate Change (IPCC). The panel comprises the world's top scientists, economists, and other experts. In 1992, the United Nations Conference on Environment and Development met in Rio de Janeiro, Brazil (known as the Rio Earth Summit), and established the "Framework Convention on Climate Change" (UNFCCC), the "Convention on Biological Diversity," and the "United Nations Convention to Combat Desertification." The United States became a party to UNFCCC, which set voluntary emissions reduction goals.

With the lack of success under the UNFCCC, nations met in Kyoto, Japan, in 1997 to establish mandatory reductions in greenhouse emissions. This resulted in the Kyoto Protocol, which the United States conspicuously did not sign due to political concerns about competitiveness of American businesses. The UN also hosts annual conferences of the parties, one of the most notable being in Paris in 2015 that culminated in the Paris Climate Change Agreement. At these conferences, delegates from most countries come together to discuss climate change mitigation through international cooperation.

## 1. The Greenhouse Effect

The driving force behind warming temperatures is the greenhouse effect. This is a natural phenomenon where heat from the sun is trapped due to the ozone layer and greenhouse gases (GHGs). While GHGs are essential to warm the planet to some extent, human activities have released an alarming amount of GHGs at a faster rate than at any other time in the past hundreds of thousands of years, raising the temperature of the earth of 1.3°F over the past century. In the United States, fossil fuel usage contributes about 76 percent of the GHGs released into the atmosphere, so this usage has come under scrutiny. If usage can be reduced, we will emit fewer GHGs.

There is no longer any doubt that most of the warming experienced since the 1950s is due to an increase in GHG emissions. All models show an increase of global temperatures. If humans do nothing to curb GHG emissions, the earth's average global temperature is expected to increase by 2.7°F by the year 2100. Land and polar regions are expected to bear higher temperature increases than the average projection. Even if activities return to the levels of GHG emissions in 2000, the earth would still warm 1°F over the next one hundred years. The problem is exacerbated by the long lifetime of GHGs and the slow cycling of heat from the ocean to the atmosphere.

## 2. The Significance of Climate Change

Climate change is a complex process that, if not mitigated, will have marked effects on the environment, society, and economy. Although the effects will be both positive and negative, most experts feel the benefits are far outweighed by the potential disadvantages to the world's ecosystems, economy, and health. Rising temperatures will intensify the earth's water cycle, causing faster evaporation. This means there will be more water in the air that will contribute to more intense storms. Areas with rain will have even more rain, increasing the chance of flooding. Flooding may lead to more diseases like cholera if untreated water mixes with drinking water. Flooding may also contaminate water supplies by washing chemicals and toxins into freshwater. Areas with low levels of precipitation will have more chance of drought.

Temperatures will increase, creating more severe heat waves and fewer cold spells. As hurricanes and typhoons are energized by warm sea surfaces, the world can expect more intense storms like Hurricane Sandy. Warming seas means polar ice sheets, the largest surface features on the planet, will melt at a rapid rate and raise the sea level by six inches to two feet by the end of this century. A rise in sea level could render coastal lands uninhabitable and lower property values of all coastal land. The changes will result in a loss of biodiversity, changes in species distribution, and delicate species in fragile ecosystems may face extinction. Species that thrive in warm temperatures, such as mosquitoes or ticks, will proliferate, and the world can expect to see higher rates of infectious diseases like malaria, West Nile virus, dengue fever, and Lyme disease. Warmer temperatures may also lead to more heat-related deaths, instances of heat cramps, heat exhaustion, and heat stroke in humans.

Agriculture will be affected. Colder regions will see longer growing seasons, but warmer regions may experience higher temperatures that do not allow certain crops to grow. Livestock may be stressed and yield less meat, eggs, or milk, and owners of fisheries may lose profits if they harvest fish like salmon that need colder water. Warmer regions will have a higher irrigation demand, requiring more water and energy. To cool buildings during hotter summers, energy bills will be more expensive. The increased

Fig. 24.1 Malaria research.

demand in hotter weather will stress the capacity of power plants, transmission grids, and distribution systems, resulting in brownouts. Power plants also require vast amounts of water, so more water will be required to provide energy needs. If a city's infrastructure is damaged from an intensified storm, wildfire, or flood, taxpayers will have to cover the cost of repairs. From a global perspective, developing countries will have fewer resources and be more negatively impacted by natural disasters. If extreme weather events lead to food and water shortages, these countries could face social disruption and political instability. The following case involves a species that is expected to be adversely impacted by climate change.

## *Defenders of Wildlife v. Jewell*
### US District Court for the District of Montana

*Who is suing?* _____

*Who is being sued?* _____

*For what?* _____

*What is the issue on appeal?* _____

The Court vacates the United States Fish & Wildlife Service's (Service) withdrawal of its proposed rule to list the distinct population segment of the North American wolverine as threatened under the Endangered Species Act (ESA), and remands this matter to the Service for further consideration consistent with this order. The North American wolverine, *Gulo gulo luscus*, is the largest terrestrial member of what is commonly known as the weasel family. Compact, stout, and uncannily strong, the wolverine has been known to kill prey many times its size. The wolverine is custom-built for life in mountainous, snowy environments, and relies upon snow for its existence at the most fundamental level. The wolverine displays an "obligate" relationship with snow for natal denning purposes, meaning the wolverine requires snow in order to reproduce. It is estimated that no more than 300 individuals live in the contiguous United States.

The effort to list the wolverine as a threatened or endangered species began over twenty years ago. Based upon both the most sophisticated and best available science for projecting the future impacts of climate change on wolverine habitat, the Service concluded in its Proposed Rule that the primary threat to the wolverine is from habitat and range loss due to climate warming and the wolverine distinct population segment presently meets the definition of a threatened species due to the likelihood of habitat loss caused by climate change resulting in population decline leading to breakdown of metapopulation dynamics. Accordingly, the Service proposed listing the wolverine as threatened under the ESA.

Eighteen months after initiating the process to list the wolverine as a threatened species, the Service withdrew the Proposed Rule, concluding "that the factors affecting the distinct population segment as identified in the proposed rule are not as significant as believed at the time of the proposed rule's publication." In the Withdrawal, the Service determined that based on new information and further analysis of the existing and new data, factors affecting the distinct population segment cited in the proposed listing rule do not place the wolverine in danger of extinction now or likely to become so in the foreseeable future. Plaintiffs, consisting of some twenty-four conservation and wildlife advocacy groups, commenced this litigation after the Service published the Withdrawal.

The ESA requires the Service to determine whether any species is an endangered species or a threatened species "solely on the basis of the best scientific and commercial data available ... after conducting a review of the status of the species." Why did the Service make the decision it did in the Proposed Rule, based on what it determined to be the best available science, and reject that decision eighteen months later? Based on the record, the Court suspects that a possible answer to this question can be found in the immense political pressure that was brought to bear on this issue, particularly by a handful of western states. The Service's decision on the wolverine has profound consequences, and the reality is that, in some instances, species conservation is a political issue as much as it is a scientific one.

Plaintiffs advance two arguments in support of their motions for summary judgment: (1) the Service unlawfully ignored the best available science by dismissing the threat to the wolverine posed by climate change; (2) the Service unlawfully ignored the best available science by dismissing the threat to the wolverine posed by genetic isolation and small population size. In the Withdrawal, the Service found that it could not determine with any certainty whether climate change would impact wolverine reproductive denning because it cannot be known how the wolverine will react to changes in snowpack depth. The Service also sought certainty beyond what is required by the ESA and case law interpreting it when it demanded the precise mechanism behind the wolverine's established need for snow for reproductive denning purposes. The Service erred in criticizing the science to cloud the otherwise crystal-clear conclusion that wolverines require snow for denning purposes. The Service's analysis is not merely the product of differing interpretations among Service staff; rather, it is an implausible misinterpretation that runs counter to the intent of the study. As such, the Service's interpretation was arbitrary and capricious. If ever there was a species for which conservation depends on foregoing absolute certainty, it is the wolverine.

Plaintiffs contend that the Service's failure to recognize the threat to the wolverine posed by small population size and its likely genetic effects was arbitrary and capricious. They cite to the Withdrawal, where the Service catalogued a number of seemingly perilous circumstances related to this issue, yet concluded that none of those circumstances actually posed a threat. Because the Court fails to see how the cited circumstances can reasonably lead to the Service's conclusion, the Court will grant the Plaintiffs' motion for summary judgment and remand to the Service to reconsider its conclusions regarding wolverine population size.

The Service erred when it determined: (1) that climate change and projected spring snow cover would not impact the wolverine at the reproductive denning scale in the foreseeable future, and (2) that small population size and low genetic diversity do not pose an independent threat to wolverine viability in the United States. By incorporating these determinations into the Withdrawal, the Service's decision against listing the wolverine as threatened under the ESA is arbitrary and capricious. No greater level of certainty is needed to see the writing on the wall for this snow-dependent species standing squarely in the path of global climate change. Accordingly, this matter is remanded to the United States Fish & Wildlife Service for further consideration consistent with this order.

## Questions

1. How is climate change expected to impact the wolverine?
2. What does the court suggest caused the Service to change its mind after issuing the Proposed Rule?
3. What does the court find was improper with the Service's new position in not listing the wolverine as an endangered species?
4. What is the problem posed by small numbers of animals of a species?
5. From this brief accounting, does the judge appear to be biased? What contributes to your opinion?

## 3. US Policies on GHGs

In the United States, various energy policies to reduce GHGs were adopted by Congress with the Energy Policy Act of 2005 and the Energy Independence and Security Act (EISA) of 2007. The latter act increased fuel standards for new cars and light trucks and expanded the renewable fuel standard concerning biofuels. The programs reducing GHG emissions are voluntary and incentive based, incorporating the expertise of federal agencies with the strength of the private sector. EISA is the only federal statute that explicitly limits GHG emissions through the renewable fuel standards.

Due to costs of pollution from motor vehicle emissions, Massachusetts and other states sued the EPA in 2007 to classify $CO_2$ as an air pollutant under the Clean Air Act in *Massachusetts v. EPA*. The plaintiffs were successful, as the US Supreme Court found that GHGs were pollutants under the Clean Air Act. The EPA, therefore, has the statutory authority to regulate GHGs from new motor vehicles. In September 2009, the EPA, along with the National Highway Traffic Safety Administration (NHTSA), proposed joint rulemaking on new-vehicle GHG and fuel economy standards. As part of that rulemaking effort, the Obama administration secured memoranda of understanding from California and the automakers that federal standards be harmonized—to the extent possible—with California standards, and that California accept certain stipulations. On April 1, 2010, the EPA and NHTSA finalized the new federal regulations, which apply to model years 2012–2016.

In 2014, the EPA established more stringent vehicle emissions standards and reduced the sulfur content of gasoline beginning in 2017. The gasoline sulfur standard will make emission control systems more effective for both existing and new vehicles, and will enable more stringent vehicle emissions standards. The vehicle standards will reduce both tailpipe and evaporative emissions from passenger cars, light-duty trucks, medium-duty passenger vehicles, and some heavy-duty vehicles. The Trump administration would like to rescind or minimize the emissions standards, as it feels the standards detract from economic performance.

The lack of meaningful federal action to address GHGs due to their contribution to climate change has led to a number of state initiatives. On the production side, policies designed to impose a cost on the extraction, refinement, and use of fossil fuels are related to climate change. Legislative actions may include gas taxes, carbon taxes, climate fees, and energy severance taxes. Energy conservation measures, including incentives for renewable electricity production and efficient household investments, can also reduce GHG emissions. Other programs offering incentives to homeowners and retailers for improving the energy efficiency of existing buildings can lead to reductions in GHG emissions.

The state of California has been the leader in enacting legislation and regulations addressing GHG emissions. These policies include the establishment of GHG emissions standards for new passenger cars and light trucks, a low-carbon fuel standard, and mandatory reporting of GHG emissions by major sources. The state's actions, however, have been controversial, as shown by the following lawsuit.

### *Rocky Mountain Farmers Union v. Corey*
US Court of Appeals for the Ninth Circuit, San Francisco

*Who is suing?* _____

*Who is being sued?* _____

*For what?* _____

*What is the issue on appeal?* _____

Plaintiffs-Appellees Rocky Mountain Farmers Union and others contend that California's Low Carbon Fuel Standard (Fuel Standard) violated the dormant Commerce Clause and was preempted by Section 211(o) of the Clean Air Act, known as the federal Renewable Fuel Standard. We hold that the Fuel Standard's regulation of ethanol does not facially discriminate against out-of-state commerce, and its initial crude-oil provisions did not discriminate against out-of-state crude oil in purpose or practical effect. Further, the Fuel Standard does not violate the dormant Commerce Clause's prohibition on extraterritorial regulation. We vacate the preliminary injunction and remand to the district court to consider whether the Fuel Standard's ethanol provisions discriminate in purpose or in practical effect.

California has long been in the vanguard of efforts to protect the environment, with a particular concern for emissions from the transportation sector. Section 209(a) of the Clean Air Act expressly prohibited state regulation of emissions from motor vehicles.

But the same section allowed California to adopt its own standards if it determined that the State standards will be, in the aggregate, at least as protective of public health and welfare as applicable Federal standards. Other states could choose to follow either the federal or the California standards, but they could not adopt standards of their own. Continuing its tradition of leadership, the California legislature enacted the Global Warming Solutions Act of 2006. California resolved to reduce its greenhouse gas (GHG) emissions to their 1990 level by the year 2020, and the legislature empowered defendant California Air Resources Board (CARB) to design emissions-reduction measures to meet this goal. CARB was required to consider "the relative contribution of each source or source category to statewide greenhouse gas emissions." In California, transportation emissions account for more than 40% of GHG emissions, the state's largest single source.

CARB adopted a three-part approach designed to lower GHG emissions from the transportation sector: (1) reducing emissions at the tailpipe by establishing progressively stricter emissions limits for new vehicles (Tailpipe Standards); (2) integrating regional land use, housing, and transportation planning to reduce the number of "vehicle miles traveled" each year (VMT Standards); and (3) lowering the embedded GHGs in transportation fuel by adopting the Fuel Standard to reduce the quality of GHGs emitted in the production of transportation fuel. The Tailpipe and VMT Standards aim to lower the consumption of GHG-generating transportation fuels. The Fuel Standard, by contrast, is directed at creating an alternate path to emissions reduction by reducing the carbon intensity of transportation fuels that are burned in California.

To comply with the Fuel Standard, a fuel blender must keep the average carbon intensity of its total volume of fuel below the Fuel Standard's annual limit. Fuels generate credits or deficits, depending on whether their carbon intensity is higher or lower than the annual cap. Credits may be used to offset deficits, may be sold to other blenders, or may be carried forward to comply with the carbon intensity cap in later years. With these offsets, a blender selling high carbon intensity fuels can comply with the Fuel Standard by purchasing credits from other regulated parties; no regulated party is required to sell any particular fuel or blend of fuels with a certain carbon intensity or origin. To build a durable and effective marketplace to stimulate the development of alternative fuels, the Fuel Standard created a market for trading, banking, and borrowing Fuel Standard credits.

The Fuel Standard uses a "lifecycle analysis" to determine the total carbon intensity of a given transportation fuel. Because GHGs mix in the atmosphere, all emissions related to transportation fuels used in California pose the same local risk to California citizens. One ton of carbon dioxide emitted when fuel is produced in Iowa or Brazil harms Californians as much as one emitted when fuel is consumed in Sacramento. The Tailpipe Standards control only emissions within California. Without lifecycle analysis, all GHGs emitted before the fuel enters a vehicle's gas tank would be excluded from California's regulation. Similarly, the climate-change benefits of biofuels such as ethanol, which mostly come before combustion, would be ignored if CARB's regulatory focus were limited to emissions produced when fuels are consumed in California. CARB designed the Fuel Standard to account for emissions associated with all aspects of the production, refining, and transportation of a fuel, with the aim of reducing total, well-to-wheel GHG emissions. When these emissions are measured, CARB assigns a cumulative carbon intensity value to an individual fuel lifecycle, which is called a "pathway."

CARB has performed lifecycle analyses of fuels made from petroleum, natural gas, hydrogen, electricity, corn, sugarcane, used cooking oil, and tallow. Fuels made from these feedstocks generate or avoid emissions at different stages of their production, transportation, and use, depending on when the conversion to fuel requires or displaces energy. An accurate comparison is possible only when it is based on the entire lifecycle emissions of each fuel pathway.

Ethanol is an alcohol produced through fermentation and distillation of a variety of organic feedstocks. To determine the total carbon intensity values for each ethanol pathway, the model used by CARB considers the carbon intensity of factors including: (1) growth and transportation of the feedstock, with a credit for the GHGs absorbed during photosynthesis; (2) efficiency of production; (3) type of electricity used to power the plant; (4) fuel used for thermal energy; (5) milling process used; (6) offsetting value of an animal-feed co-product called distillers' grains that displaces demand for feed that would generate its own emissions in production; (7) transportation of the fuel to the blender in California; and (8) conversion of land to agricultural use. The Fuel Standard also regulates crude oil and derivatives sold in California.

The Fuel Standard performs lifecycle analysis to measure the carbon intensity of all fuel pathways. When it is relevant to that measurement, the Fuel Standard considers location, but only to the extent that location affects the actual GHG emissions attributable to a default pathway. Under dormant Commerce Clause precedent, if an out-of-state ethanol pathway does impose higher costs on California by virtue of its greater GHG emissions, there is a nondiscriminatory reason for its higher carbon intensity value. Stated another way, if producers of out-of-state ethanol actually cause more GHG emissions for each unit produced, CARB can base its regulatory treatment on these emissions.

Comparing all sources of ethanol and all factors that contribute to the carbon intensity of an ethanol pathway, it appears that CARB's method of lifecycle analysis treats ethanol the same regardless of origin, showing a nondiscriminatory reason for the unequal results of this analysis. We conclude: (1) that all sources of ethanol compete in the California market and are therefore relevant to comparison; (2) that all of the factors included in the lifecycle analysis are relevant to determining which forms of ethanol are similarly situated; (3) that the lifecycle analysis used by CARB, including the specific factors to which Plaintiffs object, does not discriminate against out-of-state commerce.

The district court held that the Fuel Standard regulated extraterritorial conduct because: (1) by treating fuels based on lifecycle emissions, it "attempts to control" out-of-state conduct; (2) California's attempt to take "legal and political responsibility" for worldwide carbon emissions caused by transportation fuels used in California was an improper extension of California's police power to other states; (3) the Fuel Standard regulates the channels of interstate commerce by compelling producers to submit changes in their transportation routes to CARB to qualify for an altered pathway; and (4) if each state enacted a regulation similar to the Fuel Standard, it would result in economic Balkanization. We disagree. The Fuel Standard regulates only the California market. Firms in any location may elect to respond to the incentives provided by the Fuel Standard if they wish to gain market share in California, but no firm must meet a particular carbon intensity standard, and no jurisdiction need adopt a particular regulatory standard for its producers to gain access to California.

The California legislature has determined that the state faces tremendous risks from climate change. To combat these risks, the California legislature and its regulatory arm CARB chose to institute a market-based solution that recognizes the costs of harmful carbon emissions. The Fuel Standard's ethanol provisions are not facially discriminatory, so we reverse that portion of the district court's decision and remand for entry of partial summary judgment in favor of CARB. We also reverse the district court's decision that the Fuel Standard is an impermissible extraterritorial regulation and we direct that an order of partial summary judgment be entered in favor of CARB on those grounds. We remand the cause to the district court with instructions to vacate the preliminary injunction.

## Questions

1. Given constitutional requirements for uniformity among the states, why can California adopt its own air quality regulations?
2. Why does California worry so much about GHGs?
3. Do the CARB regulations only affect fuel use? If not, what other facet is addressed?
4. Why was a life-cycle analysis selected for the fuel standard?
5. What was the issue involving calculation of an ethanol pathway?
6. What is a problem with regulating extraterritorial activities?
7. What if the fuel standard failed to measure carbon intensity of all fuel pathways?
8. What was the effect of CARB's fuel standard on ethanol produced in Iowa or Brazil?

## 4. Looking into the Future

For proponents of limits on GHGs, various policy options are available. The policy design that has gained the most traction is a comprehensive cap-and-trade system: emission allowances would be required to cover all emissions in a given year; the number of allowances would be limited in each year (establishing the cap); entities with extra allowances could bank those for future use or trade them on a secondary market. The quantity of emissions would be controlled, but the price would be determined by the market. Cap-and-trade was the preferred approach of the Obama administration, as well as many environmental groups; moreover, several states have established or are in the process of developing their own regional cap-and-trade systems.

Other policy options include proposals for a carbon tax. Instead of setting the quantity of emissions allowed in a given year, the policy would set the price. In this manner, the market would determine the quantity of emissions. Those entities that could reduce emissions at a price below the level of the tax would make reductions, while those entities with higher costs would simply pay the tax. Carbon tax proposals have gained little support in Congress, but are the preferred approaches of many stakeholders who are concerned about the overall costs of a GHG reduction policy on the US economy.

For persons and businesses looking to forestall policies to control GHGs, two main avenues have been proposed. First, various bills and proposals have been circulated to directly limit the EPA's authority to regulate GHGs under the Clean Air Act. Some of these would preclude regulation of specific sectors (e.g., power plants, agriculture) while others would completely preempt the EPA from regulating GHGs under the act. For the moment, the American public seems willing to accept air pollution and is not overly concerned about GHGs.

## Paris Climate Change Agreement

Although the United Nations Framework Convention on Climate Change (UNCCC) adopted in 1992 had set GHG mitigation norms to prevent or limit atmospheric warming, it was not achieving desired results. The UNCCC's parties continued to meet and in 2015 successfully negotiated the Paris Agreement. Its objectives included enhancing the implementation of the UNCCC, strengthening the global response to the threat of climate change, and efforts to eradicate poverty. It diverges from earlier climate change efforts by focusing on nationally determined responses to climate change.

Under the Paris Agreement, countries have the same core obligations but flexibility in developing their implementation of economy-wide emission reduction or limitation targets. Developed countries are expected to provide financial resources to assist developing countries with respect to both mitigation and adaptation in continuation of existing obligations under the Convention. The Agreement has met nearly universal acceptance, with 195 signatories.

President Obama, together with Chinese president Xi Jinping, ratified this agreement in Hangzhou, China, in September 2016. However, the US ratification was without any action by the Senate. As such, it is an executive agreement rather than a treaty, which requires a two-thirds positive vote by the US Senate. Previous executive agreements have included the 1979 Long-Range Transboundary Air Pollution Convention, the 1991 US-Canada Air Quality Agreement, and the 1993 North American Agreement on Environmental Cooperation. However, with the election of President Trump, it remains unclear whether the United States will undertake efforts to reduce GHG contributions and ascribe to the provisions of the Paris Agreement.

# Greenwashing

Greenwashing is the unjustified appropriation of an environmental virtue by a company, industry, government, politician, or nongovernmental organization to create a pro-environmental image, sell a product or a policy, or to try and rehabilitate their standing with the public and decision makers after being embroiled in controversy. It describes a marketing strategy whereby companies use deceptive marketing or promotional materials to promote a perception that products or policies are environmentally friendly. This can involve selective disclosure of positive information and the withholding of negative information to present a positive environmental image. Business firms may use an environmentally friendly appearance to cover an environmentally unfriendly substance. In other situations, firms may change names or labels of harmful products to evoke the natural environment. In some cases, greenwashing involves multimillion-dollar advertising campaigns to portray companies as eco-friendly.

Firms, governments, and organizations may engage in greenwashing while seeking investments and profits. Another reason for greenwashing is that organizations want to impress others. In trying to make a statement, organizations may overly state their cause in a manner that constitutes greenwashing. Terra Choice Environmental Marketing, Inc. lists six sins of greenwashing:

- *Sin of the hidden trade-off.*
- *Sin of no proof.*
- *Sin of vagueness.*
- *Sin of irrelevance.*
- *Sin of fibbing.*
- *Sin of the lesser of two evils.*

Several laws provide guidance on the use of environmental marketing claims. Under the Federal Trade Commission Act, guides for the use of environmental marketing claims have been promulgated. The provisions of the Lanham Act proscribe false advertising. State legislatures are increasingly concerned about false claims of environmentally friendly products, and are enacting legislation to address greenwashing. Most state legislatures have adopted state consumer protection laws with provisions that can thwart greenwashing. A case from California discloses how a plaintiff can proceed against a firm making a dubious claim.

### *Koh v. S.C. Johnson & Son, Inc.*
US District Court, Northern District of California

*Who is suing?* _____

*Who is being sued?* _____

*For what?* _____

*What is the issue on appeal?* _____

Plaintiff Wayne Koh brings this suit, on behalf of himself and all others similarly situated, against defendant S. C. Johnson & Son, Inc. (SCJ) asserting claims under California's Unfair Competition Law; California's False Advertising Law; the Consumers Legal Remedies Act; common law fraud; and unjust enrichment. Defendant's motion to dismiss the first amended complaint came on for hearing by this court. Having considered the papers submitted by the parties and the arguments of counsel at oral argument, the motion is denied.

This case arises out of allegations of so-called "greenwashing," the practice of making one's products seem more environmentally friendly than in actuality. SCJ is a manufacturer of household cleaning products including Windex, a multi-purpose cleaner designed for cleaning glass and other reflective surfaces, and Shout, a stain remover. On January 16, 2008, SCJ began marketing and selling Windex in packaging that prominently displays a certain label (the Greenlist label) which is the subject of this lawsuit. Since then, SCJ has used this labeling on other products, including Shout. Plaintiff alleges that the Greenlist label is deceptively designed to look like a third party seal of approval, which it is not, and it falsely represents that the products are environmentally friendly.

The front of the Greenlist label has a green background and says, "Greenlist™ Ingredients," under a stylized drawing of two leaves and a stem. On the reverse side of the label, which is read through the back of the Windex packaging, there is the following text: "Greenlist™ is a rating system that promotes the use of environmentally responsible ingredients. For additional information, visit www.scjohnson.com."

Plaintiff alleges that, among today's environmentally-conscious consumers, products seen as "green," or "environmentally friendly," often command a premium price and take market share away from similar, non-green products. SCJ's products face competition from "ecofriendly" brands such as SimpleGreen and Seventh Generation. In addition, in early January 2008, just before SCJ began using the Greenlist label on Windex, its major competitor, Clorox, Co., announced that it was launching a line of Green Works cleaning products that had received a seal of approval from the Sierra Club. By using the Greenlist label, plaintiff alleges, SCJ is able to charge consumers as much as 50% more than its competitors' products that are not falsely portrayed as green. Plaintiff alleges that he would not have purchased Greenlist-labeled Windex at its premium price if he had known that Greenlist was actually created by SCJ, not a third party, and that Windex is not environmentally friendly.

Defendant raises two main arguments in support of dismissing the complaint: (1) plaintiff has not sufficiently alleged injury, and (2) no reasonable consumer could have found the Greenlist label misleading. Under the California Unfair Competition Law and California's False Advertising Law, suit may only be brought by a person who has suffered injury in fact and has lost money or property as a result of a violation. Courts have held that being induced to purchase a product one would not otherwise have purchased is not loss of money or property within the meaning of the statute as long as one still receives the benefit of the bargain. Here, however, plaintiff has sufficiently alleged that he did not receive the benefit of the bargain in that Windex cost more than similar products without misleading labeling.

On its second argument, defendant points out that the Greenlist label makes no mention of a third party, describes Greenlist as a "rating system" not a seal of approval, and directs consumers to SCJ's own website for further information. Whether a business practice is deceptive will usually be a question of fact not appropriate for decision on demurrer. Here, plaintiff's allegations are sufficient to create a question of fact as to whether the Greenlist label was deceptive. Given the context described in the complaint, it is plausible that a reasonable consumer would interpret the Greenlist label as being from a third party. In addition, guidelines issued by the Federal Trade Commission provide that a product label containing an "environmental seal," such as a globe icon with the text "Earth Smart" around it, is likely to convey to consumers that the product is environmentally superior to other products and would be deceptive if the manufacturer cannot substantiate this broad claim. Thus, while the attributes identified by defendant are relevant to the inquiry and may weaken the case for deceptiveness, they do not allow the court to rule on the issue as a matter of law.

## Questions

1. What did the court find greenwashing to include?
2. How many separate laws were allegedly involved with the greenwashing claim?
3. Doing a search of "False Advertising," California law has 168 entries, Georgia has 34, Florida has 42, and South Carolina has 9. What are the differences?
4. Should sellers or consumers (or both groups) want regulations on false advertising?

## Discussion Questions

1. How do GHGs affect climate change?
2. Why are some groups opposed to California's low-carbon fuel standard?
3. Is a life-cycle analysis of the carbon intensity of a given transportation fuel reasonable for establishing a fuel standard?

4. What is the reason some groups support a carbon tax?
5. What obligations does the United States have under the Paris Agreement since it was not ratified by the Senate?
6. How should a government address deceptive marketing or promotional materials that falsely promote the perception that products or policies are environmentally friendly?

# Image Credit

Copyright in the Public Domain.

# Section Five

---

# Regulations for Public Health

# CHAPTER TWENTY-FIVE

## Public Health Regulation and Medical Malpractice

---

### Learning Objectives

- *Assess why medical treatment in the United States is so costly.*
- *Discuss why medical malpractice is a controversial public health topic.*
- *Relate the significance of HIPAA to persons who have access to medical documents.*
- *Describe why governments can require persons to disclose they are infected with HIV.*
- *Identify why governments want to regulate conduct associated with obesity.*

Societies regulate issues dealing with public health to reduce risks that could adversely affect their human populations. Through the dissemination of information, inoculation and vaccination programs, monitoring of health threats, interventions to contain pathogens, and assistance to individuals afflicted with an illness, public health officials provide services to augment well-being. Their organized efforts prevent disease, promote health, and prolong life. Of course, public health efforts cost money, so governments must make choices to determine what programs and activities they will undertake.

With the adoption of the Patient Protection and Affordable Care Act of 2010 (Obamacare), considerable controversy has accompanied governmental decisions concerning public health. Should governments require persons to have health insurance? How much should governments pay in providing health care for the poor and the elderly? Another issue involves the provision of mental health services for indigents or persons who decline treatment. Failure to provide help to individuals with mental problems contributes to crime and tragedies such as the mass shootings that have become more common in recent years.

Controversies also involve evaluating the risks of injury and illness. Risk assessments should be based on objective and reliable scientific evidence. Four factors are generally considered: nature of the risk, duration of the risk, probability of harm, and severity of harm. Yet scientists do not agree on the dangers posed by various situations and diseases. Moreover, experts may not agree on what information to use in calculating risk. For example, in calculating health damages from exposure to particulate matter from air pollutants, governments have decided that pollution above a threshold level should be prohibited. This means that the air quality standards allow harmful pollutants to be released into the air, and, from time to time, concentrations above recommended levels occur. Moreover, even if particulate matter concentrations are below established thresholds, some people experiencing long-term exposure will develop health problems. Thus, our air pollution standards address risks by precluding egregious pollution and allowing pollutants in the air, even though they may adversely affect people.

Governments also make decisions on whether they should interfere with people's liberties by passing legislation to preclude persons from engaging in selected risky activities. For example, should governments impose reporting requirements on persons who test HIV-positive? Or should a state require a helmet for persons riding bicycles on public roads? Given the competing liberty and safety risks, differences of opinions lead to differing legislative rules among states.

# Public Health Regulation

The United States spends twice per capita on health care than other major industrialized countries. Approximately $10,000 per person of national income goes toward health care and spending. Medicare and Medicaid account for 37 percent of the funds spent on health care, and private insurance covers 33 percent. While some contend that managed care helps control costs, many patients and doctors say governmental requirements are detracting from our quality of care.

## 1. Health Care Reform in 2010

In 2010, Congress passed two major health care bills that transformed health care in the United States: (1) the Patient Protection and Affordable Care Act (Obamacare); and (2) the Health Care and Education Reconciliation Act. The first act included a series of authorities and responsibilities for the Department of Health and Human Services and called on the department to publish information regarding these new authorities. The Obama administration asserted that the reforms would make health care more affordable, make health insurers more accountable, expand health coverage to all Americans, and make the health system sustainable, stabilizing family budgets, the federal budget, and the economy. Three aspects were significant.

I.   The Act helped millions Americans afford health care who did not have it and made coverage more affordable for many more.

II.  The legislation ended discrimination against Americans with preexisting conditions, a problem that kept some employees at current jobs they did not enjoy.

III. Coverage was extended to more children, as workplace and retiree health insurance plans can now allow parents to add their children under age 27 to their health coverage on a tax-free basis.

Obamacare has become a political issue, and its amendment or repeal will remain troublesome as revised legislation may reduce or eliminate insurance coverage for millions of Americans.

## 2.  Health Insurance Portability and Accountability Act (HIPAA)

HIPAA was passed by Congress in 1996; it has two major parts. The first part protects health insurance coverage for workers and their families when they change or lose their jobs. The second part requires the establishment of national standards for electronic health care transactions and national identifiers for providers, health insurance plans, and employers. The HIPAA Privacy Rule regulates the use and disclosure of Protected Health Information held by covered entities. While information may be disclosed to facilitate treatment, payment, or health care operations without a patient's express written authorization, any other disclosure of protected health information requires the covered entity to obtain written authorization from the individual. These privacy provisions may be supplemented by state law so long as the state provisions are not an obstacle to accomplishing HIPAA's provisions.

*Bryant v. Jackson*
Superior Court of Massachusetts

*Who is suing?* _____

*Who is being sued?* _____

*For what?* _____

*What is the issue on appeal?* _____

Plaintiff Daphne Bryant, a one-time patient at Brigham and Women's Hospital (BWH), claims that her confidential medical information was wrongfully discovered and disclosed by a hospital employee to unrelated third parties. She sues the employee, defendant Shona Jackson, for negligence and claims that BWH is vicariously liable for Jackson's negligence. Bryant also sues defendants Christine Collins and BWH for negligent supervision and training of Jackson. Finally, Bryant sues BWH for violation of Massachusetts General Laws (G.L.) ch. 93A in disclosing her HIV condition. BWH and Collins move for summary judgment contending that they cannot be held vicariously liable for the conduct of Jackson. In addition, BWH and Collins contend that there is insufficient evidence in the record to sustain Bryant's claim for negligent supervision and training.

Bryant was a patient at BWH where she received treatment for HIV and related disorders. She had early been diagnosed as being HIV positive but she diligently kept secret her HIV diagnosis from her family (except for her mother) and others. Jackson was an employee of BWH. At the time relevant to the complaint, she was an "access facilitator" in the Patient Access Services Department. The position of access facilitator requires an employee to access patient information in order to perform her job function. The job function includes admitting patients administratively, assigning them to a unit in the hospital and assisting with appropriate billing. In the course of performing her job duties, Jackson was required to access confidential information concerning patients thousands of times per year.

As part of her employment, Jackson received training with respect to maintaining the confidentiality of patient medical information and the Health Insurance Portability and Accountability Act (HIPAA) with respect to confidentiality of patient information. The record contains a confidentiality agreement signed by Jackson stating "I agree not to disclose or discuss any patient … information with others, including friends or family who do not have a need-to-know." BWH performed periodic audits and quality checks of employees who may access patients' medical records. In addition, all employees, from the time of orientation and throughout their employment, receive informal training and reminders to maintain patient confidentiality.

Bryant complained to BWH about Jackson. Jackson was an acquaintance of Bryant who grew up with Bryant in the same neighborhood. They shared a mutual friend, Toshia Moore. Bryant complained that Jackson had revealed Bryant's confidential medical information, including that Bryant was HIV positive, to Moore when Moore was at the hospital. A formal Privacy Complaint Intake Form was prepared by BWH. BWH audited its computer system to determine whether Jackson had accessed Bryant's medical records. That audit showed that Jackson had accessed Bryant's electronic medical records on three occasions. BWH's investigation determined that Jackson had inappropriately accessed Bryant's medical records. Jackson was terminated from her employment at BWH.

Whether Jackson, after inappropriately accessing Bryant's records, disclosed to any person that Bryant was HIV positive is disputed. The credibility of Moore is at issue. In addition, the credibility of Jackson is at issue because the jury could choose to disbelieve Jackson's denial of disclosure of Bryant's HIV status, especially given Jackson's admission of discussing other issues of Bryant's health with Moore.

Collins was Jackson's supervisor. There is no evidence in the record that Collins, or anyone else at BWH, knew, prior to Bryant's complaint, of Jackson's unauthorized access of Bryant's medical information. There was no evidence that BWH's training and supervision of medical records personnel was below the standard of care required of a medical provider. Even if Jackson disseminated Bryant's confidential information, Collins and BWH contend that there is no evidence from which a jury could find that they were negligent with respect to supervising, training or hiring Jackson. I agree. Summary judgment dismissing this claim against Collins and BWH will be granted.

General Laws ch. 111, § 70F applies to information concerning HIV. The first paragraph of § 70F provides that no health care facility and no physician or health care provider shall disclose the results of a HIV test to any person other than the subject thereof without first obtaining the subject's written informed consent. The fourth paragraph of § 70F unquestionably gives a private right of action for damages to a patient against a "facility" like BWH for the disclosure of her HIV condition. Given the language of the statute and the expressed public policy to provide absolute confidentiality to HIV tests, I find that BWH can be held strictly liable under § 70F if the jury determines that Jackson disclosed Bryant's HIV status to Moore. For the reasons stated above, the motion for summary judgment of BWH is denied. The motion for summary judgment of Christine Collins is allowed.

## Questions

1. What does Bryant seek with this lawsuit?
2. Is Bryant seeking relief under HIPAA?
3. Why shouldn't Jackson's termination resolve the issue?
4. Was BWH negligent? If so, what was its negligence?
5. Why was Collins's motion for summary judgment granted?
6. Did Massachusetts overreact in enacting General Laws ch. 111, § 70F concerning HIV information?

# Medical Malpractice

A significant public health issue involves negligence liability for medical malpractice. As advances in science provide more and more information, opportunities for doing something wrong seem to increase. Medical practitioners may experience difficulties in keeping up with the latest medical advances. They may not realize that a new technique is available to treat a patient under their care. What expectations should we have about their expertise? Should we expect them to know the latest medical discoveries and to be able to employ the techniques in their practices?

A recent California lawsuit shows one of the predicaments. Jeffrey sustained an injury to his right shoulder in a motocross bike accident. Because X-rays did not identify any fracture, his primary care physician referred him to an orthopedic group. Jeffrey then had an MRI and a follow-up CT scan that showed a fracture running across the front of the socket half of his shoulder. When Jeffrey consulted with his surgeon for a shoulder repair, he was told that treatment would depend on the MRI and CT views. Meanwhile, Jeffrey's girlfriend, who worked at a hospital, secured advice from another orthopedic surgeon. The second surgeon voiced his opinion that it could be repaired.

Jeffrey's surgeon performed arthroscopic surgery. After probing the fracture with a K-wire, the surgeon decided not to put in a biodegradable screw because the screw might cause the fracture fragment to fall apart. Employing his best professional judgment, the surgeon decided that "it was best to leave things alone." However, Jeffrey disagreed. Based on the opinion of the second surgeon, who had glanced at the MRI and CT films, he was convinced that the shoulder could have been repaired. He sued his surgeon and the surgeon's orthopedic group for medical malpractice and battery. After a trial, the lawsuit was dismissed, as the jury found no malpractice and no battery. Jeffrey's actions demonstrate one of the problems accompanying increasing medical costs. People with no knowledge of medical science question their surgeon's professional judgment. Why can't we allow medical personnel to proceed with their work, rather than exposing them to a tort system that causes considerable stress and lost productivity?

## 1. Reducing Malpractice Litigation

Over the past half century, rising malpractice claims have resulted in the exit of many insurance carriers. Medical practitioners have fewer options for insurance coverage, and their medical malpractice premiums have increased significantly. Due to these increases, state legislatures have adopted reforms to limit malpractice insurers' costs. Proposals were also made for more fundamental reforms of the liability system. While the media share many examples of unfortunate medical malpractice, we might want to consider the evidence. Our total health care system costs are estimated to be more than $1 trillion per year. Of these expenditures, approximately 1 percent involves malpractice insurance premiums and litigation costs. Our costs for medical care are high, but 99 percent of these costs are due to funds expended for items other than litigation.

One cause might be the salaries of physicians. American physicians are paid considerably more than their counterparts in other developed countries. Another might be precautionary procedures ordered by the medical profession to avoid litigation. Defensive medicine may account for $46 billion a year in the United States. The evidence suggests that there are a significant number of avoidable serious injuries and deaths due to malpractice. It is estimated that as many as 250,000 Americans die each year as a result of medical errors. This suggests it is the third leading cause of death after heart disease and cancer. Substandard medical care is a problem. Lapses in substandard care are often predictable and frequently preventable. It is estimated that more Americans die of medical errors than the combined deaths from motor vehicle accidents and breast cancer.

Furthermore, few malpractice victims bring lawsuits. Only one out of twenty-one injured victims receives damages for their medical malpractice claims. One reason for not bringing a lawsuit is the expense. It has been estimated that damages of at least $100,000 are needed before it is worthwhile to sue. Therefore, most valid claims of medical malpractice are not compensated. Instead, victims must foot these costs and pass some expenses to their own insurers. This evidence suggests that because so many injured patients do not bring lawsuits, malpractice victims and their families incur significant uncompensated losses. Those victims with medical insurance pass on some of these costs to their first-party insurance providers. This means that workers' private medical insurance costs include expenses associated with medical malpractice. Second, insurers of medical practitioners are not incurring expenses for many of the injuries caused by their insured policyholders. Thus, although malpractice lawsuits may be expensive for medical practitioners and their insurers, they are enjoying a windfall of lower costs due to not paying damages to most injured patients. Medical practitioners and insurers are not paying their share of damages for injuries they have caused.

## 2. Legislative Responses to Medical Malpractice Damages

Legislatures have been active in responding to damages related to medical malpractice lawsuits. Every state has proceeded differently in selecting issues to address in an effort to respond to the problems. The most obvious reform involves caps on damages. Other reforms may act to help reduce damages in tort lawsuit, including statutes of limitations, affidavits of merit requirements, expert witness standards, and peer review panels.

Some state tort reforms have been enacted for a sufficient amount of time to make comparisons among states with reforms and those without. An evaluation of reforms dealing with damage caps, caps on attorneys' fees, limitations on joint and several liability, and mandatory collateral offset rules suggests that state tort reforms may net savings.

A number of state legislatures have decided that it is appropriate to establish caps on the amount of damages for pain and suffering. The legislative responses vary considerably, but most do not allow for the consideration of the extenuating circumstances involved in the case. This includes little consideration of who will pay for the future services needed by the injured individual. Caps may mean that family members, friends, or taxpayers will have to absorb the expenses of the wrongfully injured person, rather than the wrongdoers or the wrongdoer's insurance company.

Legislative enactments limiting damages continue to be controversial and continue to raise legal issues that lead to legal challenges. The statutes are interpreted strictly and may lead to some unintended results. The following case shows how lawyers failed to identify nonpractitioners as defendants and so did not qualify for moneys under the statutory nonpractitioner cap.

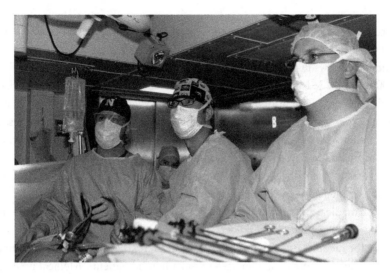

Fig. 25.1 Emergency room procedure.

### *Estate of Michelle Evette McCall*
US Court of Appeals for the Eleventh Circuit, Atlanta

*Who is suing?* _____

*Who is being sued?* _____

*For what?* _____

*What is the issue on appeal?* _____

The central question presented in this appeal is whether Florida's cap on noneconomic medical malpractice damages, Florida Statutes § 766.118, violates the Florida or United States Constitutions. The Estate of Michelle McCall, Ms. McCall's parents, and the father of Ms. McCall's son (collectively Plaintiffs) also appeal the District Court's application of that statutory cap. We conclude that the District Court did not err in applying the cap. We also conclude that Florida's statutory cap passes muster under the Equal Protection Clause of the Fourteenth Amendment.

Michelle McCall received prenatal medical care at a United States Air Force clinic as an Air Force dependent. She had a healthy and normal pregnancy until February 21 test results revealed that Ms. McCall's blood pressure was high and that she was suffering from severe preeclampsia. Ms. McCall's serious condition required that labor be induced immediately. The Air Force hospital was temporarily unavailable for obstetric and delivery services, so members of the family practice department transferred Ms. McCall to the Fort Walton Beach Medical Center instead. There, Air Force family practice doctors treated Ms. McCall for hypertension and called an Air Force obstetrician, Dr. Archibald, and asked if he could perform a cesarean section. Dr. Archibald reported that he was performing another surgery and would not be available to perform a cesarean section on Ms. McCall until after he finished that surgery.

On February 22, Dr. Archibald finally arrived to perform the cesarean section, but Ms. McCall's contractions had resumed and the Air Force family practice doctors decided to allow Ms. McCall to deliver vaginally. Dr. Archibald left the Fort Walton Medical Center. On February 23 at 1:25 a.m., Ms. McCall delivered a healthy baby boy. Ms. McCall's blood pressure began to drop rapidly and remained dangerously low over the next two and a half hours. The Air Force nurse anesthetist monitoring Ms. McCall's vital signs did not notify the family practice doctors of the drop in Ms. McCall's blood pressure. Dr. Archibald never checked the vital signs himself and relied exclusively on the nurse to inform him of any blood pressure changes or problems.

At 3:50 a.m., Dr. Archibald requested an immediate blood count and, if needed, a transfusion to compensate for the blood Ms. McCall lost during the procedure. Forty minutes later, the family practice department physician ordered the blood count test. Forty minutes after that, and over an hour after Dr. Archibald had requested immediate blood work, a nurse attempted to draw blood from Ms. McCall. Ms. McCall was unresponsive. She had gone into shock and cardiac arrest as a result of severe blood loss. It is not clear how long Ms. McCall had been in this state, since no one had monitored her or checked her status for the hour following Dr. Archibald's procedure. Ms. McCall never regained consciousness and was removed from life support on February 27.

Plaintiffs sued the United States under the Federal Tort Claims Act (FTCA). After a two-day bench trial, the District Court found the United States liable under the FTCA because the negligence of its employees proximately caused Ms. McCall's death. The District Court found that Plaintiffs' economic damages, or financial losses, amounted to $980,462.40. The court found that Plaintiffs' noneconomic damages, or nonfinancial losses, totaled $2 million, including $500,000 for Ms. McCall's son and $750,000 for each of her parents. The District Court applied Florida's statutory cap on noneconomic damages for medical malpractice claims and limited Plaintiffs' recovery of noneconomic damages to $1 million. The District Court rejected Plaintiffs' argument that they were entitled to the full $2 million in noneconomic damages because they could recover under both the $1 million cap for "practitioners" and the $1.5 million cap for "nonpractitioners." The Court also denied Plaintiffs' motion challenging the constitutionality of Florida's statutory cap under both the Florida and United States Constitutions.

On appeal, Plaintiffs challenge the District Court's rulings on both the application and constitutionality of Florida's cap on noneconomic damages for medical malpractice claims. For a personal injury or wrongful death claim arising from the medical negligence of "practitioners," Florida's statute provides:

> *(a) Regardless of the number of such practitioner defendants, noneconomic damages shall not exceed $500,000 per claimant. No practitioner shall be liable for more than $500,000 in noneconomic damages, regardless of the number of claimants.*

> *(b) Notwithstanding paragraph (a), if the negligence resulted in a permanent vegetative state or death, the total noneconomic damages recoverable from all*

*practitioners, regardless of the number of claimants, under this paragraph shall not exceed $1 million.*

*(c) The total noneconomic damages recoverable by all claimants from all practitioner defendants under this subsection shall not exceed $1 million in the aggregate.*

The District Court properly found that any noneconomic damages recoverable from the hospital based on its vicarious liability fell within the $1 million cap for "practitioners." Florida's statute expressly provides that the term "practitioner" includes any person or entity whose liability is based solely on such person or entity being vicariously liable for the actions of a practitioner. The District Court also correctly characterized the certified registered nurse anesthetist, the family practice doctors and the obstetrician who provided Ms. McCall's medical care at the Fort Walton Beach Medical Center as "practitioners."

The District Court was correct in finding that Plaintiffs did not establish that Ms. McCall's death resulted from the negligence of a "nonpractitioner." As the District Court observed, Plaintiffs' complaint did not identify any hospital staff or nurses by name except for the physicians, who are practitioners. The District Court also reported that no evidence at trial singled out a specific nonpractitioner for negligent conduct. On this record, we conclude that the District Court did not err in applying Florida's cap on noneconomic damages for medical malpractice claims.

Plaintiffs argue that Florida's statutory cap on noneconomic damages for medical malpractice claims violates the Equal Protection Clause of the Fourteenth Amendment of the United States Constitution. Under the Equal Protection Clause, social and economic legislation that does not employ suspect classifications or impinge on fundamental rights must be upheld against equal protection attack when the legislative means are rationally related to a legitimate governmental purpose. We analyze whether Florida's statutory cap is rationally related to a legitimate governmental purpose.

Plaintiffs argue that the statutory cap lacks a rational basis because the Florida legislature "had no objective, factual basis for believing" that a cap on noneconomic damages for medical malpractice claims would reduce the cost of medical malpractice insurance. That argument lacks merit. Before enacting the statutory cap, the legislature held public hearings, heard expert testimony and reviewed a separate report prepared by a Task Force on Healthcare Professional Liability Insurance. The Task Force report set forth that health care providers were changing the scope of their practice, leaving Florida, or retiring because of escalating medical malpractice premiums. The Task Force recommended that the legislature create a "per incident" medical malpractice cap to remedy the problem. We therefore conclude that Florida's statutory cap on noneconomic damages for medical malpractice claims does not violate the Equal Protection Clause of the United States Constitution.

## Questions

1. What is a bench trial?
2. Were there nonpractitioners involved in the events leading to Ms. McCall's death?
3. What is or would be the significance of having a nonpractitioner named as a defendant?
4. What is the test employed to determine whether the Florida statute violates the Equal Protection Clause of the US Constitution?
5. Why did the Florida legislature adopt the statutory cap?

# Disclosure of Disease

One controversial issue involves persons testing positive for the human immunodeficiency virus (HIV) that may lead to acquired immune deficiency syndrome (AIDS). To help curtail the spread of this virus, governments want people to be tested so that they know whether they are infected and, as a result, actions can be taken to reduce the transmission of the disease to new persons. Yet individuals may hesitate to be tested if this information can be shared with others without the individual's consent. Thus, governments have enacted statutes under which HIV/AIDS records are confidential, except for selected purposes authorized by the statute.

However, the confidentiality of this information means that persons associated with an infected individual—including future sexual partners—cannot learn about the individual's health status, unless the individual chooses to divulge the information. This is disconcerting to people who are subsequently infected with the virus. In the following case, a woman attempts to sue various governmental defendants for failing to take actions that would have assisted her in avoiding contact with a sexual partner infected with HIV.

### B.R. v. Vaughan
#### Superior Court of New Jersey, Middlesex County

*Who is suing?* _____

*Who is being sued?* _____

*For what?* _____

*What is the issue on appeal?* _____

This case comes before the court on a motion to dismiss the complaint for failure to state a claim upon which relief can be granted. It appears that this motion has highlighted a unique issue of law, as there are no applicable New Jersey decisions that directly address the duty of State agencies and/or their employees to notify a person of their partner's HIV/AIDS status when the infected individual is a client or patient of that agency or their employee.

Plaintiff had a long-term relationship with an individual named D. D. Following the end of the relationship, plaintiff discovered that D. D. had tested positive for the human immunodeficiency virus (HIV) and that he had infected her with the virus. Plaintiff brought suit against defendants Anita Vaughan, Newark Community Health Center, and others. Plaintiff alleges that defendants knew, or should have known, of D. D.'s infection and, as such, owed a duty to plaintiff to notify her that she was at risk to contract this disease. Plaintiff further alleges that the actions of defendants were reckless, willful, and wanton.

Defendants moved to dismiss, arguing that there was no duty to disclose D. D.'s HIV status as the State is constrained by the rules and regulations which generally preclude disclosure without written consent. Defendants submit that there is no allegation that this authorization was ever provided. Conversely, plaintiff argues that she pled sufficient facts in her amended complaint to put defendants on notice of her liability claims against them. Plaintiff further submits that the Appellate Division (via *Earle v. Kuklo*) imposes an affirmative duty to prevent exposing another to a contagious or infectious disease, especially with regard to HIV and acquired immune deficiency syndrome (AIDS), which the State has determined to be of paramount public importance. In support of this contention, plaintiff points to the "Notification Assistance Program" in the State, and argues that its principal objective is to elicit contacts of HIV positive individuals for the purpose of notifying them of potential exposure.

Upon a motion to dismiss for failure to state a claim upon which relief can be granted, where a plaintiff fails to allege facts sufficient to support a claim for relief, the complaint should be dismissed. Essentially, the issue before the court is whether defendants had a duty to notify plaintiff that she was at risk of exposure to the HIV virus from contact with D. D. This case is governed by the applicable statutes, namely N.J. Statutes Annotated (N.J.S.A.) §§ 26:5C-7 to -9 and § 26:5C-14.

N.J.S.A. § 26:5C-7 provides for the confidentiality of AIDS and HIV infection records and information. The records about a person who has or is suspected of having AIDS or HIV infection is confidential and shall be disclosed only for the purposes authorized by this act. Disclosure is only permitted with the "prior written consent of the person who is the subject of the record." If the prior written consent is not obtained, the records may not be disclosed except to qualified personnel, the Department, or by court order. Pursuant to the statute, unauthorized disclosure of the name of the person who has or is suspected of having an HIV or AIDS infection may result in a civil action for appropriate damages, including attorney's fees and even punitive damages "when the violation evidences wantonly reckless or intentionally malicious conduct."

The court has also reviewed the rules and regulations regarding reporting of HIV and AIDS infection as set forth by the Commissioner pursuant to N.J.S.A. § 26:5C-24. While N.J. Administrative Code § 8:57-1.1 provides a scheme for dealing with infectious and communicable diseases, it does not have application to this case, which deals with HIV and AIDS infections. Unless otherwise provided in the statute, individuals infected with HIV or AIDS have the protection of confidentiality under the law. Moreover, the purported reporting regulations, N.J. Administrative Code §§ 8:57-2.1 to -2.12, do not require notification of an HIV positive status to an outsider, but rather require a positive status be reported to the State and its agencies so that the virus can be better tracked and services may be offered to infected individuals. Plaintiff has not cited to, nor has the court found any in reviewing all of the applicable regulations, a duty on the part of the State, its agents, or employees to report an HIV positive status to a third party such as a long-term partner.

Therefore, I find that defendants had no statutory or common-law duty to notify plaintiff that she was at risk of contracting the HIV virus from D. D. Plaintiff has provided no evidence that D. D. gave written authorization for the disclosure of his HIV status. In fact, it should be noted that plaintiff provided an affidavit signed by D. D. regarding his interaction with defendants, and noticeably absent was any indication that he provided this required authorization for disclosure. Without prior written permission, defendants would be liable for an unauthorized disclosure and may be responsible for significant civil damages had they attempted to contact plaintiff. Moreover, defendants logically could not notify plaintiff that she was at risk of contracting HIV from D. D. without informing her of his test results.

Not only did defendants have no duty to disclose D. D.'s HIV status to plaintiff, but they were actually prohibited from doing so by New Jersey law. Defendants were also not under any common-law duty to notify plaintiff, as again, any such notice would violate the statute. The court finds that plaintiff's pleading fails to state a claim upon which relief can be granted even when searching liberally as there is no duty upon which the claim can be based. Accordingly, defendants' motion to dismiss plaintiff's complaint with prejudice for failure to state a claim is granted.

## Questions

1. What might be the policy objectives of N.J.S.A. § 26:5C-7's confidentiality provisions?
2. Could the N.J. Administrative Code be revised to require the state to disclose persons infected with HIV or AIDS?
3. For persons planning to engage in a sexual relationship, who should have the responsibility for protecting a person from exposure to HIV?
4. If the public feels disclosure would be beneficial, what should they do to change state policy?

# Obesity

Obesity has emerged as a major health problem. In the United States, the Centers for Disease Control and Prevention has estimated that 69 percent of adults age twenty years and over are overweight, and approximately 36 percent of adults age twenty years and over are obese. For children ages six to nineteen, more than 18 percent are obese. "Overweight" is defined as a body mass index (BMI) of 25 or higher; obesity is defined as a BMI of 30 or higher.

Obesity is a problem because it increases the risks for a number of health problems, including coronary heart disease, type 2 diabetes, cancers (endometrial, breast, and colon), hypertension (high blood pressure), dyslipidemia (for example, high total cholesterol or high levels of triglycerides), stroke, liver and gallbladder disease, sleep apnea and respiratory problems, osteoarthritis (a degeneration of cartilage and its underlying bone within a joint), and gynecological problems (abnormal menses, infertility). The health care costs of obesity in the United States exceed $190 billion per year.

Governments are now taking action to encourage behavior that will help reduce obesity. One idea is to help people reduce their consumption of sugary drinks. A portion cap rule for food service establishments was adopted by the New York City Board of Health. The portion cap rule limited the maximum self-service cup or container size for sugary drinks to 16 fluid ounces for all food service establishments. "Sugary drink" was defined as a nonalcoholic carbonated or noncarbonated beverage sweetened by the manufacturer or establishment with sugar or another caloric sweetener; has greater than 25 calories per eight fluid ounces of beverage; and does not contain more than 50 percent of milk or milk substitute by volume as an ingredient. The rule thus targeted non-diet soft drinks, sweetened teas, sweetened black coffee, hot chocolate, energy drinks, sports drinks, and sweetened juices, but contained carve-outs for alcoholic beverages, milkshakes, fruit smoothies, and mixed coffee drinks, mochas, lattes, and 100 percent fruit juices. In addition, the portion cap rule applied to restaurants, delis, fast-food franchises, movie theaters, stadiums, and street carts, but not to grocery stores, convenience stores, corner markets, gas stations, and other similar businesses.

Restaurants and others were not pleased with the rule, and successfully challenged the board of health's authority to enact such a rule. An appellate court found that the board of health overstepped the boundaries of its lawfully delegated authority when it promulgated the portion cap rule to curtail the consumption of soda drinks because it violated the state principle of separation of powers. Such a rule had to be adopted by a legislative body.

An idea that has garnered more attention is government intervention in the form of disclosure requirements. This involves identifying the caloric value of food offerings on menus and drive-through signs and vending machines posting caloric value next to the snacks displayed. While some studies have concluded that disclosure decreases the number of calories purchased, other studies found that most customers had not observed the displayed nutritional information. A related idea is to devise color-coding nutritional labels as developed by the British Food Standards Agency. Red, yellow, and green lights would express high, medium, and low levels of sugars, overall fat, saturated fat, and salt.

Other ideas to stem obesity are taxes on unhealthy food and beverage products, bans on sales in certain locales, limitations on marketing to children, litigation against fast food companies, changes in support for farm policies that support unhealthy foods, and encouraging exercise.

## Discussion Questions

1. Does current medical malpractice adequately promote the interests of physicians or patients?
2. How might medical malpractice be reformed to improve patient outcomes?
3. What might a state legislature do to reduce defensive medicine?
4. Are monetary caps on damages for medical malpractice a good idea? Why or why not?
5. What should the United States be doing to help reduce obesity?

## Image Credit

Copyright in the Public Domain.

# CHAPTER TWENTY-SIX
## Strategies to Control Diseases

---

## Learning Objectives

- *Explain categories of governmental intervention offered to control diseases.*
- *Criticize laws allowing the government to quarantine and destroy animals.*
- *Describe how governments balance required vaccination with religions freedom.*
- *Describe the balance between quarantining guide dogs to prevent the introduction of disease and the Americans with Disabilities Act.*
- *Examine how medical facilities can interfere with workers' rights to prevent the spread of disease.*

In protecting people and property, governments take actions to prevent and curtail diseases. Governmental intervention may include vaccination, quarantine, border controls, community hygiene measures, and isolation programs. These actions supplement public health practices that have gained widespread acceptance due to their effectiveness in reducing the risks of infectious diseases. Of course, implementation of these programs may interfere with property rights and may involve adverse consequences for some individuals.

# Vaccination

One of the most cost-effective public health interventions is vaccination. Vaccination programs have eliminated smallpox and drastically reduced diseases such as polio. Yet vaccination has provoked resistance over the years, including by some parents in the United States, who feel that vaccines may cause other medical problems. Some parents are demanding that their offspring not be vaccinated due to the belief that the risk of adverse consequences from being vaccinated is greater than the risk of a particular disease or for religious reasons.

### *Caviezel v. Great Neck Public Schools*
US Court of Appeals for the Second Circuit, New York

*Who is suing?* _____

*Who is being sued?* _____

*For what?* _____

*What is the issue on appeal?* _____

Plaintiffs Martina and Andreas Schenk Caviezel sued defendants under federal and state law for denying them a religious exemption from the New York requirement (N.Y. Public Health Law § 2164) that they have their children vaccinated as a condition of their attendance of public schools. In three carefully reasoned opinions, the district court ruled that (1) the Caviezels were not entitled to preliminary injunctive relief because they failed, at a hearing, to demonstrate a likelihood of success on the merits, i.e., that their opposition to vaccination was based on "genuine and sincere religious beliefs which prohibit vaccinations"; (2) dismissal was warranted of the Caviezels' First Amendment free exercise claims, as well as of their Fourteenth Amendment equal protection and due process claims; and (3) summary judgment was warranted in favor of defendants on the Caviezels' pendent claim for a religious exemption under N.Y. Public Health Law § 2164(9).

The Caviezels' challenges to the dismissal of their First Amendment and equal protection claims and the award of summary judgment on their state law exemption claim fail to clear the common hurdle erected by the district court's factual finding, made after the preliminary injunction hearing, that they failed credibly to demonstrate "that they hold genuine and sincere religious beliefs which prohibit vaccinations." That finding precludes a viable claim that they have been injured in the free exercise of religion or that the government treats sincere religious beliefs disparately in violation of the Equal Protection Clause. It also necessarily defeats a claim to a religious exemption from vaccination pursuant to N.Y. Public Health Law § 2164(9).

While the Caviezels take exception to this critical finding, to the extent the finding rests on the district court's firsthand observation of the witnesses, as well as its careful identification of evidence inconsistent with the proffered religious beliefs, we identify no clear error. Further, the district court appropriately concluded that conclusory discovery produced after the preliminary injunction hearing did not equate to admissible evidence raising triable issues of fact. Accordingly, judgment was properly granted for defendants on the Caviezels' First Amendment, equal protection, and state law claims.

In the absence of a viable First Amendment claim, the Caviezels' substantive due process challenge to New York's immunization requirement is defeated by *Jacobson v. Massachusetts* (1905) (rejecting challenge to a smallpox vaccination mandate). The Supreme Court continues to cite approvingly to *Jacobson*. The judgment of the district court is affirmed.

## Questions

1. What analysis does the court employ to examine the evidence presented by Mr. and Mrs. Caviezel about their religious beliefs?
2. Why doesn't N.Y. Public Health Law § 2164(9) help the appellants in this appeal?
3. What is the status of challenging mandatory vaccinations based on substantive due process?

## Quarantine

The practice of quarantine has long been employed to guard against the introduction of diseases and pathogens. People, animals, and objects are held for a period of time to determine whether they are infected. This practice obviously can interfere with liberty and property interests, and individuals adversely affected may seek relief claiming that an agency's actions are arbitrary and capricious.

### *Ag-Innovations, Inc. v. USDA*
United States District Court, Vermont

*Who is suing?* _____

*Who is being sued?* _____

*For what?* _____

*What is the issue on appeal?* _____

The United States Department of Agriculture (USDA or agency) issued an administrative order by which it seized and destroyed plaintiffs' imported East Friesian milk sheep and any associated sperm and embryos (germ plasma). This order was issued in conjunction with a Declaration of Extraordinary Emergency which stated that a transmissible spongiform encephalopathy (TSE) of foreign origin had been detected in several of plaintiffs' sheep. In a related action, the plaintiffs were ultimately unsuccessful in avoiding the destruction of their seized flock. In this action, the plaintiffs challenge the legality of quarantining certain animals and areas of the plaintiffs' property for a period of four years.

The plaintiffs request a declaratory ruling reversing the agency's quarantine order and awarding costs, fees and other appropriate relief. As framed by the plaintiffs, the remaining question before the Court is whether the Secretary and USDA can offer any rational justification for their imposition of a quarantine of plaintiffs' farm premises. Accordingly, the parties recognize this motion looks at the legality of the temporary, attendant quarantine imposed on plaintiffs' property and restrictions placed on their ability to raise certain forms of livestock. The Administrative Procedure Act (APA) provides the standard of review of the USDA's quarantine action. Under the APA, this Court reviews errors of law de novo. Regarding other agency findings, conclusions, and actions, the reviewing court shall hold them unlawful and set them aside if they are arbitrary, capricious, an abuse of discretion, or otherwise not in accordance with law. An agency's decision is entitled to a presumption of regularity, and the burden of proof is on the party challenging the agency's decision.

In mid-July 2000, the USDA issued and published in the Federal Register a Declaration of Extraordinary Emergency which stated a TSE of foreign origin had been detected in several sheep in Vermont and any sheep affected or exposed, and their germ plasma, had to be destroyed. Under 7 U.S.C. § 8306(c)(1), the USDA has broad authority to take actions such as imposing a quarantine where such action is necessary to prevent the dissemination of disease, such as could be caused by the type of prion proteins at issue in this case. This Court already has determined the agency's issuance of the Declaration of Extraordinary Emergency was not arbitrary and capricious. Examining the administrative record, this Court noted:

I.   1. BSE [bovine spongiform encephalopathy] can be transmitted to sheep by feeding them infected cattle brain, even in very small amounts (0.5 g).

II.   2. BSE in sheep cannot be differentiated from scrapie, the naturally occurring TSE of sheep and goats. ... Although scrapie is not considered a human health risk, BSE is the most likely cause of variant Creutzfeldt-Jakob [sic] Disease (vCJD), a fatal human disease. ...

III.   4. If BSE occurs naturally and behaves like scrapie (i.e., is transmitted from one sheep to another), bans on the feeding of mammalian protein to sheep will not prevent the spread of the disease. ...

IV.   6. 65 head of sheep were imported into the United States from Belgium in 1996. ... The imported sheep could have been exposed to BSE and could be incubating the disease. ...

V.   8. Six of nine of the sheep with interpretable test results have some evidence of brain lesions. ...

VI.   9. Eliminating the possibility of risk associated with these sheep may take longer than a decade. ... The stakes with the imported sheep are high as BSE is considered a potential human pathogen.

In short, the administrative record contains sufficient facts to support the Secretary's Declaration of Extraordinary Emergency because the continued presence of the plaintiffs' sheep posed a serious and substantial risk of spreading disease as contemplated by federal law. These underlying considerations, as well as subsequent, undisputed facts, establish the legality of the agency's quarantine under the arbitrary and capricious standard.

Two of the plaintiffs' sheep did test positive for an abnormal prion protein. Evidence suggests that abnormal prion proteins in sheep can be transmitted during the lambing process to pasture lands, where they may survive for years. These are among the factors which supply sufficient reliable evidence to support the agency's decision to impose a quarantine. Based, therefore, on the information, the agency's quarantine is not arbitrary and capricious. A reviewing court must generally be at its most deferential when an agency is making predictions, within its area of special expertise, at the frontiers of science. The defendants' motion for judgment is granted, and the plaintiffs' motion for judgment is denied.

## Questions

1. Why were plaintiffs' sheep quarantined?
2. What must a plaintiff show to gain damages and other relief?
3. What is the danger posed by sheep affected by BSE?
4. What if no sheep had tested positive for an abnormal prion protein?

# Border Controls

Countries have regulations on the entry of people, animals, and products in order to prevent the introduction of diseases. With widespread international commerce and travel, considerable resources may be needed to avoid the introduction of a disease organism. In the United States, the Centers for Disease Control and Prevention's (CDC's) Division of Global Migration and Quarantine is charged with preventing the introduction, transmission, or spread of communicable diseases from foreign countries into the United States. The CDC also regulates the importation of infectious biological agents, infectious substances, and vectors of human disease. Turning to the preservation of the nation's livestock and poultry populations, the Animal and Plant Health Inspection Service (APHIS) is charged with a similar task. The service has adopted a three-tier system to develop countermeasures to address disease outbreaks.

Federal border controls to prevent the introduction of diseases and disease organisms must comply with federal constitutional requirements and may be affected by federal statutes. The following case shows a state restriction that did not fully account for the federal Americans with Disabilities Act.

### Crowder v. Kitagawa
#### US Court of Appeals for the Ninth Circuit, San Francisco

*Who is suing?* _____

*Who is being sued?* _____

*For what?* _____

*What is the issue on appeal?* _____

The plaintiffs are a class of visually-impaired persons who use guide dogs. They seek exemption from Hawaii's imposition of a 120-day quarantine on carnivorous animals entering the state. They contend Hawaii's quarantine, designed to prevent the importation of rabies, violates the Americans with Disabilities Act (ADA) and their constitutional rights of travel, equal protection, and substantive due process. The district court rejected all these claims and entered summary judgment in favor of Hawaii. We hold that, without reasonable modifications to its quarantine requirement for the benefit of visually-impaired individuals who rely on guide dogs, Hawaii's quarantine requirement effectively prevents such persons from enjoying the benefits of state services and activities in violation of the ADA.

Hawaii is one of the few places in the world which is completely free from rabies. To protect the state from the importation of the rabies disease, the Hawaii legislature enacted Hawaii Revised Statute § 142-2. Pursuant to § 142-2, the Hawaii Department of Agriculture established a 120-day quarantine in a quarantine station for dogs, cats and other carnivorous animals entering Hawaii from any area that is not considered rabies free. Upon written request, a disabled person seeking to bring a guide dog into the state may stay free of charge for the 120-day quarantine period in one of two apartments and a cottage at the quarantine station. After an initial 10-day observation period, a guide dog may train with its owner on the station grounds and may train off the station grounds for up to four hours a day, three days a week, if accompanied by a department inspector. During the time a guide dog is outside the quarantine station, however, it may have no contact with other animals or humans. After the 120-day quarantine period, if the guide dog is found not to have rabies, the dog is released to its owner.

Vernon Crowder, a resident of California, and Stephanie Good, a resident of Hawaii, are visually-impaired users of guide dogs. They filed suit against the State of Hawaii and various governmental officials (collectively Hawaii). The evidence produced in support of the parties' motions for summary judgment established that the state's quarantine requirement denies visually-impaired persons the ability to make meaningful use of services the state provides. The plaintiffs rely upon their guide dogs to assist them in negotiating public streets and using transportation systems. The quarantine also renders guide dogs susceptible to irretrievable loss of their training.

The parties agree that the quarantine does not guarantee that rabies will not be imported into Hawaii by quarantined animals. The rabies disease can have an incubation period longer than 120 days. In support of their contention that Hawaii's quarantine requirement can be reasonably modified for the benefit of visually-impaired users of guide dogs, the plaintiffs contended that more effective alternative means were available to prevent the importation of rabies by guide dogs. Such alternatives include a vaccine-based system by which "dead" vaccines can be administered to the animals by veterinarians, who can then certify the vaccinations by fitting the animals with identifying microchips. The animals can be tested before admission into Hawaii by use of rabies virus antibody titers to ensure against the disease.

The plaintiffs allege Hawaii's quarantine system violates the ADA, which provides that no qualified individual with a disability shall by reason of such disability be excluded from participation in or be denied the benefits of the services, programs or activities of a public entity, or be subjected to discrimination by any such entity. Section 12131(2) defines "qualified individual with a disability" as "an individual with a disability who, with or without reasonable modifications to rules, policies or practices, removal of architectural barriers, or the provision of auxiliary aides and services, meets the essential eligibility requirements for the receipt of services or the participation in programs or activities provided by a public entity."

The ADA precludes exclusion from/denial of benefits of public services, as well as discrimination by a public entity. Congress intended to prohibit outright discrimination, as well as those forms of discrimination which deny disabled persons public services disproportionately due to their disability. In section 12101(a)(5), Congress declared its intent to address outright intentional exclusion as well as the discriminatory effects of architectural, transportation, and communication barriers, overprotective rules and policies, and failure to make modifications to existing facilities and practices. It is thus clear that Congress intended the ADA to cover at least some so-called disparate impact cases of discrimination, for the barriers to full participation listed above are almost all facially neutral but may work to effectuate discrimination against disabled persons.

Although Hawaii's quarantine requirement applies equally to all persons entering the state with a dog, its enforcement burdens visually-impaired persons in a manner different and greater than it burdens others. Because of the unique dependence upon guide dogs among many of the visually-impaired, Hawaii's quarantine effectively denies these persons, the plaintiffs in this case, meaningful access to state services, programs, and activities while such services, programs, and activities remain open and easily accessible by others. The quarantine, therefore, discriminates against the plaintiffs by reason of their disability.

During the four days of each week of the quarantine period when guide dogs must remain in the quarantine station, this denial of services, programs, and activities is especially acute. On the other three days when the dogs are allowed out of the quarantine station grounds, the negative impact of the regulation is only slightly alleviated, because during these days the regulations require that the guide dogs avoid all physical contact with other humans or animals. This effectively precludes visually-impaired persons from using a variety of public services, such as public transportation, public parks, government buildings and facilities, and tourist attractions, where humans or animals are inevitably present.

We conclude that Hawaii's quarantine requirement is a policy, practice or procedure which discriminates against visually-impaired individuals by denying them meaningful access to state services, programs and activities by reason of their disability in violation of the ADA. When a state's policies, practices or procedures discriminate against the disabled in violation of the ADA, Department of Justice regulations require reasonable modifications in such policies, practices or procedures when the modifications are necessary to avoid discrimination on the basis of disability, unless the public entity can demonstrate that making the modifications would fundamentally alter the nature of the service, program, or activity. We reverse the district court's grant of summary judgment in favor of Hawaii. We remand this case to the district court for determination of the factual dispute whether the plaintiffs' proposed modifications to Hawaii's quarantine are reasonable under the ADA.

## Questions

1. What two laws were considered in this case?
2. Did the selected method of quarantine guarantee that rabies would not be imported to the islands, and is this important?
3. What two distinct phenomena are prohibited by the ADA?
4. How did the case end? What is next?

# Community Hygiene Measures

Controlling disease also involves community hygiene measures, under which natural and social factors are considered in managing and promoting public health. For poor communities and developing countries, public health benefits may be achieved through improvements in water supply, sanitation, nutrition, and education. All countries need to consider occupational hygiene, in which persons manage workplaces to remove situations that impair health and the well-being of workers. The following case involving a community hygiene measure of a flu vaccination program shows how the implementation of a measure must be balanced against competing rights.

**Service Employees International Union v. Los Robles Regional Medical Center**
US District Court for the Northern District of California

*Who is suing?* _____

*Who is being sued?* _____

*For what?* _____

*What is the issue on appeal?* _____

Plaintiffs Service Employees International Union and others (SEIU) seek injunctive relief requiring Defendants Riverside Healthcare Community Hospital and others (Hospitals) to refrain from implementing a mandatory H1N1 and seasonal flu vaccination policy for Registered Nurses (RNs) and other healthcare workers (excluding physicians) pending arbitration pursuant to the parties' Collective Bargaining Agreement (CBA). Plaintiffs request an injunction. The Hospitals seek to implement a strengthened influenza prevention policy for their employees. The proposed policy does not mandate vaccination, but it expresses management's desire that all employees be vaccinated. Employees who choose to decline the vaccine must sign a declination form. The form asks employees if they are refusing the vaccination because they already have been vaccinated or for "other" reasons. Employees are not required to specify their "other" reason for declining vaccination. The vast majority of employees already have chosen to be immunized.

Although the Hospitals have required employees to be vaccinated or sign a declination form, as required by California law, the new policy requires that employees who have not been vaccinated wear a surgical mask in all patient care areas. This requirement is consistent with other existing infection-control protocols at the Hospitals, pursuant to which employees who have patient contact submit to annual tuberculosis tests and mask fits and wear gloves, gowns, and masks in various settings, such as surgery, isolation and quarantine rooms. As in the case of an employee's failure to comply with any other patient-care protocol, an employee is subject to discipline only if he or she declines both the vaccination and the mask and otherwise fails to cooperate.

In order to monitor compliance with the new policy's mask requirement, the Hospitals have adopted various means of identification. Employees who receive the seasonal flu vaccination at Good Samaritan Hospital and San Jose Health Care System

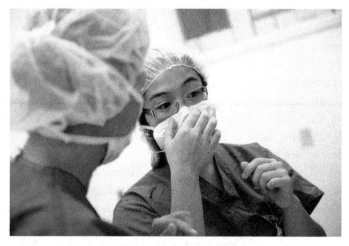

Fig. 26.1 Using masks to prevent the spread of disease.

wear a Red Cross sticker on their badge. At Riverside Health Care System, vaccinated employees use "I'm vaccinated because I care!" badge holders, and unvaccinated employees use "I wear because I care!" badge holders depicting a health care worker wearing a surgical mask; posters explaining the significance of the badge holders are posted around the hospital. At West Hills Hospital, unvaccinated employees have a purpose mark on the back of their badge; there is no marking at all on the front.

The Hospitals did not bargain with SEIU prior to announcing the new policy. SEIU filed the instant action alleging that the Hospitals have violated and are continuing to violate Section 301 of the Labor Management Relations Act and the CBA by refusing to halt implementation of the new policy pending exhaustion of the dispute resolution procedures, including arbitration, required by the CBA. SEIU next filed the instant application for injunctive relief. The parties also agreed that the new policy would not be implemented until the date set by the Court for oral argument on SEIU's application.

The standard for issuing a temporary restraining order is the same as that for issuing a preliminary injunction. In the Ninth Circuit, a party seeking a preliminary injunction must show either (1) a likelihood of success on the merits and the possibility of irreparable injury, or (2) the existence of serious questions going to the merits and the balance of hardships tipping in the movant's favor. These formulations represent two points on a sliding scale in which the required degree of irreparable harm increases as the probability of success decreases.

SEIU seeks an order requiring the Hospitals to maintain the status quo and exhaust the dispute resolution and arbitration procedures set forth in the CBA prior to any implementation of the new policy. It claims that without such relief, employees will be deprived of the opportunity to meet the Hospitals' legitimate public health goals by less intrusive means. Once injected, the vaccine and its additives cannot be taken back, and the policy requires employees who refuse vaccination to wear masks and ID badges indicating that they have not been vaccinated, which stigmatizes them. SEIU also contends that the Hospitals' unilateral implementation of the policy undermines its authority and standing with its members, and that the CBA either bars such implementation outright or at the very least requires bargaining.

These claims are not insubstantial. However, the policy the Hospitals seek to implement directly implicates public health, and it is supported by the clinical judgment of infection control experts at the Hospitals. Its goal is to protect patients from exposure to illnesses to which they may be more susceptible than non-patients. Provided that the dispute resolution procedures in the CBA are implemented on an expedited basis, the equities appear to weigh against injunctive relief.

The anecdotal evidence that the policy is being implemented in a way that stigmatizes employees who choose not to be vaccinated is unsettling. The Hospitals argue that the badge stickers and masks worn by employees who have not been vaccinated allow managers to determine which employees have been vaccinated. However, it appears that the procedures used by at least some of the Hospitals have had the collateral and unnecessary effect of calling the employees' status to the attention of patients and the public.

Because its jurisdiction in the present circumstances is extremely limited, the Court will decline to intervene in the parties' dispute at the present time. However, the Court expects that both parties will move expeditiously to resolve their disagreements pursuant to the CBA. Moreover, pending the process required by the CBA, the Court expects that Defendants will implement the new policy in a manner that serves management's legitimate interest in identifying employees who have not been vaccinated but at the same time does not call undue and inappropriate attention to an individual employee's status. It is hereby ordered that Plaintiffs' application for injunctive relief pending arbitration is denied without prejudice, subject to the following conditions: (1) that the parties engage in the expedited arbitration set forth in the CBA; and (2) that the parties meet and confer forthwith to eliminate any stigmatizing procedures associated with the new vaccination policy.

# Question

1. How does the court characterize the defendants' actions?
2. Are the requirements for injunctive relief in this case similar to injunctive relief in cases involving private nuisance?
3. What led the court to decline to issue injunctive relief?
4. Could a company such as Microsoft institute a similar vaccination program?
5. Does arbitration seem to constitute a reasonable procedure for resolving this dispute?

# Isolation

For contagious diseases, governments may enact regulations to preclude infected persons from spreading a disease to others. Such regulations markedly interfere with an individual's liberty interest, and thus responses that restrict movement must be balanced with personal freedoms. Protecting the general public is challenging, as shown by the following case, in which an uncooperative patient was placed in a criminal justice facility.

### *City of Milwaukee v. Washington*
Wisconsin Supreme Court

*Who is suing?* _____

*Who is being sued?* _____

*For what?* _____

*What is the issue on appeal?* _____

Ruby Washington appeals from the trial court's order directing that she be confined under Wisconsin Statutes § 252.07(9) for tuberculosis treatment. The only issue on appeal is where she should be confined. We affirm. Washington has pulmonary tuberculosis, which if not treated properly is not only dangerous to the infected person but also is dangerous to others, who can inhale the bacteria expelled by an infected person. The City of Milwaukee tuberculosis program manager testified at a hearing before the trial court that tuberculosis can get into the air by an infected person "coughing, laughing, singing, talking, and sneezing." Although a person suffering from pulmonary tuberculosis who is on appropriate drug-therapy may be noncommunicable, that person can become communicable unless he or she completes the course of treatment. Wisconsin Statutes § 252.07 sets out procedures designed to protect both the public and those afflicted with the disease.

Washington did not cooperate with attempts to help her overcome her pulmonary tuberculosis and to keep her from infecting others. She was living in a homeless shelter on June 17, when she was first diagnosed as having the disease. Washington was started on medication for her tuberculosis on June 21, and was given bus tickets so she could go to the tuberculosis clinic and take her medication "under direct observation" of the clinic staff. This did not work, however, because Washington missed two appointments and "disappeared from public view."

On August 22, Washington was found at the Aurora Sinai Medical Center, where she had gone to give birth. When she threatened to leave the hospital despite her tuberculosis, she was kept at the hospital in inpatient confinement against her will until, several days later, she and the City of Milwaukee stipulated that she would stay at the medical center for at least one month or until she was no longer contagious, and that after her release she would continue a course of supervised treatment for some nine months to ensure that she was cured.

On September 27, the trial court issued an order permitting Washington's release from the hospital, "but only on the condition that she strictly comply" with City orders that she fulfill and complete her course of treatment, and that this compliance be assured by having public-health staff see Washington take her prescribed medications. The order also required that Washington live with her sister, at whose home Washington "shall continuously reside and remain available for contact at that address until such time as in the judgment of the City of Milwaukee Health Department, her treatment is complete and she is cured of the disease of tuberculosis." Further, the order recited that if Washington "fails to fully and completely comply with the provisions of this Order, she may be subject to imprisonment, to renewed isolation and inpatient confinement pursuant to Wisconsin Statutes § 252.07 and/ or to such other and additional sanctions for contempt of court as this Court may determine."

Washington was released from Aurora Sinai Medical Center on September 27, and, on that very day, left her sister's home. Further, she did not comply with the required treatment-regimen. On September 29, Washington was arrested for violating the trial court's order, and was taken to the Milwaukee County Criminal Justice Facility.

The trial court held a hearing on October 5, and, on that day, issued the order from which Washington appeals. The order directed that Washington "be confined in the Milwaukee County Criminal Justice Facility" unless otherwise ordered, and directed that Washington "shall fully comply" with her treatment regimen. Uncontradicted testimony at the October 5 hearing established that the required treatment and observation would take "nine cumulative months" from October 5. If that were not done, the City's tuberculosis program manager told the trial court that both the public and Washington would suffer serious consequences: "Washington's personal consequences could include death, could include severe illness." She would again become incapacitated at some point, probably very weak and debiled, not feel very well at all. The consequences for the public would be transmission of tuberculosis to people. The order also set a later date for trial-court review of Washington's condition and circumstances.

Washington does not dispute either that she has pulmonary tuberculosis or that she must complete her course of treatment to get fully well and not be a danger to others in the community. She contended before the trial court, however, and argues on appeal, that she should not be at the criminal-justice facility, but, rather, at the hospital or some other non-jail-type facility, even if that required that she be guarded twenty-four hours a day. The trial court rejected that contention:

> There has been noncompliance and the risk of the community is way too high to allow her to just walk out the door today. If you can find some other locked facility for your client that would agree to take her, the Court would be happy to order her placed somewhere else, and I'm sure the City would agree. The problem is that I need to have a locked facility where she's going to stay put. With respect to the suggestion that I place a guard at the hospital and allow her to stay at the hospital for the remainder of her treatment, I refuse to require tax payers to pay for 24 hour around the clock guard at her door to make sure she stays put. I don't think that's appropriate. Miss Washington was given an opportunity to receive treatment in the community and she failed to do that.

We agree.

## Questions

1. Where was Washington's disease first detected?
2. How did the government learn Washington was not complying with instructions?

3. Why was Washington arrested?
4. What is the justification for the confinement?

# Global Efforts: The World Health Organization

International trade and travel present many health challenges. People can transmit diseases and spread infectious diseases to new communities. Animals also can transmit diseases and have been the source of a number of diseases that adversely affect humans. Physical items brought to new countries may contain pests or disease organisms that can lead to new infestations. Public health officials are compelled to use their best efforts to contain diseases and pests and to protect people and environments from future damages, without overly infringing upon the rights of individuals and societies.

In 1946, the World Health Organization (WHO) was established as a specialized United Nations agency for the coordination of international health activities. WHO adopted international health regulations, resolutions and agreements pertaining to health, and regulations concerning sanitary, diagnostic, and labeling standards. WHO's conventions and regulations are binding on member countries, unless the country opts out. An example of WHO's successful efforts of containing a disease is the severe acute respiratory syndrome (SARS) outbreak in 2003. WHO coordinated an international investigation and worked closely with health authorities to contain the disease.

International health regulations, adopted in 2005, address public health risks and health emergencies. These have been adopted by 195 countries. Through these regulations, WHO attempts to balance health regulations with international trade interests and human rights. Countries have a responsibility to report all "events that may constitute a public health emergency of international concern." For example, if there is an outbreak of avian influenza, the country needs to report to WHO. The United States has accepted the international health regulations with a reservation that they be implemented under our principles of federalism. The US Department of Health and Human Services is responsible for carrying out the requirements of these international regulations.

For some diseases, WHO has adopted formal guidelines. One such disease is tuberculosis (TB), and WHO guidelines address the disease with instructions for air travel. These guidelines provide a summary of practices that are to be used to manage patients with infectious TB. Physicians should inform infectious TB patients that they must not travel by air until after treatment. If an aircraft is delayed on the ground, the ventilation system should be operating.

Under WHO's auspices, the Global Outbreak Alert and Response Network brings together a technical collaboration of existing institutions and networks for pooling human and technical resources for the rapid identification, confirmation, and response to outbreaks of international importance. The network provides an operational framework to link this expertise and skill to keep the international community alert to the threat of outbreaks. The network has helped to build consensuses on guiding principles for international outbreak alerts and responses. It also establishes operational protocols to standardize field logistics, security, communications, and streamlined administrative processes to ensure rapid mobilization of field teams.

Yet many developing countries continue to be challenged by outbreaks of infectious diseases due to limitations on funding and the lack of an infrastructure to implement and deliver interventions. Because of the movement of goods, food items, and people among countries, diseases not only adversely affect local populations, but also are carried to distant areas. While the WHO has extensive emergency public health powers to respond to infectious disease threats, it lacks enforceable legal powers to require member states to compel actions. Instead, it works with national and regional public health agencies to avert global health threats, issue emergency guidance, and seek compliance from member nations. When the WHO fails to take timely action, an outbreak can result in a disease unnecessarily spreading to new locations.

In the 2014 outbreak of the Ebola viral disease (Ebola) in a number of West African countries, it was only after the disease killed nearly one thousand people that the WHO finally declared the outbreak. The WHO's declaration made it a Public Health Emergency of International Concern under the International Health Regulations. This was more than six months after two countries had confirmed the presence of Ebola and more than three months after Médecins Sans Frontières (Doctors without Borders) had issued a warning that Ebola was out of control. Moreover, WHO's declaration was after the United Nations had established its Mission for Ebola Emergency Response that led the United States and the World Bank to mobilize efforts to address the outbreak. The Ebola outbreak exposed a gap in our international infectious disease regime that needs addressing before an outbreak of some other disease requires expeditious action.

Events in the United States exposed other issues. The Centers for Disease Control and Prevention (CDC) issued voluntary national guidance on quarantine and isolation procedures for persons exposed to or infected with Ebola. However, the CDC's guidance was rejected by several states, including some with notable entry points of travelers from the affected areas. Moreover, governors of some states announced emergency quarantine and isolation measures that were unlawful. A few individuals were denied their rights by medical and governmental personnel. While quarantine and isolation requirements are in place, they appear to be poorly understood. Perhaps medical facilities and governmental officials need more guidance on what actions can and should be taken in the event of an outbreak of a dangerous disease.

## Discussion Questions

1. When should a religious belief allow parents to decline to have their minor children vaccinated?
2. Are the powers of the US federal government excessive when dealing with a possible disease outbreak? Why or why not?
3. Are the border controls of the US federal government sufficient in view of all the invasive species that continually are introduced into our country?
4. What rights do employees of a medical facility surrender so that the facility can meet health objectives?

## Image Credit

Copyright in the Public Domain.

# CHAPTER TWENTY-SEVEN
## Keeping Food Products Safe

---

## Learning Objectives

- *Summarize US governmental efforts to keep food products safe.*
- *Describe how US governments protect people from dangers associated with raw milk.*
- *Explain how a state law prohibiting deceptive acts applies to food products.*
- *Describe equitable indemnification.*
- *Construct damages sustained when the government issues a notice of inspection.*

## Regulatory Overview

D espite numerous efforts to keep food products safe, the Centers for Disease Control and Prevention estimates that more than 9 million persons in the United States become ill each year due to pathogens transmitted through food products. Plant products were responsible for more than half of the illnesses in the United States. However, greater numbers of hospitalizations were caused by pathogens in land animals, with dairy products accounting for 16 percent of the hospitalizations. Pathogens in land animals also accounted for the most deaths, with poultry responsible for 19 percent of the deaths. Yet these numbers must be related to amounts consumed and how many people actually ingested each food category. The study reporting these

Fig. 27.1 Keeping food safe at fish markets, such as the Tsukiji Market, can be challenging.

data concluded that most foodborne illnesses were attributable to food commodities that constitute a major portion of the American diet.

The Federal Food, Drug, and Cosmetic Act (FDCA) provides the regulatory framework to safeguard humans from unsafe food products. This act is administered by the Food and Drug Administration (FDA). A majority of meat, poultry, and egg products are inspected by personnel of the US Department of Agriculture's Food Safety Inspection Service. Under the Department of Commerce, the National Oceanic and Atmospheric Administration oversees the inspection of fish, shellfish, and fishery products. The FDA is in charge of problems related to food items that are adulterated or misbranded. An adulterated food is one containing a poisonous or deleterious substance that may render it injurious to health. A food is "misbranded" if its labeling is "false or misleading."

In January 2011, the United States adopted the Food Safety Modernization Act, which updated numerous food safety provisions of the FDCA. This legislation requires the secretary of Health and Human Services to develop "science-based minimum standards for conducting a hazard analysis, documenting hazards, implementing preventive controls, and documenting the implementation of the preventive controls." Persons and firms dealing with foods need to identify and evaluate known or reasonably foreseeable hazards that may be associated with their facility. Moreover, the FDA is required to identify high-risk facilities, including foreign facilities, and allocate inspection resources to inspect such facilities. The Food Safety Modernization Act also encourages the FDA to establish a program to provide for the expedited review and importation of food from importers.

Consumer and grassroots movements have challenged existing regulatory regimes and have created controversies on the role of governments in protecting the public from unwholesome foods. The use of food additives and the consumption of raw milk are two issues being debated.

# Food Additives

Many of our food products contain additives and other substances. Thousands of "generally recognized as safe substances" are allowed as additives, as well as other categories of substances, including color additives and pesticides. Their introduction into food for human consumption is regulated under the FDCA, and each additive is only allowed if there is an affirmative determination that it is safe. However, a study by the Pew Charitable Trusts published in 2013 claims that three-quarters of the additives directly added to food lack sufficient data to establish a safe level of exposure. Even more additives lack reasonable studies on their effects on human reproduction and development. Given these data, groups expressing safety concerns about food additives have a basis for their arguments.

A California court considered an allegation that caffeine was a food additive in a beverage called "JOOSE." The case shows multiple causes of actions against a company that marketed a product without divulging sufficient information to inform consumers of the risks associated with the product.

### *Cuevas v. United Brands Company, Inc.*
United States District Court, Southern District of California

*Who is suing?* _____

*Who is being sued?* _____

*For what?* _____

*What is the issue on appeal?* _____

Defendant United Brands Company, Inc. (United Brands or Defendant) has filed a motion to dismiss Plaintiff's Amended Complaint. For the reasons discussed below, Defendant's motion to dismiss is granted in part and denied in part.

Plaintiff Breanna Cuevas (Plaintiff) brings this action on behalf of herself and a purported class of similarly situated individuals. Plaintiff alleges that Defendant engaged in deceptive business practices in connection with the marketing of its flavored caffeinated alcoholic beverage called "JOOSE" (the Product). JOOSE contained between 9.9 to 12 percent alcohol by volume in addition to approximately 124.95 milligrams of caffeine. An 8-ounce cup of coffee contains 100 to 200 milligrams of caffeine and a 12-ounce Coke has 35 milligrams of caffeine.

After JOOSE went on the market, the FDA sent Defendant a warning letter stating: "FDA is aware that, based on the publicly available literature, a number of qualified experts have concerns about the safety of caffeinated alcoholic beverages. Moreover, the agency is not aware of data or other information to establish the safety of the relevant conditions of use for your product." The FDA stated that, as used in Defendant's product, caffeine was an unsafe food additive, rendering the product adulterated under section 402(a)(2)(C) of the Federal Food, Drug, and Cosmetic Act. The FDA voiced concerns regarding the safety of caffeine when used in the presence of alcohol because studies indicated that caffeine reduces subjects' subjective perception of intoxication but does not improve diminished motor coordination or slower visual reaction times. The FDA gave Defendant 15 days from receipt of the letter to respond in writing. Defendant ceased shipping JOOSE and expected to have the product off retail store shelves in one month.

Plaintiff had purchased a can of "Dragon JOOSE" for $5.00 from a 7-Eleven in Corona, California and consumed the beverage. Plaintiff also purchased two cans of "JOOSE Watermelon" for $8.00 from a 7-Eleven located in Ontario, California. Plaintiff consumed those beverages as well. Plaintiff alleges that she saw Product advertising and looked at the Product's labeling prior to purchasing the beverages.

According to Plaintiff, nothing in United Brands' packaging, labeling, advertising, marketing, promotion, or sale of the Products disclosed, or adequately disclosed, the amount of caffeine in the Products or the risks associated with caffeine as used in the Products. Plaintiff claims that the amount of caffeine in the Products and the risks associated with caffeine as used in the Products were material facts that would have affected her decisions to purchase the Products. Plaintiff alleges that she was deceived by Defendant into purchasing the Products. Plaintiff claims that she suffered an economic injury because the Products had significantly less value than was reflected in the price Plaintiff paid for them. In fact, had Plaintiff known the true facts about the Products as set forth above, she would not have purchased them at all.

The proposed class consists of all persons who during the Class Period purchased the Products for personal use and not for purposes of further retail sale or distribution. Plaintiff's Amended Complaint asserts the following claims: (1) violation of California's Unfair Competition Law (UCL), (2) violation of California's Consumer Legal Remedies Act (CLRA), (3) breach of express and implied warranties; and (4) violation of the federal Magnuson-Moss Warranty Act. Defendant moves to dismiss the Amended Complaint for failure to state a claim. The Court grants the motion to dismiss as to Plaintiff's breach of express warranty claim but otherwise denies the motion.

Under the UCL, "unfair competition" is defined as including any "unlawful, unfair or fraudulent business act or practice" and "unfair, deceptive, untrue, or misleading advertising." Plaintiff's allegations are sufficient to state an "unlawful," "fraudulent," and "unfair" business practice. An "unlawful" business act under the UCL is any business practice that is prohibited by law, whether civil or criminal, statutory or judicially made, federal, state, or local. Plaintiff has stated a claim that Defendant violated the CLRA.

The CLRA prohibits specified "unfair or deceptive acts or practices undertaken by any person in a transaction intended to result or which results in the sale or lease of goods or services to any consumer." A fraudulent omission is actionable under the CLRA if the omission is contrary to a representation actually made by the defendant or is an omission of a fact the defendant was obligated to disclose. A duty to disclose exists when the defendant (i) is in a fiduciary relationship with the plaintiff; (ii) had exclusive knowledge of material facts not known to the plaintiff; (iii) actively conceals a material fact from the plaintiff; or (iv) makes partial representations but also suppresses some material fact. The Amended Complaint suggests that Defendant had superior knowledge regarding the risks of consuming caffeine and alcohol simultaneously and therefore had a duty to disclose those material facts to unsuspecting consumers.

A fraudulent business practice under the UCL is one which is likely to deceive the public. The alleged fraudulent omissions that support the CLRA claim also support a claim of fraudulent conduct under the UCL. Based on the allegations of the Amended Complaint, members of the public were likely to be deceived by Defendant's failure to disclose material facts regarding the risks associated with caffeine in alcoholic beverages such as Defendant's Products. Under California law, "unfair" business practices exist either when the harm to the consumer outweighs the utility of the practice to the defendant or when a business practice violates public policy as declared by specific constitutional statutory or regulatory provisions. Plaintiff's fraudulent omission/CLRA claim satisfies the "unfair" prong as well.

Plaintiff contends that Defendant breached an express warranty. Plaintiff does not allege that Defendant made any express representations or warranties regarding the safety of consuming caffeine with alcohol. Therefore, Plaintiff's express warranty claim is dismissed.

A warranty that goods shall be merchantable is implied in a contract for their sale if the seller is a merchant with respect to goods of that kind. Merchantable goods are fit for the ordinary purposes for which such goods are used. Defendant argues that Plaintiff cannot state a cause of action for breach of implied warranty because her claim is barred by California Civil Code § 1714.45 as alcohol is a listed common consumer product and is inherently unsafe. The Court disagrees.

Plaintiff's claims are not based on the inherent dangers of alcohol but on the undisclosed effects of caffeine and alcohol combined. In this case, Plaintiff claims that Defendant's alcoholic beverage was adulterated with caffeine. Plaintiff alleges that the addition of caffeine made the alcoholic beverage unreasonably dangerous. Accordingly, § 1714.45 does not bar Plaintiff's implied warranty claim.

Plaintiff also alleges that Defendant violated the federal Magnuson-Moss Warranty Act (MMWA). The MMWA authorizes a civil suit by a consumer to enforce the terms of an implied or express warranty and, for the most part, calls for the application of state written and implied warranty law, not the creation of additional federal law. Because Plaintiff has stated an implied warranty claim, Plaintiff has also stated a claim under the MMWA.

For the reasons discussed above, Defendant's motion to dismiss is granted as to the breach of express warranty claim only. The motion to dismiss is otherwise denied.

Defendant shall file an answer to the Amended Complaint within 15 days of the entry of this order.

## Questions

1. What damage was alleged by the plaintiff?
2. What is the problem with adding caffeine to alcohol?
3. What was the deceit related to sales of JOOSE?
4. Was there evidence that the defendant may have breached the implied warranty of merchantability?
5. Do the facts suggest that the defendant could remedy the problems identified by the plaintiff in this lawsuit?

# Raw Milk

Of all of the food commodity sectors in the United States, no sector is more committed to public health than the dairy industry. Due to illnesses in the early 1900s, when raw milk was a major source of human disease—including tuberculosis and scarlet fever—governments responded. Under the federal Pasteurized Milk Ordinance written in 1924, the milk industry achieved an enviable safety record. Yet in the last decade, a grassroots movement to allow people to purchase raw milk has created a debate about health issues involving dairy products. People claim that raw milk tastes better and is healthier. It is true that the pasteurization of milk slightly reduces the nutritional value of milk and diminishes a few of the vitamins found in milk, notably thiamine, vitamin B12, and vitamin C. However, the basis for pasteurization is to kill harmful bacteria that cause tuberculosis, diphtheria, severe streptococcal infections, typhoid fever, and other food-borne illnesses.

A total of 81 outbreaks of illness due to unpasteurized dairy products were reported to the Centers for Disease Control and Prevention (CDC) for the 2007–2012 time period. These outbreaks resulted in 979 illnesses and 73 hospitalizations. Most of these illnesses were caused by *Campylobacter* or *Salmonella*. For every outbreak and every illness reported, many others occur, as most illnesses are not part of recognized outbreaks. Given these events, what is the role of the government in preventing people from being exposed to risky unpasteurized dairy products? Congress has decided to preclude the sale of raw milk across state lines. However, states are able to allow the sale of raw milk, and whether to allow sales of products made from unpasteurized milk is controversial. The following case shows the significance of federal law that prevents raw milk from being sold across state borders and highlights some of the misinformation that accompanies sales of raw milk products.

### *United States v. Organic Pastures Dairy Co.*
United States District Court, Eastern District of California

*Who is suing?* _____

*Who is being sued?* _____

*For what?* _____

*What is the issue on appeal?* _____

This matter is before the Court on the government's motion for summary judgment and entry of a permanent injunction. The government seeks to permanently enjoin Defendants Organic Pastures Dairy Company (Organic Pastures) and Mark McAfee from distributing and/or introducing raw milk across state lines, in contravention of the Federal Food, Drug, and Cosmetic Act (FDCA). The government's request for injunctive relief is based on separate agreements signed by Defendants three years earlier resolving criminal cases against them. In the agreements, Defendants acknowledged that Organic Pastures' employees violated the FDCA by distributing raw milk to out-of-state customers four years ago.

Defendants do not dispute the liability portions of the United States' motion. Instead, they oppose the breadth of the government's proposed relief, arguing the terms of the permanent injunction are duplicative of their criminal plea arrangements, impose on California's regulation of the raw milk industry, are financially crippling, and constitute a personal attack on Mr. McAfee. Defendants also contend that they ceased distributing raw milk into interstate commerce following their criminal pleas; therefore, the permanent injunction is unnecessary.

Defendant Organic Pastures is a California Corporation engaged in milking cows and packaging, labeling, selling, and distributing raw milk and raw milk products including cream, butter, buttermilk, and colostrum. It has over 60,000 customers in California, selling its products to retailers, including national retailer "Whole Foods Market," and via its website. Defendant McAfee is the cofounder and managing member of Organic Pastures. He is responsible for the day-to-day operations of Organic Pastures, including all manufacturing and distributing operations.

While this case was pending, Defendant Organic Pastures faced similar charges in a criminal action involving similar conduct. The criminal matter concluded in settlement by plea agreement and was approved by a judge. Pursuant to the plea agreement, Defendant Organic Pastures pled guilty to two counts of misdemeanor introduction and delivery for introduction into interstate commerce of misbranded food. Defendant McAfee entered into a deferred prosecution agreement whereby he agreed to the filing of a two-count information charging him and Organic Pastures with the same violations.

In these agreements, both Defendants admitted that: (1) on two separate occasions one or more of defendant Organic Pastures' agents or employees, with the knowledge and consent of Organic Pastures, caused a box of raw milk and dairy products, labeled as or otherwise represented to be "pet food," to be sent by defendant Organic Pastures into interstate commerce, knowing that the intended use of such foods and/or dietary supplements was for human consumption; and (2) Organic Pastures' raw milk and raw milk products were foods and/or dietary supplements, and were misbranded when so introduced into or delivered for introduction into interstate commerce, in that they were falsely and misleadingly labeled as, or otherwise represented to be "pet food," when they were actually intended for human consumption in violation of federal law.

According to the United States, Defendants' history of distributing raw milk and raw milk products across state lines establishes that Defendants violated 21 U.S.C. § 331(a) and 42 U.S.C. § 264. The United States also contends that Defendants marketing of raw milk as a "therapeutic cure" for asthma and other health conditions violated 21 U.S.C. § 331(d)'s bar on "unapproved new drugs." Pursuant to 21 U.S.C. § 332(b), the United States seeks an injunction forbidding Defendants from engaging in either of these practices.

Defendants acknowledge that they introduced and/or distributed raw milk into interstate commerce four years ago. Here, the unopposed evidence shows that Defendants have violated the FDCA by distributing misbranded raw milk at least two times since four years ago; it also demonstrates that Defendants impermissibly promoted the therapeutic benefits/capabilities of raw milk. Because the government has established that Defendants violated § 331(a) and (d) of the FDCA, the government is entitled to an injunction if it also establishes a cognizable danger of recurrent violations. The probability of future violations may be inferred from past unlawful conduct.

The government asserts that because Defendants actively violated the FDCA by shipping raw milk to out-of-state customers, they are reasonably likely to violate the FDCA in the future. The government applies the same reasoning to Defendants promotion of raw milk and raw milk products as a "therapeutic cure" for various health conditions. On the government's account, Defendants have flouted the law for years, and the record is replete with evidence suggesting that Defendants are likely to resume their illegal conduct.

Defendants contend that even if their past conduct violated the FDCA, they ceased much of the behavior complained of by the government years ago. Although Defendants' progress towards improvement and their intention to comply with FDCA requirements are relevant to the inquiry, the Ninth Circuit Court of Appeals has emphasized that a past pattern of activity bears heavily on whether the offender is likely to violate the FDCA in the future. Courts have also recognized the carry-over effects of marketing and promotional claims in actions arising under the FDCA.

Given the history of admitted violations by Defendants, as well as their acknowledgments concerning the promotion of raw milk's therapeutic effects, the government has established a likelihood of additional FDCA violations. Given the uncontested facts, Defendants cannot satisfy the burden to establish that there is no reasonable expectation that the wrong will be repeated. Here, the government has demonstrated that Defendants violated 21 U.S.C. § 331(a) and (d), which prohibit distributing raw milk across state lines and marketing raw milk's health benefits. The government has also established a likelihood of additional FDCA violations under Ninth Circuit precedent. Therefore, the Government's motion for summary judgment is granted and Defendants shall be permanently enjoined from distribution of its products across state lines.

## Questions

1. Did the products sold by the defendants cause a health problem?
2. What were the two different violations?
3. Was the fact that there was a criminal action against these defendants significant?
4. Is the government's requested injunction necessary?
5. Should the FDCA's regulation that prohibits the sale of unpasteurized milk (also known as raw milk) across state lines (21 C.F.R. § 1240.61) be amended to permit the sale of raw milk across state lines, so long as the sale is legal in both the seller's state and the destination state?

# Indemnification

When there are multiple parties involved in transactions and torts, decisions must be made on how much responsibility accrues to each party. In the following case, Sizzler Steak House paid all the damages and sought indemnification from the supplier responsible for the tainted meat.

### *Estate of Brianna Kriefall v. Sizzler USA Franchise, Inc.*
Supreme Court of Wisconsin

*Who is suing?* _____

*Who is being sued?* _____

*For what?* _____

*What is the issue on appeal?* _____

This is a review of a published decision of the court of appeals that affirmed in part and reversed in part the judgment of the Circuit Court for Milwaukee County. The questions before this court stem from damages sustained because of food contaminated by E. coli 0157:H7 pathogens at two Sizzler Steak House restaurants in the Milwaukee area. The plaintiffs in the underlying actions settled years ago, and the claims now before us relate to the apportionment of liability and costs among those who were defendants in the underlying actions. We affirm the decision of the court of appeals on all issues. Sizzler is entitled to indemnity from Excel for the entirety of Sizzler's $1.5 million advance partial payment to the Kriefall family because the payment was not voluntary and the jury found that Sizzler was zero percent liable for the E. coli contamination.

Approximately 150 people became ill from ingesting food contaminated with E. coli at two Sizzler Steak House restaurants in the Milwaukee area. Their illnesses ranged from diarrhea and cramps to, in the case of three-year-old Brianna Kriefall, death. Excel Corporation processed and distributed the contaminated meat that was the source of the E. coli pathogens. Excel's contaminated meat was distributed to franchisees of Sizzler USA Franchise, Inc. (Sizzler), including, E&B Management Co. (E&B). Many of those sickened by the Milwaukee E. coli contamination asserted claims against Excel, Sizzler, E&B, E&B's shareholders, and Sysco Food Services, the local distributor for Excel's meats. One group, the Kriefall plaintiffs, settled with Excel, E&B, Sizzler, and their insurers. The Kriefalls received $10.5 million, including $8.5 million in settlement of claims against Excel, and $2 million in settlement of claims against E&B and Sizzler. Excel paid the entire $10.5 million amount. The jury found that Excel was 80 percent liable, E&B was 20 percent liable, and Sizzler was not liable. The parties then sought to apply certain contractual and common law doctrines in the assignment of the ultimate responsibility for the settlement amounts among themselves.

In regard to Sizzler's claim for equitable indemnification, we are asked to review the court of appeals' reversal of the circuit court's discretionary denial of equitable relief to Sizzler. Discretionary decisions are upheld if they are based on the relevant facts and apply a proper standard of law. However, an exercise of discretion based on an erroneous application of the law is an erroneous exercise of discretion.

Indemnification can arise by contract or it can be based on equitable principles. Contractual indemnification assigns the risk for a potential loss as part of the bargain of the parties. Equitable indemnification seeks to shift the burden of payment to the party who, in equity, should pay. Equitable indemnification shifts the entire loss from one person who has been compelled to pay it to another who, on the basis of equitable principles, should bear the loss. No shared liability for the debt is required to support indemnification.

Sizzler seeks equitable indemnification from Excel for its pre-settlement payment of $1.5 million to the Kriefall family. Sizzler made this payment under an agreement entitled an "Advance Partial Payment Pursuant to Wisconsin Statutes § 885.285." The circuit court concluded that, "the law does not allow for Sizzler's recovery of the $1.5 million as equitable indemnity." However, the court of appeals reversed the circuit court's denial of equitable relief, reasoning that Sizzler's payment to the Kriefalls was sufficiently involuntary to satisfy the requirement that a party seeking equitable indemnification must not have voluntarily paid the sum that it now seeks to recover. We agree with the conclusion of the court of appeals.

Equitable indemnity is possible when one party is exposed to liability for the wrongful acts of another. In order to be eligible for equitable indemnification for the $1.5 million payment Sizzler paid to the Kriefall family, Sizzler must show that it in whole or in part, has discharged a duty which is owed by Sizzler but which as between Sizzler and another should have been discharged by the other. The discharge-of-a-duty requirement ensures that a party who voluntarily pays the obligation of another will not be equitably indemnified. Potential liability will defeat the conclusion that a payment was voluntary.

Based on the circumstances herein presented and controlling legal principles, we conclude that Sizzler's payments to the Kriefalls were not made voluntarily. First, at the time of the payments, Sizzler was a named defendant in the Kriefalls' lawsuit, which alleged that the plaintiffs had suffered substantial injuries at a Sizzler restaurant. Second, no apportionment of fault had yet been made, and at the time of Sizzler's payment, Excel denied any liability for the E. coli contamination. Therefore, the specter of potential liability hung heavy over Sizzler at the time of its payment to the Kriefall family.

Moreover, the jury's allocation of fault demonstrates that the considerations necessary to invoke equitable indemnification are present. As between Excel and Sizzler, who was found not liable, Sizzler's payment, if unreimbursed would benefit the tortfeasor, Excel. Sizzler made a payment in contemplation of potential liability for injuries for which Sizzler was later determined to have no responsibility. We agree with the court of appeals that the circuit court erroneously exercised its discretion when it failed to apply the relevant principles of law to Sizzler's claim for equitable indemnification.

We further conclude that, as between Excel and Sizzler, no persuasive argument has been made that Sizzler should be equitably indemnified for only 80 percent of the payment it made to the Kriefall family, as Excel urges. Excel argues that because it was determined to be only 80 percent liable, it should not be required to pay Sizzler for the full amount, suggesting that Sizzler's claim for indemnification should be partially satisfied by E&B. However, Excel's argument ignores the purpose of equitable indemnification, which is to shift the entire obligation to pay from one who has paid to another who, in equity, should be held liable. We offer no opinion about Excel's seeking equitable relief from E&B. That question is not before us. However, as between Excel and Sizzler, equity entitles Sizzler to shift the entire burden of its payment to the Kriefalls to Excel.

We affirm the decision of the court of appeals. Sizzler is entitled to indemnity from Excel for the entirety of Sizzler's $1.5 million advance partial payment to the Kriefall family because the payment was not voluntary and the jury found that Sizzler was zero percent liable for the E. coli contamination.

## Questions

1. Why didn't the Wisconsin Supreme Court defer to the circuit court's discretion?
2. How much of the $10.5 million should Excel be liable for?
3. What is the difference between contractual indemnification and equitable indemnification?
4. Why had Sizzler made the $1.5 million payment?

5. How much of the $1.5 million could Sizzler collect from Excel if the jury had found Sizzler 20 percent liable for the damages?

# Suspending Inspection Due to Safety

Under federal law, all meat processing plants must develop and implement controls to address food safety hazards under a Hazard Analysis and Critical Control Point plan. The Food Safety and Inspection Service (FSIS) employs nearly 8,000 persons to inspect 6,200 establishments. Slaughter facilities cannot conduct slaughter operations if FSIS inspection personnel are not present. If an establishment fails to maintain sanitation, does not follow its HACCP plan, or violates other regulations, FSIS can issue a citation, withhold the mark of inspection from meat products, or suspend the assignment of inspectors. Whenever the FSIS chooses to withhold the mark of inspection or suspend the assignment of inspectors, the establishment cannot slaughter any animals.

In the following case, an establishment was found to be connected to an outbreak of *Salmonella* and the FSIS issued a Notice of Suspension under which the inspectors withdrew. The facility stopped slaughtering chickens and commenced actions that would bring it into compliance. After coming into compliance and recommencing slaughtering, the facility again ceased operations to more thoroughly eradicate a facility-wide infestation of cockroaches. Subsequently, the facility submitted a coverage claim with its insurer. The insurer balked at paying for damages associated with the second stoppage, and raised issues about what damages were covered by its insurance policy.

### *Foster Poultry Farms, Inc. v. Certain Underwriters at Lloyd's, London*
United States District Court, California

*Who is suing?* _____

*Who is being sued?* _____

*For what?* _____

*What is the issue on appeal?* _____

After conducting a four-day bench trial, the court finds in favor of plaintiff Foster Poultry Farms, Inc. (Foster) on its breach of contract claim in the amount of $2,706,398. Foster is a poultry producer with its largest chicken processing plant in Livingston, California. The facility is comprised of two processing areas (Plant 1 and Plant 2) that share a common packaging floor. Defendant Certain Underwriters at Lloyd's, London, issued a product contamination insurance policy to Foster that covered an Insured Event.

On October 7, 2013, the United States Department of Agriculture Food Safety and Inspection Service (USDA or FSIS) issued a Public Health Alert after 278 illnesses had been reported due to a continuing salmonella outbreak. The Public Health Alert warned consumers that consumption of "chicken produced by Foster Farms plants were the likely source of this outbreak of Salmonella Heidelberg infections." On January 8, 2014, the FSIS issued a Notice of Suspension (NOS) that suspended the assignment of its inspectors at the Livingston facility and withheld marks of inspection for chicken produced there. The FSIS issued the NOS because of egregious insanitary conditions observed whereby products produced at the facility may have been rendered adulterated in violation of the Poultry Products Inspection Act. As a result of the NOS, the FSIS denied Foster's request to apply marks of inspection to 1.3 million pounds of chicken produced on January 7 and 8, 2014.

After the FSIS approved Foster's Verification Plan in response to the NOS, the FSIS verbally placed the NOS in abeyance on January 10, 2014 and sent a written "Notice of Suspension Held in Abeyance" (Abeyance Notice) on January 13. Foster resumed operations in Plant 2 on January 11 and 12 and completed two full production shifts. Late in the morning on January 12, Foster voluntarily ceased operations at the Livingston facility and did not resume operations until January 22, 2014. Foster submitted a coverage claim with defendant for over $12 million in losses purportedly incurred as a result of the NOS. Foster claimed coverage under the Government Recall provisions, and instituted this action for declaratory relief and breach of the insurance contract. The court already found that Foster is entitled to coverage under the Policy. It is entitled to judgment in its favor on its breach of contract claim if it sustained loss covered by the Policy.

A pivotal dispute between the parties is whether the Insured Event extends for the entire duration the Livingston facility was not processing chicken from January 8 to 22. Foster contends there was a single shutdown from January 8 to 22 and that this entire period constitutes the Insured Event. Defendant argues that if the Insured Event was the initial shutdown mandated by the NOS, and the second voluntary shutdown Foster elected to impose on January 12 is not part of that Insured Event.

The USDA's NOS informed Foster that the "suspension will remain in effect until such time as you provide adequate written assurances of corrective and preventative measures to assure that meat and poultry products will be produced under sanitary conditions." On January 10, Foster submitted a response via email and was notified that the NOS was in abeyance. The following day, on January 11, Foster resumed operations in Plant 2, but then found two dead or dying cockroaches in a production area of Plant 2. Approximately ten hours later, Foster's plant manager decided to temporarily cease operations. None of the evidence at trial establishes that the USDA's decision to place the NOS in abeyance was dependent on or influenced by Foster's decision to voluntarily cease operations on January 12.

The insured has the burden of proving that the claimed loss falls within the scope of the policy. Foster is entitled to seek only those losses covered by the Policy, which the Policy defines in relevant part as "reasonable and necessary expenses incurred by the Insured ... and which arise solely and directly out of the Insured Event." The NOS did not require Foster to cease operations on January 12 and the FSIS's Notice of Abeyance was not dependent on Foster's decision to voluntarily cease operations. The court finds that its concern for doing the least damage to its brand while eradicating the facility-wide infestation was the key consideration leading to its decision to voluntarily cease operations. Accordingly, Foster has not carried its burden of proving that the second shutdown arose solely and directly out of the NOS and conditions described in it.

Foster seeks loss under the Policy for "Recall Expenses," "Loss of Gross Profit," and "Increased Cost of Working." Defendant does not dispute the award of Recall Expenses in the amount of $11,733 in landfill fees to dispose of the chicken produced on January 7 and 8 and $7,500 in trucking fees to move that chicken to the landfill. Foster also seeks $74,791 in public relations (PR) expenses. It is impossible for the court to distinguish the PR expenses that arose solely and directly out of the Insured Event from those that were incurred from the second shutdown. Because Foster has the burden of proof and the only evidence before the court is that the PR expenses arising solely and directly out of the Insured Event are limited to $14,958, the court will award Foster that amount.

It is undisputed that Foster's inability to sell the 1.3 million pounds of chicken that the USDA refused to approve for sale arose solely and directly out of the Insured Event. The court will therefore award Foster $1,047,700 in loss of gross profit for chicken that did not receive the USDA's marks of inspection pursuant to the NOS. According to the evidence at trial, Foster produces organic and conventional chicken and is able to sell organic chicken at a higher profit margin. Because Foster did not submit any evidence challenging this allocation, the court will award plaintiff only $3,726 for its claimed loss of gross profit resulting from downgrading its organic chicken. As a result of both shutdowns, Foster was unable to fill a substantial number of firm orders for chicken. The court will award plaintiff $346,164 in loss of gross profit based on unfilled orders arising solely and directly out of the Insured Event.

Foster seeks loss of gross profit for customer credits and claims resulting from the shutdowns. Only $54,241 arose solely and directly out of the Insured Event so the court will therefore award this amount. Foster also seeks over $1 million as a result of Winco's alleged decision to cease ordering certain chicken products sooner than it had agreed because of the NOS. The court finds plaintiff lost gross profits of $1,107,550 based on Winco's early exit. Foster next seeks over $3 million for incremental labor costs incurred to process and package as much product as possible at the other facilities during both the Insured Event and the second shutdown. The court will award plaintiff loss of gross profit attributable to incremental labor costs in the amount of $11,457. Foster seeks substantial losses for remediation and cleanup expenses and supplies. Foster has thus carried its burden of proving that the remediation cost of $101,369 in "Increased Cost of Working" for supplies and pest control services that arose solely and directly out of the Insured Event.

For the reasons stated herein, the court hereby finds for Foster on its breach of contract claim and finds that Foster suffered Loss in the amount of $2,706,398 covered by the Policy.

## Questions

1. After the court found an Insured Event, what was the controversy?
2. Who made the decision to stop operations on January 12? Whom do you think was consulted?
3. How could this controversy have been avoided?
4. What explains the difference between the $12 million requested and the $2.7 million awarded by the court?
5. Had Foster fully prepared its data to support its various damage requests?

# Discussion Questions

1. Should consumers be able to sue sellers of food products for a deceptive label, or should such actions be handled by the government? Why?
2. Is raw milk wholesome? Is it healthier than regular milk?
3. Who should pay for regulatory costs associated with health problems from raw milk? Explain your reasoning.
4. When a restaurant sells a contaminated food product that injures a person, should it settle prior to a determination of whether it or its supplier is liable? Why?
5. What insurance coverage should a food company purchase with regards to the safety of its food products?

# CHAPTER TWENTY-EIGHT
## Public Health and Civil Liberties

## Learning Objectives

- *Summarize the two major requirements of the Americans with Disabilities Act.*
- *Defend the abridgement of free speech in regulating tobacco products.*
- *Criticize laws compelling people to give samples to further criminal investigations.*
- *Recognize how the rights of incompetent persons are protected.*

G overnments have choices and make decisions when addressing public health issues and civil liberties. Internationally, a number of declarations are important in affirming that people have rights that no government should abridge. The United States has ratified the International Covenant on Civil and Political Rights (1966), the Convention on Elimination of All Forms of Racial Discrimination (1966), and the Convention against Torture and Other Cruel, Inhuman, or Degrading Treatment or Punishment (1994). The United States has not ratified the Convention on the Elimination of All Forms of Discrimination against Women (1979) or the Convention on the Rights of the Child (1989).

However, our constitutional and statutory provisions on property, liberty, and privacy interests embody important protections that cannot be abridged by government. A look at four civil liberties dealing with public health discloses contemporary issues that affect the rights and freedoms of Americans. The first issue concerns the Americans with Disabilities Act, which prohibits types of discrimination based on disability. The second is the First Amendment's freedom of speech and whether sellers of tobacco products can be forced to place warnings including graphic images on their products. The third is whether a person's property interest requires the government to return or destroy a felon's blood sample, and a fourth issue involves governmental actions to address mental illness.

# The Americans with Disabilities Act

The Americans with Disabilities Act (ADA) has been described as the emancipation proclamation for 43 million Americans with disabilities. Title I of the ADA prohibits discrimination against qualified individuals with disabilities in private and public employment. The ADA applies to such activities as hiring, firing, promoting, compensating, recruiting, training, and other terms, conditions, and privileges of employment. This law goes beyond most other employment discrimination legislation. It not only prohibits "discrimination" in the traditional sense of that term, but also requires "reasonable accommodation" of individuals with disabilities, unless the accommodation would impose an "undue hardship" on the employer. The objectives of the ADA are (a) to eliminate discrimination against people with disabilities; (b) to fully integrate them into American economic life; and (c) to transfer the cost of supporting individuals with disabilities from the public to the private sector.

Those who employ fifteen people or more are covered. The definition of an employer includes every agent of an employer, thus creating individual liability on the part of every manager. Subchapter I of the ADA describes rules prohibiting discrimination in employment and requires employers to engage in reasonable accommodation of disability. Subchapter I also defines "disability" with respect to an individual to cover: (a) a physical or mental impairment that substantially limits one or more of the major life activities; (b) a record of such an impairment; or (c) being regarded as having such an impairment. Subchapter III prohibits discrimination to qualified individuals with a disability in the provision of public services.

Congress declined to provide an exhaustive list of disabilities. Rather, the ADA was drafted to include virtually every physical or mental condition that fits within any one of the three prongs of the definition. The ADA does exclude a few impairments from the term disability, including compulsive gambling, kleptomania, pyromania, transvestism, gender identity disorders not resulting from physical impairments, other sexual behavior disorders, and psychoactive substance use disorders resulting from current illegal use of drugs.

Impairment also does not include ordinary physical characteristics such as race, age, eye color, left-handedness, baldness, or educational, environmental, economic, or cultural disadvantages. Some examples of disability include: the inability to read because of a learning disorder or dyslexia, heart disease, alcoholism, sleep disorders, epilepsy, nicotine withdrawal, phobias, AIDs, and significant disfigurement that prevents a person from being hired.

# 1. Reasonable Accommodations

The ADA requires employers to make reasonable accommodations for any prospective employee with a disability to perform the essential function of the job. The ADA contemplates that the employer will need to consult the applicant or employee about what reasonable accommodation would allow him or her to be fully effective. Reasonable accommodations include: (1) making existing facilities used by employees readily accessible to and usable by individuals with disabilities; (2) job restructuring; (3) part-time or modified work schedules; (4) acquisition or modification of equipment or devices; (5) providing qualified readers or interpreters; (6) special training materials; and (7) different policies or programs.

# 2. ADA-Qualified Individual with a Disability (QID)

While you are not required to hire someone who is not qualified, the ADA's duty to provide reasonable accommodations only applies to qualified individuals with a disability (QID). A QID is someone who, with or without reasonable accommodation, can perform the essential functions of the job. This means that every possible affected employer should prepare written job descriptions that list only the essential functions of the job. Essential functions of the job means only those functions without which the job could not be accomplished.

In attempting to prohibit all forms of employment discrimination against individuals with disabilities, the ADA lists seven forms of discrimination.

I.   Limiting, segregating, or classifying an applicant or employee in a way that hinders their opportunity or diminishes their status because of the disability.

II.   Participating in a contractual arrangement or a relationship that has the effect of subjecting applicants or employees to discrimination. Providing insurance benefits for employees but excluding those with disabilities would be an example.

III.   Using standards, criteria, or administrative methods that have the effect of discriminating on the basis of disability or that perpetuate past discrimination.

IV.   Denying equal jobs or benefits to individuals because they are related or have an association with a disabled individual.

V.   Not making reasonable accommodations to the known physical or mental limitations of a QID applicant or employee unless you can prove that the accommodation would impose an undue hardship on your business.

VI.   Using employment tests or having qualifications for the job that screen out individuals with disabilities, rather than what is actually essential for the job.

VII.   Requiring a preemployment medical examination or asking an applicant about their physical or mental condition.

The following case looks at a claim that an employee was dismissed in violation of the ADA due to his infection with HIV.

### *Lundy v. Phillips Staffing*
US District Court for the District of South Carolina

*Who is suing?* _____

*Who is being sued?* _____

*For what?* _____

*What is the issue on appeal?* _____

The plaintiff, Walter Lundy (Lundy), brought this action against the defendant, Phillips Staffing (Phillips), alleging discrimination under the Americans with Disabilities Act (ADA). Specifically, Lundy alleges that Phillips fired him after it discovered that he was infected with the human immunodeficiency virus (HIV). Phillips has moved for summary judgment, asserting a nondiscriminatory reason for Lundy's discharge—withholding information on a medical questionnaire. Now before the court is the magistrate judge's Report recommending that the court deny Phillips's motion. The Report has no presumptive weight. The court is charged with conducting a de novo review of those portions of the Report to which either party specifically objects. Then, the court may accept, reject, or modify the Report or recommit the matter to the magistrate judge.

During the summer of 2011, Lundy was contacted by Phillips to fill a position at Hubbell Lighting (Hubbell). As part of the intake process, Lundy completed a Post Offer Medical Questionnaire, which asked if he had any other disease, condition or impairment which is permanent in nature. Lundy answered "no," understanding the question to refer to conditions that would impact his work, partially due to a statement on the questionnaire that the purpose of this form is to insure that you will be able to safely and successfully perform all job functions. However, the questionnaire also stated that failure to answer this questionnaire truthfully may result in your termination for falsifying documents.

Lundy began working for Hubbell as an unloader. By all accounts, Lundy performed his job well and Hubbell decided to consider him for a forklift operator position. To get the position, Lundy had to apply for a commercial driver's license, which required a routine medical exam. In response to a question about his medications during that exam, Lundy indicated that he was taking medication for HIV and had been diagnosed in 2003. The medical report certified that Lundy was fit to receive a commercial driver's license, but also noted that he was taking a prescription for HIV. A Phillips representative reviewed the medical report and, after comparing the report to Lundy's Post Offer Medical Questionnaire, concluded that Lundy did not fill out the questionnaire truthfully and should be terminated. Shortly thereafter, Phillips terminated Lundy's employment.

Summary judgment is appropriate if the court is satisfied that no genuine issues of material fact exist and that the movant is entitled to judgment as a matter of law. To survive summary judgment, Lundy must first establish a prima facie case of discrimination by showing: (1) he "was a qualified individual with a disability"; (2) he was discharged; (3) he was fulfilling his employer's legitimate expectations at the time of discharge; and (4) the circumstances of his discharge raise a reasonable inference of unlawful discrimination. If Lundy makes this showing, then the burden shifts to Phillips to produce a legitimate, non-discriminatory reason for the termination. If Phillips meets this burden, then the presumption of discrimination created by the prima facie case disappears from the case and Lundy must prove that Phillips's proffered justification is pretextual.

The Report recommends denying Phillips's motion for summary judgment because there is a question of material fact as to the true motivation behind Lundy's termination. Specifically, the Report finds that there is a question of fact as to whether Phillips reasonably concluded that Lundy lied on the questionnaire because (1) Lundy's understanding that the form was asking for conditions that would affect his job performance may be reasonable, (2) Phillips has not defined the term "any other disease, condition or impairment which is permanent in nature," and (3) the parties dispute whether Phillips agents made comments during Lundy's termination meeting regarding his HIV status. According to the Report, these issues are enough to suggest that Phillips's reason for firing Lundy may have been pretextual.

Phillips objects to the Report's analysis, asserting that (1) Lundy is not a member of an ADA protected class, (2) Lundy was not meeting legitimate job expectations, and (3) Lundy did not present sufficient evidence to suggest pretext. First, Phillips objects to the Report's finding that Lundy's asymptomatic HIV qualifies as a disability under the ADA because Lundy has not demonstrated that his HIV affects a major life activity, as required under the ADA. Lundy has shown that he has HIV, which is a physical impairment that has a constant and detrimental effect on the infected person's hemic and lymphatic systems from the moment of infection. The lymph nodes play a key role in the body's immune response system, a major life activity.

Next, Phillips argues that Lundy was not meeting legitimate job expectations because one such expectation is that employees complete their paperwork truthfully. The court agrees that the legitimate expectations prong encompasses compliance with company rules, along with general job performance. However, while on summary judgment, an employer is free to assert that the job expectation prong has not been met, nothing prohibits the employee from countering this assertion with evidence that demonstrates (or at least creates a question of fact) that the proffered "expectation" is not, in fact, legitimate at all. In this case, the record suggests that Lundy's general job performance was more than adequate. Lundy offers evidence that this company rule, or at least the way in which Phillips enforces it, is not legitimate. The court finds that Lundy has presented enough evidence to create a question of fact as to whether Phillips is using this company rule to hide a discriminatory purpose.

Finally, Phillips asserts that Lundy has not presented sufficient evidence of discrimination to show that his termination was due to unlawful discrimination. Specifically, Phillips objects to the Report's reliance on the purported statements Phillips representatives made at Lundy's termination meeting. For the reasons stated above, the court finds Lundy's testimony regarding statements made at his termination meeting plausible and material. There are contradictions between the non-discriminatory rationale for firing Lundy currently propounded by Phillips and the statements allegedly made by Phillips representatives during Lundy's termination meeting. Such contradictions between an employer's proffered explanation and the contemporaneous statements of the employer are convincing evidence of pretext and combined with the plaintiff's prima facie case, can be enough to permit the trier of fact to conclude that the employer unlawfully discriminated. The court agrees with the Report's apt analysis and incorporates it herein. Accordingly, Phillips's motion for summary judgment is denied.

## Questions

1.  If the court can reject the magistrate judge's report, what is its value?
2.  What does Lundy need to show to qualify for relief under the ADA?
3.  What proof was offered by Lundy to show a disability?
4.  What if Lundy is lying about the statements made at his termination meeting?

# Freedom of Speech

Americans are very protective of their First Amendment free-speech rights. Congress and governmental agencies may have difficulties in devising regulations to advance public health objectives that do not offend commercial free speech. In the following case, the court found the federal government's proposed graphic warnings for cigarette packages violated the free speech rights of cigarette companies.

### R.J. Reynolds Tobacco Company v. Food & Drug Administration
US Court of Appeals for the District of Columbia Circuit, Washington

*Who is suing?* _____

*Who is being sued?* _____

*For what?* _____

*What is the issue on appeal?* _____

The Family Smoking Prevention and Tobacco Control Act (Act) directed the Secretary of the U.S. Department of Health and Human Services to issue regulations requiring all cigarette packages manufactured or sold in the United States to bear one of nine new textual warnings, as well as "color graphics depicting the negative health consequences of smoking." Pursuant to this authority, the Food and Drug Administration (FDA) initiated a rulemaking proceeding through which it selected the nine images that would accompany the statutorily-prescribed warnings. Five tobacco companies (Companies) challenged the rule, alleging that FDA's proposed graphic warnings violated the First Amendment. The district court granted the Companies' motion for an injunction and summary judgment. FDA appeals and we affirm.

The Act gives FDA the authority to regulate the manufacture and sale of tobacco products, including cigarettes. In addition to requiring cigarette packages and advertisements to bear one of nine new warning statements, the Act mandates that the new warning labels comprise the top 50 percent of the front and rear panels of cigarette packages and 20 percent of the area of each cigarette advertisement. The Act directs the Secretary to issue final regulations identifying the graphic component of the warnings.

Pursuant to the statutory directive, FDA issued a Proposed Rule. FDA asserted the government's "substantial interest in reducing the number of Americans, particularly children and adolescents, who use cigarettes and other tobacco products in order to prevent the life-threatening health consequences associated with tobacco use." FDA promulgated the final set of nine images, one for each warning statement, without firm conclusions about the "long-term, real-world effects" of the proposed warnings, but claimed the existing scientific literature "provides a substantial basis for our conclusion that the required warnings will effectively communicate the health risks of smoking, thereby encouraging smoking cessation and discouraging smoking initiation."

The only question before us is whether FDA's promulgation of the graphic warning labels violates the First Amendment. Both the right to speak and the right to refrain from speaking are "complementary components of the broader concept of individual freedom of mind" protected by the First Amendment. Any attempt by the government either to compel individuals to express certain views or to subsidize speech to which they object is subject to strict scrutiny. This case contains elements of compulsion and forced subsidization. The Companies contend that, to the extent the graphic warnings go beyond the textual warnings to shame and repulse smokers and denigrate smoking as an antisocial act, the message is ideological and not informational. This case raises novel questions about the scope of the government's authority to force the manufacturer of a product to go beyond making purely factual and accurate commercial disclosures by making "every single pack of cigarettes in the country a mini billboard" for the government's anti-smoking message.

The FDA contends that the district court erred by failing to apply the intermediate-level scrutiny generally afforded to commercial speech, and that the graphic warnings pass constitutional muster under the *Central Hudson* case. Under *Central Hudson*, the government must first show that its asserted interest is "substantial." If so, the Court must determine "whether the regulation directly advances the governmental interest asserted, and whether it is not more extensive than is necessary to serve that interest." The Administrative Procedure Act (APA) requires us to hold unlawful and set aside agency action, findings, and conclusions found to be unsupported by substantial evidence.

A review of the statute and the administrative record makes clear that the graphic warnings are intended to encourage current smokers to quit and dissuade other consumers from ever buying cigarettes. The only explicitly asserted interest in either the Proposed or Final Rule is an interest in reducing smoking rates. Assuming FDA's interest in reducing smoking rates is substantial, we next evaluate whether FDA has offered substantial evidence showing that the graphic warning requirements directly advance the governmental interest asserted. The requirement that a restriction directly advance the asserted interest is "critical," because without it, the government could interfere with commercial speech in the service of other objectives that could not themselves justify a burden on commercial expression. FDA has not provided a shred of evidence, much less the "substantial evidence" required by the APA, showing that the graphic warnings will "directly advance" its interest in reducing the number of Americans who smoke.

FDA's Regulatory Impact Analysis estimated the new warnings would reduce U.S. smoking rates by a mere 0.088%, a number the FDA concedes is "not statistically distinguishable from zero." FDA has thus presented us with only two studies that directly evaluate the impact of graphic warnings on actual smoking rates, and neither set of data shows that the graphic warnings will "directly" advance its interest in reducing smoking rates "to a material degree."

The First Amendment requires the government not only to state a substantial interest justifying a regulation on commercial speech, but also to show that its regulation directly advances that goal. FDA failed to present any data showing that enacting their proposed graphic warnings will accomplish the agency's stated objective of reducing smoking rates. The Rule thus cannot pass muster under *Central Hudson*. The APA directs that we shall set aside the agency action found to be contrary to a constitutional right. We therefore vacate the graphic warning requirements and remand to the agency.

## Questions

1. Why did the FDA develop graphic images for cigarette packages?
2. Does the case involve the right to speak or something else?
3. Are all governmental restrictions on speech treated the same? Why or why not?
4. Why wasn't the government's substantial interest in reducing smoking sufficient to justify the requirement of graphic warnings?
5. What should the FDA do next?

## Protecting the Privacy of Property Interests

American jurisprudence entails significant protections for property interests and privacy. Our federal and state constitutions accord individuals special protection for their rights, and Americans view these rights as being very important. Persons convicted of crimes lose some of their rights, including the right to not divulge personal information available from blood samples that enable governments to establish DNA profiles for crime enforcement purposes. In the following case, a convicted felon argues that his property interest in his blood should enable him to obtain back the sample that had been taken by the government. The court was not sympathetic to his argument.

### *United States v. Kriesel*
US Court of Appeals for the Ninth Circuit, San Francisco

*Who is suing?* _____

*Who is being sued?* _____

*For what?* _____

*What is the issue on appeal?* _____

Government and commercial entities enjoy increasing capacity to obtain, store, and analyze information about people, giving rise to increasing concerns about privacy. Nowhere is that upward spiral more evident than in litigation calling into question practices relating to identifying people through their deoxyribonucleic acid (DNA) sequences. The appellant here, Thomas Kriesel, pled guilty to a drug conspiracy charge, and was sentenced to a term of imprisonment followed by a term of supervised release. One condition of his supervised release required him to provide a blood sample for analysis of his DNA, and inclusion of his DNA profile into the government's Combined DNA Index System (CODIS) database. Now that Kriesel has completed

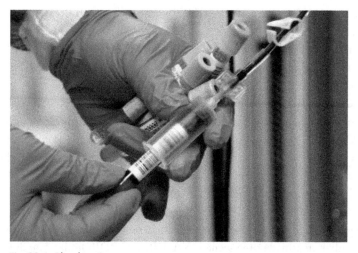

Fig. 28.1 Blood testing.

his term of supervised release, he has made an unusual invocation of Federal Rule of Criminal Procedure 41(g) asking the government to return the blood sample. He has no remaining objection to the government's retention of the information in his DNA profile, which the government analyzed from the extracted blood sample, and which it currently stores in the CODIS database.

Kriesel argued to the district court that the government had no legitimate reason for retaining the blood sample—which of course has within it not only the limited information the government has analyzed for his DNA profile, but his entire unanalyzed genome. The district court ruled the government had a legitimate purpose in retaining the blood samples that generate the CODIS profiles in order to ensure that the matches to forensic evidence, identified through CODIS searches, are accurate. The court found no reason at this time to believe the government would use the blood for other purposes, many of which are already prohibited by statute. The district court therefore granted judgment to the government, and we affirm on a similar basis.

The CODIS database stores DNA profiles of convicted federal felons on supervised release and others who have had brushes with the law. These DNA profiles are commonly generated from blood samples. The blood is collected from offenders and then sent to the Federal DNA Database Unit (FDDU). The FDDU extracts the DNA molecules from each blood sample, analyzes the molecules, generates a profile of identifying characteristics, and uploads the profile to CODIS. In addition to storing the profiles in CODIS, the FDDU retains offenders' physical blood samples to help ensure accurate matches to DNA found at crime scenes.

Blood cells in the samples contain two types of DNA: the biologically important coding (or non-junk) DNA, and the biologically unimportant non-coding (or junk) DNA. We held in *United States v. Kincade* that the government may extract junk DNA from samples, and use it to generate profiles for inclusion in CODIS, because present scientific understanding indicates that junk DNA reveals no sensitive, private genetic or medical information. It is useful, however, for identification purposes. The government uses only junk DNA to generate the CODIS profile. The CODIS system searches for matches between offenders' DNA and crime scene evidence. It is when a match is found that the actual sample is tested. This verifies that the person whose profile CODIS matched to the crime scene evidence is the same person who provided the original blood sample.

The FBI retains Kriesel's blood sample as part of its implementation of quality and accuracy standards developed pursuant to Congressional directives. The primary value of CODIS is to link unidentified DNA samples collected from crime scenes to the DNA of known offenders in the system. Forensic laboratories around the country analyze DNA from those samples to generate a profile that can be matched to known offenders' DNA. The process produces accurate identifications because it is extremely unlikely two people will have the same profile. The goal of the CODIS system is to find what the government calls a "Candidate Match," a putative match between an identified offender and unidentified crime scene DNA. When CODIS finds a Candidate Match, the FDDU receives a CODIS Match Report. At this point the original blood sample is used for confirmation.

In deciding the Rule 41(g) issues, the district court first ruled that the blood sample was property within the meaning of the Rule, and that Kriesel, because of his concerns about the private information the sample's non-junk DNA in the sample could reveal, was sufficiently aggrieved to seek its return. The district court denied the Rule 41(g) motion, however, because the government had shown a sufficient reason for retaining the sample. It ruled that the use of the "Match Confirmation" process to ensure the accuracy of the system satisfied the government's burden to justify retention. The court observed that Kriesel's sample was an integral part of the database, and that Rule 41 should not be permitted to undermine it. The court recognized that if Kriesel and other offenders whose DNA profiles were included in CODIS were able to petition successfully for the return of their blood samples, then "offenders' identities would be released without Match Report confirmations" and "CODIS's integrity would erode."

Kriesel's primary argument is that the district court erred in concluding that retaining his blood sample is reasonable. Although the district court did so because retention allows the government to ensure the accuracy of putative matches between offenders and unidentified DNA, Kriesel contends the "Match Confirmation" process is not a reasonable justification because it is not necessary to ensure the accuracy of Candidate Matches. The government explained to the district court how and why it uses the blood sample to ensure it has accurately determined the identity of the person associated with the DNA profile stored in CODIS. This "Match Confirmation" process ensures that the system is working accurately. It also enables pre-arrest confirmation of a match. The Match Confirmation process is also a method of long-term quality control.

Because the government obtained Kriesel's sample as a condition of his supervised release from custody, the remaining question under Rule 41 is whether the government's justification for retention of the sample disappeared when Kriesel completed the term of supervised release. The question is whether the record of a felon's DNA could be retained once those formerly on supervised release had "wholly cleared their debt to society." In this case, Kriesel's completion of his sentence did not eliminate the government's interest in retaining the DNA profile in CODIS, and Kriesel no longer argues that it did. The need to identify DNA found at a crime scene is critical and accuracy matters. The retention of the blood samples further those goals by ensuring the accuracy of the CODIS profile match, which is the function served by the "Match Conformation."

We have previously stressed that if scientific discoveries make clear that junk DNA reveals more about individuals than we have previously understood, we should reconsider the government's DNA collection programs. We affirm the district court's holding that the government's continued retention of Kriesel's blood sample is reasonable under the circumstances presented on this record.

## Questions

1. What is the government's purpose for retaining blood samples?
2. Why isn't the retention of information of a felon's DNA profile sufficient for the government?
3. Do convicted felons have a property right in their blood?
4. Why does the court allow the government to keep felons' blood samples?
5. Do felons ever "clear their debt to society?"

# Treating the Mentally Ill

Addressing issues accompanying mental illness is challenging. Governments have responsibilities in assisting the mentally ill to obtain treatment and in protecting society from actions by the mentally ill. Simultaneously, individuals who are mentally ill have rights. The following case shows a court evaluating the rights of an individual to make her own decisions in refusing treatment with the government's concerns that, left untreated, the individual would place greater costs on society.

### *Guardianship of L.H.*
Appeals Court of Massachusetts

*Who is suing?* _____

*Who is being sued?* _____

*For what?* _____

*What is the issue on appeal?* _____

L. H. appeals from a decree and findings of the Probate and Family Court that she was not competent to make medical decisions and would benefit from a proposed treatment plan to use the antipsychotic drug Risperdal, and that she would consent to use of that drug were she competent. L. H. also appeals from the judge's subsequent allowance of a motion to reinstate and to modify the treatment plan to allow for the administration by injection of Risperdal. We affirm. We conclude that the evidence in these substituted judgment proceedings and the probate judge's findings established by a preponderance that L. H. was in need of treatment with antipsychotic drugs. At the time these proceedings commenced, L. H., a 57 year-old woman, was living at the Lowell Health Care Center (LHCC), having previously been a resident in a nursing home in New York.

LHCC staff members (collectively, petitioners) filed a petition in the Probate and Family Court seeking appointment of a guardian for L. H. pursuant to Massachusetts General Laws Chapter 190B, § 5-303. The petition later was amended to include a proposed antipsychotic treatment plan. Dr. Anthony Joseph, a psychiatrist, completed and signed the statutorily required medical certificates and supporting documentation that detail L. H.'s physical and mental condition and, we conclude, justified the petition undertaken.

A hearing was held and the witnesses included Dr. Joseph of LHCC; Dr. David Rosmarin, an independent forensic psychiatrist retained by L. H.'s court-appointed counsel; L. H.; and her court-appointed temporary guardian. Dr. Joseph provided a psychiatric diagnosis of borderline personality disorder, mood disorder, anxiety, and excessive compulsiveness, among other mental ailments. He noted that behavioral modification treatment had been ineffective. This psychiatrist testified that treatment with an antipsychotic medicine was proposed to decrease L. H.'s agitation and paranoia so that ensuing behavioral treatment could become more effective, with the goal of returning L. H. to a supportive living environment in New York. While acknowledging that the proposed antipsychotic medicine, Risperdal, had side effects, the psychiatrist stated his medical opinion that it would be the preferred drug for L. H., and that the medication's side effects relative to its overall effectiveness were within tolerable ranges. Regarding L. H.'s prognosis if left untreated, Dr. Joseph predicted that she would "continue the way she is," and added that he "would be very concerned about what kind of facility she would end up in New York, how long they would keep her."

The second psychiatric expert witness, Dr. Rosmarin, also stated medical opinions that tended to support the position that L. H. would benefit from the proposed treatment plan. This psychiatrist diagnosed L. H. as having a personality disorder with obsessive compulsive symptoms and suggested she could benefit from treatment with antipsychotic medicine, although at a lower dose than was proposed: "This lady needs very careful management but with a very careful behavioral plan in concert possibly with two kinds of medications. One would be a very low dose of antipsychotic. I don't have an objection to that."

L. H. testified in opposition to the treatment plan and to the use of antipsychotic medications. L. H. acknowledged that she had been homeless, suffers from MS, requires the use of a wheelchair, and needs physical assistance in her living situation. However, she did not believe guardianship was warranted, and she protested the use of antipsychotic drugs. She stated that when she previously had been treated with the proposed antipsychotic Risperdal, she had experienced severe side effects and "would rather be dead than go on Risperdal again." The guardian testified he had met with L. H., consulted with LHCC staff, and spoken with L. H.'s sister on three or four occasions. Based on those discussions, the guardian stated, "I think she needs some supervision and she needs some medication."

At the conclusion of the hearing, the judge found the testimony of the two physicians proffered are really not diametrically opposed. They both appear to agree that treatment is needed, continuation of the guardianship is warranted and that the treatment plan as proposed, actually by both physicians, involves both medical treatment, a psychotropic drug treatment, together with a behavioral treatment. In his findings of fact, the judge acknowledged L. H.'s stated preference against the proposed antipsychotic medication, but found, listing the *Rogers* decisional factors, "that if L. H. could rationally evaluate the side effects described, she would choose the Treatment Plan subject to the explanation that the use of the drugs would be properly managed and that efforts would be made to continue to monitor the dosage within the lowest optimum range."

Accordingly, the judge authorized the proposed treatment plan and appointed a permanent guardian and *Rogers* monitor for L. H. The plan expired. Subsequently, staff of LHCC, as the petitioners, filed a motion in the Probate and Family Court to reinstate the *Rogers* order and to modify it to allow an injectable form of the antipsychotic medication to be administered because L. H. was refusing to take Risperdal orally. The testimony at this hearing reflected L. H.'s persistent mental disabilities. Dr. Joseph supported the modification of the treatment plan modification to include injectable medication, stating, "Most likely she would become much less paranoid, much less agitated and would have a much improved quality of life in terms of her sense of well-being and satisfaction." The prognosis without antipsychotic medication was as follows: "Without treatment, she would continue to be agitated, dysphoric with a very impaired quality of life and it's very likely she would end up in a chronic state psychiatric facility." L. H. strenuously objected to antipsychotic treatment.

The judge allowed the motion to reinstate the *Rogers* order and to continue the treatment plan, and to modify the order for treatment to allow for an injectable form of drug administration. The judge carefully weighed the applicable factors set forth in *Rogers*, including (1) L. H.'s expressed preferences to decline treatment with Risperdal; (2) consideration of L. H.'s family, including that the guardian, who endorsed the plan, had spoken with L. H.'s sister; (3) the balancing of adverse side effects against the benefits of treatment; (4) the prognosis without treatment; and (5) the prognosis with treatment. The judge also considered other relevant factors, including L. H.'s physical condition and living arrangement and the goal of greater physical independence. Based on our review of the evidence, we agree that the guardianship and the treatment with antipsychotic medication were appropriate, and if competent, L. H. would consent thereto.

## Questions

1. Is the judgment being appealed founded on common law or statutory law?
2. How did the state provide L. H. an opportunity to be heard in the proceedings?
3. What kind of evidence justified intervention through an order requiring the use of Risperdal?
4. Why weren't L. H.'s objections sufficient to allow her to avoid treatment with Risperdal?
5. Who weighed the testimony and made the decision regarding treatment with Risperdal?
6. Is this a fair resolution for persons with medical issues similar to those documented for the individual in this case?

# Payment for Medical Intervention

With the advent of governmental involvement in health care, individuals and companies are objecting to requirements of medical interventions that are contrary to their beliefs. Several years ago, the issue was whether pharmacists could refuse to fill prescriptions for emergency contraception. Some states reacted to the issue by enacting legislation requiring pharmacists to provide medication to patients, or prohibiting pharmacists from obstructing patient access to medication. Other states enacted statutes that allow pharmacists to refuse to assist patients with prescriptions they object to, based on religious or moral reasons, with the consequences that some patients may not receive emergency contraception in time for it to be effective. Public opinion seems to support the position that pharmacists and pharmacies should dispense contraception to patients without discrimination or delay.

A more recent moral and religious issue is whether private companies should have to provide medical insurance coverage that pays for contraception. The US Supreme Court decided that the Religious Freedom Restoration Act offers owners of private corporations protection from legislation that burdens the exercise of the owners' religious beliefs. Owners who have religious objections to abortifacients do not need to provide health insurance for contraceptive measures that would prevent an already fertilized egg from further development.

# Discussion Questions

1.  What is the purpose of the ADA? Do the regulations fulfill congressional objectives?
2.  What types of reasonable accommodations should an employer be required to make?
3.  Despite the ADA, can companies find ways not to employ workers with qualifying disabilities? How?
4.  Should the federal government make another attempt to incorporate graphic labels on tobacco products? What should they do to support their new initiative?
5.  You are in charge of rendering assistance to a parent or close relative who is gradually becoming mentally disabled. How would you decide when to take steps and have yourself designated as the guardian of this individual?
6.  Your state passes a law that requires eggs from chickens raised in cages be labeled as "Eggs produced by chickens in cages." Does this offend sellers' First Amendment rights? Why or why not?

# Image Credit

# CHAPTER TWENTY-NINE

## Other Issues Concerning Public Well-Being

## Learning Objectives

- *Recognize limits on the dismissal of whistleblowers.*
- *Describe how governments can require a medical exam for employment despite a person's right to privacy.*
- *Explain the status of medical marijuana in states that authorize its some uses.*
- *Explain the tradeoffs in allowing private medical records to be used in litigation involving a plaintiff's mental and emotional health.*
- *Critique the imposition of prison terms on corporate officers.*

## Introduction

In earlier public health chapters, we have addressed medical malpractice, controlling diseases, food safety, and civil liberties to highlight governmental actions employed to protect people. Several additional issues concerning public well-being can be identified that are important to Americans. Governments evaluate risks and costs to enact provisions responding to social needs. The first issue involves whistleblower protection to shield employees who disclose information on violations or dangers to public health and safety. Another topic involves the use of employment exams, and whether their provisions are arbitrary and capricious. A third involves the use of medical marijuana, while the fourth is an exception to the privacy of personal medical records when a plaintiff's mental and emotional health is an issue in the litigation. A final topic is punishment for firms and individuals who flaunt our food safety regulations.

# Whistleblowing

At common law and by statute, states have adopted whistleblowing principles to encourage reporting problems that might result in unsafe situations or less-than-optimal outcomes. The following case shows a government official reporting a water conservation violation by a politician and subsequent retaliatory action by his boss.

### *Shaw v. Southwest Kansas Groundwater Management District Three*
Court of Appeals of Kansas

*Who is suing?* _____

*Who is being sued?* _____

*For what?* _____

*What is the issue on appeal?* _____

Leland Kent Shaw appeals the district court's order granting summary judgment to Southwest Kansas Groundwater Management District Three (GMD) on Shaw's retaliatory discharge claim. For the reasons stated herein, we reverse the district court's order granting summary judgment and remand for further proceedings. GMD is an organization created pursuant to Kansas Statutes Annotated to ensure the proper management and conservation of Kansas' groundwater resources. Water users within GMD's district are not to allow "waste of water." One of the definitions of "waste of water" is "the escaping and draining of water intended for irrigation use from the authorized place of use." Pursuant to Kansas Administrative Regulations (K.A.R.) § 5-23-11, if a representative of a district finds that a water use violation exists, the representative shall issue a written directive to the violator stating the nature of the violation and directing the violator to come into compliance with these rules and regulations.

GMD is governed by a board of directors (Board). The Board employs an executive director to manage the day-to-day operations of the district. For 15 years, Steve Frost served as GMD's executive director. Subsequently, Steven C. "Hank" Hansen became GMD's executive director and was given a 3-year employment contract. Shaw was hired by GMD and worked as a conservationist. One of Shaw's duties as a conservationist was to perform field investigations regarding alleged waste of water violations. For 15 years, Frost supervised Shaw and evaluated Shaw's performance as "exceptional" and routinely recommended Shaw for salary and position advancements. When Hansen

Fig. 29.1 Irrigation runoff.

replaced Frost as GMD's executive director, Hansen continued to evaluate Shaw as an exemplary employee for three years.

Shaw observed evidence that he believed constituted a waste of water from farmland operated by Peterson, the Board's president. Shaw observed water runoff from the field into the adjacent roadway caused by the field's irrigation system. No effort was made to prevent the waste of water or to retain the water on the land with a berm or a dike. Shaw called his office and notified Janet King, a GMD employee, of the violation and its location. King apparently informed Hansen of Shaw's finding because when Shaw returned to the office, Hansen told Shaw that he did not want Peterson to receive a formal notice about the violation. Hansen sent an e-mail to Shaw and King in which he explained that he had contacted Peterson about the water drainage problem. Hansen stated that because Peterson was aware of the situation and was on course to remedy the problem, Hansen did not want a legal notice filed against Peterson.

A month later Shaw told Shirley Spanier, a former GMD employee, about Hansen's order prohibiting him from sending notice to Peterson. Spanier contacted several members of the Board and told them she believed it was wrong for Hansen to refuse to issue a notice to Peterson. The Board decided to investigate and asked Shaw to meet with the Board's executive committee. At the meeting, the parties discussed Peterson's alleged waste of water violation and how Shaw did not agree with Hansen's handling of the situation. According to Shaw, Peterson admitted at the meeting that a violation had occurred and that he expected to receive a notice. Shortly thereafter, Hansen fired Shaw without warning. Hansen gave Shaw a termination letter and an evaluation documenting four deficient job performances or misconduct by Shaw and stating that Shaw had shown a disregard for the authority of the executive director.

Shaw filed a petition against GMD for retaliatory discharge. The petition alleged that Shaw was terminated in retaliation for his actions that constituted protected internal whistleblowing. Specifically, the petition alleged that Hansen fired Shaw because he had complained to the Board about Hansen's order prohibiting him from sending notice to Peterson about his waste of water violation. GMD filed a motion for summary judgment and argued that Shaw's actions were not whistleblowing, or if they were, Hansen did not violate clearly defined and applicable rules, regulations, or laws. The district court granted GMD's motion for summary judgment, ruling that Shaw's complaint did not constitute whistleblowing. The district court found that under Kansas law "a report must be made to an outside agency in order to qualify as whistle blowing."

On appeal, Shaw argues the district court erred in granting GMD's motion for summary judgment. Shaw argues that internal whistleblowing is actionable under Kansas law. Kansas follows the common-law employment-at-will doctrine, which allows an employer to terminate an employee for good cause, no cause, or even for wrongful cause. To prevail on a retaliatory discharge claim, an employee must demonstrate that he or she falls within one of the exceptions to the employment-at-will doctrine. One of those exceptions is termination for whistleblowing. Our Supreme Court first recognized the whistleblower exception as including termination of an employee in retaliation for the good-faith reporting of a serious infraction of rules, regulations, or the law pertaining to public health and safety and the general welfare by a coworker or an employer to either company management or law enforcement officials is an actionable tort.

GMD urges this court to affirm the district court's decision as right because Hansen's decision to withhold the written directive against Peterson was discretionary and, therefore, not a violation of K.A.R. § 5-23-11. While it is true that a party may file a written complaint with the district alleging a water use violation, the plain language of the regulation clearly states that once the representative of the district finds a violation, the representative "shall issue a written directive to the violator." Here, Shaw personally observed water runoff from Peterson's field into the adjacent roadway caused by the field's irrigation system. Shaw completed his investigation and reported the violation to the office. Once Hansen became aware that a violation existed, the decision whether to issue a written directive to Peterson was not discretionary.

In summary, the district court erred by concluding that under Kansas law, a report must be made to an outside agency in order to qualify as whistleblowing. Accordingly, we reverse the district court's order granting summary judgment in GMD's favor and remand for further proceedings. Reversed and remanded.

## Questions

1. What evidence did Shaw introduce to support his claim for retaliatory discharge?
2. Does Kansas have a whistleblowing statute?
3. Did Hansen violate any law? If so, is this important?
4. What if Shaw had only "average" performance evaluations?

5. What if Shaw was in his first year of employment when these actions occurred?
6. Why do you think the district court erred in granting summary judgment?

# Employment Exams

Many firms use employment exams to discern qualifications of applicants for employment. Care must be used in structuring these exams, and care must be used not to violate the Americans with Disabilities Act (ADA) or state law. The following case shows a state law that precludes disqualification of employment based on an arbitrary and capricious exam.

### In the Matter of the Application of Peter Hawkins
Supreme Court of New York, New York County

*Who is suing?* _____

*Who is being sued?* _____

*For what?* _____

*What is the issue on appeal?* _____

The application of petitioner for an order annulling and reversing the final determination of respondent New York City Civil Service Commission (CSC) affirming the disqualification of petitioner from employment as a New York City police officer is denied and the proceeding is dismissed. The motion by respondents to dismiss the petition is granted.

Petitioner Peter Hawkins was a candidate for the civil service title of police officer. As part of a pre-employment investigation, petitioner underwent a physical examination performed by respondent New York City Police Department (NYPD). Petitioner revealed that he was previously diagnosed with an extra heartbeat. An EKG was administered that resulted in abnormal results. Petitioner was placed on medical review and directed to produce any pertinent medical records regarding his cardiac condition prior to his next examination.

Petitioner was subsequently evaluated by NYPD cardiologist Dr. Berkowitz, at which time petitioner submitted additional medical documentation. Petitioner submitted a photocopy of: (1) a Holter monitor report that confirmed the presence of occasional isolated ventricular premature beats, however the arrhythmia was prevalent through the entire twenty-four hour period; (2) the result of a stress test study that indicated frequent ventricular ectopy; (3) the results of two EKG studies that indicated moderately reduced global left ventricular function, moderate diastolic dysfunction with elevated left ventricular filling pressures, and moderate prolapse of both leaflets of the mitral valve; (4) handwritten progress reports; and (5) a narrative report from Dr. Stephen Vlay. Based on the review of medical records of petitioner and a physical examination of petitioner, Dr. Berkowitz recommended that petitioner be disqualified from further consideration as a police officer.

By Notice of Medical Disqualification petitioner was disqualified from employment as a police officer. The stated basis for disqualification was cardiomyopathy. Petitioner appealed the disqualification to the CSC and submitted medical documentation in support of his appeal. Petitioner submitted an opinion letter from Dr. Vlay who opined that petitioner "has excellent exercise performance" and that petitioner would be able to perform the duties of a police officer. Dr. Vlay further opined that petitioner is New York Heart Association functional class I, by which there is no limitation of physical activity and ordinary activity does not cause undue fatigue, palpitations, or shortness of breath. Dr. Rakesh Patel provided a second opinion that indicated petitioner could engage in a moderate intensity exercise program.

In opposition, NYPD submitted a letter from its supervising chief surgeon, Dr. Eli J. Kleinman, who opined that applicants with cardiomyopathy "cannot be expected to safely perform the essential duties of police officer, as the nature of their condition can pose a serious threat to themselves and the public." Dr. Kleinman requested that CSC affirm the medical disqualification of petitioner. CSC conducted a hearing, considered the arguments and testimony of both parties, and, based on its review, concluded that the record supported the medical disqualification of petitioner. The CSC affirmed the decision of NYPD to medically disqualify petitioner from employment as an NYPD police officer.

Petitioner avers that the employment disqualification was unreasonable, arbitrary, and capricious, and violated the Civil Service Law and Executive Law. In opposition, respondents move to dismiss the petition in its entirety on the grounds that: (1) the petition fails to state a cause of action; (2) the actions of respondents were rational; (3) petitioner failed to show that the CSC abused its discretion; and (4) petitioner failed to show that respondents violated Executive Law § 296. In reply, petitioner maintains that the determination was unreasonable, arbitrary, and capricious.

A court may not disturb an administrative decision unless the action of an agency was arbitrary and capricious, was in violation of lawful procedures, or was made in excess of its jurisdiction. A court may not substitute its judgment for that of the board or body it reviews unless the decision under review is arbitrary and unreasonable and constitutes an abuse of discretion. An arbitrary action is one "without sound basis in reason" and without regard to the facts.

In determining the fitness of candidates for civil service employment, an agency is afforded wide discretion, which is to be sustained unless it has been clearly abused. A determination of the Civil Service Commission is rational and must be upheld so long as it is based on evidence in the record. In determining whether a candidate is medically qualified to serve as a police officer, the appointing authority is entitled to rely upon the findings of its own medical personnel, even if those findings are contrary to those of professionals retained by the candidate.

In the instant proceeding, the CSC relied on evidence in the record to support the medical disqualification of petitioner. The determination followed an extensive review and appeal process in which copious documentation was submitted by petitioner and petitioner was examined by both private and NYPD physicians. The disqualification rested on the documented history of petitioner having cardiovascular disease. This court finds that the determination of CSC was neither arbitrary nor capricious. Accordingly, final determination is sustained on review.

Under New York Executive Law § 292(21), a disability is defined as "(a) a physical, mental or medical impairment which prevents the exercise of a normal bodily function or is demonstrable by medically accepted clinical or laboratory diagnostic techniques or (b) a record of such an impairment or (c) a condition regarded by others as such an impairment." In dealing with employment matters, the term disability shall be limited to disabilities which, "upon the provisions of reasonable accommodations, do not prevent the complainant from performing in a reasonable manner the activities involved in the job or occupation sought or held." Thus, a person whose condition prohibits him from performing employment duties in a reasonable manner is not considered disabled under the statute.

Here, the record demonstrates that the cardiovascular disease of petitioner does not fall within the definition of the term "disability" as contemplated by Executive Law § 292. The heart condition of petitioner, coupled with the risks and stress imposed by the responsibilities and duties of being a police officer, poses a serious threat to his ability to reasonably and safely perform the essential functions of a police officer. The conclusions of NYPD were not based on mere speculation or upon the existence of an asymptomatic disorder, but were based on a careful review of the medical records of petitioner. The conclusions constitute individualized findings that petitioner suffers from a heart condition that prevents him from performing in a reasonable manner the particular activities involved in employment as a police officer. Accordingly, the medical disqualification of petitioner did not constitute an unlawful discrimination by respondents.

Accordingly, the application of petitioner is denied and the motion by respondents to dismiss the petition is granted.

## Questions

1. Why was this preemployment exam reasonable?
2. What must a rejected employment applicant show to overturn a preemployment exam result?
3. What is the significance of New York's legal definition of "disability?"
4. If the petitioner had raised the Americans with Disability law, would the result be the same? Why?
5. If the petitioner had raised a due process claim, how would the court respond, and why?

# Medical Marijuana

Our country is changing its approaches in regulating marijuana. Changes include state laws to regulate the production and sale of small amounts used for medical purposes. This legislation raises several difficult issues, one of which is whether a private business can terminate persons who are using marijuana as allowed under state law but in violation of the federal Controlled Substances Act.

### *Coats v. Dish Network, LLC*
#### Supreme Court of Colorado

*Who is suing?* _____

*Who is being sued?* _____

*For what?* _____

*What is the issue on appeal?* _____

This case requires us to determine whether the use of medical marijuana in compliance with Colorado's Medical Marijuana Amendment, Colorado Constitution article XVIII, § 14, but in violation of federal law, is a "lawful activity" under Colorado Revised Statutes section 24-34-402.5, Colorado's "lawful activities statute." This statute generally makes it an unfair and discriminatory labor practice to discharge an employee based on the employee's "lawful" out-side-of-work activities.

Petitioner Brandon Coats claims respondent Dish Network, LLC (Dish) violated section 24-34-402.5 by discharging him due to his state-licensed use of medical marijuana at home during nonworking hours. He argues that the Medical Marijuana Amendment makes such use "lawful" for purposes of section 24-34-402.5, notwithstanding any federal laws prohibiting medical marijuana use. The trial court dismissed Coats's complaint and the court of appeals affirmed.

Brandon Coats is a quadriplegic and has been confined to a wheelchair since he was a teenager. In 2009, he registered for and obtained a state-issued license to use medical marijuana to treat painful muscle spasms caused by his quadriplegia. Coats consumes medical marijuana at home, after work, and in accordance with his license and Colorado state law. For three years, Coats worked for respondent Dish as a telephone customer service representative. Then Coats tested positive for tetrahydrocannabinol, a component of medical marijuana, during a random drug test. Coats informed Dish that he was a registered medical marijuana patient and planned to continue using medical marijuana. On June 7, 2010, Dish fired Coats for violating the company's drug policy.

Coats then filed a wrongful termination claim against Dish under section 24-34-402.5, which generally prohibits employers from discharging an employee based on his engagement in "lawful activities" off the premises of the employer during nonworking hours. Coats contended that Dish violated the statute by terminating him based on his out-side-of-work medical marijuana use, which he argued was "lawful" under the state's Medical Marijuana Amendment and its implementing legislation. Dish filed a motion to dismiss, arguing that Coats's medical marijuana use was not "lawful" for purposes of the statute under either federal or state law.

The trial court dismissed Coats's claim. It rejected Coats's argument that the Medical Marijuana Amendment made his use a "lawful activity" for purposes of section 24-34-402.5. The court of appeals affirmed based on the prohibition of marijuana use under the federal Controlled Substances Act (CSA). Looking to the plain language of section 24-34-402.5, the majority found that the term "lawful" means "that which is 'permitted by law.'" Applying that plain meaning, the majority reasoned that to be "lawful" for purposes of section 24-34-402.5, activities that are governed by both state and federal law must "be permitted by, and not contrary to, both state and federal law." Given that the federal CSA prohibits all marijuana use, the majority concluded that Coats's conduct was not "lawful activity" protected by the statute. We granted review of the court of appeals' opinion and now affirm the opinion of the court of appeals.

The "lawful activities statute" provides that "it shall be a discriminatory or unfair employment practice for an employer to terminate the employment of any employee due to that employee's engaging in any lawful activity off the premises of the employer during nonworking hours," unless certain exceptions apply. By its terms the statute protects only "lawful" activities. However, the statute does not define the term "lawful." Coats contends that the General Assembly intended the term "lawful" here to mean "lawful under Colorado state law," which, he asserts, recognizes medical marijuana use as "lawful." We do not read the term "lawful" to be so restrictive. Nothing in the language of the statute limits the term "lawful" to state law. Instead, the term is used in its general, unrestricted sense, indicating that a "lawful" activity is that which complies with applicable "law," including state and federal law. We therefore decline Coats's invitation to engraft a state law limitation onto the statutory language.

Coats does not dispute that the federal CSA prohibits medical marijuana use. The CSA lists marijuana as a Schedule I substance, meaning federal law designates it as having no medical accepted use, a high risk of abuse, and a lack of accepted safety for use under medical supervision. This makes the use, possession, or manufacture of marijuana a federal criminal offense, except where used for federally-approved research projects. There is no exception for marijuana use for medicinal purposes, or for marijuana use conducted in accordance with state law. Coats's use of medical marijuana was unlawful under federal law and thus not protected by section 24-34-402.5. Having decided this case on the basis of the prohibition under federal law, we decline to address the issue of whether Colorado's Medical Marijuana Amendment deems medical marijuana use "lawful" by conferring a right to such use. For the reasons stated above, we affirm the decision of the court of appeals.

## Questions

1. If marijuana use is illegal under federal law, how can a state adopt a medical marijuana amendment and implementing legislation?

2. How could the Colorado "lawful activities statute" be changed to apply only to state law?

3. Should companies contemplate changing their drug policies in states with medical marijuana laws?

4. Why doesn't Congress remove marijuana from Schedule I of the Controlled Substances Act?

# Privacy of Medical Records

The age-old tradition of doctor-patient privilege has been a mainstay of privacy protection for information on an individual's medical records. Moreover, in the Health Insurance Portability and Accountability Act of 1996 (HIPAA), Congress promulgated rules governing the doctor-patient privilege by ushering in a strong federal policy in favor of protecting the privacy of patient medical records. However, there are exceptions to the privacy protections. In the following case, the medical records of an individual alleging damages based upon emotional pain and suffering were found to involve issues that required the limited disclosure of her medical information for the purposes of the lawsuit.

### *Johnson v. Federal Express Corporation*
US District Court for the Middle District of Pennsylvania

*Who is suing?* _____

*Who is being sued?* _____

*For what?* _____

*What is the issue on appeal?* _____

This case comes before the court for resolution of a discovery dispute regarding whether the plaintiff's medical records are properly subject to disclosure and inspection by counsel for the defendants. For the reasons set forth below, we find that the allegations in the plaintiff's complaint put her medical condition at issue in this case, and, therefore, require disclosure of these records to defense counsel. However, in recognition of the privacy interest implicated by medical records, we will place reasonable limitations on the further dissemination of these records by defense counsel in the course of this litigation.

The plaintiff, Cathalene Johnson, has filed a complaint against the defendant, Federal Express Corporation (Fed Ex), alleging that Fed Ex discriminated against her in her employment with that company based upon her gender and race. Included among Johnson's prayers for relief is a demand for damages based upon emotional pain and suffering and the loss of enjoyment of life, elements of damage that go directly to the plaintiff's physical and emotional state at the time of the events set forth in her complaint.

Consequently, Fed Ex has sought access to the treatment records of Johnson's primary care physician and endocrinologist in discovery in order to determine whether those records shed light on the extent to which Johnson has exhibited physical and emotional symptoms as a result of the allegedly discriminatory actions of her employer. Johnson has resisted this discovery demand, asserting the physician-patient privilege in an effort to avoid disclosure of any of these medical records. The dispute between the parties on this discovery question was then referred to this court for resolution. We have now completed our "in camera" review of this material.

This in camera review reveals that these records contain matters which we deem relevant to the issues in this lawsuit. Specifically, the records contain numerous reports by the plaintiff to her physicians regarding her general psychological state. In some of these records, Johnson specifically ties her emotional state to stress at her work in ways that are relevant both to the plaintiff's claims and to Fed Ex's defense of those claims. The records also identify some other chronic medical complaints of Johnson's, complaints which may independently account for some symptoms of stress and fatigue identified by the plaintiff. Further, the records may be relevant in that they may reflect instances in which Johnson did not report any particular emotional or psychological complaints while employed with Fed Ex. Despite their undoubted relevance on these scores, the records are also interspersed with matters of a less relevant, and more personal nature, involving women's health issues and other similar matters. Oftentimes these relevant and non-pertinent matters are interspersed in the records in a way which makes redaction difficult or unwieldy.

Having conducted this review, we will order the medical records released to defense counsel for defense preparations in this lawsuit, since the records contain relevant information which cannot be reasonably gleaned from the documents through some simple form of redaction. However, in order to preserve Johnson's medical privacy, we will further direct that the contents of these medical records may be used by counsel solely for preparation of this litigation, and may not be further disclosed to Johnson's supervisors at Fed Ex without prior approval of the court.

In the context of a request for access to medical records of a plaintiff in an employment discrimination lawsuit, this court has previously defined for us the standards which control our evaluation of such discovery disputes. In this setting, we have repeatedly held that when a plaintiff puts her mental and emotional health at issue in a civil lawsuit she implicitly waives the protection of the doctor-patient privilege with respect to her medical records.

Thus, while courts consistently hold that it would be unfair to allow plaintiffs to unilaterally determine the amount of harm defendant caused, without allowing the defendant or the fact-finder to argue, consider and weigh other relevant factors of emotional stress, it is also well recognized that the plaintiff has a privacy interest in maintaining the confidentiality of her records of health treatment. Finding that the plaintiff's assertions of claims for emotional distress put these medical matters at issue in this litigation, we conclude that the plaintiff has waived any broad claim of privilege. We further conclude that the plaintiff's medical records are relevant to the issues raised by her claims in this lawsuit, and, therefore, direct that the medical records be provided to defense counsel subject to a protective order requiring defense counsel to maintain confidentiality of the records by not disclosing any portion of the contents to anyone other than the court, the attorneys (and their staff) involved in the matter, and expert witnesses; by not releasing any portion of the records to third-parties, including Johnson's coworkers and supervisors, without prior express approval of the court; by destroying the records at the conclusion of the litigation; and by not using the information contained in the records for purposes other than prosecuting this lawsuit.

## Questions

1. Why are the medical records of a plaintiff's primary care physician not usually available in a lawsuit?
2. Why did the court find an exception to this rule?
3. Why does the court employ an in camera review?
4. Is court-imposed secrecy as directed in this case the best resolution for the conflicting interests?

# Enforcing Food Safety Regulations

We previously learned how important our federal laws were in providing safe food products. However, sometimes there will be violations that need to be addressed. While federal law provides for penalties, how severe should they be to assure compliance? The following case shows the government resorting to drastic measures to force noncomplying corporate officers to accept responsibility for their actions.

### *United States of America v. DeCoster*
US Court of Appeals for the Eight Circuit, St. Louis

*Who is suing?* _____

*Who is being sued?* _____

*For what?* _____

*What is the issue on appeal?* _____

Austin "Jack" DeCoster and Peter DeCoster both pled guilty, as "responsible corporate officers" of Quality Egg, LLC, to misdemeanor violations of 21 U.S.C. § 331(a) for introducing eggs that had been adulterated with salmonella enteritidis into interstate commerce. The district court sentenced Jack and Peter to three months imprisonment. The DeCosters appeal, arguing that their prison sentences are unconstitutional. We affirm.

Jack DeCoster owned Quality Egg, LLC, an Iowa egg production company. Jack's son Peter DeCoster served as the company's chief operating officer. Quality Egg operated six farm sites with 73 barns which were filled with five million egg-laying hens. It also had 24 barns which were filled with young chickens. Additionally, the company owned several processing plants where eggs were cleaned, packed, and shipped. Quality Egg did not test or divert eggs from the market before July 2010 despite receiving multiple positive environmental and hen test results of salmonella. The Centers for Disease Control and Prevention estimated that about 56,000 Americans fell ill with salmonellosis in 2010 after consuming contaminated eggs, and federal and state officials determined that the salmonella outbreak had originated at Quality Egg's facilities.

The FDA inspected the Quality Egg operations in August 2010. Investigators discovered live and dead rodents and frogs in the laying areas, feed areas, conveyer belts, and outside the buildings. They found holes in the walls and baseboards of the feed and laying buildings. The investigators discovered that some rodent traps were broken, and others had dead rodents in them. In one building near the laying hens, manure was found piled to the rafters; it had pushed a screen out of the door which allowed rodents into the building. Investigators also observed employees not wearing or changing protective clothing and not cleaning or sanitizing equipment. The FDA concluded that Quality Egg had failed to comply with its written plans for biosecurity and salmonella prevention. The agency also discovered that the contamination had spread throughout all of the Quality Egg facilities. In October 2010 the FDA instructed Quality Egg to euthanize every hen, remove the manure, repair its facilities, and disinfect its barns to prevent the risk of another outbreak.

The government then began a criminal investigation of the company's food safety practices and filed a criminal information against Quality Egg and both of the DeCosters. The investigation revealed that Quality Egg previously had falsified records about food safety measures and had lied to auditors for several years about pest control measures and sanitation practices. Although its food safety plan stated that Quality Egg performed flock testing to identify and control salmonella, no flock testing was ever done. Quality Egg's employees had also bribed a USDA inspector in 2010 to release eggs for sale which had been retained or "red tagged" for failing to meet minimum quality grade standards. Quality Egg also misled state regulators and retail customers by changing the packing dates of its eggs and selling the misbranded eggs into interstate commerce.

Quality Egg pled guilty to: (1) a felony for bribing a USDA inspector, (2) a felony for introducing misbranded eggs into interstate commerce with intent to defraud and mislead, and (3) a misdemeanor for introducing adulterated eggs into interstate commerce. Jack and Peter each pled guilty to misdemeanor violations as responsible corporate officers under the Food Drug & Cosmetic Act (FDCA). Before sentencing, the DeCosters argued that sentences of incarceration would be unconstitutional because they had not known that the eggs were contaminated at the time they were shipped. The district court determined that although nothing in the record indicated that Peter and Jack had actual knowledge that the eggs they sold were infected with salmonella, the record demonstrated that their safety and sanitation procedures were "egregious," that they ignored the positive salmonella environmental test results before July 2010 by not testing their eggs, and that they knew that their employees had deceived and bribed USDA inspectors.

Under the FDCA responsible corporate officer concept, individuals who by reason of their position in the corporation have the responsibility and authority to take necessary measures to prevent or remedy violations of the FDCA and fail to do so, may be held criminally liable as "responsible corporate agents," regardless of whether they were aware of or intended to cause the violation. The FDCA punishes inaction where the law imposes a duty because, according to Congress, the public interest in the purity of its food is so great as to warrant the imposition of the highest standard of care on distributors.

The DeCosters argue that their prison sentences are unconstitutional because they did not personally commit wrongful acts. Officer liability under the FDCA is not equivalent to vicarious liability. Under vicarious liability, a supervisory party is held liable for the actionable conduct of a subordinate based on the relationship between the two parties. Under the FDCA, in contrast, a corporate officer is held accountable not for the acts or omissions of others, but rather for his own failure to prevent or remedy the conditions which gave rise to the charges against him. Thus, some measure of blameworthiness is imported directly to the corporate officer. Here, as owner of Quality Egg, Jack decided which barns were subject to salmonella environmental testing, and as chief operating officer, Peter coordinated many of the company's salmonella prevention and rodent control efforts. We conclude that the record here shows that the DeCosters are liable for negligently failing to prevent the salmonella outbreak.

On this record, the DeCosters' three month prison sentences are not grossly disproportionate to the gravity of their misdemeanor offenses. We conclude that the district court's sentences in this case do not violate the Eighth Amendment. For these reasons the judgments of the district court are affirmed.

## Questions

1. What were the connections of each of the defendants to the operations of the poultry operations?
2. Why weren't the activities of Quality Egg that contributed to salmonella detected earlier?
3. Are the provisions of the FDCA important to the court's decision? Why or why not?

4. What should corporate officers and owners need to know before they can be criminally liable for infractions by their business?

## Discussion Questions

1. Should felons lose their right to vote? Maine and Vermont do not take away felons' right to vote, even while they are incarcerated. In other states, including Florida, Georgia, and Virginia, felons and ex-felons permanently lose their right to vote. It is estimated that 5.3 million Americans have lost their right to vote due to a felony conviction.

2. You are an inspector for a state health department. You inspect a food production facility and give it a passing score despite the fact that you lack the training in how to inspect one part of its production process. Products from the facility are contaminated and lead to the death of three people. Can you be held accountable for your accident? Why or why not?

3. You want to bring a lawsuit for wrongful termination against your former employer, but realize that your case would be severely undercut if privileged information about your past substance abuse was disclosed. What should you do, and why?

## Image Credit

Copyright in the Public Domain.